SIR EDWARD WATKIN, 1819–1901

The Last of the Railway Kings

Sir Edward Watkin, aged about 65

SIR EDWARD WATKIN, 1819–1901

The Last of the Railway Kings

John Neville Greaves

The Book Guild Ltd
Sussex, England

First published in Great Britain in 2005 by
The Book Guild Ltd
25 High Street
Lewes, East Sussex
BN7 2LU

Typesetting in Times by
Acorn Bookwork Ltd, Salisbury, Wiltshire

Printed in Great Britain by
CPI Bath

A catalogue record for this book is available from
The British Library.

ISBN 1 85776 888 4

CONTENTS

ACKNOWLEDGEMENTS

I am primarily indebted to the late George Dow, to whom I owe the original inspiration for this study of Sir Edward William Watkin. I am grateful also to the public library network of Great Britain for materials obtained readily, and quickly, sometimes beyond the call of duty. My particular thanks are due to the staff at Nantwich, and also at Folkestone, Manchester Central, Salford, North Lincolnshire, Lincoln Cathedral, North Yorkshire, Birmingham City, Glasgow City, Kent County Council at Deal, The Kentish Studies Centre, Maidstone, and the archivists at the Universities of Oxford, Manchester and Nottingham; the Manchester Grammar School; and the towns of Oldham, Rochdale, Bolton and Caernarfon for help; also the County Record Offices of Devon, West Sussex, Cheshire, Lancashire, Norfolk and the London Metropolitan Archives. Other bodies who have been helpful are the Bibliotheque nationale de France, Paris; the House of Lords Record Office; The Reform Club, London; the Hayward Gallery at the Royal Festival Hall; the *Railway Magazine* archivist; the Register Offices at Southport and Macclesfield; and of course the British Library (St Pancras and Colindale) and the Public Record Office at Kew. Generous assistance was provided by the Curator of the Marylebone Cricket Club, Stephen Green; by the Earl of Harrowby, Sandon Hall (access to Mss, and introduction to the Governor-General of Canada); and by the Marquess of Salisbury for access to the Watkin Correspondence at Hatfield House. I am grateful, too, to Dr Sheridan Gilley of Durham University for his guidance throughout, and to the staff of St Deiniol's Residential Library, Hawarden. The Revd Greg Forster, Rector of Northenden, was unfailingly helpful, with his parish archives and close connection with Rose Hill Home, of which he was Chaplain; as were Alec Farrow and Pauline Franklin, with local knowledge of Salford and Altrincham respectively, to Helen Matthews, with details of the Fripp family of painters, and to Susan Watkin for help with the family tree. I could not have managed without the various people who came to my help with information technology, particularly Jonathan and Dr Renate Greaves, Archie Bell and Jane Coates.

I have appreciated warmly the assistance of descendants of Absolom and Edward Watkin: Dorothea Worsley-Taylor for her help and friendship, and Magdalene Goffin, to whom my indebtedness is obvious from the text. Finally, my gratitude to Iris, who had to share the first eighteen months of our marriage with Sir Edward.

John Greaves

ILLUSTRATION ACKNOWLEDGEMENTS

The author gratefully acknowledges the source of, and copyright permission, where applicable, to use the illustrations in this book

Miss Dorothea Worsley-Taylor 9, 11, 26–29
Mrs Magdalene Goffin 3
Andrew R.G.Dow 21, 32, 33, 39, 46, 47, 49, 50
The National Archives (PRO) Kent 22, 35
The National Archives of Canada 14, 15, 16, 18
Gwynedd Archives, Caernarfon 44, 45
Birmingham City Library 7, 13
Manchester Central Library 34
Nottingham City Library 48
City of Salford Libraries 1
Nottingham University Department of Mss and Special
  Collections 12
The Illustrated London News 10, 24, 41
Willow Publishing, Timperley, Cheshire 25
The Allan Sommerfield Collection 19
The Brian Hilton Collection 51

INTRODUCTION

This study of one of the nineteenth century's most prominent railway managers – the last of the railway kings – was first conceived in the early 1960s on a reading of George Dow's monumental history of the Great Central Railway, though its completion had to wait for retirement from a demanding working life.

Edward William Watkin was born six years before the opening of the world's first public locomotive-hauled railway, and died four years after the building of Britain's last complete main line, which he himself had envisaged and devised for a major part of his working life.

Watkin was a splendid example of the Victorian entrepreneur. He was Victorian in that he was exactly contemporary with the Queen (his life-span was only forty-four days shorter than hers), and as an entrepreneur he was one of those who seized the opportunities of the rapid industrial development, made possible by steam power, and the burgeoning capitalism of the early nineteenth century. He was imbued with the indomitable self-confidence of those whose horizons were unlimited, and for whom all things were possible, given energy and determination.

He came from modest farming and mercantile stock, but was brought up amidst the enthusiasm of his father Absolom for literature and involvement in the social and political developments of the time. He was born in Salford, and the proximity of Manchester, the world's first industrial city, brought his father, a textile merchant, into close contact with the civil unrest and turmoil in that molten casting of a new form of human society. The year of Watkin's birth, 1819, saw the 'Peterloo Massacre' in central Manchester, and it was no surprise that, following his father's example, he threw himself into the task of supporting the interests and civil dignity of the workforce of the growing industries, and of keeping alight the ideals of culture and education amidst the smoke and grime.

His main life work was the chairmanship of the Manchester,

Sheffield and Lincolnshire Railway, but he had a profound influence on the South Eastern, the Metropolitan, and the Great Eastern Railways, as well as on the railways and politics of the Canadian Federation, and as a Member of Parliament for a total of twenty-four years. Like many supremely confident Victorian explorers, he aroused much opposition in his lifetime. While most historians concede some good qualities in his character, the main drift of twentieth-century historical references to him, at least in railway histories, categorise his career as a failure and in very uncomplimentary terms; adjectives such as overbearing, manipulative, over-ambitious and duplicitous are used of his management style. No attempt has been made to examine his personality, or to determine what was his paradigm of interpretation of the world in which he pursued his various aims; in short, what kind of man he really was.

An early discovery in research was that all his personal papers had been destroyed by his daughter-in-law just before her death in 1944.[1] This meant reliance on other men's papers and biographies, the mentions in railway histories and journals, and many newspaper accounts, magazine articles, and records of his speeches and letters. Because of the comparative lack of his own reflections on events, I have quoted extensively from his own words, so as to give a clearer picture of his character, 'warts and all'. Fortunately, Watkin was of sufficient importance to his contemporaries to merit a large number of such mentions and reports, though a biographer has to construct a framework for them 'if they are not to become merely an unimaginative compilation of facts, rather than a product of human intelligence'.[2]

Michael Robbins[3] points out that in the absence of personal documents, to record the subject's observations on the important events in which he was involved, the historian is reliant on primary sources, such as contemporary records and the minutes of board meetings, which are already a distillation of what was discussed, and individual contributions which were, in the case of news-

---

[1]Possibly, like Henry James, 'to frustrate as utterly as possible the post-mortem exploiter' (quoted, John Stallworthy, in John Batchelor (ed.), *The Art of Literary Biography* (OUP, 1995), p.28), but equally possibly to obliterate the memory of a less-than-fulfilling marriage.

[2]S.W. Fairweather, in his Introduction to G.R. Stevens' history, *Canadian National Railways, 1836–1896* (Vol 1), p.xv.

[3]In *Points and Signals* (George Allen and Unwin Ltd., 1967), Chapter 2, p.18.

papers, especially on politics, subject to editorial bias. Within such limitations, Robbins set out the craft of the historian in four principles:

1. To decide what questions should be asked and answered.
2. To seek out and assemble facts, in order to throw light on the questions.
3. To select those facts which supply the answers to the questions.
4. To arrange them and present them in such a way as to secure the greatest possible measure of acceptance.

I hope I have made a credible case for Watkin's place in English social and industrial history. If he does fall short of 'genius', and 'greatness' and indeed 'nobility', it is not, in my estimation, by very far.

John Greaves
September 2003

1

The Social Background

Edward William Watkin was a quintessential Victorian. He was born in the same year as Victoria – 1819 – on 26 September, and died in the same year – 1901. He personified the spirit of the age in believing that what was scientifically conceivable was perfectly achievable, given imagination, energy and perseverance. The England into which they were born was a rapidly changing society: it was emerging from the Napoleonic wars, the impact of industrialisation was increasing, there was a sudden surge in the pace of life with the railway revolution, and great conflicts appeared in the land as mass poverty and unemployment spread. There was a buoyant belief in progress, together with a great nostalgia for the past. The Romantic movement in the arts, and religious revivals, showed a reaction against the static rationalism of the eighteenth century. The American and French Revolutions, based on equality, liberty and democracy, had aroused the fear of similar movements in Britain. The 'Peterloo Massacre' in Manchester in 1819, in which a popular demonstration against the government was put down by the military, was seen to be a sign of the times.

In manufacturing, steam, generated from coal, and replacing water and wind power, was transforming both the rate of production and the living and working conditions of the population. Along with this was the adoption for the first time of the theories of Adam Smith; the institution of a market economy free from social and political control, in which prices of commodities and labour found their own level through free competition.

Manchester, the world's first industrial city, became 'a grim utilitarian place – the city of long chimneys'.[1] Alexis de Tocqueville,

---

[1]Michael Harrison in A.J. Kidd and K.W. Roberts, (eds), *City, Class and Culture* (Manchester University Press, 1985), p.120.

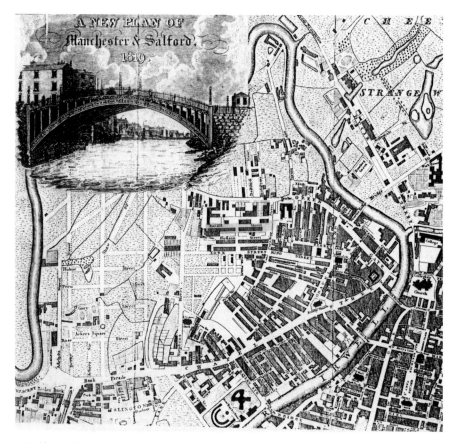

1 Salford, 1819

on his visit to Manchester in 1835, wrote of the six-storey factories
'which keep air and light out of the human habitations which they
dominate...from this foul drain...the greatest stream of human
industry flows out to fertilize the whole world. From this filthy
sewer gold flows.'[2] Even so, Disraeli could say later that 'Manchester is as great a human exploit as Athens.'[3]

The textile business of John Watkin (1752–1812) had been established in Manchester in the late eighteenth century. He was the son

---

[2]Quoted, Gary Messenger, *Manchester in the Victorian Age* (Manchester University Press,
1985), p.140.

[3]In *Coningsby*. Quoted, N.J. Frangopulo, *Rich Inheritance: A Guide to the History of Manchester* (Manchester Education Committee, 1962), p.24.

2

of John Watkin (1734–1809), a yeoman farmer at Audlem, near Nantwich in Cheshire. The family had come originally, via Shropshire, from Wales, but the farm could not support all John Watkin's eleven children, and some had to seek their livelihood elsewhere.[4] Thomas Watkin, another of the sons, went to London and became a private in the First Regiment of Guards, and afterwards an innkeeper there, where his son Absolom was born in 1787. In 1801 Absolom was offered a job with his Uncle John in his Manchester cotton firm,[5] and by April 1807 he had bought out the business and changed it to his own name. He bought a house in Salford, where he was listed in the 1819/20 Street Directory as a 'Manufacturer and Gent.' living at No.19 Ravald Street, which ran between Broughton Street and Paradise Street.[6] Absolom married Elizabeth Makinson, daughter of a proprietor of an 'Adventure School', on 3 November in her parish church, St John's, Deansgate, Manchester.[7]

From the age of twenty-three Absolom kept a daily journal of events and reflections, from which all our knowledge of his son Edward William, born in Ravald Street, is derived. Absolom's heart and soul were not in his business: his 'great and enduring pleasure'[8] was books, and the scope of his reading testifies to a lively and enterprising intelligence. He wrote in his journal of his close involvement in the social and political activities of those eventful times. These included founder-membership of the council of the Anti-Corn Law League; helping to write the famous protest against the conduct of the yeomanry at the 'Peterloo Massacre'; drawing up the petition in favour of the Reform Bill of 1832 and being the scribe of the various groups to which he belonged. He also wrote the loyal address to Queen Victoria on the occasion of her marriage.[9] 'His library was a fine one, and for an ordinary private citizen of those days was large.'[10] It contained history, grammar, politics, travel, medicine, poetry, biography, and works

---

[4]Magdalene Goffin, *The Diaries of Absolom Watkin: A Manchester Man 1787–1861* (Stroud: Alan Sutton Publishing Ltd, 1993), p.xi.

[5]*Ibid,* p.3.

[6]It was finally obliterated in the development of Trinity Way in the 1980s.

[7]*Ibid,* pp.3, 6, 11 and 14.

[8]*Ibid,* p.3.

[9]*Ibid,* p.208.

[10]A.E. Watkin, *Absolom Watkin: Extracts from his Journal, 1814–1861* (London: T. Fisher Unwin, 1920), p.8.

on religion, science and philosophy. Edward spoke admiringly in later years of the range and depth of his father's library, which he inherited and treasured himself.[11]

Amongst the political ferment of which Manchester was the main generator was the agitation against the Corn Laws, and the formation of the Liberal Party, intent on bridging the gap between rich and poor and on social justice. This philanthropy was based not so much on *The Rights of Man*, or a revolutionary reaction against social inferiority, and certainly not on manufacturing utility (contented labour as the engine of capitalism), as on a Christian doctrine of man. Thus Absolom wrote to John Bright about the Crimean War: 'For liberty, for civilisation and progress, for justice and for truth...our battle is for the welfare of the whole human race, and our trust is in the righteousness of our cause, and in his aid who has called us to this glorious work.'[12] 'Absolom had a strong belief that it was Christianity that promoted the happiness and contentment of mankind.'[13] John Vincent claimed that 'It is necessary to insist upon the Christian dimension of Liberalism...for many Liberals, politics was not an autonomous activity, but one deriving from a religious centre.'[14]

'Accounts of Victorian Manchester which portrayed it as a money-grubbing cultural desert or as a battleground between rich and poor were always...wide of the mark. [It] saw the creation of an almost endless stream of societies catering for an ever-widening range of cultural and intellectual interests.'[15] The first free lending library in Britain opened there in 1852 (6 September), and England's oldest privately-endowed library (Chetham's) was open to the general public. Absolom was a member of several groups devoted to the study and debate of literary and social issues. The weekly Literary and Scientific Club was an informal group of friends meeting in each others' houses: more public and formal were The Literary and Philosophical Society of Manchester, and

---

[11]E.W. Watkin, *Catalogue of the Library at Rose Hill* (Manchester: Henry Blacklock, 1891).
[12]A.E. Watkin, p.14.
[13]Michael J. Turner, *Reform and Respectability: The Making of a Middle-Class Liberalism in Early Nineteenth Century Manchester* (Manchester: The Chetham Society, 1995), p.30.
[14]John Vincent, *The Formation of the Liberal Party, 1857-1868* (Constable, 1966), pp.xvi and xvii.
[15]Michael E. Rose, in Kidd and Roberts, pp. 110 and 112.

the Manchester Athenaeum, in the foundation of which he played a leading part.[16] From these groups sprang J.E. Taylor, who co-founded and edited *The Manchester Guardian* on 5 May 1821, and Archibald Prentice, a muslin merchant, who, unsuccessfully, offered Absolom the editorship of *The Manchester Gazette.*[17] Absolom was a founder-member in 1830 of The Society For the Preservation of Ancient Footpaths, a precursor of the Commons, Open Spaces and Footpaths Preservation Society of 1865, which was part of the establishment of the National Trust in 1895. He became a JP, a County Magistrate for Lancaster, and a director of the Commercial Bank of England in the city.

He was also a lay preacher in the Methodist New Connexion, a branch of Methodism which separated from the main body in 1797, but to which it returned in 1932, after forming, with two other bodies, the United Methodists in 1907.[18] He had started reading the Fathers of the Church and later writers, and worshipping with other denominations – Cross Street Unitarian Chapel; the 'Old Church' (later, at the formation of the Manchester Diocese on 1 September 1847, the Cathedral) – so-called to distinguish it from St Ann's Church (1712); and Mulberry Street Roman Catholic Chapel.[19] His transition to Anglicanism is not recorded; it was possibly between the years 1818 and 1825. The baptism of each of his children as Anglicans is noted by him, but not their confirmation, though that is not critical: his second son, John, must have been confirmed to be ordained, and Edward almost certainly to become a lay chairman of the Church Congress. Edward never lost his 'tender regard' for Methodism; many years later he accompanied a deputation to the Secretary of State for War from the Methodist Army and Navy Committee, to argue for the rights of Wesleyans in the armed forces. 'In his earnestness and excitement he spoke of "our" rights...and what "we" should unceasingly demand, much to the amusement of the deputation.'[20]

Edward grew up with a great sympathy for Absolom's ideals and aims, and was drawn early to an involvement in social and

---

[16]A.E. Watkin, p.10.
[17]Goffin, p.20.
[18]*Ibid*, p.8.
[19]*Ibid*, pp.10, 11, 12 and 27.
[20]*The Methodist Recorder*, 18 April 1901.

5

2 Absolom Watkin, Sir Edward's Father   3 Elizabeth Watkin, Sir Edward's Mother, aged 31

political activities. In two monographs, entitled *Fragment No.1* (1874) and *Fragment No.2* (1878),[21] he wrote a sketch of his father's life. He studied Absolom's journal, setting himself to learn Dr Byrom's shorthand (even by then out of date) in order to decipher certain parts of it. In his introduction to the first book, he wrote:

> Today [21 October 1873] I have read the autobiography of John Stuart Mill, and especially the chapter on his hereditary want of belief in Christian doctrine. Yesterday I read Lord Derby's speech at Liverpool, in which he declaimed against 'coating with moral whitewash' the race of 'black men.' Hence I feel stirred afresh to give to a circle of relatives and friends an insight into the life of a man who was neither a Lord nor a philosopher, but simply a Christian, who believed in Christianising all men, whether black or white; a man who, as a scholar, was erudite; as a speaker, always able, and at times

[21]Published at the time by Alex Ireland, Pall Mall, Manchester.

eloquent; as a politician, enlightened; but still a man who only now and then emerged into the sight and hearing of the great world. For *he* thought it reward enough to have health and strength enough to 'go about doing good', working harder for other people than himself, and doing it modestly and unobtrusively.[22]

This gives a rare insight into Edward's own convictions and motivations, and also shows that, like Gladstone, he found time to read enlightening books in the midst of a punishing load of work. Both of Absolom's other sons showed this characteristic of selfless service: John (1821–70) went to St Edmund's Hall, Oxford, to train for Holy Orders, and after a curacy at Long Benton in the Diocese of Durham (at that time), became Vicar of Stixwould in the Diocese of Lincoln until his death. Alfred (1825–75) served for many years on the City Council in Manchester, being elected as Mayor in 1873–74.

One of the most deeply impressive events for the young Edward Watkin must have been the opening of the Liverpool and Manchester Railway, on 15 September 1830, eleven days before his eleventh birthday.[23] Absolom took him frequently to watch the continuing construction of the railway,[24] and the century's most revolutionary sign of the changing times became a formative part of Edward's life.

---

[22]*Fragment No.1*, p.4.
[23]Goffin, p.121.
[24]C. Hamilton Ellis, *British Railway History* (George Allen and Unwin, 1953 (2 Vols.), Vol. 1, 1830–1876, p. 177.

2

Infancy and Youth

Absolom's first reference in the journal to his eldest son as a
sentient participant in his life dates from June 1826, when they
walked together by the brook in Prestwich, some five miles from
their house. Absolom was then preoccupied with financial worries,
and perhaps much of the meditative atmosphere sank into the
mind of the seven-year-old who was later to administer the receipt
and expenditure of millions of pounds.[1]

On 18 June of the following year Absolom noted, on a visit to
Audlem, walking after breakfast with his wife and Edward and
two others, that he read poetry as they went along.[2] Three days
later he recorded a family outing from Nantwich, where one of his
relatives lived, to nearby Beeston Castle. The walk up to the castle
was, and is, sharply inclined, but Absolom was 'Quite pleased with
the enthusiastic ardour of my little Edward'. The old lady
caretaker in the cottage at the foot of the hill had told the lad of
the presence of a deep well in the castle ruins, and he came to his
father 'with sparkling eyes and a countenance full of smiles' to tell
him he had found it. Absolom wrote, 'If this boy is not spoiled by
the folly of those about him, he will assuredly prove superior to
the herd of mankind.'[3] Again, on 26 April 1828, he took Edward
for an evening walk in Prestwich Clough. The beautiful scene was
enhanced by the ringing of the parish church bells, and as they
each gathered a large handful of anemones, Edward began to
repeat Moore's song 'Sweet Evening Bells', which had come into

---

[1]Goffin, p.70.
[2]A.E. Watkin, p.118
[3]Goffin, p.81.

4 Beeston Castle, Cheshire

Absolom's mind, too. As they walked home under the moon and the stars they talked of the universe and its Author, and were happy.[4]

Absolom's knowledge of the writings of Thomas Moore (1779–1852), 'Ireland's National Poet' – who was a controversial figure both in literature and in politics – indicates his literary judgement and taste. Listed in Edward's catalogue of 1891 of the books in the library at Rose Hill are six books, published between 1818 and 1853, of Thomas Moore's writings. The poem which moved them both reads:

Those evening bells! Those evening bells!
How many a tale their music tells,
Of youth, and home, and that sweet time,
When last I heard their soothing chime!

Those joyous hours are passed away!
And many a heart that then was gay
Within the tomb now darkly dwells,
And hears no more those evening bells!

And so 'twill be when I am gone!
That tuneful peals will still ring on,

---

[4]*Ibid*, pp 95 and 96.

9

While other bards shall walk these dells,
And sing your praise, sweet evening bells!

This is too sweet, perhaps, for twenty-first century tastes, and a little early in life for Edward to reflect upon *les temps perdu*,[5] but Moore's poetry was praised by such contemporaries as Byron, and Tennyson, who expressed amazement that such perfect poetry as 'Oft in the Stilly Night' should actually exist.[6] Moore had an influence on Edward in other ways; he is listed by him as a possible Chairman for the Manchester Athenaeum soirée of October 1845; and Moore's political opinions on the relationship of Ireland with Great Britain, as distinguished from the Catholic/Nationalist views of Daniel O'Connell and those of the Fenians, resembled closely those expressed by Watkin during the Home Rule debates in the 1880s and 1890s.

One of his walks with his father, on 30 April 1832, was to the new house and grounds, Rose Hill, that Absolom was buying at Northen, later known as Northenden, on the southern bank of the River Mersey in Cheshire. It was a farm, and Absolom commented on how eager young Edward was to start farming. A farmer, like his great-grandfather, Edward was not to be, but he was clearly taking a keen interest in the opportunities to hand. Another influential event about that time was the procession through Salford on 9 August 1832 to mark the passing of the Reform Bill.[7] There is no record of the conversation between father and son on that day, but the meaning of the occasion would have been explained to the boy.

At the age of fourteen, Edward started work in his father's warehouse; his brother John joined him before his thirteenth birthday.[8] John was later to reproach his father for not giving him a better education, though he did eventually go to Oxford and become a priest of the Church of England, being later awarded a Doctorate of Civil Law by the university.[9] *The Railway Magazine*,

---

[5]Absolom added that although he 'could feel all that the poet describes, [he] did not feel that life is less valuable or less pleasurable than it was then', (A.E. Watkin, p.123).

[6]Brendan Clifford, *The Life and Poems of Thomas Moore* (Belfast: Athol Books, 1993), p.79 and p.8.

[7]Goffin, p.144.

[8]*Ibid*, p.167.

[9]*Ibid*, p.374.

in its obituary of Edward, stated that Edward went to the grammar school in Manchester. However, the family lived in Salford, which had a grammar school of its own, indeed more than one from time to time. Records of pupils' names have not survived, so it is possible that he attended one of the several such schools which came and went during that period. Manchester Grammar School records have survived, and it is clear that Edward did not attend there.[10] His brothers John and Alfred attended a school in Nantwich for a while, and in Audlem for a year or two.[11] It seems strange that Absolom did not pay for his boys to attend public schools, as did so many of the newly wealthy merchants of the day, but perhaps his constant anxiety about the precariousness of his business and his wife's carelessness in matters financial, as well as her general untidiness and unpredictability,[12] did not give him the confidence to do so. It cost something like £261 per year to send a boy to Eton.[13] In 1839 Absolom calculated that he had spent £200 over the previous seven years on the education of his four children – just over £7 per annum each.[14] Edward's daughter was at school in Paris for a time,[15] and Alfred's son Edgar (1860–1908) went to Harrow.[16]

On 30 January 1835 Absolom took Edward and John to 'The Club' to hear James Buckingham, an MP[17] and a well-known author and traveller, who gave a lecture on the advantage of Free Trade. Drawing lessons from the example of ancient Palmyra, the speaker exhorted his hearers to cherish free institutions, to extend education accompanied by moral and religious instruction, to labour to make the mass of the people happy, and individually to determine to do something to preserve and increase the greatness and happiness of our great and happy country. This was powerful fare for a fifteen-year-old. It clearly made a lasting impression on Edward, for all those principles were to be found in his public

---

[10]Private letter from the School Archivist, Ian Bailey, 1997.
[11]Goffin, p.294.
[12]Ibid, several references, including pp.96, 244, 343 and 346.
[13]Roy Jenkins, *Gladstone* (London: Macmillan, 1995), p.10.
[14]Goffin, p.214.
[15]Mentioned in the course of his Report to the MSLR half-yearly shareholders' meeting, 16 January 1867 (PRO RAIL 463/73, p.27).
[16]Magdalene Goffin, private letter, 2002.
[17]1786–1855. The first MP for Sheffield, 1832–1837 (*DNB*, Vol. vii, p.202), (A.E. Watkin, p.175).

words and actions throughout his life. At the end of the meeting, Edward and John were introduced to Mr Buckingham. Not many weeks later, in April, Edward undertook his first public duty. There was a by-election in Manchester, when he acted as 'check-clerk' for Mr C. Poulett-Thomson, who was elected.[18]

In Absolom's journal for June of that year, the first signs of headstrong rebellion appeared. Edward was beginning to assert his independence, and both he and John were becoming 'rude and indifferent'.[19] On 3 October 1836, just at a time when Absolom was feeling more depressed than usual about his abilities as a businessman and the disorganised state of his domestic affairs, Edward began the day by behaving 'very insolently, both to his mother and to [him]'. He provoked Absolom to boxing him on the ear, and telling him that if he wanted to leave he could do so, but while he stayed with his parents he should behave properly. After breakfast he took Edward into another room and explained to him his plans for the family, and that if he thought he could do better elsewhere he would promote his interests as far as he could, but would not submit to improper treatment from any of his children.[20] Not long afterwards, John caught some of his brother's defiance, behaving so badly at the warehouse that Absolom dismissed him, whereupon Edward declared himself unwell and Absolom had to work alone. However, John became bored at home and, promising not to give any further trouble, pleaded with his father to let him return. On 6 August 1837, Absolom recorded that 'the boys trouble me with their violence', but conceded that it was from thoughtlessness rather than bad intentions.[21]

A further outbreak of insolence occurred one day when Absolom set out with William Grime to dine with Richard Cobden, and Edward was put out that he was not invited. Though

---

[18]Charles Edward Poulett-Thomson (1799–1841) sat for Dover from 1826 to 1832, when he was elected simultaneously for Dover and Manchester, and chose the latter. He was re-elected in 1835 and in 1837, when his opponent was Gladstone. He was President of the Board of Trade until 1834, and again from 1835 until appointed, from destiny's inexhaustible fund of coincidences, as Governor-General of Canada in 1839. There he was charged with implementing the policy of his predecessor, Lord Durham, which he did 'with great skill and courage'. The new Constitution, joining the Upper and Lower Provinces of Canada, came into force on 10 February 1841, and laid the foundation of the Confederation, in which Edward was to play a significant part, in 1867, (*DNB*, Vol. lvi, p.237)

[19]Goffin, p.173.
[20]*Ibid*, pp. 178 and 179.
[21]*Ibid*, p.185.

only nineteen years old, he was mature enough to consider himself as fit company for the great man. Later in life, he was become a friend of Cobden's, and published his reminiscences of him in his book *Alderman Cobden of Manchester*.[22] However, on his return home, Absolom found an apologetic letter from Edward, which gave his father 'real pleasure'.[23] Cobden's house was in Quay Street, on the corner of Byrom Street opposite the Opera House in Manchester. In 1851 it was to become the first home of Owens' College, the foundation of the University of Manchester. One of the speakers at the Athenaeum in 1836 read a paper in which he included what must have been one of the earliest proposals for a University in Manchester.[24] According to the *Grimsby Times* of 30 April 1880, quoting the *Manchester Examiner*, 'It was as a result of a conversation between [Sir Edward] and the late Mr Alexander Kay (quondam Mayor of Manchester), that Mr John Owens determined to devote his bequests to the foundation of the College which bears his name – the forerunner of the new Victorian University.'

After further bouts of rudeness, insolence and laziness from Edward and John, Absolom confided to his journal that all his children except Alfred caused him anxiety. His eldest child, Elizabeth (1817–63) suffered from some sort of chronic nervous indisposition. The close companionship that Absolom and Edward had enjoyed in earlier years had turned into irritation and hostility.[25] The time was approaching, however, for Edward to channel his energy and talents more creatively.

Social agitation, particularly against the 1815 Corn Laws, and their depressing influence on trade and employment, was increasing. Absolom had spoken as a member of the Anti-Corn Law Association to a meeting of 3,000 people in the Corn Exchange. In September 1838, Feargus O'Connor, the Chartist leader, addressed a meeting on Kersal Moor, Salford, estimated at over a quarter of a million. He had openly incited his followers to armed rebellion, and torchlight meetings had taken place where

---

[22]Ward, Lock, 1891.
[23]Goffin, p.187.
[24]Messenger, p.52.
[25]Goffin, p.207.

some had worn tricolour cockades and caps of liberty.[26] The Chartists were a working-class movement for parliamentary reform, named after the People's Charter, drafted by the London radical William Lovett in May 1838. It contained six demands:

1. Universal manhood suffrage.
2. Equal electoral districts.
3. Vote by ballot.
4. Annually-elected parliaments.
5. Payment of members of parliament.
6. Abolition of the property qualification for membership.[27]

Richard Cobden and John Bright were working hard for a repeal of the Corn Laws. Free Trade was the watchword, and the establishment of what would later be called Free Market Capitalism was in motion. Cobden owned all the spare land in St Peter's Field, the scene of the notorious 'Peterloo Massacre' in 1819, and in order to accommodate meetings of the supporters of the rapidly-growing Anti-Corn Law Association,[28] he offered some of the land for the building of a 'Free Trade Hall'.

A temporary wooden building was first erected, the work of 100 men in 11 days. With room for 4,000 people, it was 100 feet long and 105 feet wide.[29] In 1843 an even larger, brick-built, Free Trade Hall was built on the site, replaced in 1856 by a stone building. On 13 January 1840 a grand banquet for all members was held there, for 3,000 people, with many others arriving after dinner to hear the speeches. Absolom reckoned there were nearly 5,000 present. 'The speeches were not worthy of the occasion', he noted wearily afterwards.

The Association was anxious not to lose support to the Chartists, who were regarded by Liberals as too revolutionary; in order to cultivate the working classes, an Operative Anti-Corn Law Association was formed, and Edward Watkin was one of its leading spirits. He organised a second banquet, in the same place,

[26]*Ibid*, pp.199 and 202,
[27]*Encyclopaedia Britannica*, 1995, Vol. 3, pp.132 and 133.
[28]Later, in 1839, the Anti-Corn Law League, the national activities of which were directed from its offices in Manchester. John Morley, *The Life of Richard Cobden* (London: T. Fisher Unwin, 1879, 1910 Edition), p.149.
[29]Goffin, p.209.

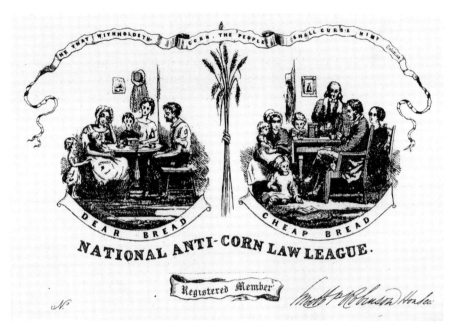

5 National Anti-Corn Law League Membership Certificate

for the day after the one his father had attended, and 5,000 'operatives' sat down to dinner. The radical Samuel Bamford (1788–1872) wrote delightedly that the poor were usually shunned by the rich, and '[that] had filled the working classes with a fierce contempt of anyone wearing a decent coat'. Now for the first time 'the two classes had come together to shake hands and to look manfully in each other's faces'.[30] The triumph of that meeting laid the foundation for Edward's ability to conceive and organise successfully the 'great occasion' in pursuit of his aims and ideals, an ability so often to be demonstrated over the coming fifty years.

Archibald Prentice, the son of a Scottish farmer, settled in Manchester in 1824, and purchased *Cowdroy's Gazette*. This failed, but it was incorporated into a new newspaper called the *Manchester Times*. In 1845 this was sold to three other radical, anti-Corn Law gentlemen, and in 1848 a union took place between this paper and the *Manchester Examiner*. The *Examiner*, a Liberal newspaper,

---

[30]Goffin, p.210.

had been founded two years before by John Bright, the Presbyterian Minister The Revd Dr William McKerrow, and Edward Watkin. The *Examiner and Times* was published by Alexander Ireland and Company, but when the Liberal split over Home Rule took place in 1886, it became a Unionist paper, and after changing hands twice in the 1890s published its last issue on 12 March 1894.[31] Of the many newspapers founded in those early years, not all were of such noble policy or editorial quality, some being given to strong language and libellous assertions, and most were fairly short-lived.

Prentice worked tirelessly in Anti-Corn Law League activities, and stayed with Absolom at Rose Hill in order to speak at meetings in neighbouring Gatley and Cheadle. It was at the Gatley meeting in spring 1840 that Edward made his first public speech. Absolom's reaction to his son's high profile and burgeoning achievements was half proud and half critical: such activities were to the detriment of time spent at the warehouse.[32] Soon after Easter, Absolom was to bewail that his business was in a critical state, but the boys continued to neglect it in favour of Anti-Corn Law activities. In July, however, Edward relieved the home pressures on Absolom by taking his sister Elizabeth to Lytham for a holiday. [33]

June 1841 saw a General Election, and Sir Robert Peel became Tory Prime Minister for the second time. The contest in Manchester was a three-cornered one – the Anti-Corn Law League, the Chartists and 'The Irish'. The League was organised into districts, each with own association and leader: Edward had been made Chairman of a district of The Operative Anti-Corn-Law Association. He, with his brother John, led a violent scrap in Stevenson Square against the Chartists and the Irish repealers, which he thoroughly enjoyed, presaging his notorious verbal confrontations with the various Chairmen of railways whose interests challenged those of his own.[34] Despite his belligerence, Edward arranged a 'Conciliation Meeting' between his group and representatives of

---

[31]T. Swindells, *Manchester Streets and Manchester Men* (Didsbury: E.J. Morton, 1907), pp. 53–5.
[32]Goffin, p.211.
[33]*Ibid*, p.215.
[34]*Ibid*, p.217.

16

the Chartists – an early example of the contrast in his character between his tendency to attack opponents with great vigour, and his gifts for reconciliation and sharing a broadness of vision.

Cobden warned of the danger of 'fraternisation' of this kind. While agreeing that some sort of agreement to avoid disruption of each other's meetings would be desirable, their respective aims remained quite different. 'They had no knowledge at all of our question – to relieve the widow and orphan from the cruelties of the bread tax, and to strike the fetters from the hands of our suffering workmen.' He urged Edward to 'try to carry a resolution expressing a wish that the working classes be not misled by ignorant or designing men', some of whom were 'the hired tools of the Duke of Buckingham…spies bribed to lead the people into treasonable causes'.[35] The working classes, he argued, 'wanted a leader of character and firmness', and asked his opinion of Sharman Crawford, 'as honest as day, and unswerving as a rock', and Colonel Thompson, 'who has many qualities that befit him for a popular champion', as possible candidates for such a position. It is worth conjecturing why Edward, with such trust and support, did not see that he could fulfil that role. Honest and principled and strong-minded he certainly was, and had he given himself wholly to politics, he could have used his gifts of mass persuasion, his concern for the common man, and his love of a battle to change the course of nineteenth-century working-class participation in democracy.

'You and your little band are doing wonders by keeping alive the Anti-Corn Law agitation,' Cobden wrote and suggested starting another Universal Suffrage newspaper, either in London or Manchester, advocating democratic principles, and asked Edward, who was all of twenty-two years old at this time, if such a newspaper could be supported.[36] It is possible that this suggestion was behind the foundation of the *Manchester Examiner*. The editorial preface of the first issue, dated Saturday, 10 January 1846, was indicative of the glowing idealism of the times:

---

[35] *Letters from the Late Richard Cobden, MP, to Sir E.W. Watkin. MP, From 1837 to 1864.* (Unpublished; bound collection by Watkin himself), letters dated 9 October 1841, 24 October 1841 and 19 January 1841.
[36] *Ibid*, letter dated 9 October 1841.

In commencing a journal, which it is hoped may become an instrument for good in this populous and important district, we are conscious that we have undertaken a task of much labour and of no little responsibility. It has appeared to us that in this county...there is still a wide field for the exertions of men who are sincerely desirous of advancing the public weal; and we have taken our present position, in the hope, and with the resolve, that our labours shall avail something in the struggles and triumphs of our time...in the cause of justice and of truth.

In the meantime, the Chartists had not forgotten Edward's attack upon them in Stevenson Square. At a meeting in the Hall of Science on 12 March 1842, violence broke out between the factions, and men were badly hurt and furniture smashed. In his newspaper *The Northern Star,* Feargus O'Connor accused Edward of having incited the Irish to attack the Chartists, as if, with O'Connor as their leader, they needed anyone else to encourage them to violence.[37]

Absolom, further disturbed at the extent to which Edward was getting involved in such violent activities, suggested that year that the lad took a holiday in Italy with his friend George Wall. He asked Richard Cobden for introductions for the two of them, and in his reply,[38] Cobden was helpful, but shrewd enough to discern Absolom's motivation: 'I should be very glad,' he wrote, 'to be able to render any service, in any way you wish, to your son, Edward, for whose character, talents, and energy I have the greatest respect. Am I correct in the supposition that you are actuated by a prudent desire to withdraw him for a short season from the vortex of political excitement into which his ardour has plunged him?'[39] He offered the help of contacts in Paris and Marseilles, and his brother-in-law for possible introductions in Genoa and 'the other places you mention'.[40] Edward and George Wall left for Italy on 26 April 1842, and arrived home from

[37]A.E. Watkin, p.214.
[38]Cobden, Letters, 22 April 1842.
[39]Goffin, pp. 219.
[40]Unfortunately, Absolom's letter has not survived.

Naples on 11 June 1842.[41] Cobden wrote on 22 June, having had a letter from Edward after his return, commenting on the brief time he had been away that he 'must have been an expeditious tourist'.[42] Wall later married Alice Makinson, Edward's cousin, popular in the family as a spirited pianist. He and Alice eventually went to live in Ceylon, where he became a prominent coffee planter.[43]

In his absence, the Chartists had presented a huge petition to Parliament, bearing over three million signatures. It included a condemnation of the new Poor Law, a request for legislation to limit hours of work in the factories, and a demand for 'one man, one vote'. Stagnation of trade was worse, and beggary increased on the streets. An Irish Chartist declared that if the Charter were not gained 'in three hundred suns', a bloody revolution would ensue.

In accordance with strict economic principles, the mine owners lowered the weekly wage for all workers, and the manufacturers also reduced their wages. Many were in a precarious position financially, and saw reducing wages as a way to stay in business and a preferable alternative both to themselves and their otherwise redundant workforce. The living standard of the working classes in 1842 was better than it had been twenty years before. Friedrich Engels, in that year, remarked that the English worker had a standard of living that would have been the envy of his counter-part in France or Germany.[44] But comparisons are also contextual: to the workers themselves the predominant perception was that of gross inequality of wealth and opportunity. Unrest continued to develop, and on Sunday, 14 August, 500 Grenadier Guards, 36 Royal Horse Artillerymen, and 2 six-pounder guns arrived in the town, by the Queen's proclamation. The Borough and County Magistrates declared that all meetings and processions were illegal, and, if necessary, would be put down and dispersed by force. Manchester was already full of trade unionists gathered for a convention: it was the anniversary of Peterloo, and the authorities were preparing for the worst. By September, peace had been

---

[41]A.E. Watkin, p.215.
[42]Cobden, Letters, p.26.
[43]Goffin, pp.242 and 254.
[44]Ibid, p.212.

restored and people had gone back to work, but Absolom felt that the prospects for the future were 'gloomy and uncertain'.[45]

Amidst all these upheavals, the future was being forged in an unlikely manner. That November, in Cologne, the twenty-two-year-old Friedrich Engels introduced himself to Karl Marx. Engels (1820–95), who was born in Barmen, 'the Manchester of Germany',[46] was on his way to Manchester to work as the agent of his father, a Rhenish cotton manufacturer, in the offices of Ermen and Engels. He had already come to the conclusion that the proletariat would rise in a social revolution which would be the bloodiest ever waged, and he was shortly to accuse the 'English bourgeoisie...of murder, robbery, and all sorts of other crimes on a grand scale'. Engels was to inspire Marx to construct a new 'metaphysic', which, with Social Darwinism via Nietzsche, was to provide one of the two main alternative paradigms of interpretation of reality for the twentieth century to that of the Christian faith.

Edward himself was to become further involved in Manchester's cultural development.

[45] *Ibid*, pp.227 and 229.
[46] Frangopulo, p.150.

3

Cultural Involvement

The Manchester Athenaeum, which Absolom had helped to found in 1835[1] for the encouragement of discussion of the arts, sciences and technology, was much more to his taste than his life as a merchant. Edward had become a member, on a date not shown in the minutes, and at the Board of Directors meeting of 27 April 1843, he was appointed with eight others to a sub-committee charged with organising a bazaar to raise funds for the running of the society, which was in acute financial embarrassment. On 11 May, Edward appears in the minutes for the first time as a director. He acted as secretary to the committee when it reported back to the Board meeting on 29 June 1843, proposing a general meeting of all Athenaeum members for the bazaar project, over which the Mayor of Manchester (Alderman Kershaw) would preside. The event raised nearly two thousand pounds, and at the meeting of 13 October the Board expressed its 'deep sense of gratitude to Edward Watkin and Peter Berlyn for their unwearied exertions'.

The minutes of the meeting of 26 October (the Board clearly believed in keeping itself busy), recorded thanks to Edward Watkin, who had sold three of his shares in the Athenaeum to a Mr Thomas Baker, and given half the proceeds of the transaction, five pounds, to the Athenaeum library. At about that time, Edward appears to have organised a 'Grand Literary Soirée', and invited Charles Dickens to preside. Dickens came for the occasion with his sister Fanny and her husband Henry Burnett, who lived in Manchester. Absolom had for some weeks been reading *Martin Chuzzlewit* to the family as the instalments came out. At a meeting

---

[1] 31 October. The opening meeting was held, at the Royal Institution, on 11 January 1836.

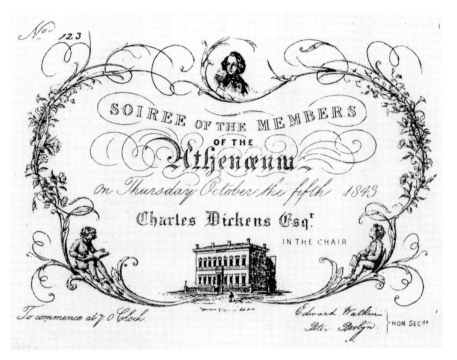

6 Athenæum Soirée ticket, 1843

on the evening prior to the event, to discuss the arrangements for it, Edward asked Dickens, who had just returned from a reading tour of the of the USA, for his American impressions. In reply, he spoke well of the American universities, and said that the feeling against slavery was stronger than most people imagined, and that it was growing.[2] That very day Edward received a note from Cobden to say that Benjamin Disraeli and his wife were staying at the Mosley Arms Hotel, and suggesting that they be invited to the soirée.[3] Edward lost no time in going to the hotel, where Mrs Disraeli met him, her husband having gone out. She assured him that they would both come, and when Edward added that they would like her husband to say something, she replied that 'Benjamin would speak: he could always speak at ten minutes'

---

[2]Goffin, pp.234, 235.
[3]*Ibid*, p.236.

notice'. And so he did.[4] Disraeli spoke of the importance of the education of the poor, amidst the clanking and whirring of machinery. It was on this visit that Dickens conceived *A Christmas Carol*,[5] when 'the complete story flashed into his mind in a great gust of creative imagination'.[6]

About this time, Edward, backed by some of his friends from the Athenaeum, agitated for a Saturday half-day holiday for the workers in shops and businesses in Manchester, and had obtained a consensus for the idea. This, of course, affected his father's business, and thereafter Absolom found it increasingly difficult to persuade himself that it was worthwhile going into Manchester to work on a Saturday morning.[7] In his journal he wrote: 'Today, the giving of a half-day holiday on Saturdays for people employed in warehouses etc., was commenced. About five hundred warehouses were closed at 1, 2, or 3 o'clock.'[8] Until then, the workers, or 'operatives', and of course the employers, had only one day off per week, and that was the 'Sabbath', on which any kind of activity was severely proscribed.

Akin to his perception of the plight of the operatives, and their daily grind in the conditions of the time, Edward saw also the need for public parks, open spaces in cities where they could have access to trees and grass and relaxation in more 'natural' surroundings. In 1843, as spokesman of the committee urging these facilities, he published a pamphlet, *A Plea for Public Parks*, 'the earliest evidence of local agitation for public parks'.[9] Enough money was raised by their activities to open Queen's Park, Harpurhey, in 1846; Peel Park, Salford; and Philips Park, in the Bradford district of Manchester.[10] All these still serve their intended purpose, though in a far less polluted atmosphere.

Absolom Watkin attended, on 8 August 1844, a public meeting on the subject of public parks and gardens in Manchester. The

---

[4]*The Grimsby Times*, 30 April 1880, quoting *The Manchester Examiner*.
[5]Though G.K. Chesterton implied that it originated in the December, in the 'very London fog'. (*Encyclopaedia Britannica*, 1955, Vol. 7, pp.331 and 336).
[6]Goffin, p.237.
[7]*Ibid*, p.239.
[8]A.E. Watkin, p.229.
[9]*Parks for the People: Manchester and its Parks, 1846–1926* (Manchester City Art Galleries, 1987), p.10.
[10]Named after Mark Philips – also spelt Phillips indiscriminately in the literature – who was the MP for Manchester.

23

Mayor introduced him to Lord Francis Egerton of Tatton Hall, Knutsford, one of the three leading speakers with Canon R.C. Clifton[11] and Mark Philips. Egerton of Tatton was an enlightened aristocrat who freely acknowledged the extent to which he owed his wealth to the labouring classes, and believed that the wealth of the mill and mine owners, and the new railways promoters, carried with it certain responsibilities and a duty to 'promote the general happiness'.[12] There is a pleasant public park in the churchyard of St John's Church, which was demolished in 1931,[13] and the plinth of a cross in its centre records that 22,000 people are buried there, including one 'William Marsden who originated the half-day holiday'. This is shorthand for 'the citizen who presided over the official committee which received the petition from Edward Watkin and his colleagues in September 1843'. Marsden (1820–48) was in support of the cause, and a monument to him and his achievements during his short life stood in St John's Church under the South Gallery.[14] The parents of the first Sir Robert Peel and John Owens are also buried there.

On 31 July 1844, Absolom and Edward attended the wedding of a Miss Hannah Mellor, daughter of Jonathan Mellor, a cotton manufacturer and friend of Absolom, who lived at Hope House, Oldham, and was a magistrate of that town.[15] This occasion was to have important consequences, for after another bout of 'unpardonable insolence' and extreme tiresomeness on Edward's part, following which Absolom had seen him off on a holiday to Ireland with one of Mellor's sons, it emerged that some of Edward's tensions were occasioned by his courting Mary Briggs Mellor. Mary Mellor's baptism[16] was recorded on 9 November 1823 at Oldham, by a priest called Fallowfield, as the daughter of Jonathan Mellor, described as a spinner, and Mary Mellor of Glodwick, Oldham. Jonathan Mellor (1783–1849) was a man of substance and high integrity. He was a Justice of the Peace, and High Constable in 1819, the year of Peterloo, when he was given

---

[11]Rural Dean of Manchester, and first Rector, and for 62 years, of St John's Church, Deansgate, founded in 1768, and where Absolom was married in November 1814.
[12]*Parks for the People*, p.10.
[13]Manchester Central Library, Greaves Collection.
[14]William E.A. Axon, *The Annals of Manchester* (Manchester: John Heywood, 1886), p.245.
[15]Goffin, p.241.
[16]She was born on 23 January 1823.

blank warrants by the Home Office so that he could arrest anyone he suspected. He refused to use them, regarding them as a dangerous legal weapon. He could remember, at the age of six, being blessed by John Wesley – his vicar having taken him personally to the meeting – when the founder of Methodism went to Oldham to open the Methodist chapel there.

On 3 July 1844, Edward, for the soirée committee, dutifully reported back to the Board of the Athenaeum and recommended another soirée, which duly took place in October. This time he suggested that an attractive group of speakers would be Disraeli, Lord John Manners and George Sydney Smythe. The invitation of Disraeli again is a little surprising. The relevance of a Tory reform movement like Young England to Manchester Liberalism is not totally obvious, and Cobden questioned it immediately: 'Those Young Englanders are sad political humbugs', he wrote to Edward on 9 July. He conceded that the tactic could help the Athenaeum, but 'did not like the idea of Manchester throwing itself too exclusively upon the patronage of the landed aristocracy'. The creed of 'Young England' was a benevolent feudalism, a 'romantic, aristocratic, nostalgic and escapist'[17] coalition of the upper and lower classes against the manufacturers and the radicals – much the sort of people who supported the Athenaeum. They represented a 'deeply-felt and sincere protest against the ugliness of contemporary England, its centralising tendencies, its vulgar utilitarianism and its meritocracy'.[18]

The actual event, which took place on 3 October, was chaired by Disraeli, and was a very good one.[19] In 1872, Disraeli returned to Manchester, 'and delivered one of the most remarkable polemics of the nineteenth century'.[20] The Free Trade Hall, and Manchester generally, might be expected to be Gladstone's territory, not his rival's. But Disraeli seems to have been relaxed there, and popular, and how much of this was due to his welcome at the Manchester Athenaeum's soirées of 1843 and 1844 can only be conjectured. In 1846, he had invented the phrase 'The Manchester School', with

---

[17]*Encyclopaedia Britannica* (1995 Edition), Vol 4, p.127c.
[18]Goffin, p.242.
[19]*The Grimsby Times,* 3 October 1844.
[20]Roy Jenkins, *Gladstone* (London: Macmillan, 1995), p.353.

which the policy of Free Trade has ever since been identified.[21] At the Board meeting of October 1844, Edward proposed, successfully, the granting of life membership to Benjamin Disraeli and the Hon. George Sydney Smythe, among others.

Autumnal gloom, and what we might today call 'Seasonal Affective Disorder', seemed to descend on the family that year, and Edward was ill and tetchy.[22] To compound the gloom, Edward's brother John had written home to say that everything at Oxford was too much for him; he was 'labouring under a dark depression of spirits', and asked that one of his brothers come to him at once. Edward responded and set out for Oxford immediately. He came back with John two days later, and the student was sufficiently recovered to return to Oxford in mid-January. Part of Edward's acute tension came from his realisation that his income was not large enough to support his marriage to Mary Mellor and keep her in 'the manner to which she was accustomed'. He knew he would have to find a much better-paid position than that of partner in a modest family warehouse business.

Absolom's youngest child, Alfred (1825–75), kept the family calm by reading to them during these stressful periods, and was working with his brothers in the business. He had grown up to be a sociable and witty young man, and loved boxing, shooting, and entertaining his friends to convivial evenings which too often ended in over-indulgence. He was later to marry another of Jonathan Mellor's daughters, Hester Anne (1827–91)[23], and become Mayor of Manchester, and his descendants became distinguished in their own right.

In the Athenaeum minutes for 26 April 1845, Alexander Ireland appears for the first time as a director. As with Edward, the minutes show no record of his election to the Board. No doubt such matters were dealt with discreetly 'off the record'. Ireland (1810–92), a well-known writer and publisher, had settled in Manchester, from Edinburgh, in 1843, and in 1846 took over the *Manchester Examiner* from Edward and his two co-founders. He married, as his second wife, Anne Nicholson (d.1893), herself an authoress of note. She was the sister of Henry Alleyn Nicholson

---

[21]Frangopulo, p.50.
[22]Goffin, p.244.
[23]*Ibid*, pp.244 and 246.

(1844–99), professor of physical sciences at Durham University and elsewhere. Their son, John Nicholson Ireland (1879–1962), trained at the Royal College of Music, graduated from Durham University in 1905, received an honorary doctorate there in 1932, and became one of England's best-known composers.

On 14 February 1845, Edward proposed 'a vigorous and combined effort for the covering of the mortgage debt' at the Athenaeum. Powers were given to a sub-committee to think of something, and at the Board meeting of 7 May, acting as amanuensis and spokesman of the sub-committee, he moved the holding of 'a Grand Soirée in the Free Trade Hall in...October next', and that the chairman, vice-chairman and secretary be appointed to a committee to procure a chairman for the occasion, and 'to apply only to the following persons, in the order here placed: Thomas Carlyle, Sergeant Talfourd[24] (who accepted), Lord Morpeth, Thomas Moore, Douglas Jerrold'. He also moved a vote of thanks to the Chairman for his efforts to induce Thomas Babington Macaulay to perform that office. This proposal, worded as it is in such a directive manner, bears Edward's own stamp; at the age of twenty-four, he was perhaps already exhibiting tendencies which would be recognised, thirty of forty years on, by the shareholders of various railway companies.

Edward was clearly playing an influential role in the affairs of the Athenaeum, and in the impact it was having on Manchester through the national figures appearing at its functions. It is clear, also, that the Athenaeum was a formative part of his experience. The record of the subjects of speakers at its meetings probably shows much of his influence, for he appears consistently as a member of the Board's sub-committee for the formation of policy on lectures and books and newspapers. Titles of the lectures include: French and German Literature; Astronomy; English Opera; Elocution; Latest Discoveries in Science; Man's Moral and Intellectual Development; The Nature and Value of Imaginative Literature; Improvements in the Steam Engine and Mechanical Science as Applied to the Arts; Civilisation; India (on which Edward later wrote a monograph); and Education. The last subject appeared in several lectures over the period.[25] His attendance at

---

[24]Thomas Noon Talfourd, Sergeant at Law, one of Her Majesty's Judges.
[25]*Manchester Athenaeum Addresses, 1835-1885* (Manchester: 1888) pp. 67 ff.

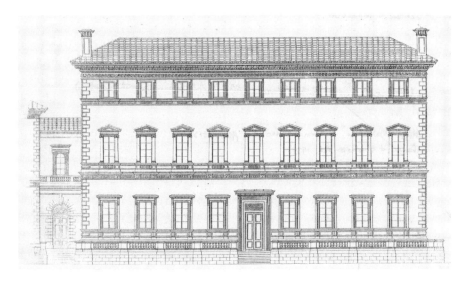

7 Charles Barry's design for the (London) Reform Club of which Watkin was a member; used by the architect also for the contemporary (1837) Manchester Athenæum of which Watkin was a director

Board meetings, which had been almost total, did not stop entirely when he left the family business in autumn 1845. He appears in the minutes of annual general meetings for the election of new directors, and on other signal occasions, and his influence was still to be perceived in its proceedings, particularly, for example, in the choice of presidents for subsequent soirées. He was not actually present at the special meeting of 8 April 1846, but the chairman was asked to approach a number of worthy gentlemen in order of preference, a list which clearly followed the lines of thinking Edward had established. These were: Thomas Babington Macaulay, Thomas Carlyle, The Archbishop of Dublin (Dr Richard Whately), The Bishop of Norwich, Edward Stanley,[26] Sir Edward Lytton Bulmer (sic), Bart., and Lord Francis Francis Egerton.

At the soirée of 22 January 1875, the speakers were the Lord

---

[26]This gentleman's inclusion is probably explained by his having been, until 1837, the incumbent of the parish of Alderley, Cheshire. Absolom recorded that the Revd Edward Stanley's Address on leaving his Alderley parishioners was 'excellent' (A.E. Watkin, p.192: Journal entry for 17 September 1837).

Chief Justice Sir Alexander E. Cockburn, the Marquis and March-ioness of Salisbury, and Lord Houghton (better known as Monckton Milnes, the poet and social reformer). Edward is recorded as seconding a resolution of thanks to the Lord Chief Justice, pointing out the benefits which the Athenaeum had brought to the people of Manchester.[27]

In the meantime, Mary Mellor and Edward were married, at Oldham Parish Church on 3 September 1845,[28] and after a week's honeymoon in Chester, moved into a rented house in Failsworth. They were not there long, however, and by January were living in Woodlands Cottage, Lower Broughton, one of his father's cottages.[29] At the end of August 1845, Edward had consulted his father about an offer he had received to become the Secretary of the newly-authorised Trent Valley Railway Company, at a salary of £500 per year. Absolom had advised him to accept it.[30] The die was cast.

---

[27]*Manchester Athenaeum Addresses, 1835–1885,* p.133.
[28]Edward's occupation was given as 'Commission Agent'.
[29]Goffin, p.251.
[30]*Ibid,* p.247.

4

The Trent Valley Railway: The Embryo Railway King

Edward's decision to accept the invitation to become the Secretary of the newly formed Trent Valley Railway Company was to lead to his huge impact on the transport history of England and Canada, and in various other parts of the globe. The Trent Valley Company had been conceived as a way of providing the Manchester and Birmingham Railway with a direct line to London by avoiding Birmingham – going from Stone (originally, later from Stafford) to Rugby, where it connected with the London and Birmingham Railway. The project was first mooted in 1835 by George Stephenson, and was referred to at the half-yearly meeting of the M&BR on 2 April 1838. At a public meeting of 'bankers, merchants, manufacturers and traders of the borough of Manchester…held at the Town Hall on the 26th of that month, the Boroughreeve of Manchester in the chair, a resolution was passed to support the proposal for the most immediate and direct means of communication by railway between this district, which may be termed the metropolis of trade, and the great metropolis of the country.'[1] This resolution was supported by the Town Council of the Borough of Manchester, the Mayor in the chair, at a meeting of the council on 8 April 1838, and at a second public meeting on the following day. The prayer of the petition was presented to Parliament in 1839, but met with great opposition, mainly from the London and Birmingham Railway, which offered to give the supporters of the Trent Valley scheme £20,000 to abandon their

---

[1] *Trent Valley Railway: Origin and Progress of the Undertaking* (Official Publication, Manchester: Cave and Sever, 18 St Ann's Street, 1845), p.4.

30

intentions.[2] Others also opposed it: Sir John Eardley Eardley Wilmot[3] could not see why the whole trade between Manchester and London should be taken from Birmingham, and Lord Sandon opposed the second reading, on 14 May 1839, on the ground that 'The pride of Manchester demanded to have a line to itself', and he questioned whether 'saving a distance of twelve miles and in time of half an hour, should be effected against the wishes of the landowners'.[4] Such was the opposition, in fact, that George Stephenson was to say later that the company's expenditure on legal fees was almost as much in total as the eventual cost of building the line.[5]

Due to the forces arrayed against it, and the tortuous parliamentary procedures, the Bill was not passed until the 1839 session, and, although a shareholders' meeting on 4 September had resolved to pursue their aim, a meeting on 11 January 1841 decided to dissolve the company, known officially as the Manchester and Birmingham Extension Railway, and re-form under another name – The Stafford and Rugby Extension Company.[6] However, on 17 March 1841, Parliament turned down the new Bill, and the project lapsed. The shareholders, still undismayed – as befitted the Mancunian spirit of the day – revived their attempt in spring 1844, under yet another new name, that of the The Trent Valley Railway Company. This time they were supported by the London and Birmingham, The Grand Junction – which ran from Earlestown on the Liverpool and Manchester Railway, via Crewe and Stafford, to Birmingham – and the Manchester and Birmingham itself. In fact, they all contributed large sums, in the region of £200,000 to £250,000, towards its cost, presumably having perceived in the interval the possibilities of such a route.

The line was to run through very flat country, involving several level crossings of roads but only one significant engineering work – Shugborough Tunnel, some four miles from Stafford. The Earl of Lichfield, permitting the line through his estate, insisted that it did

---

[2] Peter Lee, *The Trent Valley Railway, Rugby to Stafford, 1847–1966* (Trent Valley Publications, 1988), p.4.

[3] Conservative Member for Warwickshire North from 1832, until appointed Governor of Van Diemen's Land in 1842.

[4] Cave and Sever, p.8.

[5] Adrian Vaughan, *Railwaymen, Politics and Money* (John Murray, 1997), p.123.

[6] Cave and Sever, pp.22 and 23.

so in a tunnel, and that the tunnel mouths be suitably ancient in design. Thus, one end imitated the entrance to a medieval castle, and the other an Egyptian temple.[7] It ran from Rugby Station, on the London and Birmingham Railway, via Nuneaton, Atherstone, Tamworth, Lichfield, Rugeley, Colwich and Stafford. Its length was given variously as 62½ miles,[8] 52 miles,[9] and 54 miles 67 chains.[10] The higher figures are probably due to taking Stone as the northern end – as at first intended – rather than Stafford, as it was finally built. It is given as 51 miles in today's timetables.

The Bill was passed on 21 July 1845, in an Act which provided also that the company could lease itself to the L&B, The Grand Junction and the M&B, or to any one of them.[11] Incorporated into the Bill was the Act regulating level crossings – The Railway Clauses Consolidation Act of 1845,[12] which compelled trains to pass over level crossings adjoining railway stations at a speed not exceeding four miles an hour. The nature of railway operation was changing so rapidly at that time that it is very surprising that such a regulation remained in force for over fifty years after 1845. It was not revoked until 1898, when the LNWR was charged with a breach of the Act. The 1898 Bill was deposited by the North Staffordshire Railway, whose line from Colwich Junction through Sandon to Stoke on Trent was parallel in part to the Trent Valley line.[13]

The first sod of the undertaking was turned by Sir Robert Peel, who was coming towards the end of his second term as Prime Minister. His home was near Tamworth, and the ceremony took place in a field known as Carmel Close, about half a mile from the town, on 13 November 1845. At this ceremony, Edward Watkin pushed the wheelbarrow carrying the spade which was used by Sir Robert for the ritual. The *Illustrated London News,* reporting the occasion on 15 November 1845, carried a picture of this implement and a detailed description. The whole of the 'blade', made of electro-silver, was in the form of an heraldic shield, and carried the

[7]Anthony Burton, *The Railway Builders* (John Murray, 1992), p.47.
[8]Norman Webster, *Britain's First Trunk Line* (Adams and Dart, 1972), p.156.
[9]*Illustrated London News,* 22 November 1845.
[10]Cave and Sever, p.3.
[11]Peter Lee, p.4.
[12]*Ibid.*
[13]*Railway Magazine,* January 1899, self-quoted, January 1999.

arms, crest and motto of the Rt. Hon. Baronet, and on the reverse side was engraved the official seal of the Trent Valley Railway Company and 'the names of the Chairman, the Directors, Engineer, Solicitor, and the Secretary...' Further coverage by the *ILN* came at the opening of the line on 26 June 1847, in the edition of 3 July.[14] 'The line was opened with eclat when a remarkable speech was made by Sir Robert Peel, comparing the present enterprise with that of the great Roman emperor Julius Agricola, who had chosen the same route as the railway.'

Among those present at the opening was Viscount Sandon, MP, who must have had a change of heart after his initial objections. Perhaps he had further reflected on a letter to him from Sir Robert dated 12 December,[15] a reply to a communication from the noble Lord (rather an anxious one, judging from the way Sir Robert repeats his assurances), declaring that he had not pledged his support to either the promoters of the Trent Line, or the objectors to it. He confided: 'I would rather the line was *not* made – for it cuts in two that part of my property which I most wish to be exempt from the intrusion of a Rail Road. On the other hand,' he continued, 'if the interests of my constituents and the neighbourhood are to be promoted by the line, I must consult them, rather than my own private feelings.' He said that he was able to support or object to one line rather than another. Such a discussion of clash of interest must have taken place many times in those pioneering days. Peel went on to note other quandaries: 'I have not given my consent to the line, for that part of my property above referred to, and am in that embarassing position situation in which many others are placed, of having to treat with the Company for land taken and injury done – and then to decide as a Member of Parliament on the merits of their proposal'[16] – this was a question of 'declaring an interest'. However, because of his eventual commitment, the railway became generously spoken of as 'Peel's Line'.[17]

Absolom Watkin's impressions of the opening festivities were

---

[14]Page 3.
[15]No year shown – assumed to be 1838.
[16]Harrowby Mss Trust, Sandon Hall, Stafford. By kind permission.
[17]Peter Lee, p.4.

recorded in his journal: 'About five hundred persons[18] sat down at two o'clock to a splendid dejeuner in a huge building run up for the purpose and hung with pink and white calico and ornamented with evergreens and flags. We also had a military band...I enjoyed the day very much.'[19]

The full opening of the line to traffic was on Wednesday, 1 December 1847. Reporting on that occasion, the *Illustrated London News*,[20] listing the stations on the line, stated that it passed through 'Thugborough Tunnel', and thanked the Secretary of the line, 'Mr Watkins', for the help given to the artist for the illustrations. The *Staffordshire Advertiser* (8 May 1847) expressed the thanks of its staff to Watkin for 'his great courtesy in affording us every facility for minutely inspecting the line, and his imparting full information' on the undertaking. From 1 December, the LNWR declared that it would be running its trains between London and the North over the new line, and that the clocks on every station on their system would be set to Greenwich Time, pointing out that this worked out at seven minutes before Birmingham time, twelve minutes before Liverpool, ten before Manchester and Preston, and twelve before Chester time.[21] On the twenty-third, Aberdeen sustained 'the irrevocable loss' of eight minutes and twenty-two seconds.[22]

As the new railway company was floated in Manchester, a comparison of the men named in the prospectus and the successive committees of the project discloses how Edward came to be offered the post of Secretary. James Aspinall Turner was a close associate of Absolom Watkin: he was a shareholder with him of the Bank of England in Manchester.[23] Another prominent name in the Manchester cotton trade was Tootal. Henry and Edward Tootal (eventually Deputy Chairman) were directors of the Trent Valley

---

[18]Six hundred, according to the *Staffordshire Advertiser* (26 June 1847), which listed the most distinguished guests, followed by others 'of the highest respectability', including Captain Huish and Edward Watkin.

[19]Goffin, p.264.

[20]4 December 1847.

[21]Peter Lee, p.5.

[22]J.J. Waterman, *The Aberdeen Railway and the Great North of Scotland Railway in the 1840s* (University of Aberdeen, September 1873), p.17.

[23]Goffin, pp.270, 352, 358 and 366.

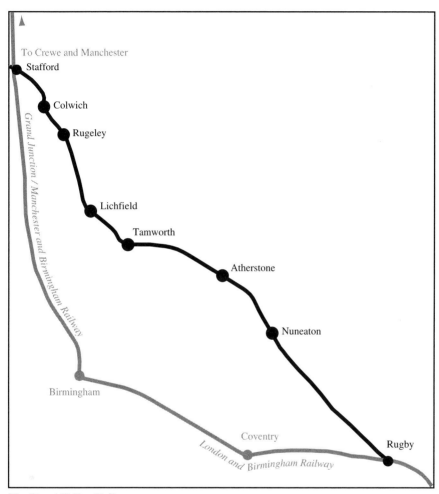

The Trent Valley Railway

Company[24] and Absolom was well known to them.[25] Edward Tootal was admitted as a life member of the Manchester Athenaeum on 26 October 1843. The admiration of any of these gentlemen for the public activities of Absolom's eldest son would lead them to see him as a likely candidate.

Given the way that rail traffic was developing, and that the Trent Valley Company had formed itself into an important segment of the commercially busiest corridor in the country, it is not surprising that its prospects were very promising. It was not to last as a separate unit for long. In spring 1846 the line was bought by the London and Birmingham Railway, acting for itself and for the Manchester and Birmingham and Grand Junction Railways, just before these three companies came together to form the LNWR on 16 July 1846. Cuthbert Hamilton Ellis[26] was of the opinion that the Trent Valley Railway was the *reason* for the former enemies coming together in this way; it represented a common interest and a common potential threat of competition if absorbed by a rival company. If he is right, this rather insignificant length of track, linking no great centres of industry or population, gave rise to the largest capital investment company in the world at that time. History has always given Edward the credit for the surprisingly high sale price (after three or four offers had been turned down, the Trent Valley raising its price each time).[27] This was given variously as £440,000,[28] £500,000[29] and £438,000[30]. Considering that the three companies had already contributed over half that amount each for the building of the line only three years before, it is perhaps a high figure. One historian has observed that from it one would think that the Trent Valley's rails were made of gold, rather than iron.[31] In view of the traffic later to traverse what eventually became Britain's West Coast Main line, perhaps symbolically they were.

Despite the high price, but presumably because it was a bargain

[24]Cave and Sever, p.47.
[25]Goffin, p.264.
[26]In his *British Railway History,* (2 Vols.), Vol. 1. (George Allen and Unwin, 1953), p.177.
[27]*Blackburn Telegraph,* 15 April 1901.
[28]*Railway Magazine,* April 1901, p.411.
[29]*Manchester Guardian,* 15 April 1901.
[30]Watkin's own figure, in *Canada and the States,* p.321.
[31]Roger Lloyd, *Railwaymen's Gallery* (George Allen and Unwin, 1953), p.91.

anyway, Edward received from the LNWR in January 1848 a 'very panegyrical' letter, thanking him for his help in the negotiations.[32] Edward himself, however, paid a very high personal price for the operation. As Secretary of the company, he was responsible for winding up the company's business, balancing the books and paying off the shareholders. This he tackled with characteristic application and disregard for proper food and rest. In his own account, he explained that 'In the Spring of 1846 it became necessary to give each shareholder his share of principal and profit. It was arranged that the shareholders should call at the office in Norfolk Street, Manchester, for their cheques on and after a day in April' of that year. The book-keeper reported a balancing error in the books of 1s 10d. Edward observed that any error, even of one penny, could conceal errors by the hundred. They stayed up over the two nights left to them before the settlement day, and did discover over a hundred errors in debit and credit. Still not having had anything to eat or drink ('A beefsteak and a pint of stout would have saved me from ten years, more or less, of suffering, weakness, and all kinds of misery'), he began to receive the shareholders.

'They got their cheques and went away satisfied. About noon, Mr Henry Houldsworth, the father of the present member for Manchester, called for his cheque, and, chatting with him at the time, as I was making the upstroke of the letter "H" in "Houldsworth", I felt as if my whole body was forced up into my head, and that it was ready to burst.' He raised his head, and the strange feeling went away. He tried again and the same thing happened, repeatedly, until 'with a face as white as paper, that alarmed those about me, I fell forward on the desk'. He was given water, but was not able to swallow it. 'I never lost entire consciousness, but I thought I was going to die. I never can forget all that in those moments passed through my brain.'[33]

After being taken to the room of a surgeon, an old friend, in Mosley Street, and given brandy and soda water (a drink he had never had before) and a biscuit, he felt much better and declared himself fit to carry on. His medical adviser, however, sent him

---

[32]Goffin, p.270.
[33]E.W. Watkin, *Canada and the States*, p.322.

home (Woodlands Cottage, Lower Broughton) to rest, but did not prevent him from calling at the office to see how the clerks were coping. Alarmed by his appearance, some of them said, Watkin found out later, 'We shall never see him again'. 'But they did', wrote Edward, 'shaky and seedy as he was, for many a long day.'[34]

'What weakness, what nonsense,' he said to himself the next day, feeling ready for work; and after putting in some time at the office was brought to his senses by his affectionate wife who, prompted by Mr Smith, the surgeon, persuaded him to stop at once or he would have 'brain fever'. The words were hardly out of her mouth when he felt he could do no more. 'Alas, my *nerve* was gone', he wrote. 'Often have I sneered at "bilious subjects", "dyspepsia", and that long string of woes which one hears of, in such luxuriance of description, usually over breakfast, at Clifton, Tonbridge, or Harrogate. Like the old Duchess of Marlborough, too, I used to "thank God I was born before nerves came into fashion." '[35]

After some years of 'struggling with this nerve-demon, the child of overwork', he wrote down the sequence of events in the hope that others might be spared the suffering he had inflicted on himself. Deranged digestion, jangling nerves, sleepless nights on end, the bed shaking from the violent palpitations of the heart, pillow drenched with sweat, suddenly afraid – 'not before real dangers but at phantasms and shadows, nay, actually at your own horrid self'. 'But most of all,' he goes on in this agony of self-analysis,

> if you are of a stubborn, dogged temper, and are blessed with a strong desire to 'get on' – to feel yourself unable to make some effort at all, to find yourself breaking down before all the world in others, and to learn, at last, in consequence, almost to hate the half-dead and failing carcase tied to your still living will. This, not for months only, but for YEARS. Years, too, in what ought to be your prime of manhood. Ah! Old age and incapacity at thirty is a bitter, bitter, punishment.

---

[34] *Ibid*, p.323.
[35] *Ibid*, pp.324 and 325.

...Indeed, a lady of a certain age could hardly feel more abashed at the sudden production of her baptismal certificate than I – a man, a matter-of-fact man, a plain, hard-headed, unimaginative man of business – do, at this confession. Suffice it to say, that in the last four years I have lived the life of a soul in purgatory or an inhabitant of the 'Inferno'...The history of my derangements is told above in one word: that word is – OVERWORK.[36]

He became convinced that functional derangement had become organic disease, and that his days were numbered. Nothing seemed to do him any good. Yet as Roy Jenkins remarks on Gladstone, in his biography, 'Vast energy, plus, as it turned out, exceptional longevity, is not necessarily connected with good health.'[37] 'This acute episode sounds like a vasovagal (fainting) attack which can be brought on by acute stress...In those days the diagnosis may have been one of "neurasthenia" but the label these days would probably be "anxiety state".'[38] He set sail for convalescence in the United States on 16 August 1851, to stay with some Manchester Quaker friends.

He returned from North America on 7 October, very much improved in health, and began to write an account of his trip, based on his letters from across the Atlantic to the banker George Carr Glyn, Chairman of the LNWR. Referred to by Edward simply as 'a very little book', it was published on 1 January 1852 by the stationer/politician W.H. Smith, and promptly sold out.[39] Richard Cobden complimented him upon it, though observing that he appeared to have worked very hard on what was supposed to be a holiday. He wrote, 'You could not have done a wiser and more patriotic service than to make the people of this country better acquainted with what is going in the United States. It is from that quarter, and not from barbarous Russia, or fickle France, that we have to expect formidable rivalry – and yet that

---

[36]*Ibid*, pp.326 and 327.

[37]Roy Jenkins, *Gladstone* (London: Macmillan, 1995), p.221.

[38]Private letter, 21 November 2000, from Stephen Tomlinson, Professor of Medicine at the University of Manchester, who remarked that Sir Edward clearly had insight when he suggested that "Alas, my nerve had gone", and undoubtedly managed it appropriately, and in some sense as it would have been today.

[39]E.W. Watkin, p.331.

8 Richard Cobden, at the age of 57

country is less studied or understood in England than is the history of ancient Egypt or Greece...What you saw there [was] that we were being fast distanced by our young rival.'[40]

Watkin's book shows him to have engaged in a fairly lengthy geographical and economic survey of the country, with ten pages devoted to the moral and financial implications of slavery, including figures for the number of church buildings, and communicant members in the various Christian denominations – 1 in 5.5 of the population. 'This country', he observed, '...possesses all the elements which are usually considered as contributing to civilisation and to power. It has far outstripped us in the rate of its progress.'[41]

Well might Cobden rebuke Watkin mildly for his restless energy during his recuperation. Absolom's journal records several instances, during the period after the winding-up of the Trent Valley Company and Edward's appointment by the LNWR as assistant to its manager, of his being unsettled, worn out and dejected. This was having a bad effect on his wife Mary, who, on

[40]Cobden, *Letters to E.W. Watkin* dated 6 and 8 January 1852.
[41]E.W. Watkin, pp.334–9.

40

at least one occasion, was 'very ill, sick, and hysterical'.[42] By this time they had a son, Alfred Mellor, who was born on 18 August 1846, and by June 1850 a daughter, Harriette Sayer. At the beginning of July 1848, Edward and Mary moved to London, and in November Absolom and Edward went to visit the Devonshire village where Absolom's mother had been brought up. They stayed two days in Bath, visited Walcot church, where she had been married, and then to Ashbrittle, her 'native place'.[43] Later in his life, Edward, who had been very fond of his grandmother, had two elaborate stained glass windows put into Ashbrittle church to honour her and his father. These are still in place. The first is a reproduction of Holman Hunt's *Light of the World*, spread over three lights, with the words from Revelation Chapter 3, verse 20: *Behold, I stand at the Door and Knock*. 'Absolom Watkin, died 1861. In Memoriam'. The second is a representation of the Crucifixion, spread over three lights, with the words, under the three figures, *Scanta* (sic) *Maria B.D.* [?], *Salvator Mundi*, and *Sanctus Johannes*. 'Presented by Lady Watkin and her dau. Mrs Harriette Sayer Worsley in memory of Betty Sayer Widow of Th.Watkin Born 1750 and once of this parish. 1887.' The Sayer family married into the Goddard family, whose descendants still farm at Ashbrittle. A long-established industrial pumping company, now run by Charles Doble, who lives in the Old Rectory at Ashbrittle, played a part in Edward Watkin's Channel Tunnel endeavours in the 1880s.[44]

Edward was taken into the employment of the LNWR at a fairly high level. In February 1849 he was appointed Secretary of Committees, reporting directly to the Board of Directors, and was issued with a free ticket to travel, as his duties required, on the system.[45] The number of committees included in that description was in excess of ten, covering all aspects of the running of the company.[46] In addition there were various sub-committees: including Canal, Church and School, and Permanent Way. It was established by the directors that his salary would be £600 per

---

[42]Goffin, pp. 268, 275 and 279.
[43]*Ibid*, pp.282 and 283.
[44]Private letters to author dated 6 July and 13 August 1998.
[45]Minutes of Board meeting held on 10 February 1849, Minute 751, (PRO RAIL 410/20).
[46]Listed in meeting of 12 May 1849, Minutes 805, 806, 818–22; and 11 May 1850, Minute 1842.

annum[47], 'exclusive of any temporary allowance from Branch Lines'.[48] This provision gave rise to many extra responsibilities in those expanding times, taking Watkin onto the committees of the Coventry, Nuneaton, Birmingham and Leicester; the Buckinghamshire; the Warwick to Stratford-upon-Avon; the Worcester and Hereford; the Oxford, Worcester and Wolverhampton; and the Shrewsbury and Crewe, with several others as they emerged. On all of these, Watkin's reports and recommendations were adopted by the Board.[49] In the negotiations with the Great Western Railway over the Oxford, Worcester and Wolverhampton Railway, Watkin proposed a complete union of interests and a cessation of hostility. There had been much heat generated by the discussion of the gauge to which the line should be built, starting, as it did in Great Western territory, with Brunel's gauge of 7' 0¼ " and connecting with the LNWR with the 'narrow' gauge, later 'standard', of 4' 8½". Because of his skill in these negotiations, his colleagues nicknamed him 'Nimble Ned'.[50]

Thus Watkin seems to have had, in the most prominent school of the time, a first-class programme of training in how to run a railway, from practical details to top management. The Board's discussions of proposals to amalgamate with the Midland Railway,[51] and to acquire the North Staffordshire Railway *in toto*,[52] would give him first-hand experience of grand strategy and competitiveness. Apparently the Board of Directors and Mark Huish were confident of their protégé's abilities at this time, though Edward was later to pay full credit to George Carr Glyn (1797–1873), the banker, and chairman of the LNWR, later Lord Wolverton, for his education in railway management. On 24 July 1873 he announced to the shareholders of the South Eastern Railway the death of Wolverton, acknowledging that 'It was under the Chairmanship of Lord Wolverton...that I first acquired some knowledge of railway working and railway policy, and, at a far

---

[47]By July 1852 this had increased to £1,000, (Goffin, p.319).
[48]Meeting of 12 May 1849, Minute 830.
[49]Meetings of 12 May 1849, Minutes 834, 837 and 838; 13 October 1850, Minute 995 (PRO RAIL 410/21); of 10 July 1852, Minute 1838; and 4 August 1852, Minute 1858 (PRO RAIL 410/22).
[50]*The Looking Glass,* Manchester, April 1878, p.12.
[51]At the meeting of 18 September 1852, Minute 1884.
[52]9 October 1852, Minute No.1908.

later date, it was his wish – a wish that induced me to accept the responsibility – that I became the chairman of a great undertaking on the other side of the Atlantic.' His name 'will stand out as conspicuously or more so than that of Stephenson or any of the other pioneers of our noble industry...We must see how much the public at large, and mankind at large, owe to Lord Wolverton for bringing the people of this country to risk their savings in the prosecution of railways (cheers).'[53]

Mark Huish (1808–67) was one of the first railway managers, and therefore one of the pioneers in management of a large-scale modern industrial joint stock company.[54] He was foremost in the development of traffic cartels which divided receipts between participating companies. When the most significant of these, the so-called 'Euston Square Confederacy' ('a bold and imaginative piece of strategic planning'[55]) collapsed in 1857, largely due to the reorganisation of agreements involving Edward Watkin, he was made the scapegoat by a group of LNWR directors, led by Richard Moon (later to become one of the most formidable and successful of railway chairmen), George Glyn, the Chairman, and Absolom's friend Edward Tootal, and in 1858 Huish was forced to resign. He was a master strategist of railway diplomacy, but having such a comprehensive grasp of how things could best be done, and great enthusiasm in pursuing it, he found it difficult to delegate authority and responsibility.

The parallels with Watkin have not been lost on historians. Such epithets as 'wily' and 'crafty', liberally sprinkled about in much writing on Huish,[56] have been also used of Watkin,[57] with some justification. Other adjectives, doubtfully applicable to Huish, have been used of Watkin with far less truth: 'vain, petulant, ruthless, dishonourable', 'unscrupulous', 'rapacious', and 'a liar'.[58] References to Watkin's having taken over Huish's mantle as the 'Railway Machiavelli' are acceptable only if it is borne in mind

[53]PRO RAIL 1110 425, p.747.
[54]T.R. Gourvish, *Mark Huish and the London and North Western Railway – A Study of Management* (Leicester University Press, 1972).
[55]*Ibid,* p.259.
[56]Richard Hough, *Six Great Railwaymen* (Hamish Hamilton, 1955), p.111.
[57]C. Hamilton Ellis, *British Railway History* (George Allen and Unwin, 1953), Vol. 1, p.309.
[58]Jack Simmons, *The Victorian Railway* (Thames and Hudson, 1991), pp.113 and 263; and George Dow, *Great Central* (London: Locomotive Publishing Company, 1959, 1962 and 1965, 3 Vols.),Vol. 1, p.182.

that the Florentine political philosopher's recommendations were not totally without scruple. The Prince was advised to adhere to virtue – fidelity, friendship, humanity and religion – as far as possible in government and diplomacy, resorting to sheer expediency only when the stability or very existence of the commonwealth was threatened.[59]

In the meantime, Absolom records that Edward's mood was far from rested, or restful: '2 March 1851: Edward enraged and everyone uncomfortable.' Magdalene Goffin comments that the 1850s was a decade of opportunity for those who were sufficiently intelligent or tough. Edward had the qualities, but the going was rough for him and for his family. Oswald Spengler regarded capitalism as 'economic Darwinism'. He blamed the English for it, in its pitching the rich against the poor,[61] contrasting it with the Prussian hierarchical state. There certainly was a Darwinian tinge to business endeavour in those pioneering days. 'The world of the British railway magnate in the eighteen-fifties was a fantastic bedlam of extreme competition. There were no rules and no principles. Competition alone was king. To succeed in it a man must have nerve and skill and a strong body.'[62] Only those fitted for the fierce competition and pace of progress survived. Edward was in the process of developing his survival skills, and the learning curve was very steep indeed. He himself said at the time, 'I felt the price I was paying for the privilege of labour and its remuneration. But I thought, ever, of my wife and little babies and the thought roused me to a kind of desperation, and made me feel for the time as if I could trample weakness under foot, and tear out, break in pieces, those miserable, over-sensitive organs, which chained, cramped and hindered me.'[63]

With a touch of irony, his wife Mary was involved in an accident on his railway on 5 August 1852. Her train to London was in collision with a light engine between Madeley and Stafford. The train engine concerned, *Scorpion*, had been given a pilot engine, *Velocipede*, for the 9.30 a.m. Liverpool to London

[59]Machiavelli, *The Prince* (London: Penguin Books, 1981), p.56.
[60]Goffin, p.303.
[61]Spengler, *Preusentum und Sozialismus* (Munich, 1920), p.111. Quoted, Giles MacDonogh, *Prussia: The Perversion of an Idea* (Mandarin Press, 1994), p.283.
[62]Roger Lloyd, *Railwaymen's Gallery* (George Allen and Unwin, 1953), p.57.
[63]E.W. Watkin, p.330.

9 Mary Briggs Watkin, Edward's wife, about 1846

train, which was exceptionally loaded to twelve carriages and two brake vans for the Crewe to Stafford section. After the train had negotiated Madeley bank, the pilot engine, according to normal practice, was detached, and ran on ahead to cross over to the down line and return to Crewe. Unfortunately, the train caught up with the pilot engine at Hatton Coal Wharf, about $10\frac{3}{4}$ miles north of Stafford, before it had had time to complete the maneouvre and there was a crash.[64] Mary suffered no more than a severe shaking, but two people were killed and several injured. She recuperated with Absolom and his wife at Rose Hill, taking with her her two-year-old daughter and her nurse. In June 1848, Edward and Mary, who had until then been living in Cheadle, moved to London, and in March 1853 moved again to Tavistock Square, only a few hundred yards from the Euston headquarters of the LNWR.[65] However, in December of that year Absolom records that Edward was still stressed, and fidgety and out of humour; his two children were being looked after by

---

[64] *The Staffordshire Advertiser,* Saturday, 7 August 1852. Goffin, pp.319 and 320.
[65] Goffin, pp.279 and 324.

45

their nurse, Miss Mellor, part of the time, and they were often at Rose Hill. He was contemplating leaving the LNWR, and was weighing up the merits of the various companies eager to employ him.[66]

On 4 November 1853, at a Board meeting in Manchester of the Manchester, Sheffield and Lincolnshire Railway, the Deputy Chairman, John Chapman, was given full powers to find a successor as general manager of the company to James Allport, who had resigned on 20 July to become General Manager of the Midland Railway. Chapman reported back only one week later to say that he had secured an acceptance of the post from Edward Watkin of the LNWR. His appointment would take place on 1 January 1854, or 'from such earlier date as his present commitments allowed'.[67]

That was the date of his taking up the post, but Watkin rendered some services to the MS&LR during the December (for which he was paid £100) – one of them being the settlement of a dispute of over a year with the Midland Railway, which had caused the suspension of train services at Eckington Station, near Sheffield. Another was the negotiation of the reduction of tolls which the LNWR charged on MS&LR traffic between Ardwick Junction and Manchester London Road Station.[68] Edward's contract was for five years and his salary £1,200 a year – the same as Allport's – plus 1⅛ per cent of all increases in net earnings, or savings on working expenses, taking the year ended 30 June 1853 as the starting point.

After spending much time at Rose Hill between 1851 and 1853,[69] Edward and the family moved in July 1854 to a house in Wash Lane, Timperley.[70] This was Moatfield House, built a couple of years earlier in the grounds of Riddings Hall, a fifteenth-century moated farmhouse within 450 yards of the Manchester, South Junction and Altrincham Railway station there, and thus only seven or so miles and a twenty-minute journey from the MS&LR headquarters at London Road Station. The house was of consider-

---

[66] *Ibid*, pp.323, 324, and 338.
[67] Dow, Vol. 1, p.156.
[68] *Ibid*, pp.156 and 157.
[69] They moved back to Rose Hill in 1858, to look after Absolom, living there permanently after his death in 1861. Goffin, p.371.
[70] Goffin, p.343.

10 Edward Watkin, c1864

11 Watkin Family Group, c1865: Edward, Mary, Alfred and Harriette

able size: the 1861 Census recorded that the owner was an East India Company merchant, who had a resident staff of a governess, a housekeeper, a cook and a number of maids.[71]

---

[71]The house was demolished in 1904, but the named gateposts are still there.

5

The Manchester, Sheffield and Lincolnshire Railway, 1831–1861

Whatever else determines Edward Watkin's place in history, the MS&LR and its development was his main work, in terms of length of time, covering, as it did, over forty years of his working life. The first railway between the great industrial cities of Manchester and Sheffield had its origin in the attempts of a group of business men – inspired by the overwhelming commercial success of the Liverpool and Manchester Railway, opened in 1830 – to improve the movement of manufactures and raw material between them. The canal system operating at the beginning of the century, which ran via Ashton-under-Lyne, Huddersfield, Wakefield, Barnsley and Rotherham, not the most direct of routes but dictated by the intervening Pennine massif, involved a journey of eight days. The best route by horse and cart took two whole days.[1]

Various new canal and composite canal/rail schemes were proposed, but opinions gradually veered towards a rail route throughout, starting with schemes which included inclined planes involving the use of rope haulage, but developing towards the idea of a tunnel to pierce the final part of the Pennine ridge. The proprietors of the Sheffield and Manchester Railway held the first of several planning meetings in Manchester in October 1831, but by June 1833 the project was defeated by the estimated expenditure and the physical difficulties of tunnelling in such wild and unpredictable moorland, and the shareholders were paid off. However, only two and a half years later, the new railway system, with locomotives hauling vehicles on iron rails throughout, had estab-

---

[1]Dow, *Great Central*, Vol. 1, p.1.

lished its superiority over all other modes of transport. Groups of influential men from Sheffield, Manchester, Ashton-under-Lyne and Stalybridge held a series of meetings in 1836, and after a survey of the best route, involving 'only two miles of tunnelling', launched the prospectus for the 'Sheffield, Ashton under Lyne and Manchester Railway' (SAM), with a proposed capital of £800,000. It declared that the new line 'would be available to a population as numerous (with perhaps one or two exceptions) as is connected by any railway in the kingdom'. This figure was given as 456,892.[2] The line was to run from London Road, Manchester, to near the cattle market in Sheffield, a distance of $40\frac{3}{4}$ miles.

The decision to site the headquarters of the railway in Manchester caused one Sheffield officer to resign, but throughout the life of the company, even through two changes of name, it was to be referred to colloquially as 'The Sheffield Company'. The Bill for its incorporation was deposited in 1836, and the ground was broken, to mark the beginning of construction, near the middle of the proposed line, by the western entrance of the eventual summit tunnel at Woodhead. This ceremony took place on 1 October 1838, in unwonted fine weather. The lines were built eastwards and westwards to the tunnel site, trains running from both ends, and the distance between, until the tunnel was completed, was accomplished by transferring the passengers to coach and horses. The Woodhead tunnel, taking six years to complete, was considered one of the great engineering achievements of its time. Its length of 3 miles 22 yards made it the longest railway tunnel in the world.[3] The cost was in the region of £200,000, and the number of men employed on the work, living in stone huts on the wild and bleak moors, was said to have reached 1,500, though the average was about 400. *The Sheffield Iris* declared that 'the tunnel itself is a wondrous triumph of art over nature', being bored so accurately from both ends as to meet 'within a few inches', and straight enough to enable an observer to see 'daylight at the other end like a small burning taper.'[4] The ticket collector at Woodhead Station

[2]*Ibid*, pp.15, 17, 18 and 20.
[3]Martin Bairstow, *The Sheffield, Ashton under Lyne and Manchester Railway* (published by the author, 1986), p.19.
[4]George Dow, *The First Railway Between Manchester and Sheffield* (The London and North Eastern Railway, 1945), p.25.

could see from his office window a train entering the tunnel at the far end, and know that he had four and a half minutes before stepping out to receive the passengers – an important calculation on one of the wild and wet days frequent at the spot.[5] The newspaper eulogy could have included the observation that the tunnel was driven at a rising gradient (west to east) of 1 in 201. Through trains between the two towns began with the formal opening on 22 December 1845, but traffic increased until the single line through the tunnel became inadequate, and a second bore was driven alongside; this was opened on 2 February 1852.

The most important further development, by far, came from talks towards absorption by the SAM of the prospected Sheffield and Lincolnshire Junction Railway, the Great Grimsby and Sheffield Junction Railway and the Grimsby Docks Company. This last, though only small, was of great antiquity, having been incorporated in 1796 as the Grimsby Haven Company at a time when Grimsby had allowed its fish trade to pass to Hull, because of lack of commitment to solving the problem of silting. The resulting conglomerate of these companies, forming a continuous line from Manchester to the North Sea, was to be known as the Manchester, Sheffield and Lincolnshire Railway from 1 January 1847.[6] There were several joint lines – owned by two or more companies – in which the MS&LR was a partner. One of the most important of the eight was opened on 1 August 1849. This was the Manchester South Junction and Altrincham Railway, which had been jointly promoted in 1844 by the SAM and Manchester and Birmingham railways. It ran from their joint station at Store Street (later renamed London Road) to make connection with the Liverpool and Manchester Railway at Liverpool Road Junction, and then a branch line of $7\frac{3}{4}$ miles from Castlefield Junction (so-called because of the nearby fort of Celtic origin) to Altrincham.

In 1849 the railway world was shocked by the downfall of George Hudson on charges of fraud. The most prominent of the 'Railway Kings' after George Stephenson, Hudson (1800–71) had ruled with a rod of wrought iron over four of the major companies of the time: the Midland; the York, Newcastle and Berwick; the

[5]Personal conversation with retired employee, Mr Tom Davies, Crowden, on 25 August 1988.
[6]George Dow, *Great Central*, Vol. 1, p.84.

Eastern Counties; and the York and North Midland. He was thus in financial control of the whole railway system east of the Pennines as far south as the Thames, and with a monopoly of the services in Nottingham, Leicester and Derbyshire.[7] Hudson's place as the so-called 'Railway Machiavelli' was taken by Captain Mark Huish of the London and North Western Railway, who perceived that in order to hold and develop traffic to the North and the Midlands he must regard the Great Northern and the Great Western as his main enemies. To disadvantage the Great Northern, a railway 'which every other company in England had struggled to strangle at birth'[8] (its enemy at the start having been Hudson), in 1850 he made secret treaties with six companies: the Midland (in disarray after Hudson's departure), the East Lancashire, the Eastern Counties, the North British, the Lancashire and Yorkshire (like the MS&LR a cross-country line serving South Lancashire and Yorkshire, extending from Blackpool and Liverpool to Goole), and the MS&L, though the last two stood more to gain from befriending the Great Northern. The purpose of the alliance was to maximise profits by minimising competition. Such 'common purse' agreements were illegal, and against the interests of the travelling public.

Because of such empire-building, it was clear to the MS&L Board that there was an urgent need for a general manager big enough to manage its affairs in the brutal world of this gladiatorial pit. They invited James Joseph Allport (1811–92), a man who was 'destined to become one of the greatest railway general managers of all time'.[9] George Hudson had recognised his abilities early, and made him superintendent of the York, Newcastle and Berwick Railway. Allport was appointed to the MS&LR on 9 November 1849, and urged to take up his duties at the earliest possible moment. This proved to be 1 January 1850, and his appointment occasioned an outburst of criticism at the choice of 'one of Hudson's pupils'.[10] Looking at the state of affairs he had inherited, Allport felt he had to enter into the traffic agreements proposed by Huish, a move which bedevilled MS&L/GNR relations for years

---

[7]Jack Simmons, *The Railways of Britain* (London: Sheldrake Press, 1986), p.20.
[8]Roger Lloyd, p.63
[9]Dow, Vol. 1, p.138.
[10]*Ibid.*

afterwards. At that time, the GNR was completing the line from London to Peterborough, which connected with its route from Boston to Lincoln, and in the near future hoped to complete access to Doncaster by means of its link between Peterborough and Retford.

Huish correctly discerned that if the GNR and MS&L reached any agreement, there would emerge, from where they crossed at Retford, the rival route he feared from Manchester to London. Huish thus made overtures of traffic-sharing to this hitherto-negligible company, 'The Sheffield', in which Allport and the directors acquiesced in 1850. It was thus that the MS&L became part of the 'Euston Square Confederacy', one of the more notorious of the inter-company agreements of the second half of the nineteenth century which were to come under the scrutiny of the anti-monopoly legislation. This move of Allport's was bound to cause friction with the GNR where that company came face to face with the MS&L. The Chairman of the 'Sheffield', Lord Yarborough, made overtures to his GN opposite number, Edmund Denison, regarding the possibility of the common use of the GNR station at Lincoln and the MS&LR ones at Sheffield, Retford, Gainsborough and Grimsby, but his terms were rejected contemptuously. However, during this period, MS&L services, especially for passengers, were improving. The new electric telegraph was installed on an increasing number of routes, stations were rebuilt and train services were extended. The traffic receipts for 1851 were £397,000, an increase of £38,000 over the previous year. A new dock was opened in Grimsby in March 1852 as well as the second Woodhead tunnel.

Allport's reign on the MS&L was brief. In 1853 the Midland Railway offered him the post of General Manager, and he resigned on 20 July of that year. At the half-yearly meeting held on 31 August, the directors were able to declare that revenue from both passenger and goods traffic was following encouraging trends.[11] Watkin was offered the post of General Manager of the MS&L, which he took up from 1 January 1854. Captain Huish and those at the helm of the LNWR were sorry to lose him. In gratitude for his services to the LNWR, its officers raised a sum by

---

[11] *Ibid*, pp.138, 146, 151–3 and 154.

subscription and bought plate worth £750. The presentation was made on 3 April at a dinner held in Edward's honour at the London Tavern, with his parents and his brother John and his wife. The plate was on display at a large assembly of guests in Edward and Mary's new house in Timperley in July 1854.[12]

He was early involved in expansionist measures for the MS&LR. On 7 May 1855, Absolom recorded that he went to a meeting in the committee room of the Victoria Hotel in London at which Edward was examined by a parliamentary committee, representing the Board of Trade, for one of the MS&LR extension lines. He wrote that 'Edward...gave his evidence clearly and well.'[13]

Huish's Euston Square agreement had to be dismantled hastily once it had become public knowledge, and he then approached the GNR with terms for dividing traffic which would have frozen out the Midland and the MS&L. The GN Board was wiser than to trust him, however, and informed Watkin of the attempt. The result was the signing of the GN/MS&L Agreement of 8 July 1857.[14] 'Denison's masterly blow was to win Watkin to his side, and thereby destroy the anti-GNR alliance.'[15] About this time, Watkin asked John Chapman, the Deputy Chairman of the MS&LR, about his future with the company, in advance of the expiry, in 1858, of his contract as General Manager.

George Carr Glyn had asked him in 1855 to spend some seven weeks sorting out the affairs of the Grand Trunk Railway of Canada, but the MS&L Board had discouraged him from spending so much time away. At a special meeting of the directors, held in the Euston Hotel, London on 16 June 1857 (to consider the company's relationship with the LNWR), the question arose 'of a new arrangement with Mr Watkin in order to secure his services after the termination of his present agreement.' Chapman read Watkin's letter stating the conditions 'on which he was willing to continue his services with the Company if desired by the Board', offering a further period of three, five, or seven years.

After some discussion, with Watkin present, it was resolved

---

[12]Goffin, p.338.
[13]A.E. Watkin.
[14]Frank Dixon, *The Manchester South Junction and Altrincham Railway* (Oakwood Press, 1973), pp.18 and 19.
[15]Roger Lloyd, p.71.

unanimously that a new agreement be entered into for a period of seven years, beginning 1 January 1859, the date when his present agreement was due to expire, 'at a fixed rate of £1,200 per annum with a percentage at the rate of £1.2s.6d upon all increase of net earnings over those of the year ending 31 December 1857'. He was to be responsible for the proper conduct and management of the railway 'but not to be required to give his whole time to the Company'.[16] Chapman was charged 'in his individual capacity, and not necessarily as a Director...to be the sole judge of whether or not Mr Watkin gave sufficient time to the Company'. The minutes passed on to the next business, having unknowingly laid the foundation for a remarkable pluralistic and controversial career.[17] By 1861, Watkin was auditor to the Oldham, Ashton under Lyne and Guide Bridge Junction Railway, and was representative of the MS&L on three railways, and a director of four others – the West Midland (successor to the Oxford, Worcester, and Wolverhampton); the Hereford, Hay, and Brecon; the Boston, Sleaford and Midland Counties; and the Grand Trunk of Canada.[18]

The agreement with the Great Northern, representing hostility from one of its former assistant managers, prompted the LNWR to retaliate where it would have most effect – at the joint station in Manchester (London Road). MS&L clerks were ejected from their booking offices, their windows boarded up, and trains were obstructed.[19] Another 'battlefront' in the hostilities was at the MSJA Board meetings. These were chaired alternately by the two companies, and resolutions taken under the MS&L chairman would be reversed at the next meeting, and then re-affirmed at the one following that. Huish himself was not much interested in attending those meetings, but Watkin was, and often turned up for an LNW-chaired session, to be requested to leave.[20] Matters came to such an impasse that an Act was passed on 23 July 1858 for the appointment of an arbitrator 'to affirm, modify, or negative such

[16]It is not difficult to reconstruct the main content of Watkin's letter here.
[17]PRO RAIL 463/3, Minute 520.
[18]Dow, Vol. 1, p.185.
[19]Frank Dixon, p.20.
[20]Ibid.

resolutions as could only be carried by the casting vote of the chairman, which is abolished'.[21]

The militancy with which these skirmishes were organised was not unusual. Early railway managers were often ex-naval or army officers, and Captain Huish was an obvious example. A former soldier on the North London Railway described its workers as 'a regular little army'. Both organisations ran under a high discipline and according to a detailed 'Rule Book'.[22] This comparison would have commended itself to Watkin, especially after Lord Palmerston's offer to him to go to the army in the Crimea, and his subsequent interest in military matters throughout his time in Parliament. The charge that he was 'vain and autocratic' [23] could be levelled at many in the field of railway management, or indeed any enterprise requiring disciplined teamwork, large-scale organisation and periodic revitalisation.

The inter-company relations of those days were often aggressive. In 1857 Watkin wrote to the Lancashire and Yorkshire Railway at Hunt's Bank, Manchester, to complain that the track was unsafe on their Penistone to Huddersfield line. The reply gave in some detail the results of an examination of the route, in a rather leisurely manner, to which Watkin wrote again to say that it was the L&Y's responsibility to maintain safety, not his company's, and asking them, in a highly perfunctory manner, to note that he had brought it to their attention. This provoked an equally terse reply, and the correspondence seems to have ended there.[24] This matter was not one of interference in another company's affairs: the MS&L had initially worked the Huddersfield and Sheffield Junction Railway and re-timed its trains on the line to connect with the new King's Cross to Manchester expresses (via Retford) on 1 August 1857. In 1859 through-coach workings were introduced between King's Cross and Huddersfield, and an Act of that year ruled that the LYR (which had absorbed the H&SJR in the early 1850s) must provide 'all reasonable facilities' for such traffic.

Watkin was right to be suspicious of the engineering of the LYR

[21]*Bradshaw's Shareholders' Manual* (Manchester: 1897), p.215.
[22]Michael Robbins, *The North London Railway* (1953), p.28, quoted by Jack Simmons, *The Railways of Britain* (London: Sheldrake Press), p.209.
[23]Dow, Vol. 2, p.183.
[24]PRO RAIL 463/3.

line between Penistone and Huddersfield. The original viaduct over Denby Dale, built of timber, had partially collapsed in 1847 and been replaced in 1880 by a stone viaduct. This itself had to be underpinned in 1881. Two arches of the Penistone viaduct collapsed on 2 February 1916, depositing 2-4-2T locomotive no. 661 (fortunately running 'light engine') into the valley. Watkin was often highly critical of civil engineering works: he berated the Wrexham, Mold, and Connah's Quay Board when a bridge carrying the Ewloe to Queensferry Road over the line collapsed only moments after the passage of Gladstone's train on 2 December 1889 when he was on his way to the opening of the Hawarden Bridge.[25]

As well as doing battle with the LNWR, Watkin was also waging an offensive against another great rival company, the Midland. The MS&L was to forge a strong link with that company in the late 1860s, but the strong-arm tactics of Captain Huish forced Watkin to make approaches to several companies in the interest of co-operation and support. He also wrote a series of letters, of considerable belligerence, to the Midland's General Manager, W.L. Newcombe, which, with the replies, were copied into a book, at Watkin's request, by a 'Mrs Rawlinson' (presumably his secretary), marked 'Private'.[26] These were on issues of disputed traffic flows in certain key areas. On 14 November 1858 Watkin wrote to Newcombe in connection with a new MSL curve west of Lincoln, connecting the GNR with the Midland line. Derby had tried to set limits to its use in the context of the MS&L's friendship with the GN. Watkin ended his letter 'It is high time that you elected which side to take, for, unfortunately, in this world people cannot continue to be on both, even though they have friends as enduring as we have been.'[27] Newcombe replied from Derby[28] with a gracious opening paragraph and ending with the words 'My company are sincerely desired to be on terms of amity and goodwill with the MS&L Company', but having made his point that '[You] are aware that we have repeat-

---

[25]James I.C. Boyd, *The Wrexham, Mold, and Connah's Quay Railway* (Oxford: The Oakwood Press, 1991), p.216.
[26]PRO RAIL 226 and 336.
[27]Dow, Vol. 1, p.256.
[28]23 August 1859.

edly brought our grievance under your notice without being able to obtain any redress'. Watkin's reply, of the following day, found him 'sorry that you take up old one-sided complaint[s] most of them, according to our conviction, being mere trumpery...we have a moral claim against your Company for £10,000 for traffic diverted from our line'.

On 1 September, he wrote to Newcombe, claiming that the MS&L's 'new system of through special service trains' would be well served if, to places like Derby, Burton, Loughborough, Leicester, Nottingham, Newark, etc., the Midland fitted its own trains into Watkin's. Carrying the war into the enemy's territory indeed! 'We shall be quite ready', he continued, 'to co-operate with you in any way in this direction, if you really will help us, and not merely promise to do so.' In other words, 'We are cheerfully hoping to run trains through the heartlands of your operation, and would like you to help us?' Four days later, following up the attack, Watkin suggested to Newcombe that a new connection be made at Woodhouse, near Sheffield. On the ninth he asked if Newcombe had laid his letter before the Midland directors; were they disposed to improve the accommodation between the two lines? However: 'If you tell me frankly that it's "no use", I should cease to pester you on these subjects.' Newcombe's response[29] reported that the directors had considered the proposal, and would be glad 'to see the improvements at Woodhouse completed' – at the cost of the MSL. Watkin's predictable reply, three days later, was that the improvement would be of mutual advantage, and the cost ought therefore to be in some 'fair proportions'. His reminder of 29 September was met on 6 October with a repetition of Derby's terms.

A dispute over traffic in fish and game arose in Watkin's next letter.[30] 'I should think that you are "making game" of me,' he said. 'About this time last year you wrote to me about the "game" traffic and I replied showing that the whole affair was a matter of a few pounds...and you kept silent thereafter. I have no doubt the fish grumble is the same. We give you fair play and *more*. Pray do not', he went on, 'get into the way of making groundless

---

[29] 9 September.
[30] 29 September.

57

complaints as it discourages those who would work cordially with you, if you would let them. And *so far as meaning something else than the complaint itself*, he concluded, darkly, 'is only too transparent [sic] and therefore is not likely to deceive even Yours faithfully, E. Watkin.' Newcombe[31] repeated the Midland's first grievance (of December 1858), and pointed out that just as Watkin had treated the matter then as something of a joke, so he seemed disposed to do so again. He did not want to trouble Watkin with groundless complaints, but to advise him of the habitual practice of the MS&LR of diverting traffic to their lines from those of the Midland. He was giving them the opportunity to set matters right. 'If you are bent on misconstruing these frank and friendly remonstrations...taking no steps meanwhile to remedy the grievances of which we complain, I don't see how those friendly relations which ought to subsist between our two companies can well be expected to be maintained.'

It is surprising that so comparatively early in the development of the country's railway system the Midland should see the business of traffic flows as a matter of mutually satisfying arrangement between companies, rather than one of competition to the benefit of the user. Clearly some general managers were already set in their thinking, and to have in their midst one still energetically pursuing further development was an incomprehensible irritation. On 6 October, Watkin wrote asking for actual figures relating to the loss of traffic in game, promising to take up the matter. Until then, he 'must consider still that the whole matter is a joke, and not a very happy one on your part'. Responding to Newcombe's reply, Watkin denied that any traffic belonging fairly to the Midland was being diverted to any other route. 'You are now getting far more than you are entitled to in face of the legislation of 1858.'[32] But he also believed that the public could send the traffic whichever way they pleased. He was 'heartily sick of groundless and unjust complaints which clearly show either that it is desired to set up a quarrel with the best friend your company ever had [!], or that you really do not know when you are well off,

---

[31]6 October.

[32]The Act of 23 July of that year, The Great Northern and Manchester Sheffield and Lincolnshire Traffic Arrangement Bill, (C. Hamilton Ellis, *British Railway History* (George Allen and Unwin, 1953, 2 Vols.), Vol. 1. p.237).

and are anxious to make your position worse. I write most seriously, and hope you will take it in the same spirit.' And so the correspondence went on, back and forth in the same vein, exchanging long lists and tables of figures, until Newcombe wrote, on 21 January 1860, to Seymour Clarke, General Manager of the Great Northern, complaining about their setting up in competition with the Midland for goods traffic in the West Riding of Yorkshire. Clarke replied, under the same date, 'We have been working with the MS&L of late, and it is natural that we should carry the traffic that offers itself.'

The correspondence between Watkin and Derby became considerably firmer with Newcombe's replacement by James Allport on 7 May 1860. Allport resumed as general manager at Derby after three years as managing director of a shipbuilding firm in Jarrow, where he had gone after suffering some 'occultation' after the break up of Huish's empire.[33] He immediately began to demand facts and figures on traffic rates, wresting the initiative from Watkin, and putting him on the back foot, urging a reply. In his reply, from the 'Victoria Hotel, London', Watkin answered the various questions raised, adding: 'Practically speaking, the Great Northern and our Company [are] for traffic purposes one.' (An interesting admission.) 'However, if we do anything wrong in the opinion of the Midland, I think it would be more desirable for you to communicate with our chief partner and head of the firm the Great Northern...and hit one of your own size.'

The boxing analogy is revealing. There was a strong pugilistic streak in the family. Edward's youngest brother, Alfred, was a capable boxer in his youth and Edward's chalet in North Wales was equipped, in an out-house, with a suspended punchball, at least in Edward's son's time. Family photographs from the early years of the twentieth century show various unidentified burly gentlemen with boxing gloves, squaring up to it or to each other. It is difficult to imagine that this characteristic was inherited from Absolom. It is more likely to have come from his mother's family, the Makinsons, various members of which made their mark in sport.

In Edward the tendency was sublimated to an intellectual form

[33] *Ibid*, p.237.

of sparring, and his more respectful tone towards Allport, as compared with his predecessor, indicates his recognition of someone more his own 'weight and size'. An examination of an In Memoriam tribute to Alfred in 1875 is in fact illuminating.[34] It credits him, recently deceased after his year as Mayor of Manchester, and having declined, through ill-health, an invitation to serve for a second term, with having 'attained considerable skill' as a boxer, one who would 'stand up and be pounded at by the best boxers of the day'. He is described as regarding as a conclusive argument, a 'good head-punching', believing that 'fisticuffs were the readiest solution of all sophistry...not because he shirked the conflict of opinion as conducted by words and ideas, but because when his blood had been sufficiently wrought-up by words, he wanted the simpler satisfaction of deeds'.

Clearly Edward's character, being more cerebral and wide-ranging, did not go so far, but this offers some insight into his conduct of his affairs. Other parallels may be observed later in the same article: 'A bull-terrier hanging-on kind of hardihood was the basis of his character.' 'He hated public softness – he hated it so much, and looked out so keenly for its detection and exposure, that he was not unfrequently [sic] betrayed into injustice. But what a reparation he made when he was once proven wrong!...he could not bear the idea of ill-will. No man esteemed more highly the favourable verdict of his fellows, and yet no man studied so little the likeliest mode of retaining it.' The similarities are close enough for us to understand better, perhaps, some of the contradictions in Edward's character.

Allport replied at equal length on 2 June 1860, asserting that as the MS&L/GN actions were taking from the Midland some of its traffic: 'You cannot object to our taking steps to maintain our receipts from sources which will be new to us': firmly matching Watkin's Free Market position. This letter contained questions regarding rates charged by the MS&L between Sheffield and Manchester and Sheffield and Liverpool – unveiled threats to Watkin's territory. He wrote again on 18 June, expressing 'regret that you do not enter into any reply to my letter, as although you may flatter yourself that you have a complete answer to it, you

---

[34]In *The Critic* (one of the many Manchester-based journals of the nineteenth century), 2 July 1875, p.412.

afford me no opportunity of accepting your explanation [of the West Riding traffic]'. The next day, Watkin wrote to Seymour Clarke: 'I have received *another* threatening letter from Mr Allport, who evidently considers he can settle with you and bully us. This we cannot admit of and I shall be therefore obliged if you will postpone any meeting with him until after our next Joint Committee when it must be decided what course to take for the protection of both our interests.' He replied to Allport on 28 June, though not to the question of Sheffield/Manchester traffic, and referring again to his co-operation with the GNR. Allport, on 30 June, again displaying his own 'almost pathological love of inter-company quarrelling',[35] wrote 'You say you have a reply to my letter which you are quite sure would be satisfactory – I wish you would give me the reply to enable me to judge for myself.' This letter is the last in the series, Watkin apparently having ducked out of the ring.[36]

On 28 June 1861 the MS&LR Board, expressing its gratitude for Watkin's successful efforts during the current parliamentary session, granted him, at Chapman's recommendation, £500 and a period of leave of absence 'to enable him to recoup his strength'.[37] Richard Cobden had written to Watkin, after landing from a journey from New York then going on to London using the MS&L and GNR route, testifying to the 'model management of the line'.[38] The year 1861 marked an important turning-point in Watkin's life, as he crossed the Atlantic and became involved in North American railways and politics. Not everyone's idea of a way of recouping strength, but his idea of 'rest' was involvement in fresh arduousness.

---

[35]C. Hamilton Ellis, Vol. 1, p.235. This historian refers to Allport as 'The Bismarck of Railway Politics' (*Ibid.*, p.331).
[36]PRO RAIL 226 and 336.
[37]PRO RAIL 463/6, Minute No. 45.
[38]*Letters from the Late Richard Cobden, MP, to Sir Edward Watkin, MP, from 1837 to 1864* (privately bound). Collection of Miss Dorothea Worsley-Taylor. Letter of 3 October 1859.

6

Canada, 1861–1868

The Spirit of Capitalism came to be seen by many as exciting, romantic, almost aesthetic...The romance of spanning the whole continent of North America by a railway, even across vast stretches where customers were few, destroyed the fortunes of many...while virtually all who built railways in more secure and limited confines prospered. A man could dream of building new cities, creating new industries, achieving great things never even imagined before...The spirit of capitalism came to be linked to the spirit of invention and creativity.[1]

The question of the unity of the British Colony in North America, gained by Wolfe's victory over the French in 1759, was a concern of the administration from the outset. The colony had 60,000 French settlers with French customs and laws, and the intention of the British Government at first was to impose a rigid uniformity of English laws and customs. It was realised fairly early that this policy would have been imprudent, and from 1774 until 1783 the religious and legal rights of the new subjects were secured by Parliament. However, 1783 saw the recognition of American Independence, and a consequent influx into Canada of loyalists from the United Sates. Within a few years, some 50,000 of them had settled, with grants from England of land and money, in Upper Canada. In order to provide the loyalists with representative institutions, the Canada Act was passed in 1791, dividing the country into two provinces – Upper and Lower (French) Canada.

---

[1]Michael Novak, *The Catholic Ethic and the Spirit of Capitalism* (New York: The Free Press, 1993), p.25.

But many British also settled in the lower province, and Lower Canada became a centre of racial and religious strife. With an utter divergence of religion and culture, the two sides became bitter and jealous, so that social intercourse, intermarriage and a mutual trust of the legal processes became almost impossible. The French were distrusted and repressed; the English were violent and exasperated. Thus arose a highly dangerous crisis.

The Colonial Office sent out the Earl of Durham[2] as Lord High Commissioner and Governor-General of British North America to report on the state of affairs. His report, dated 31 January 1839, ran to 246 pages, and proposed a legislative union of Upper and Lower Canada, in the hope that, in working together in the framework of a 'free colony', the two peoples would produce a united people who were loyal to the colony, and a safeguard against annexation by the United States.[3] The British Government, not without misgivings among both Tories and Whigs, accepted this proposal, and on 13 June 1841 the first Parliament of the United Provinces came into effect.

The fear of annexation by the United States was not groundless. In 1812, as an extension of the war with Napoleon, Britain was at war with the USA, and there were numerous invasions and border battles in Eastern Canada. The US was beginning to feel its economic and expansionist strength, and covetous eyes were being cast on the British colonies, especially on British Columbia, with its fertile strip of land, isolated and neglected, beyond the Rocky Mountains. 'There is plenty of evidence that the aggressive political groups in the US were prepared to go to almost any ends to "liberate" and absorb British North America piece by piece.'[4]

'It was becoming plain...that if the colonies hoped to retain their right against the United States, in fisheries as in other matters, if they hoped to retain their very existence, they must cease to depend on Great Britain, and find their strength in unity'.[5] The lines of communication, burgeoning business and social cohesion were developing South to North and not East to

---

[2]John George Lambton, 1792–1840.
[3]*A Report on Canada* (London: Methuen. Reprint, 1902), Introduction, pp.v–xv.
[4]Richard Hough, *Six Great Railwaymen* (Hamish Hamilton, 1955), chapter on George Stephenson of the Canadian Pacific Railway, pp.158 and 159.
[5]Arthur R.M. Lower, *Colony to Nation: A History of Canada* (Toronto: Longmans, Green and Co., 1946), p.319.

West. This would further social and economic integration between the two countries, if allowed to grow unchecked. Both the British Government and the Canadian political leaders began to see the need for a full-scale unification of the whole of British North America, to form a 'Commonwealth'. On 8 March 1848, Lord Elgin (Governor-General, 1847–54), entrusted to the leaders of the two communities the task of forming an administration which would take into account the right of the Canadian people as a whole to 'legal and fiscal autonomy enabling them to determine their own future'.[6] It soon became clear that further union was indeed desirable. In 1860, the Prince of Wales, with the Duke of Newcastle, as Secretary of State for the Colonies, visited Canada – a 'triumphant progress'[7] – and rallied the cause, and thought began to be given to the idea of a unification of the Canadian states on an East–West line of communication, by a transcontinental railway.

The Grand Trunk Railway of Canada was projected in 1852. It was to be the longest, and perhaps the costliest[8] railway in the world, but quickly became known as the world's most complete commercial failure. It was a pioneer in several ways: in design and management, and in the economic interrelationship between Britain, the United States and Canada; and it was the first experience for Canadians of 'big business'. The widespread construction of railways in Britain had been followed closely in Canada: businessmen in Portland, Halifax, St John's, Quebec and Ontario who had seen that railways were bringing increased prosperity to the US and Britain, were interested in furthering trade and development by connecting the towns with an 'intercolonial' railway. But not many were keen on investing money in a business which would not produce dividends until several years later. In 1851, the Premier of Nova Scotia, Joseph Howe, asked Morton Peto, builder of several railways in England and France, to look at the possibilities. Peto joined up with three other railway contractors, including Thomas Brassey, and in April 1853 the contractors issued a prospectus.

---

[6]Robert Borden, *Canada in the Commonwealth* (Oxford University Press, 1929), pp. 83–6.
[7]E.W. Watkin, *Canada and the States* (London: Ward, Lock and Co., 1887), p.ix.
[8]Kenneth McNaught, *The Pelican History of Canada* (London: Penguin Books Ltd., 1982 p.115.

Unfortunately, the gauge decided upon was 5' 6". The US had eventually standardised on 4' 8½". The reasons given for this departure from the rapidly emerging standard gauge were partly to do with arguments concerning smoothness of riding, larger and more powerful locomotives, and greater capacity of goods and passenger vehicles per axle. Commercial interests in Portland argued that a unique gauge would ensure that traffic would not have to be shared with rival concerns to the south. The decision proved to be an 'unmitigated evil',[9] for it was without value in attracting or withholding traffic for Portland, Montreal or Quebec. In railway building in the 1850s there were errors in track-laying, component design and construction, drainage, and proper alignment of curves, so that there was endless trouble with trains even when they were running. Another feature of the early economic difficulties was that, unlike in Great Britain, most freight consisted of goods of low value, moving over great distances only slowly. The bankers Baring and Glyn, financiers of the Grand Trunk, overestimated badly the prospect of the returns: enormous stretches of railway, running through sparsely populated land, with little in the way of large-scale industry or centres of population, presented a very different picture from their British experience. From the outset, the Grand Trunk, in denying the natural channels of trade, 'was trying to make water run uphill'.[10] The Provincial Government must bear a large proportion of the blame for the early failures; most British investors assumed, wrongly, that as the project had been in the government's direct interest and encouragement, it had guaranteed the success of the railway.

The truth was that the company's relationship with the Province of Canada had deteriorated badly: political leeches had moved in on the enterprise, and underhand deals were syphoning off such money as it had. Over the first five years of operation (1855–59), the ratio of outlays to receipts averaged 89.8%.[11] The reports to shareholders were so dismaying that one of them, H.C. Chapman, a Lancashireman, went to make his own investigation over several

---

[9]A.W. Currie, *The Grand Trunk Railway of Canada* (University of Toronto Press, 1958), pp.3, 5 and 57.

[10]*Ibid*, pp.59, 61, 63 and 69.

[11]G.R. Stevens, *Canadian National Railways: Sixty Years of Trial and Error. 1836-1896.* (Toronto: Clarke, Irwin and Co.Ltd., 1960, (2 Vols), Vol. 1, pp.286 and 287.

weeks in the summer of 1860: 'I could not have brought myself to believe that such a system of peculation, extravagance and mendacity could have so long been permitted to exist', he wrote. 'The explanation I receive is that the Grand Trunk has been used for political purposes and that [its] money has been spent in bribery and corruption. It is the general opinion in Canada', he concluded, 'that, as the executive is at present constituted, it will never be worked either honestly or purely as a commercial concern'.[12] Thus for the first few years after its completion, the Grand Trunk verged on bankruptcy, and Baring and Glyn had to come to its rescue in 1860 with £800,000. A shareholders' meeting held in January 1861, after hearing the figures and debating for four hours, set up a committee of seven, including representatives of investors in Manchester and Liverpool. This committee urged all investors to sign a petition requesting help from the Canadian Government, to be signed 'in London, Liverpool, Birmingham, Manchester, Leeds, Bristol, Glasgow, Edinburgh or Dublin'. In July of that year the committee, after a meeting in which the company was described by one speaker as 'currently in a hopeless state of bankruptcy', reported that the petition had been presented and that In order 'to straighten out the Company's affairs…a man of great skill, experience, and energy should proceed at once to Canada. This man would take over the entire supervision of the Company and negotiate with the Government.'[13] The response of the London Board was to invite Edward Watkin to undertake this responsibility.

Watkin had previously shown an interest in specific railway matters on the other side of the Atlantic, ignited during his 'convalescent' visit in 1851. He was asked in 1854 by George Carr Glyn and Thomas Baring to go to Canada for a few weeks to look into the state of management of the Grand Trunk Railway, but as he had been appointed only that year as General Manager of the MS&LR, he could not go. He wrote to Samuel Cunard[14] on 5 June 1858, commending the projected railway from Quebec to Halifax on military grounds, as equivalent to trebling the value of

---

[12]*Ibid*, p.287.
[13]Currie, pp.71, 74, 77, 83 and 78.
[14]The founder of the first regular transatlantic steamship line, who was born in Halifax, Nova Scotia.

the number of troops in the country. 'The entire frontier...from Lake Huron to Halifax, more than 1,200 miles in length would have a parallel line', enabling the deployment of troops within thirty six hours at any point. He pointed out that the American lines of railway ran, in the main, at right angles to the frontier, with no equivalent parallel to that which the proposed Intercolonial would give the Confederacy.[15]

On this new invitation, he expressed serious doubts about the possibility of success. His current responsibilities and anxieties, and the lack of prospects of increased traffic for years to come on the GTR, all seemed over-daunting. 'The discipline and traffic of the line could easily be put on a sound basis...and expenses...- could be kept down...Any man thoroughly versed in railways and quite up to business...and the management of men...and to serious negotiation, could easily accomplish this.' But all this, he thought, would be insufficient to satisfy the shareholders, and he would not advise Glyn and Baring 'to tie their reputations to any man, however able or experienced, if it involved a sort of moral guarantee [of] any sudden improvement...likely...to raise the value of the property in the market'. 'The only way to make it a success over years', he suggested, 'though it would be, to many...chimerical...incomprehensible...or visionary', lay through its extension to the Pacific.

However, after consulting the Duke of Newcastle, who 'utterly concurred' with the idea, he 'accepted the mission offered' to him. He had made the acquaintance of the Duke in January 1847, when, as Lord Lincoln, the latter had stood for election in Manchester. Though a Conservative, he had aligned himself with Sir Robert Peel and the principle of Free Trade, and was accordingly in disgrace with his father. His opponent was John Bright, an old Anti-Corn Law League warrior, and Watkin had sought an interview with Lincoln in order to avoid an unnecessary opposition. Lincoln withdrew for other reasons, however.[16] Their next meeting was on a train between Rugby and Derby in the spring of 1852. The Duke was reading a copy of Edward's 'little book' on

---

[15]Edward Watkin Papers (Canada Archives, Ottawa, A519.
[16]E.W. Watkin, *Canada and the States,* pp. 12–14, 11, 6 and 7.

12 The 5th Duke of Newcastle, Henry P.F Pelham-Clinton, 1811–1864, aged 45

the United States and Canada, written in the previous year,[17] and they talked about US politics.[18] Watkin's name had again come to the attention of the Duke in 1854, when Palmerston had suggested that he was a suitable person to sort out the mess in the organisation of the army in the Crimea.

They next met in 1857, when Watkin sought an interview, as Manager of the MS&LR, because one of its locomotives had set fire to part of one of the Duke's plantations. The Duke had written about the incident to Lord Yarborough, Chairman of the MS&L, in what Watkin felt was 'a very haughty manner', and intended to take up the quarrel. He described his meeting, at the mansion in Portman Square, London: 'I waited some time; but at last in stalked the Duke, looking very awful indeed – so stern and severe – that I could not help smiling, and saying, "The burnt coppice, your Grace." Upon this he laughed, held out his hand,

[17]E.W. Watkin, *A Trip to the United States and Canada* (London: W.H. Smith, 1 January 1852).
[18]A.W. Currie, 'Sir Edward Watkin: A Canadian View', *Journal of Transport History* , Volume 3, Pt. I, 1957, p.33.

placed me beside him, and we had a very long discussion, not about the fire, but about the colliery he was sinking...at Shireoaks. [Then] we talked once more about Canada, the United States, and the Colonies generally.'[19]

They then met more and more frequently on business, and the year after the Duke's return from his visit to Canada, 1861, he read an article by Watkin in the *Illustrated London News* of 16 February 1861, written during Watkin's stint of two or so years as its editor. In the leading article, under the heading 'A British Railway from the Atlantic to the Pacific', Watkin quoted Queen Victoria, from her speech proroguing Parliament in 1858: 'I hope that its new Colony in the Pacific [British Columbia] may be but one step in the career of steady progress by which my dominions in North America may be ultimately peopled in an unbroken chain from the Atlantic to the Pacific by a loyal and industrious population.' These words, argued Watkin, 'found a fervent echo in the national heart'. Such an aspiration 'speaks of a great outspread of solid prosperity and of rational liberty, of the diffusion of our civilisation, and of the extension of our moral empire'. These four virtues adumbrate Watkin's political credo, and underpinned everything he tried to achieve, both in business and in politics. 'How is this hope to be realised, not a century hence but in our own time?' he asked. After outlining the great riches of the country, and the present disposition of its two and a half million people, he went on to argue the physical possibility of a continuous railway right across the country. The cost, estimated at between twenty and twenty-five million pounds, though large, 'is only six per cent of the amount we have laid out on completing our own railway system in this little country'. He judged that 'such a work was too costly and too difficult for the grasp of private enterprise. To accomplish it, the whole help of both the local and Imperial Parliament must be given. That help once offered...private enterprise would flock to the undertaking, and a people would go on to colonise on the broad trade laid open to their industry.But...Parliament must take the initiative, for the work is great, and its utility is in all senses Imperial.' He urged upon all who were interested to establish 'an unbroken line of road and

---

[19]E.W. Watkin, *Canada and the States*, p.10.

railway from the Atlantic to the Pacific through British Territory'.[20]

Before he left for Canada in 1861, Watkin had a long interview with the Duke of Newcastle, on 17 July. They discussed the problems of the North American continent, and the future of Canada, and the Duke described the idea of an iron road, onwards to the Pacific, as 'a grand conception'. The union of all the provinces and territories in 'one great British America' was the necessary, the logical, result of completing the Intercolonial Railway, and he authorised Watkin to say that the Colonial Office supported such works.[21] He re-affirmed to the Duke[22] his vision of a railway stretching from the Atlantic to the Pacific, urging Imperial financial investment in a line from Halifax to Vancouver's Island, 'connecting the two great oceans of the world with a line under British sway'. He suggested calling the line 'The Queen Victoria Road', as the project was 'essentially an imperial one'.[23]

Back in Manchester from his initial visit in November 1861, Watkin persuaded the City Council, of which he was a member for the Exchange ward, to petition Her Majesty's Government for financial aid to build a railway from Truro, Nova Scotia, to Riviere du Loup, on the St Lawrence River north of Quebec. This petition, while part of the larger aim, was based particularly on military concerns, because the Civil War in the USA was arousing fresh concern over Britain's defence of British North America. Watkin's argument was that the proposed railway would make it possible to cut the normal British garrison in Canada by half, and thus save £200,000 every year. In addition to this, £25,000 would be saved annually in the carriage of mail through the US, necessary because transport between Canada and the Atlantic ports was not then available.

A special meeting of investors was held in London on 9 August 1862. Watkin expressed his belief that the Canadian Legislature would deal fairly and honestly with the Grand Trunk, and that the responsibility for any failure of the intended extension of the

---

[20]*Illustrated London News,* Saturday, 16 February 1861, pp.135 and 136.
[21]E.W. Watkin, p.65x.
[22]8 November 1862.
[23]Edward Watkin Papers, Canada Archives, Ottawa. A519.

company to Halifax would lie with the Province.[24] 'It is no exaggeration to say that as Supervising Manager and later as President of the Grand Trunk, Watkin faced two tremendous tasks: he had to bring the company safely through the turbulence of Canadian politics in the immediate Confederation period, and he had to reconstruct the railway physically. Thus he was at once politician and business executive, statesman and railway director. Both roles fascinated him.' The important Intercolonial Conference at Quebec in 1861 was a piece of his stage-management.[25] He did not, however, accept the Presidency with absolute self-confidence. He wrote to the Duke, 'hoping that his Grace will give him his confidence as he assumed the office'.[26]

In July 1862, a committee of investigation reported to the investors, making several recommendations, which were upheld by Watkin. The basic statement was that the company needed five years as a breathing space, to clear up its burden of floating debts and to build up its physical assets and earning power. All interested groups were urged to make concessions for a while, so that the company could overcome the difficulties which it had experienced from the beginning. Until this was achieved it was felt that it would be quite unproductive to seek help from the Canadian Government, except through advances on the carriage of mail, troop and military supplies. Equivalent to a loan of £1,500,000, this would help the company to re-equip, but, like the proposal for government representation on a 'delegated commission, with representation from all interested parties', this was turned down by the government.[27] The position became so bad that would-be users of the railway's facilities were fearful of losing their freight because of seizure of the rolling-stock by creditors. Only Watkin's skill at temporising had prevented seizure of parts of the railway's assets. In one instance creditors to the sum of £7,000 were held off by his assumption of personal responsibility for the debt.[28] Having established the background, Watkin set about making sweeping changes

---

[24]Currie, *Grand Trunk*, pp.79 , 84 and 85.
[25]Arthur R.M. Lower, *Colony to Nation: A History of Canada* (Toronto: Longmans Green and Company, 1946), pp.299, 300 and 313.
[26]Watkin to the Duke of Newcastle, 6 November 1862; from 21 Old Broad Street, London, the HQ of the Atlantic and Pacific Postal and Telegraph Company Ltd. (Edward Watkin Papers, Canada Archives, Ottawa, A519).
[27]Currie, *Grand Trunk*, pp.80 and 81.
[28]*Ibid*, p.84.

10 A typical station on the Grand Trunk Railway of Canada

in every department of the railway, making it more cost-effective
and offering a better service. He was ruthless in getting rid of
dishonest and superfluous staff.[29] 'Able, ambitious, grandiose,
Watkin came and swept through a reorganisation of the Grand
Trunk.'[30]

Despite the problems, the Grand Trunk did begin to improve.
During 1861 it extended its sidings at 23 stations, and bought
docks at Quebec. It converted 40 tenders weighing 18 or 19 tons
each from 4 to 8 wheels, the high axle-loads of which had been
accused of the unacceptable number of rail breakages during the
preceding winter. In 1862 it had become obvious that Watkin –
'energetic, honest, eloquent and influential' – had driven the
bailiffs from the door. 'The Grand Trunk shareholders were unanimous that the Company could not afford to be without him. On
21 October of that year he became President.'[31] By early 1864,

[29]G.R. Stevens, p.293.

[30]W.L. Morton, *The Union of British North America: The Critical Years, 1857–1873* (Toronto:
McClelland and Stewart Limited, 1964), p.95.

[31]Succeeding Thomas Baring (G.R. Stevens, pp.296 and 295.)

after five years in which gross annual revenues had increased from £505,000 to £912,000, the fleet of freight wagons and locomotives had become totally inadequate for the traffic. In 1865, Watkin declared that, given the right equipment, the railway could raise its gross revenues from £30,000 a week to £40,000, saying that farmers and traders were constantly demanding an improved service.[32]

In 1862 the Grand Trunk acquired some notoriety in a court case, brought about by some unguarded words from its President. Critics among the shareholders, notably one J.C. Conybeare[33] raised awkward questions about the railway's involvement with a line which ran between Port Huron and Detroit. This had been a speculative flotation by Baring, Glyn and one or two others, with the intention of its being leased, when up and running, by the Grand Trunk. The lease was made on 30 March 1860, but the line was not in profit and had not fulfilled its traffic expectations. Watkin, in reply, defended stoutly the intentions of Baring and Glyn, pointing out, not for the first time, that they had on several occasions intervened to help the Grand Trunk to continue in business. He set out the financial facts of the case in detail (though without specific reference to the lease by the company of the Detroit and Port Huron), saying that Baring and Glyn's methods of raising capital by their own personal efforts on behalf of the company – procedures criticised by Conybeare in a pamphlet as being in bad faith – were in fact to the benefit of the company. In his address to the shareholders, Watkin said that in his view Conybeare's pamphlet was libellous, and looked very much like an attempt to extort money; whereupon Conybeare sued Watkin for slander. At the hearing, the Lord Chief Justice interrupted Conybeare's opening speech, after one and a half hours of it, and expressed disgust at his childish motives. He suggested that all imputations, on both sides, be withdrawn, and dismissed the jury.[34]

Despite these problems, Watkin pursued other amalgamations in

[32]Currie, *Grand Trunk*, pp.99 and 100.
[33]Winner of the Chancellor's Prize for Undergraduate Poetry when he was at Cambridge, (Currie, p.83).
[34]Currie, *Grand Trunk*, pp.102–4.

that year, with the Great Western and the Buffalo and Lake Huron Railways, giving as his reasons the avoidance of 'wasteful competition between railways, to enable them to meet water competition and retain to British companies traffic which would otherwise be handed over to American railways at the Niagara frontier'. He said 'the unified concern would press for the construction of the Intercolonial railway with the assistance of the governments concerned'. The Canadian legislature refused to authorise the proposed amalgamation, claiming that it was monopolistic. However, in June 1864 the Grand Trunk did go ahead with amalgamation with the Buffalo and Lake Huron line on its own, as its charter did not entail legislative action. With other improved connections, including the provision of a third rail between the Grand Trunk's 5' 6" gauge rails to allow the passage of standard-gauge stock, traffic[35] could run through Canada to connect one part of the US to another.[36]

One of the barriers to the plans of both the Grand Trunk and the Colonial Office was the huge stretch of land owned by the Hudson's Bay Company. This company was incorporated by Royal Charter in 1670, which made it the legal owner of all the lands which drained into Hudson's Bay, an area as great as European Russia,[37] giving it title to the soil and exclusive licence to trade from the Rockies to the Bay and north to the Arctic and in Labrador. Its domain included what is now Washington and Oregon, until American settlers moved in and challenged its authority. The Treaty of Oregon in 1846 established the US–Canadian border at the 49th Parallel.[38] The 286 proprietors in England enjoyed many years of 10% and 15% dividends.[39] But circumstances were changing, and agitation arose in 1848, and again in 1855, against the huge influence of the company, whose monopoly position was beginning to be seen as anachronistic. The objections were explicitly on the grounds of its contradiction of the principles of Free Trade; its proprietary rights over a vast area; its

---

[35]The final change of gauge on the Grand Trunk to 4'8½" did not take place until 1873. (Currie, p.121).
[36]*Ibid*, pp.105–6.
[37]Douglas MacKay, *The Honourable Company: A History of The Hudson's Bay Company* (London; Cassell and Co., 1937), p.305.
[38]Pam Hobbs and Michael Algar, *Canada* (M.P.C. Hunter, undated –1996?), p.35.
[39]*Ibid*.

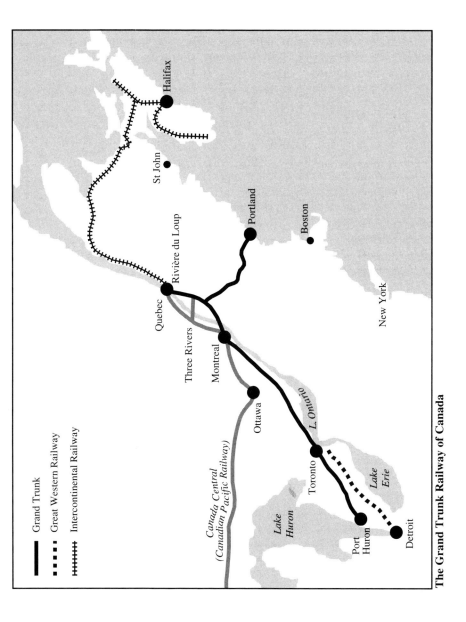

The Grand Trunk Railway of Canada

75

relationship with the native Indians; and its highly important position in any consideration of East–West communication.[40] In 1862 the Duke of Newcastle secured the co-operation of Henry Hulse Berens, Governor of the company from 1858 to 1863, to the idea of 'the improvement of the communication across the Territory of the Company, and for the settlement of the country'. 'Newcastle eased the way for [Thomas] Baring the banker, and Watkin, the Grand Trunk Railway promoter, to open negotiations with the Hudson's Bay Company.'[41]

Watkin had really sunk his teeth into the necessity for Canadian unification of a transcontinental railway. He told Baring, on his way to Canada in May 1862, 'We *must* make this matter go, now.'[42] Whenever in England, between his weeks in Canada, he was a consistent advocate of the union of the British North American states, and 'acted as a liaison between the delegates and the Duke'.[43] In 1861 the influential British North American Association had been formed, and its members included Joseph Howe, Baring, Glyn and Watkin. On 19 March 1862, the directors of the Hudson's Bay Company were invited to join, an idea 'generally associated with Howe' but which 'we can be reasonably sure Watkin had a hand in'.[44] The company would naturally require substantial compensation for the surrendering of its power over such a large tract of land, and the Duke told Watkin[45] that it would be willing to sell its whole rights for a sum of £1,500,000. He added, however, that as the prospects of any immediate or substantial return were slender, he could not view the proposal in so favourable a light as Watkin.[46] In other words, the British Government would not be prepared to finance the proposal. Watkin thereupon pursued the possibility of raising private capital for the purchase, urging upon Baring and Glyn the necessity of the completion of an intercolonial railway for the welfare of the Grand Trunk. Baring, however, did not want to get embroiled in Newcas-

[40]Elaine Allan Mitchell, 'Edward Watkin and the Buying-Out of the Hudson's Bay Company', *Canadian Historical Review*, Vol. xxxiv, No.3, September 1953, p.219.
[41]MacKay, p.306.
[42]5 May 1862 (Mitchell, p.231).
[43]*Ibid*, p.247.
[44]Mitchell, p.227.
[45]14 August 1862 (Mitchell, p.233).
[46]E.W. Watkin, pp.128 and 129.

tle's political aims, and as Glyn was unwilling to break ranks, they refused. Watkin appears not to have familiarised the Duke with this difficulty, not surprisingly, but he went ahead himself.[47] Mitchell suggests, from Watkin's own references in his book, that his confidence in doing so was based on his continuing conviction that the Colonial Office would take it over for the country (Gladstone had approved the 'intercolonial'), and that there was sufficient support in Canada. She states, not implausibly, that his commitment to success, and the possibility of enhancing his reputation, would not allow him to lose the chance.[48]

Watkin's first idea was to encourage fifteen persons to purchase £100,000 worth of stock, but the Hudson's Bay company was not willing to accept such a speculative scheme. He thus fell back on his alternative, and handed over the purchase to the newly founded International Finance Society. Berens wrote in midsummer 1863 to the Duke, telling him that the terms 'have been agreed upon by which the whole interests of the Hudson's Bay Company are to be transferred to the parties represented by Mr Edward Watkin'. The proprietors were paid the sum of £1.5 million – £300 per share – which was more than half as much again as their value on the stock market.[49] The company was re-organised, with Sir Edmund Walker Head, formerly Governor-General of Canada, as Governor, '[at] the suggestion – almost the personal request, according to Watkin – of the Duke of Newcastle'.[50] The International Finance Society then set up a subsidiary company to build a telegraph line to the Pacific.[51] Watkin's fingerprints are detectable all over each of these arrangements.

In November 1869, 'the transaction was concluded with the prorogations of the Crown sustained, the aspirations of a people fulfilled, and the interests of Capital protected'. 'It was probably the greatest single transfer of a territory ever accomplished unheralded by war.'[52] In that month a 'Deed of Surrender' was signed,

[47]Mitchell, pp.234 –7.
[48]*Ibid*, p.238.
[49]MacKay, pp.306 and 307.
[50]Chester Martin, *Foundations of Canadian Nationhood* (University of Toronto Press, 1955), p.413.
[51]W.L. Morton, p.95.
[52]MacKay, pp.311 and 312.

but the final implementation of all its agreements was not until 1925, after which the company operated as a private trading corporation.[53] 'Rupert's Land' became part of the Dominion in 1869, Manitoba and the parts of the North-West Territories in 1870.

But the removal of that immense barrier to the dream of a continuous connection from the Atlantic to the Pacific had been achieved in 1863. 'Watkin claimed a considerable share of the credit for British North American Union by his action in removing the obstacle of the HBCo.'[54] By any examination of the evidence, and after conceding some ground to those who have accused him of immodesty,[55] he was not mistaken.

Although the government had been reluctant all along to loan or grant money to the Grand Trunk, it realised a collapse of the railway's operations would have disastrous results, both on the movement of mails and its military use in the repulsion of cross-border raids from the USA. It therefore entered into long and tediously drawn out discussions about fair rates for these operations, from which some beneficial conclusions emerged. The attempts to achieve some government support, and the concomitant efforts of politicians to harness the backing of the railway and its employees, led to the involvement of the Grand Trunk in party politics. This inevitably drew charges of undue interference in Canada's affairs by 'resident Agents of a distant proprietary' from those who felt they had they had been injured by the process.[56]

The Grand Trunk came in for some bad feeling in the minds of many Canadians; 'the lowest level of public morality at the time' gave foundation for the appearance of what Watkin dubbed a 'rascally element'.[57] He himself aroused some aversion in government circles by intervening in political affairs generally, in the too assiduous pursuit of his Colonial Office mandate. Opposed to tariffs as a matter of principle, he expressed in 1864 his support for the 1854 'Reciprocity Treaty', which had abolished customs duty on natural products between Canada and the US, and which

---

[53] *The Hudson's Bay Company, Incorporated 2 May 1670. A Brief History* (London: Hudson's Bay House, 1934), p.37.
[54] Mitchell, p.220.
[55] e.g., Arthur R.M. Lower, p.320.
[56] Currie, *Grand Trunk,* pp. 84 –9.
[57] *Ibid,* pp.89 and 94.

was due to terminate in 1866. He was concerned also that goods between Britain and Canada via the US might incur US duty.[58] Conversely, there was feeling among the shareholders that there had been too much interference by the provincial government in the affairs of the Grand Trunk. The new breed of shareholders, who bought their shares from the first generation at a discount, were intent only on squeezing the last farthing out of the railway. This threatened the wider interests of the company and its relationship with the political forces in Canada. Watkin and Richard Potter, his assistant,[59] 'by constant and courageous resistance, rescued the Company, and put it on the road to prosperity, but earned nothing but the dislike and disavowal of those whom they served'.[60]

John A. MacDonald, the future joint first Prime Minister of the Dominion, declared, in Quebec, to cheers on 7 March 1865, that it was 'of the greatest possible importance that Canada should not be unrepresented in England at the present time'. He wrote to Watkin in London to encourage him. 'You say that you have been snubbed for interfering in Canadian affairs', he said. 'I hope that you will disregard the snubbings and continue...'[61]

In 1864, Watkin told the shareholders that 'it was Britain's duty to support everything which tended to give breadth and solidity to her North American colonies. The statesmen engaged in the task of confederation would have the cordial good wishes and, wherever possible, the earnest support of the Company.' All statesmen were agreed, said Watkin, that if the desired federation of the colonies were to be effected, they must be physically connected with each other. The Intercolonial Railway would be effectively an extension of the Grand Trunk, and it would run through an area where there were abundant deposits of coal, the most important requirement for manufacturing. At the same meeting he went on to expound the importance for the Canadian trade of federation, in setting up a market independent of the US, developing her resources and in every respect strengthening her ties with Britain and British trade. He added that if the Canadian

---

[58]G.R. Stevens, p.298.
[59]Father of Beatrice Webb of the Fabian Society.
[60]G.R. Stevens, p.296.
[61]Chester Martin, pp.365 and 366.

Government were to make an important concession, presumably in guarantee of bond interest, 'certain parties interested in stocks and bonds would undertake to raise the capital for an intercolonial railway'. Government support, again, failed to materialise, but construction of the Intercolonial Railway formed part of the Confederation arrangement in 1867.[62]

By December 1865, the company felt that its credit had been re-established. Traffic had risen by over 50% in less than three years, and the operating rate had improved by ten points.[63] It had borrowed £190,000 from Canadian sources for the purchase of equipment: 'A sign of a return of confidence in the railway', observed Watkin. It was paying off its debts punctually, and was able to make purchases for cash, and in the cheapest market. He assured investors that their willingness to postpone their claims under the Arrangements Act had been vindicated by results.[64] Unfortunately, the end of the American Civil War saw a reduction of trade with the US, and the stock market crisis of 1866, together with suspicions of speculation in Grand Trunk shares, put a damper on Watkin's habitual optimism for a while. In these circumstances of yet further disappointment, some shareholders became critical of Watkin's management. In 1865, they pointed out, the Grand Trunk's operating ratio (of outlay to receipts) was 55%, net of losses on US currency and extraordinary renewals. Its rival, the Great Western, returned a rate of 41%. Watkin replied that he had crossed the Atlantic twelve times,[65] in order to scruti-nise every part of the company's expenditure, but had concluded that its costs could not be cut further. He wanted to raise tolls, but US railways had refused to co-operate. It is true that the Grand Trunk's problems were associated with attempts by some in the US to starve it of capital and force the British Colonies to seek economic union. But the Grand Trunk had 228 miles of its line in the US and needed to keep on fairly good terms with that country.

In 1867, a far more formidable critic appeared; Captain Henry W. Tyler, Chief Inspector of Railways in Britain, declared that he

---

[62]Currie, *Grand Trunk*, pp.96 and 97.
[63]Stevens, p.303.
[64]Currie, *Ibid*, p.107.
[65]His eventual total was 30 times, the last being in 1886, when he travelled on the newly-completed Transcontinental line from Montreal to Port Moody (E.W. Watkin, *Canada and the States, 1851-1886*, pp. 36 ff).

had confidence in the line, but little in the management. Its operating ratio, by this time 83%, was far too high, and the company's proposed expenditure on renewals was nowhere near sufficient.[66] In the same year, Watkin announced that Tyler had agreed to conduct an investigation into the company's affairs. Tyler, in his report submitted late in 1867, stated that the line suffered from defects in its original construction, an excess of non-paying mileage, the abrogation of the Reciprocity Treaty, and low tolls. Without new capital, he said, any improvement in the company's position would be tedious. He detailed the investment required as totalling £1,014.000, and stated that the company's credit was deplorable. 'The proprietors had spent huge sums of money...on a great highway. But Canada was deriving infinite advantages from the road. Therefore the people and Government of Canada should be asked for such reasonable assistance...as would improve the Company's credit.'

At the shareholders' meeting held in December 1867, convened to consider Tyler's Report, Watkin, instead of pointing out that 'the expert chosen to refute the management came back from Canada to support most of its recommendations',[67] launched an extended survey of the company's affairs. He declared that when he took over the Grand Trunk it had no more value than scrap iron. He had refused all pressure from Canadian interests to allow the line to be put up for auction and sold, as it would have brought the shareholders very little. It had made great progress under his management, in spite of being hampered by share-holders' demands for quick returns. In his six years in office, its capital had increased by £6,269,000 and it had earned £2,500,000 over working expenses; of this sum £925,000 had been paid to shareholders and bondholders. If this was failure he was willing to admit it.[68]

This was followed by an attack from the floor on C.J. Brydges,[69] the General Manager, but Tyler defended him, asserting that some of the critics had larger holdings in the Great Western, and some

<hr/>

[66]*Ibid*, p.111.
[67]Stevens, p.305.
[68]*Ibid*, pp. 306 and 307.
[69]'An aggressive, independent manager, drawn away from Canada's Great Western Railway by Watkin' (A.A. den Otter, *The Philosophy of Railways* (University of Toronto Press, 1997), p.108).

were maliciously stirring up trouble for the Grand Trunk. At the half-yearly shareholders' meeting in 1867 and 1868, there was renewed criticism of Baring and Glyn, Watkin and Brydges. Watkin, after repeating the numerous circumstances that had conspired to restrict the company's earning power, gave as his opinion that the basic trouble had been that British investors were deceived on the cost of construction and operation. Though he had been able to improve the railway physically, he had exhausted himself in a futile effort to put the company on its feet financially.[70] He lacked health and vigour to serve any longer as President, he said, and refused to be re-elected when his term of office expired in October 1869. He had written from Rose Hill in August 1868 to Joseph Hickson of the Grand Trunk management, saying that his critics wanted him to retire from the presidency unless he could devote the whole of his time to the company. He recommended that the issue be brought before the proprietors at the October meeting, and would be willing to resign if it served the company and not the private interests of individuals.[71] On 27 March 1869 he handed over his duties to Richard Potter, who also came from solid Lancashire stock and was a capable businessman, but he was of too fine and sensitive a nature to sustain railway management in such turbulent circumstances. Potter fared no better than his predecessor against the cabal which had snapped at Watkin for so long. Had he been 'abrupt and cavalier' with the shareholders he might have prevailed, but he sought to disarm them with sweet reasonableness. And they brought him down. He resigned the President's chair on 11 October 1876, and Captain Tyler took over from him fourteen days later.[72]

In 1871 the Canadian Government contracted to begin a Pacific railway in two years and to complete it within ten years of the entry of British Columbia into the Union. The Grand Trunk soon excluded itself from this development: it refused to agree on the proposed route, and in 1880, when the government offered the privileges and franchises to the Grand Trunk which were later enjoyed by the Canadian Pacific Railway, Tyler turned them down. He remained unmoved even when the government, through

---

[70]Currie, *Grand Trunk*, pp. 111–13.
[71]Edward Watkin Papers, Canada Archives, Ottawa. A519.
[72]G.R. Stevens, pp.307, 308 and 329.

14 The Honourable Donald A. Smith (later Lord Strathcona) driving the last spike in the Canadian Pacific Railway Transcontinental, 7 November 1885

Sir Charles Tupper, insisted that the line was essential, and that Canada would never become a nation without it.[73] Watkin's vision had eventually found public financial backing, but he was no longer there to grasp it with both hands. The government worked with a new Grand Trunk Pacific Company from 1903, which became the second transcontinental railway, under the name of the Canadian Northern Railway. The honour of the first complete East–West line had fallen to the Canadian Pacific Railway, whose last spike was struck on 7 November 1885, only twenty-four years after Watkin's advocacy as set out in the *Illustrated London News* in 1861.[74] In the summary at the end of his history of the Grand Trunk Railway, Currie wrote perceptively that it was an almost perfect example of the complex relationship between speculative capital investment, profitability, and the elusive but undeniable

[73]Donald Grant Creighton, *Dominion of the North: A History of Canada* (London: Robert Hale Limited, 1947), p.333. Currie, *Ibid*, p.307.
[74]William D. Euler, MP, *The Canada Year Book, 1936* (Ottawa: J.O. Patenaude, I.S.O. 1936), pp.653 and 654.

factor known as social utility. 'It was a financial failure – but a public asset...it was a failure as a commercial enterprise. But it made a significant contribution to the economic development of Canada.'[75]

Reference has been made to Watkin's unpopularity at certain times for his propensity to offer unsolicited advice on particular political issues. The fact remains that he has gone down in Canadian history as one of the main influences on the processes which led to the formation of the Dominion of Canada. Apart from the essential cohesive element represented by the Grand Trunk Railway, there is evidence of his creative work and influence in politics. He was an indefatigable spokesman in the House of Commons for Canadian Federation. W.L. Morton could describe him as the 'aggressive champion of Union'.[76] He arrived in Canada in August 1861 and between then and returning to England in November, he spent most of the time travelling and meeting public figures in all the provinces. 'None knew better than [he] the art of getting men together.'[77] In the September, he gave a dinner party in Montreal to the delegates of the five provinces of British North America on the subject of the desirability of a railway from the maritime provinces, Halifax and St John's to Vancouver, to form one big country, 'a country large enough to breed large ideas'.[78] At that party, Joseph Howe, Premier of Nova Scotia said, of the scattered isolation of the provinces: 'We have been more like foreigners than fellow-subjects...There are men in this room who hold the destinies of half of the Continent in their hands; and yet we never meet...we have done more good by a free talk over the table, tonight, than all the governors, general and local, could do in a year.'[79] Clearly, this is a good example of Watkin's gifts for bringing people together who ought to meet, and who had a common interest, and an illustration also, perhaps, of the manner in which his influence was impressed on events, rather than by way of recorded speeches or written papers. It is probable that other similar occurrences which influenced the great

---

[75] *Ibid*, p.481.
[76] In *The Union of British North* America, p.215.
[77] Mitchell, p.227.
[78] Watkin, p.23.
[79] *Ibid*, pp.21 and 22.

84

movement towards Confederation have gone unrecorded.

The historian Arthur Lower has observed that

> When all the impersonal factors are set out, a large gap still remains, for history, after all, consists in the interaction not of blind forces, but of human beings. It is the role of individuals which is of ultimate significance. Since so much depends on unrecorded conversation and upon likes and antipathies, this is also the most elusive.[80]

'Estimates of the importance of Watkin's part in Canadian national unity vary considerably', according to A.W. Currie,[81] who, said 'he loved to be in the swim' and to feel that he 'counted' politically, and that 'the extent of his influence on the Confederation Movement cannot be accurately assessed'.[82] He quoted Professor Chester Martin as casting doubt on the real value of Watkin's contribution. Martin used words like 'grandiose' and 'chimerical' of some of Watkin's political suggestions.[83] Currie argued that 'Confederation was brought about by forces within Canada. Only by accepting the Marxist interpretation of history without reservation can Watkin's role be magnified into a major one.'[84] Given that Marx asserted: 'History is nothing else than the process of creating man through human labour to satisfy his needs, and therefore man has evident and irrefutable proof of his own creation by himself',[85] this seems to be a curiously harsh and inapplicable judgement. The evidence for Watkin's importance is not, in any case, confined to his own account of events. Emerging from lengthy reports of arguments and debates over the uniting of the separate colonies, there are occasional glimpses of him as a leader. When, after the conference of delegates of all parties which was convened in late 1866 to discuss the legislative details of a Bill for Canadian Confederation for submission to the Imperial Government, the participants met for dinner at the Canada Club, on 5 January 1867, Watkin chaired the dinner, and 'much in

[80]Lower, p.319.
[81]A.W. Currie, 'Sir Edward Watkin: A Canadian View', pp.33 and 39.
[82]Currie, *Grand Trunk*, p.98.
[83]Martin, pp.276 and 413.
[84]*Ibid*, p.98.
[85]*Encyclopaedia Britannica*, 1977 Edition, Vol. 11, p.554.

evidence…were the British supporters', who, besides Watkin, included Thomas Baring and Lord Wharncliffe.[86]

Lower disagrees with Currie's statement, above, that Confederation was brought about by forces within Canada: 'As the Movement was not a great groundswell of popular feeling but proceeded from logical necessity, the number of persons concerned in it is relatively small.' It is true that he added doubts about whether Newcastle's part was as great as Watkin claimed, and also whether Watkin's place in the events was as great as he himself seemed to think.[87] But, on the basis of Lower's own doctrine of 'unrecorded conversations', it could be argued that only Watkin himself had access to much of the evidence. Lower's final opinion, however, was that, in assessing all those involved in the process, 'A few dwarf all others.' Three Englishmen and five Canadian (plus five secondary Canadian figures) were the main engines of the Confederation Movement. Of the Canadians he lists, George Etienne Cartier played the key role in persuading French Canada to accept the new Constitution, and John A. Macdonald, the pilot of Confederation, was the practical man who applied other men's ideas. Cartier (1814–73), who had been a French rebel in earlier days, having been banished on pain of death by Lord Durham's Ordinance of 28 June 1838, was the acknowledged leader of the majority of French-Canadians. He had become a successful corporate lawyer in Montreal when the Ordinance was lifted on 9 October of that year and being interested in railways was chosen as the solicitor for the Grand Trunk Railway in 1853.[88] Watkin and he struck up an enduring friendship.[89] Federation would have been impossible without Cartier. John A. Macdonald (1815–91), actually born in Glasgow but taken to Canada when he was five years old, was, with Cartier, the joint first Prime Minister of the Dominion. The three Englishmen were 'Newcastle, Head, and Watkin'. Sir Edmund Walker Head, as Governor-General from 1854 to 1861, had been in the 'authentic liberal imperialist' succession of Durham and Elgin; the 5th Duke of Newcastle was 'a

---

[86]Morton, p.209.

[87]Lower, p.320.

[88]Norah Story, *The Oxford Companion to Canadian History and Literature* (OUP, 1967), p.156.

[89]Who knows how much this friendship influenced Cartier to support Federation so whole-heartedly?

15 Sir John Alexander Macdonald, Joint First Prime Minister of the Dominion of Canada, c. 1871

16 Sir George Etienne Cartier, Joint First Prime Minister of the Dominion of Canada, c. 1871

clearing house for ideas and influences, and one of the major figures to hold the Colonial Secretaryship in the 19th century'. Watkin 'brought men together,' and was 'a central figure'.[90]

For his part in the unification, John A. Macdonald was awarded the honour of Knight Commander of the Order of the Bath. Cartier's award was that of Companion of the same Order, and he felt, not unwarrantably, that there was some injustice in the disparity. Watkin, according to his letter to Benjamin Disraeli dated 3 August 1867 replying to the offer of a knighthood, had been promised by the Duke of Newcastle some time before his death 'an even higher reward for his services which he alone knew the extent of', but at Watkin's own request 'this was postponed until...the great question of policy which [the Duke] had so much at heart should be finally realised in legislation'. In the same letter he refused to accept a knighthood because of Cartier's disappointment, which the Catholic French-speaking population had taken as an act of indifference towards them. He did so, he explained, in

---

[90]Lower, pp.319 and 320.

17 Sir Edward's coat of arms, 1880

order to avoid further trouble at the moment of the birth of the 'new Dominion'.[91] Disraeli replied on 8 August, accepting his 'highly creditable' refusal. He wrote again a year later, after Cartier had been awarded a baronetcy, to inform him of the substantive offer of a knighthood, which this time was accepted.[92] The *Folkestone Gazette* of 24 April 1880 recorded that Sir Edward had been made a baronet in that month, adding that the new dignity bestowed on him, 'though it may be taken as an expression of the Queen's appreciation of his recent gift to the town of Grimsby,[93] will be regarded by those best acquainted with the history of the Canadian Dominion as an instance of honours

---

[91]Watkin, pp.459, 491 and 492.

[92]*Ibid*, pp.494 and 495. *The London Gazette*, 1 September 1868; Baronetcy – 30 April 1880.

[93]The statue of the Prince Consort – see the chapter on Grimsby, *infra*.

18 Watkin, aged about 66, as painted by Sir Hubert Herkomer.
He holds a map of Canada

accidentally deferred'. The motto he adopted for his armorial device was 'Saie and Doe'.

Watkin was not above putting in a word for himself at times. Towards the end of the 1880s, he seems to have recalled the vague words of the Duke of Newcastle suggesting a rather more exalted recognition of his work in Canada. To the Marquess of Salisbury, referring to a report that the Queen's Jubilee Year was to be marked by the elevation of one or more representatives of industry to the House of Lords, set out his own case for consideration.[94] If such self-commendation seems to be less than dignified, we must remember his refusal of his own knighthood until George Cartier had been honoured appropriately, and that in 1891 he could exhibit a similar concern: on 9 June, to Salisbury, on the death of

_____

[94]Salisbury Papers, Watkin Letters, 9 May 1887, f.151. About this time he asked Macdonald to commend Joseph Hickson (1830–97) for a knighthood, successfully (1890). Hickson had been taken by Watkin from the MS&LR in 1861, to be the chief accountant of the Grand Trunk Railway; he was its General Manager from 1874 to 1891. He had married Catherine, daughter of Andrew Dow of Montreal, who sent a floral tribute to Watkin's funeral. Watkin also recommended to Salisbury his own son, Alfred Mellor Watkin, for a knighthood – a request almost immediately withdrawn, with an apology.

Sir John A. Macdonald, he suggested 'Why not make lady Macdonald a Peeress – as you did in the case of Lady Burnett-Coutts? This would gratify 2,800,000 Canadian women.'[95]

Watkin had his portrait painted several times, the most notable being that by Herkomer.[96] It was exhibited in the Royal Academy in 1887,[97] and was probably Watkin's favourite. It shows him holding on his lap a map of Canada.

[95] *Ibid*, f.161.
[96] Hubert von Herkomer,1849–1914 (knighted in 1907). He was born in Bavaria, came to England in 1857, and was naturalised. In addition to social subjects, his portraits included those of Wagner, Ruskin, and the Marquess of Salisbury. He was prodigiously versatile, working as an engraver, architect, journalist, playwright, singer, composer, actor, and a pioneer producer of films. He was an enthusiast, like Baudelaire, Scriabin and Schönberg, for the association between colour and music [DNB (OUP, 1982), p.318. *Cambridge Biographical Encyclopaedia* (CUP,1994), p.444. Magnus Magnusson, ed., *Chambers Biographical Dictionary* (Chambers, 1995), p.702].
[97] *DNB* (1911), p.603.

7

The Manchester, Sheffield and Lincolnshire Railway Development, 1863–1877

Watkin departed the M&LR in August 1861, having left, ringing in the ears of the Board, the possibility of amalgamation with the GNR or the LNWR or both. However, a chance meeting while he was away was to upset all his peace of mind. In that autumn, Allport and two other Midland men were surveying the possibility of a new line between Buxton and Manchester, when they came face to face with a dogcart carrying a MS&L director and two officers. Allport and company openly declared their purpose, and at the end of the day they had agreed on a proposal for the Midland to extend their line to New Mills, giving them access from there to 'Manchester…Lancashire, Cheshire, or beyond' over MS&L metals.[1] A special meeting of the 'Sheffield' Board was held on 11 October 1861, to which the Chairman reported that 'Mr. Allport had stated that the Midland Company had resolved upon getting access from their system to Manchester at whatever cost, and…were prepared to deposit a line between New Mills and some part of their Buxton extension…but being anxious to avoid an unnecessary expenditure were disposed to make an arrangement with this Company for the use of their lines between New Mills and Manchester.' In return, the Midland would agree that 'the whole of their traffic between stations south of Chesterfield would go over this Company's line via Beighton until the new lines were completed'. This agreement would hold for ten years, 'without prejudicing the agreement between this Company

---

[1]Frederick S. Williams, *The Midland Railway (Bemrose and Co., 1877)*, pp.156–7.

and the Great Northern Company'.[2] The agreement was made on 7 November 1861.[3] At the 15 November meeting, at which Watkin was present, a letter was read from E.B. Denison, Secretary of the Great Northern Railway, to the effect that his company had lodged an injunction to restrain the MS&L from carrying out the agreement.[4] The 'Sheffield' replied, regretting that the GNR Board 'should take so hostile a proceeding', and recommending a meeting between the two companies and the Midland, 'for mutual benefit'.

Watkin, of course, was incensed that all his badgering of the Midland had gone for nothing in his absence. He and Chapman exchanged what must have been a rather heated correspondence, the summary of which was reported by Chapman to a Finance Committee meeting on 22 November that year, and as Watkin had intimated his willingness to resign if the company wished to terminate his agreement, the Board arranged with him to cancel it, on payment to him of £3,400.[5] Dow describes Watkin's attitude as petulant, and unpleasantly reminiscent 'of his departed tutor, Huish'. But he could scarcely be expected, in view of his own resistance to the machinations of the Midland, to allow that company to take advantage in his absence of his much more pacific and malleable colleagues. His relationship with them seems, however, to have been unimpaired, for only a month later, when Watkin expressed his willingness to represent the company on the Boards of the Cheshire Midland and the Stockport and Woodley Junction railways if the directors so desired,[6] Chapman and the Board accepted his offer. Edward Underdown, the very capable Chief Accountant of the company since April 1854, was appointed as General Manager in Watkin's place, and his contract stipulated that he spent the whole of his time on the company.[7]

At the ordinary half-yearly shareholders' meeting on 30 July 1862, a motion was tabled by John Fildes, a prominent Manchester broker, that a return be furnished to the shareholders of all

---

[2]PRO RAIL 463/6, 11 October 1861, Minute 136.
[3]Minute 185 of Board meeting of 13 December 1861.
[4]Minute 159.
[5]Dow, Vol. 1, p.205.
[6]A curious offer, as technically he no longer worked for the MS&LR. An indication, perhaps, that – characteristically – he felt, on reflection, that his resignation had been over-impetuous?
[7]Dow, Vol. 1, p.205.

directorships and committee appointments held by any MS&L directors, distinguishing between those held subsidiary to or arising from being an MS&LR director and those held by an independent qualification. It is not known what Fildes' intention was in putting this motion; he was one of Watkin's keenest supporters at the time. At any rate, an amendment was moved, and carried unanimously, that 'such a return was calculated to embarrass the independent action of Boards of Directors, and thus affect injuriously the interests of Railway Companies, and that this meeting, therefore, declines to order such a return'.[8]

Watkin was invited back to the MS&LR in 1863, being unanimously elected as a director on 15 March.[9] It did not take long for him to assert himself. At the meeting of the Board on 23 October he gave notice that at the next meeting he would move 'That in view of the serious question of Policy and Finance now affecting the position and prospects of the proprietors, it is desirable that the Board reconsider its organisation as respects the offices of Chairman and Deputy Chairman.'[10] Minute 197 of the following meeting, on 6 November, recorded that he had withdrawn 'the motion notice of which he had given at the last meeting'. He may have felt his motion to have been too aggressive to Chapman, who had not been in the best of health for some time, but objectively he must have been impatient at the way matters were being led. He had become used to engaging with railway and state politics at a national level, and the Manchester scene was very provincial and leisurely by comparison. It may have been only a shot across the bows, but Chapman and his colleagues would have sensed Watkin's impatience to take firm control of the company's destiny. When, in the following year, the chairmanship became vacant, John Fildes wrote to his friend John Wintringham in Grimsby,[11] 'I think there is no doubt of Mr Watkin's being placed in the chair of the Sheffield Company (I hope that he will be unanimously), he will be a first-rate thing for the shareholders.'[12]

Watkin was elected Chairman of the company on 27 January

[8]PRO RAIL 463/6, Minute 400.
[9]MS&L Board Meeting, Minute 604. PRO RAIL 463/6.
[10]Minute 193.
[11]12 January.
[12]Wintringham Papers, North-East Lincolnshire Archives, 223/3/2. 12 January 1864.

19 Locomotive 'Watkin', with its Engineer's Saloon; sold to the LNWR in 1863 and photographed as repainted and renamed 'Carlisle' by its new owners

1864, though it is not recorded whether it was unanimously.[13] He remained so for the next thirty years, though still retaining, for five years, his presidency of the Grand Trunk Railway of Canada. A curiosity had appeared as the last item of business at the Board meeting on 9 January 1863: Charles Reboul Sacré (the Locomotive Superintendent) submitted an offer from the engineering department of the London and North Western Railway to purchase the MS&L's small engine named *Watkin*, for the sum of £800, which 'Mr Sacré recommends should be accepted', and it was accordingly agreed upon.[14] This engine, a 2-2-2WT, had been bought from the builders, George England and Company, in 1856 for £894, and had a small saloon attached for the use of the General Manager. The LNWR renamed it *Carlisle*, and it was used by the Northern Division Engineer at Manchester until it was withdrawn in 1888.

In September 1865 the MS&L Board learned that LNWR surveyors were prospecting a line between Chapel-en-le-Frith, on their Manchester to Buxton line, and Sheffield. This spurred the Board on to the completion of the Marple, New Mills and Hayfield Junction Railway. The LNW countered by placing a Bill to repeal the running powers of the MS&L between, *inter alia,* Manchester London Road and Ardwick Junction, to deprive them

---

[13]PRO RAIL 463/7, Minute 367.
[14]Minute 494.

of that first stretch of their main line from Manchester to Sheffield. Watkin's response to this latest LNW offensive was Napoleonic in its boldness. In 1866 he proposed the building of a new railway from Cornbrook on the MSJ&A to the projected Midland Railway goods branch at Ancoats, which was to join the MS&L main line near Ashbury's Station/Ardwick, thus circumnavigating the LNWR connection. The new railway would have run through the heart of Manchester, crossing Oxford Street, running behind Portland Street – where a large station was to be built – and spanning Piccadilly on a bridge near Ducie Street. The new station, with its viaduct, was estimated to cost £1.25 million, but as the cost of the land alone was declared at £617,000, this sounds over-optimistic.[15] This ambitious scheme would have linked Sheffield with Liverpool, and the Bill was passed by the House of Commons, but rejected in the Lords.[16]

The LNWR, not to be outdone, presented a Bill for a railway from its lines at Buxton to Sheffield, thus connecting Sheffield with Manchester and Liverpool over their own metals. The Sheffield, Buxton and Liverpool Railway was, said Watkin, '[a] veritable High Peak Line, evidently conceived in pique'.[17] It was withdrawn, but revived in 1867 as an LNWR 'Buxton and Sheffield Bill', and as such was passed by the Commons. Watkin then became alarmed, and offered, in return for its abandonment, running powers over the MS&L between Ardwick Junction and Sheffield. This gave the LNW access to Sheffield without the huge expenditure of its own proposal, and so the terms were accepted. This secured the first three-quarters of a mile of Watkin's main line, but the outcome of these particular skirmishings must be seen as an LNWR victory. At the 24 January 1866 half-yearly shareholders' meeting, a Mr Mallalieu proposed an increase in the remuneration of the directors, which, since 1849, had been £1,200 per annum, having been voluntarily reduced in that year from the £2,250 established in 1847. He drew comparison with six neighbouring companies: the Great Northern, with a similar capital (£14m), paid their directors £3,700; the Midland (£25.25m), paid £4,000; the LNW

---

[15]Jack Simmons *The Railway in Town and Country*, 1830–1914 (David and Charles, 1986), p.111.
[16]Dow, Vol.12 p.13.
[17]*Ibid.*

(£41m), paid £8,000 plus £2,000 to the Chairman; the Lancashire and Yorkshire (£21m), £4,000; the North Eastern (£31m), £5,000; and the Great Eastern (£23m), £4,000. He proposed £3,400, plus an additional sum for the Chairman, to be decided by the directors. This was seconded by John Fildes, and the proprietors voted 42 to 13 in favour.[18] This decision was confirmed by the directors on 24 January 1866, to take effect from 1 February.[19]

Such support from his colleagues and the shareholders runs like a leitmotif throughout Watkin's time of the MS&L and is a contrary theme to the received notion of him as an enemy of the shareholders. The opposition was present, however, in his lifetime. A year later he was to speak to the proprietors about a damaging rumour being spread in the stock exchanges of Manchester and London to the effect that the Sheffield company was not paying in full its debentures, thus causing a run to sell its shares. He had pursued its origins, he reported, and outlined the whole history of the rumour, tracing it to a small group of individuals, and concluding, 'I do not know why anybody should seek to damage me. I do not mean, in a longish life of hard work, I have never made an enemy, or have not…unintentionally…trodden upon somebody's toes. But I declare most solemnly, that I do not entertain an envious, or a spiteful, or an injurious feeling against any man living. I have received too many blessings of the Almighty to entertain any ill-feeling against any one of his creatures.'[20]

The rumour was wholly without foundation, as can be seen from the records. In the same period, in the autumn of 1866, his enemies put it around that Watkin was in serious personal financial trouble, particularly in affairs of the Humberside Ironworks Company, of which he was the Chairman. The MS&L Board, at their meeting on 21 December, with Watkin in the chair, supported him unreservedly. William Fenton (Deputy Chairman) drew attention to the 'scandalous report', and it was resolved unanimously that a letter be addressed to the Chairman and signed by the Deputy Chairman on behalf of the Board, 'expressing our abhorrence of the scandalous and iniquitous report which has been

---

[18]An attendance of 55, plus abstentions, of a total of 5,000 shareholders is interesting. The total figure was given at a Special Meeting of 25 March 1867, (PRO RAIL 463/73, p.4.).
[19]Board Minute no. 753.
[20]PRO RAIL 463/73, p.27.

20 Edward Watkin aged about 50

circulated against you throughout the length and breadth of the country'. 'Fortunately,' the letter went on, 'your position is so unassailable that the blow has been turned aside...we are aware however that the report must necessarily have caused you much painful anxiety. We beg to assure you of our sincere and profound sympathy, and we trust that your efforts...will be successful in bringing to light the machinations of the party or parties who have not hesitated, for their own base purposes, to place in jeopardy or even ruin your fame and position.' [21]

That was not the end of the matter. On 2 July 1869, Watkin called the attention of the Board to the proceedings taken against him by a Mr Jacomb, a Huddersfield solicitor. Jacomb was a shareholder of the Humberside Ironworks Company. This company, which had invited Watkin in to salvage its affairs, had fallen on hard financial times, the promoters having promised a dividend of 20% and more, but almost the whole of the public's money invested had disappeared within a few months.[22] Jacomb, after four unsuccessful attempts, had at last forced the case into Court, and Watkin invited the Board 'to make enquiries and form

[21]PRO RAIL 463/9, Minute 365.
[22]PRO RAIL 463/10, Minute 682.

their own opinions' upon the transactions involved, and his own part in them. He then retired from the chair, and in his absence it was decided unanimously: 'The Board desire to express their continued and entire confidence in he integrity of their Chairman, Sir Edward Watkin, and to convey to him their sincere sympathy in the present trial, so unjustly forced upon him.' They recorded their opinion that there was 'no necessity whatever for an enquiry to be made as suggested by the Chairman'. At the half-yearly shareholders' meeting held on 28 July, 'It was recorded unanimously that the Board congratulated the Chairman on the successful result of the action brought against him...and again desire to express their sympathy with him in this undeserved persecution for which there was not a shadow of foundation.' Sir Edward was not only exonerated, but complimented by the judge at the trial. The 'pettifogging Yorkshire Attorney opted to be nonsuited rather than accept the verdict of the jury'. [23]

This did not prevent Sir Robert Peel (1822–95, the third baronet) from attacking Watkin in the House on this matter on 7 June 1877. Watkin had asked the Attorney-General whether his attention had been drawn to the opinion expressed by the Lord Chief Justice of England, reported in *The Times* of 18 May, regarding the purchase on the stock exchange of shares for the purpose of raising the shares to a fictitious value in order to encourage others to buy them, only for them to find the shares worthless; and whether the Attorney-General intended to advise the government to take proceedings against any of the guilty parties. Sir Robert Peel then stood up to ask the Attorney-General a question – initially to use exactly the same words as Sir Edward but going on to make particular reference to the *Railway News* of 24 March 1876, which reported the circumstances of the Humberside Ironworks Company case, naming certain people, including Sir Edward.

Watkin asked the Attorney-General, before he answered the first question, for the indulgence of the House while he said a few words in reference to the one from the Rt. Hon. The Member for Tamworth. He said he thought he was within parliamentary language in describing what Peel had said as 'not a little offensive'.

---

[23] *The City Jackdaw* (Manchester), Vol. 2 (1877), p.243.

98

'He was grossly in error...had done me a grave injustice, wasted the time of the House, and extended a practice...which is not entirely to the credit of the House – namely that of bringing forward personal matters and arousing personal animosities in the shape of asking questions...The facts are very simple, and they are perfectly well known.' He referred Members to the Library, to inspect *The Times* of the autumn of 1869, where they would find the report of the trial. He had refused to allow the case to go to a referee and insisted on its going to a trial by jury. 'The jury was empanelled,' he went on, 'to try whether I...had done anything dishonourable, or fraudulent, or unfair, and they were unanimously of the opinion that no case whatever had been made out.' The Lord Chief Justice recorded that no imputation rested upon him, and the misfortunes of the undertaking 'happened mainly because the advice which I gave was not taken'. The Attorney-General would, he thought, do him the justice of admitting that the question was not fair, was not well-founded, and was libellous. It was such a question, he said, as a man would not put to me out of this House without receiving such a reply as the forms of this House would not permit me to make'.

The Attorney-General limited himself merely to a 'No' to Watkin's first question, but Watkin responded that the point was a serious one, and gave notice of moving a Resolution. The House cheered Watkin at this point.[24] *The City Jackdaw* concluded that 'Sir R. Peel's smartness had for once overstepped the mark', and observed that the bearing of an illustrious name did not mean that a man would run an illustrious career, 'but the ungenerous display of small wit, the cowardly utterance of libel in privileged places, and the distortion and suppression of fact, are things which are not usually associated with the names either of legislators or simple gentlemen'.[25] *Herepath's Railway (and Commercial) Journal,* not usually on Watkin's side, could say: 'His integrity was unquestioned.'[26]

At the 16 January 1867 half-yearly meeting, the Chairman gave his definition of a sound railway company: one which earns as a net profit the whole of the original capital cost in a period not

---

[24] *Hansard* c.1435–38.
[25] *Ibid.*
[26] 19 April 1901, p.398.

21 Manchester London Road Station, about the turn of the century. The MS&LR Offices were in the left hand third of the building and the LNWR premises in the other two thirds

exceeding twenty-five years. 'The charge cannot be made against us as the proprietors of a sound undertaking...that we have habitually entered upon a reckless, extravagant, profitless or unsound outlay...we have increased the solidity of the outlay instead of diminishing it (Applause).'[27] This may have been a prior defensive tactic, for later in the meeting, John Fildes complained about the expense proposed on the Manchester Central Station, which formed part of Watkin's newly projected line from Manchester to Liverpool. Fildes seems to have had a complex loyalty to Watkin, something which the latter now commented upon: 'I must say good-naturedly to Mr. Fildes that he reminds me very much of that pleasant story in Captain Marryat's "Peter Simple"; Mr. Handycock, a stockbroker, sometimes bullies his wife and is uncivil to everybody, and at other times he is the most pleasant, generous and sentimental of men. Mrs Handycock explains it in this way: "Why, you see, sometimes he is a bull, and sometimes he is a bear, my dear (Laughter)." Fildes replied, "I am a bull now,

[27]PRO RAIL 463/73, pp.16ff.

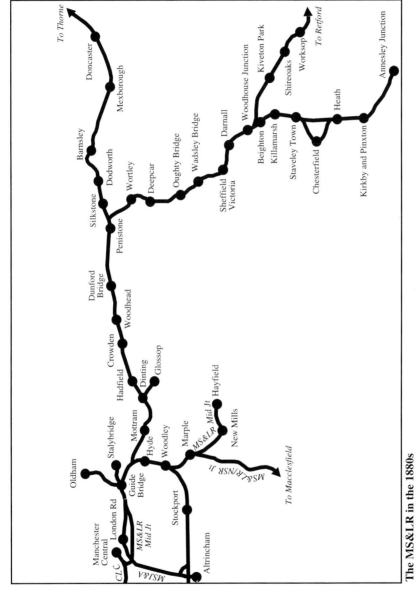

The MS&LR in the 1880s
1. Manchester - Penistone - Sheffield - Retford

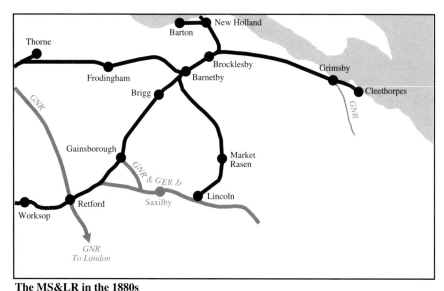

The MS&LR in the 1880s
2. Retford - Lincoln - New Holland - Grimsby

Sir (Laughter)." Watkin hoped he would not only be a bull, but become a lamb.[28]

In 1865, Watkin's generous remit from the MS&LR enabled him to accept a challenge from the South Eastern Railway, which was in need of re-organisation, and to which he now directed his main energies.

---

[28] *Ibid*, pp.29–44.

8

The South Eastern Railway, 1866–1894

The third of the most important railways of which Watkin became Chairman was the South Eastern Railway, from London to Dover, opened on 7 February 1844. The railway's historian, Adrian Gray, describes it as: 'A great railway, linking the nation's capital to the chief ferry port of Europe'.[1] Its utility would appear to have been obvious, but investors responding to its prospectus were not numerous, and the Chairman of the company, Joseph Baxendale, had to subsidise it from his own money, lending £10,000 in November 1841.[2] However, there was little doubt of its viability once it was running. The tentativeness of those early transport business endeavours, and the riskiness of some of the proposed ventures, as evidenced in the slump which followed the proliferation of schemes in the 'Railway Mania' of the middle 1840s, meant that any strong-minded individual with an ability to convince others of his confident grasp of the difficulties involved could seize power over a company. Such power sometimes became absolute, and this took place during the chairmanship of James McGregor. He was elected Chairman on 4 September 1845, and became Managing Director in the same month. 'Just as Edward Watkin came to be synonymous with the South Eastern Railway in its later years, so James McGregor was apparently the South Eastern personified in the late 1840s and the early 1850s'.[3]

The maintenance of absolute power required a supporting organisation of cronies and a compliant claque of shareholders and employees. This, and the lack of effective accountability, led McGregor's regime into malpractices such as improper share

---

[1] Adrian Gray, *South Eastern Railway* (Middleton Press, 1990), p.21.
[2] *Ibid*, p.16.
[3] *Ibid*, p.22.

22 Charing Cross Station, SER, 1870

dealings, paying dividends out of capital to cover up inefficient management, buying off opposition and withholding information from those entitled to know. Such mismanagement, and the fact that some were not taken in by McGregor, led to many factions and disputes. His ineffectiveness in meeting the challenges of the East Kent Railway, a venture promoted locally by gentry and business people in Rochester, Faversham and Canterbury because the SER failed to provide rail connections for them, resulted in the success of the EKR, and its transformation 'into the consuming monster of the London, Chatham and Dover Railway', a mistake which was to have a profound effect upon the SER. McGregor's reign, marked by patent self-interest, became more and more turbulent as time went on, punctuated by vituperative rows and boardroom scandals. Groups of shareholders, particularly those from Manchester, began to question McGregor's chairmanship. One of those shareholders, Josiah Wilson, openly criticised his methods and at the March 1850 shareholders' meeting he described the Chairman as a 'complete dictator'.

At the general meeting of March 1854, McGregor was ousted,

and then resigned also as General Manager, though remaining as a director. This served only to usher in another phase of factionalism and spitefulness. The Board divided into two groups of rivals and the minutes record 'offensive and intemperate exchanges...in a manner irreconcilable with the harmonious action of the Board', and 'inconsistent with mutual relations of personal courtesy and respect'. In 1855, McGregor was finally removed from the SER altogether, 'amid further rumours of dubious financial dealings'.

As early as 1862, some shareholders expressed their view that Edward Watkin possessed the qualities needed by the SER. On 24 January, the Lancashire shareholders of the company gathered in the Clarence Hotel, Manchester, to discuss their dissatisfaction with the SER management. At that meeting, Jonathan Mellor, a prosperous Oldham cotton manufacturer and a director of the Oldham, Ashton-under-Lyne and Guide Bridge Junction Railway as well as of the SER, inaugurated a discussion, after which Edward William Watkin was voted, by 20 votes to 18, as their candidate for the Board in the forthcoming elections. Watkin had married Mellor's sister, Mary, in 1845, and no doubt this influenced his advocacy. It was not until January 1865 that a vacancy on the Board occurred and that Watkin was elected; but by March 1865 he was already Deputy Chairman, and was elected Chairman in March the following year at a salary of £2,500.

The year 1866 was a bad one for the financial markets, on the collapse of the bankers Overend and Gurney and Company. The London, Chatham and Dover Railway was taken into Chancery, and the Humberside Ironworks, of which Watkin was Chairman, went bankrupt. There were rumours that Watkin himself was to be declared a bankrupt, but this did not happen. In later years he was to tell Lord Redesdale that he had used his own money to help the SER through the crisis. 'I became responsible for everything I had in the world to the bankers of the Company', he said.[4]

Talks of amalgamation and mutual operation with other railways were abundant in the late 1860s. Those with the LCDR evaporated because of that company's financial distress, but arrangements with the London, Brighton and South Coast Railway developed well. In his chairman's address to a special

---

[4]*Ibid,* pp.22, 24, 28 and 39.

meeting of shareholders held on 4 July 1867, Watkin explained that he had applied for powers for the companies to fuse their net receipts, keeping their capitals apart, on the recent example of the North Eastern Railway plan of 1854. This would serve, he explained, 'to ensure unity of management and a perpetual peace'.[5] One shareholder, Mr George Smith, in the following debate, pointed out that due to the Chairman, 'a man who had worked his way by his own exertions to his present high and honourable position', the SER was in good health, but the 'Brighton' was not. He commented also that 'Mr. Watkin receives £200 per annum and Mr Laing, Chairman of the Brighton line, received a salary of £2,500 a year.'[6] The Chairman objected that this was no matter for the present meeting, but on 29 August he was voted a salary of £2,500 per annum.[7]

On 28 November, the Board decided to include the LCDR in the amalgamation talks, and early in the following year an approach was made to the London and South Western Railway, but it expressed a lack of interest. A Bill for the working union of the South Eastern and Brighton companies and the London, Chatham and Dover was declared proved, but the Lords' Select Committee recommended maximum tolls as proposed by the Brighton. This would have cost the SER £60,000 a year – the equivalent of giving away £1,200,000 of its capital. The SER directors proposed that this be allowed for in the division of profits, but the proposition was not accepted. No toll clauses were in the Bill as presented to the Commons.[8]

Such a widespread movement for amalgamation and fusion of interests was a very bold step. Had all the SER's plans succeeded, it would have accomplished what the government grouping of 1923 finally achieved, and created a 'Southern Railway' fifty years before. It was hardly surprising, however, that a monopoly of that scale should prove unacceptable to Parliament in the 1860s, and influenced by opposition from the Midland Railway, the LNWR and the corporations of Brighton and Dover, the Bill was voted out. Once the agreed arrangement had been thwarted, relations

[5]PRO RAIL 1110/425, 4 July 1867, pp.511ff.
[6]Ibid, p.516.
[7]Ibid, p.518.
[8]Ibid, 27 August 1868.

between the parties became distant, and at times hostile, as the customary cut-throat competition of the time re-asserted itself.

Watkin continued to explore new ways of increasing revenue, by making plans for new branch lines, and imaginative suggestions such as the one that ladies when accompanied by a gentleman should be able to travel at half-fare,[9] and the far more important issue of workman's tickets – cheap tickets to enable workmen to travel economically to and from their places of employment.[10]

Talks of 'fusion of interest' between the SER, the LC&DR and the LB&SCR were revived in 1870, but Watkin was informed by a 'Brighton' representative that Forbes of the LCD was cool about the proposal. Progress was made by the other two companies, but Parliamentary opposition to an attempt in 1871 to merge the Lancashire and Yorkshire Railway with the LNWR (an amalgamation which actually took place in 1922) was so heated that the SER decided not to pursue the plan further. As the LCD recovered from its financial problems, relations with the South Eastern deteriorated, and remained acerbic for the next twenty or so years, notwithstanding attempts by Watkin from time to time to achieve something like operational agreements. Moves to amalgamate the two companies were made in early 1875, in January 1877, and in 1890.[11] Watkin often acted in the role of peacemaker and unifier, in spite of his reputation for 'courting controversy'.[12]

However, a correspondence published in *Herepath's Journal* of 7 January 1888 showed a complicated picture of these negotiations. Under the heading 'Southern Railways, Proposed Working Union', William Abbott, a shareholder both of the SER and the LCDR, set out, in a letter to the Chairmen of the LBSCR and the LCDR,[13] the points of advantage of a working union between those two companies and the SER:

1. The Termination of all disputes and rivalries...involving a very large wastage in competitive working, as well as heavy expenses for law and Parliamentary charges.

---

[9] Gray, p.41.
[10]C.F. Dendy Marshall, *History of the Southern Railway* (Ian Allan, 1963, 2 Vols.), Vol.2, p.307.
[11]Gray, pp.43 and 50.
[12]*Ibid*, p.39.
[13]27 December 1887.

2. The pooling of all traffic at competitive points.

3. The opening of the 16 metropolitan stations of the three companies to all the passengers using the lines of either [sic].

4. Great improvements in development of the intermediate and cross-country traffic, now so much sacrificed to...excessive accommodation.

Samuel Laing, Chairman of the LBSCR, replied[14] that he regarded the proposed union with great reserve. 'Our position with regard to the South Eastern Company was very fully and very carefully defined in my speech to our shareholders at the general meeting last January...I had hoped that the Chairman of the South Eastern Company would have been satisfied with that speech...and that our two companies might have rested in peace and tranquillity...Unfortunately, Sir Edward Watkin has thought it necessary to revive the claims in question...' James Staats Forbes, Chairman of the LCDR, expressed[15] his 'cordial adhesion' to the principle of such a working union, but two years before, a similar plan had foundered on 'the want of co-operation on the part of the Brighton Company. Another attempt made several years ago was thwarted by the withdrawal of the representatives of the South Eastern Company engaged in the promotion of this Bill'. It would seem that on the verge of losing their independence of operation, the companies suddenly became over-cautious and found excuses to withdraw from the negotiations.

Although 1874 was meant to be a 'year of truce', by the summer, rival schemes had multiplied. The Chatham Company was manoeuvring for control of the Crystal Palace and South London Railway, the SER was supporting the proposed Bromley Direct Railway, which would have given it access to a stronghold of the LCDR, and also lines from Maidstone to Ashford, and to Dungeness to strengthen its bid for cross-Channel traffic. When conciliation failed, it was Watkin's policy to compete with renewed energy. That year saw the opening of the LCD's direct line to Maidstone, which Watkin reckoned would cost his company

---

[14]4 January 1888.
[15]30 December 1887.

£15,000 a year in lost traffic. A further 'truce' was agreed on 30 July, but that, too, lasted less than a year.[16] Watkin's success in securing better harbour facilities on both sides of the Channel[17] may seem at first to be strange in view of his advocacy of a tunnel, but the tunnel would have taken years to complete, and meanwhile there was still competition to be met, and profits to be made from surface communication.

The history of the SER/LCDR rivalry, more perhaps than any other, demonstrates the policy of rivalry for the sake of it. The Chatham's port at Queenborough, Isle of Sheppey, was built by Staats Forbes for continental traffic, via Flushing, behind the back of his working agreement with Watkin for such traffic. Watkin responded by building facilities at Port Victoria on the Isle of Grain, to entice passengers away.[18] It is highly questionable whether such competition – such energetic hostility over such a relatively small area of the possible traffic to be generated – was in the best interest of the public economy. Adam Smith's principle of letting the market find its own level, and thereby creating the competition which would produce a higher quality of goods and services for the purchaser (who has thereby greater freedom of choice and would thus eliminate the inefficient) has to have some social and ethical regulation.

In those early days of the application of Smith's ideas to commerce and industry, Parliament was finding its way towards a proper and acceptable way of safeguarding the process, and ensuring healthy competition. W.E. Gladstone, as shrewd and non-partisan in this as in so many other ways, brought in a regulatory Bill controlling railway expansion as early as 1844. His Railway Act of that year also stipulated that on each line there should be operated what became known as 'Parliamentary Trains' at least once per day with a fare of no more than a penny a mile; the intention being the availability of travel to all classes. In addition, the Act reserved to the state powers to nationalise the railway system, if the companies should fail the common good.[19]

---

[16] *Ibid*, pp.39 and 42.
[17] *Men and Women of the Day: A Picture Gallery of Contemporary Portraiture* (London: Richard Bentley and Sons), p.47.
[18] C Hamilton Ellis, *British Railway History* (George Allen and Unwin; 1959), Vol. 2, pp.59–61.
[19] Roy Jenkins, *Gladstone* (Macmillan, 1995), p.68.

Not surprisingly, there was much resentment and resistance on the part of railway management to government interference in their commercial affairs. The Board of Trade was the department responsible for overseeing safety and methods of working on the railways from 1840; there was no appeal against their rulings, and sometimes these were ignored completely, as in the case of the Metropolitan District's line from Blackfriars to Mansion House, which was built in 1871 without the Board's authority. Engineers and management showed great contempt for the Board's activities. Allport of the Midland Railway replied 'pertinaciously' to one inspector's report after another; Brunel detested them and government officials of every kind. Watkin 'pursued them with virulence,' and in 1872, Richard Moon, the Chairman of the LNWR, told its shareholders that he believed 'the Board of Trade were as responsible for railway accidents as the railway companies were', on the grounds that they divided the functions of management but left all the responsibility with the companies.[20] The government was often accused of 'State interference with the companies' commercial relationship with the user'.[21] Regarding the general principle of freedom of competition, the General Manager of the North Eastern Railway assured a government Select Committee in 1872 that amalgamations had produced reductions in fares. This statement has to be taken in the context of the fact that his company, as a result of the 'absorption' of rival companies, had a virtual monopoly over the vast area between the Tees and the Scottish Border. His claim was contested by Edward Watkin – beset on all sides by rivals! – who was convinced that increased competition on certain routes had produced fare reductions.[22]

However, the hostile competition between the SER and the LCDR was, on balance, a wasteful use of resources, serving as they did a small corner of the map. Any benefits of challenge to initiative and inventiveness could have been only marginal. If Watkin had been in charge of the SER in 1853, the East Kent Railway and its development would never have been. As he said years later, the terms of the South Eastern's taking over the EKR

[20]Jack Simmons, *The Victorian Railway* (Thames and Hudson; 1991), pp.80 and 81.
[21]David Newman Smith, *The Railway and its Passengers: A Social History* (David and Charles, 1988), p.37.
[22]Newman Smith, pp.38ff.

were 'a bagatelle' – the SER could have bought up its nascent rival for virtually nothing.[23] The intermittent negotiations towards amalgamation, and their failure, have been described as 'largely a personal [struggle] between the giant of the railway world, Sir Edward Watkin, and Mr J.S. Forbes, the astute Chairman of the Chatham Company'. Both 'exceptionally able men', who bestrode their Boards of Directors, 'they were so closely matched, scheming to outwit each other at every point...that the natural compromise, the capitulation of the smaller Chatham Company, was out of the question'. 'One may regret that [Forbes's] talents were misdirected, and may deplore...his cynical disregard of ordinary standards ...and the strife which he encouraged between his company and the South Eastern. [But] one is compelled to admire...his almost impudent confidence in the...prospects of a company which had fallen so low that it could hardly deteriorate further.' [24]

Edward Cleveland-Stevens recorded that in 1875, when Watkin 'proudly called attention to the improvements of the last ten years...he was not thought to overstate the prospects of the company' when he claimed it was the 'soundest of all railways'. The same historian asserted that the SER was 'popular with an immense stream of suburban passengers', and that 'its efficiency was contrasted with the indifferent condition of the Chatham'.[25] *Herepath's Journal* stated 'We believe that most railways have an improving future before them, but very few so good as the South Eastern...The Chatham were not improving', and had lost their chance of profitable amalgamation.[26] In December 1876, another proposal was ventured, with net profits split 67% to 33% in favour of the SER. Parliamentary rules delayed the application until early in 1878, when Forbes put it to a shareholders' meeting in a peremptory speech weighted towards rejection of the scheme. One of the shareholders, William Abbott, called it 'an absolute confiscation', and the meeting rejected it unanimously.[27] Despite the inherent wastefulness in wanton competition for a compara-

---

[23]Gray, p.26.
[24]Edward Cleveland-Stevens, *English Railways: Their Development and Their Relation to the State* (London: George Routledge and Sons Ltd.,1915), pp.302–4.
[25]*Ibid*, p.305.
[26]13 February 1875, p.172; 25 March 1876, p.1184: Quoted, Cleveland-Stevens, p.306.
[27]Cleveland-Stevens, pp.308 and 309.

tively small market, the South Eastern was doing well. It produced a gross return on capital during 1870–74 of no less than 9.29%, and in January 1876 declared a dividend of 7.5%.[28] Such figures are hardly supportive of Watkin's image as a 'wrecker' of the finances of companies of which he was chairman.

The 1870s saw more and more of Watkin's energies being directed towards his vision of a Channel tunnel. The SER Board was not unanimous in supporting his submarine intentions, and the trial borings of March 1875 excited lengthy debates about expenditure. On 11 March, however, the Board agreed, with government authority, to make a grant of £20,000 towards the venture, with a proviso that the LCDR did the same, and that the company would not be bound to any further expenditure. The Board minutes record that in December 1876 Watkin told the directors that he intended to resign his seat on the MS&LR Board due to pressure of work on the South Eastern. He obviously did not do so, and it can only be assumed that he made the statement during a highly pressured moment, to be reconsidered on reflection. The MS&LR was integral to his vision.

In 1877 he ran into personal trouble with the SER Board, on two counts. In 1876 he had commissioned a new class of express passenger locomotive – the 'Ironclad' class – from John Ramsbottom, the former locomotive superintendent of the LNWR. This was a highly irregular and discourteous intervention in the domain of the locomotive engineer, James Cudworth.[29] Ramsbottom (1814–97, 'The father of the modern locomotive') had been called upon in 1872 to arbitrate in the affairs of the MS&LR in a difference of opinion with the South Yorkshire Railway.[30] His report was written from 'Harewood Lodge, Mottram, Cheshire', which was not many yards from Hill End, the residence of John Chapman, Watkin's predecessor as Chairman of the 'Sheffield'. It is not too fanciful to imagine that Watkin's invitation was put to Ramsbottom over the port during an evening shared by the three of them. Whatever the reason, Cudworth

---

[28]Gray, p.43.
[29]Though E.L. Ahrons, in *Locomotive and Train Working in the Latter Part of the Nineteenth Century* (Cambridge: W. Heffer and Sons Ltd, 1953), Vol.5, p.6, suggested that Cudworth was very set in his ways, and was not meeting the needs of the company.
[30]Dow, Vol.2, p.43.

resigned in protest, and Watkin promoted his son Alfred Mellor Watkin to the vacant position. This, and the fact that Watkin junior was elected as Member of Parliament for Grimsby on 1 August 1877 (in addition to being a director of the Metropolitan and MS&L railways), displeased the South Eastern Board. A hard-fought boardroom battle was lost by Watkin by six votes to four, in which, strangely, Alfred Watkin's uncle and godfather, Jonathan Mellor, was one of the six. Edward's relationship with this brother-in-law was chilly for a year or two after that setback. At the turbulent shareholders' meeting of 1 February 1879, Watkin said 'My brother-in-law here...Mr Mellor...has not for some few years been the most happy and agreeable of brothers-in-law.'[31] Alfred Watkin was dismissed at the beginning of September, and a new locomotive superintendent, James Stirling, from the Glasgow and South Western Railway, was appointed in March 1878.[32] As if to convict Watkin of his error, the 'Ironclad' class was a comparative failure.

Alfred was not entirely unqualified for the post. He had been appointed to the Locomotive Committee in 1875, having been apprenticed to the West Midland Railway at seventeen years of age, qualified as a driver on the MS&LR in 1865, as a loco inspector on the LC&DR in 1867, and he joined the SER Locomotive Department in 1868.[33]

Of the boardroom clash, *The Grimsby Observer* of 3 October 1877 said:

We publish the subjoined note from a director of the South Eastern Railway, Mr Joshua Fielden, with some reluctance for many reasons, but chiefly because of its bitterness. From what we have heard and seen regarding this unfortunate dispute we should say that Mr Fielden has no warrant for using the phrase 'Vote of censure on Sir Edward Watkin' in reference to what occurred. The vote of censure, if such it

---

[31]PRO RAIL 1110/425, p.1016.
[32]Gray, p.44.
[33]He had previously had experience on the Grand Trunk Railway of Canada in the Locomotive Department, from the age of 15 [E.W. Watkin, *Canada and the States* (Ward, Lock and Co.,1887), p.38).

was, was passed upon his son; and though it may be true that Sir Edward's opponents on the Board designed to hit the father through the son, it is none the less a stretch of language to characterise it as Mr Fielden does. We have no wish to enter into the dispute, and, indeed, we deprecate it altogether; but we hardly think that the directors who seek to overcome an opponent after this fashion are hardly likely to make much headway, be their cause the most just in the world.

The dispute was even more momentous than that. *The Grimsby Observer* of 19 September 1877 reported:

We are informed that in consequence of the adverse decision arrived at by the majority of the South Eastern directors to relieve Mr Alfred Watkin of his duties as locomotive superintendent, Sir Edward Watkin has tendered his resignation of the office of chairman of that company. Strenuous efforts are being made, however, by some members of the Stock Exchange to induce that gentleman to reconsider his decision, or, at all events, to postpone giving effect to it until the fusion with the Chatham and Dover Company has been completed...It is not probable that the requisition will have the effect desired, or that Sir Edward will attach any importance to opinions expressed by the Stock Exchange, when they conflict with a decision which it must be presumed would not have been arrived at except after mature consideration.

Nepotism was a normal feature of life at that time. At all grades of staff, on railways, in the mines, in banking and others, the employment of the son of one of the successful and competent older generation was seen to be the exercise of recognised sound judgement. The system worked very well when the son was good at the job. It came under bitter criticism when he was not. This would seem to have been the case with Alfred Mellor Watkin (1846–1914). In a pamphlet on railway safety,[34] written in response to a plea from a Mr Wrigley for fewer trains and a speed limit of thirty

---

[34]Alfred Mellor Watkin, *Don't Leap in the Dark* (Manchester; Cave and Sever, 1871), p.5.

miles an hour, he had written, in disagreement: 'Brought up myself to hard work, I have no respect for slow, easy-going operations', which sounds like Sir Edward, but overall he seems to have been, epigonally, of nothing like the same stuff as his father or his two grandfathers, either in his work or in his private life. He had married Catherine Elizabeth Payne Smith, daughter of the Dean of Canterbury, who was very pretty, but whose character has come down through the family as being 'rather strait-laced'. They had no children, and Sir Edward's baronetcy was to die out with him. C. Hamilton Ellis,[35] recalls that a nephew of Charles Sacré, the Chief Engineer and Locomotive Engineer on the MS&LR, told him that he remembered Alfred Watkin as being 'somewhat dim and very deaf'. Magdalene Goffin says that he 'was quite charming, but more or less just enjoying himself'.[36] She records that while he was in London he lived at the Charing Cross Hotel, where he kept two mistresses, each in her own suite, who were known as 'the ladies in waiting'.[37] He resigned from the SER board in 1877.

The second occasion of questioning Watkin's policy came in July 1878. This time it was on account of his own tendency to accumulate directorships, and the suspicion that this led to an incomplete commitment to the affairs of any of his companies. A further criticism was that he had handled badly the capitalisation of floating debentures; another was his becoming Chairman of the East London Railway – a contentious issue with the SER because it was causing strained relations with the LBSCR. Watkin's defence in this case was that John Hawkshaw, the company's Consultant Engineer, had advised him to 'interfere in the East London, to prevent its being used against the interests of the SER'. Slumbering misgivings were aroused by a reference to the Humber Ironworks, and allegations that his record with the Erie Railroad and the Hudson's Bay Company was unsatisfactory.[38]

---

[35] In his *British Railway History*, Vol.2 (where he devotes the whole of Chapter 3 to 'The Watkin Empire'), p.57.

[36] In a private letter, Magdalene Goffin to the author.

[37] Goffin, pp.373 and 374.

[38] His record on the Hudson's Bay Company speaks for itself. The Erie Railway – another company which Watkin was invited to rescue from financial difficulties – was brought to bankruptcy by the robberies of Jay Gould, James Fisk and Daniel Drew; the shareholders could not agree to his proposal to wipe clean the 'assets' that had been plundered, and he was not able to set the 'Erie' on its feet. See *The Times*, 15 April 1901.

Watkin announced to the shareholders on 25 July 1878 his intention to retire from the chair of the South Eastern in January next, to cries of 'No!'[39] In his response to the criticisms, he said 'I always admire men according to the number of their enemies. Little men hate talent and abhor success.' The little men 'snarl at the heels of others because they feel their comparative littleness. Those who succeed must be attacked'. He then detailed the instances they had given of his financial adventurism. The Erie Railway: he was asked by a unanimous vote of the Board and stockholders to come, as a public duty, to the rescue of that fraudulently-managed undertaking. He had no personal interest in the undertaking whatever, but had largely succeeded. The Humberside Ironworks Company: they did not heed his advice. The Hudson's Bay Company was badly affected by war, the Russian fur market having been one of the main elements of its trade. That was in 1863, and the undertaking had paid a good dividend since.

Samuel Fielden, a persistent opponent of Watkin, stood up to accuse the Chairman of not answering the question about his son, and of having divided loyalties. 'When you came here in 1866 you had nothing but the Manchester Sheffield and Lincolnshire Railway to take care of. You got that into a very good condition; there is no question about it; it is wonderfully well worked...It was never anticipated that you were going to take any amount of business besides...I do object', he went on, in a lengthy contribution to the debate, 'to your autocratic management'. No one spoke to support him, and when a vote of confidence was eventually proposed, it was carried with only four dissentients.[40]

The directors, however, were not pacified by the confidence of the shareholders. At a stormy meeting of the Board on 27 December 1878, Watkin received a 7–4 vote of censure for his dictatorial attitude, and the proprietors were faced, at a special meeting held on 9 January 1879, with a report from the Board, deeply regretting having to lay before them 'statements of a personal nature'. They were strong in their conviction that their discussions and decisions should be frankly accepted by the 'gentleman who presides over their deliberations'. Sir Edward

[39] PRO RAIL 1110 425, p.984.
[40] *Ibid*, p.995.

Watkin disagreed on the subject of the late Locomotive Superintendent, saying repeatedly that he had the support of the shareholders, and would if necessary appeal to them to carry out his views. 'No independent body of gentlemen can be found to conduct your business', they claimed, 'if they are to be subject to treatment so autocratic and unbecoming'. A catalogue of complaints followed, with the usual accusations of pluralism and parliamentary distractions, including his having 'supporters' on the Board, and a revealing list of the relative debenture holdings of each director. The eight who supported the above report held a total of £284,150, and the four who dissented from it held £10,940: Watkin's portion, the second lowest of all the directors, was £2,010.[41] This document was supported by one from John Shaw, Manager and Secretary of the company (from 1874, having been brought by Watkin to the SER in 1868), under instruction from the directors, listing the differences between the Chairman and the Board, in particular his exercise, in his own words, of 'supreme authority'.[42]

The *Railway Times* reported the division of the Board as 8–4 against Watkin. Yet another source of discontent was his attempt to secure a connection between the Metropolitan Railway via the East London line at New Cross. Some of the Board saw such a move as deleterious, rather than advantageous, to SER interests. Three weeks later, at the half-yearly meeting held on 1 February 1879, there was great confusion and disorder as many speakers, some for the Chairman, others against, strove for a hearing. Eventually, Lord Alfred Churchill rose to defend Watkin, congratulating him on making his case successfully before the proprietors, and trusting in their 'sound judgement and strong common sense'. The arguments of those who took the contrary view were, in his opinion, 'exceedingly shallow'. He felt guilty that he had been 'mainly responsible' for Watkin's accepting the chairmanship of the East London; Watkin had refused it 'half a dozen times before reluctantly agreeing'. This insight into the background of at least one of Watkin's various Chairmanships supports the view that practically all of them were by urgent entreaty, and not from a

[41] *Ibid*, pp.999 and 1000.
[42] *Ibid*, p.1001.

sense of gross imperialism on his part.[43] No vote of confidence was proposed, though Churchill's formal and usual vote of thanks to the Chairman for his conduct in the chair at the meeting was seconded, and carried unanimously. Watkin thanked them. He said he 'had tried – I may have failed – to do that which is right and proper and kind to everybody'. He hoped that 'when we go to our churches and chapels tomorrow there will be no rancour or ill-feeling'.

How could Watkin survive such a period of stormy opposition from his colleagues? But survive he did, for the majority of share-holders – judging him not on details, or of reports of dictatorial behaviour in the boardroom, but by the overall results of his leadership – supported his policy of strengthening the SER in London by promoting new lines, including the connection to New Cross. By July of that year the South Eastern was taking up its share in the working of the East London Line, giving it access to, *inter alia*, the Great Eastern Railway.

In April 1879 Alfred Watkin, MP, was restored to the SER Board, and one of the chief rebels against the Chairman, John Shaw, later (sometime between 18 September and 8 January 1880) relinquished his position as Manager. He continued in his role as Secretary, and Watkin brought in as General Manager Myles Fenton, from the Metropolitan Railway. Hamilton Ellis[44] paints an altogether more draconian picture of this sequence of events: a group of shareholders petitioned John Shaw, in one of Watkin's absences, to hold an extraordinary meeting, which he did. Watkin's anger at this disloyalty caused him to adjust summarily Shaw's status in the company. Possibly the Chairman's response to Shaw's opposition was exaggerated, and difficult to excuse, but it is necessary to remember Hamilton Ellis's prejudices.[45]

Gray says, without elaboration,[46] that about this time Watkin was accused of bribing the electorate, at the expense of the SER, during his successful campaign at Hythe in 1874. Certainly the charge was not proved, nor even made officially, and was probably a repetition of the false charges made against him from time to

---

[43]*Ibid*, pp.1029 ff.
[44]C. Hamilton Ellis, Vol.2, pp.57 and 58.
[45]As noted *infra*, pp.141-143.
[46]Gray, p.46

23 SER Suburban train at Greenwich, 1884. Locomotive number 144 being given the 'right away' by Stationmaster C. Spurgeon

time on that account. In July 1880 a shareholder complained about the building of the Seabrook Hotel at Hythe, at a cost of £22,998, which opened on 21 July that year. The suggestion was that it was built purely to provide Watkin with accommodation when he visited his parliamentary constituency. The irresponsibility of the accusation was demonstrated by the hotel's immediate success as a commercial venture. It needed enlarging the following year.[47]

Whatever the merits of Watkin's expansionism and his re-moralised and financially successful management of the SER, there remains the suspicion, as in the case of the MS&LR, that money spent on development and enlargement was sometimes at the expense of consolidation and improvement of what already existed. The quality of the SER rolling stock, stations and passenger services was at times something of a joke, or a scandal. In the period 1870 to 1898, the ratio of its spending on stock and

---

[47]*Ibid*, pp.46 and 233.

on new lines was 18:100, compared with, for example, the North Eastern, which was 80:100.[48] *Herepath's Journal* printed a bitter attack on the company: 'The SER starts indifferently from Cannon Street or Charing Cross and goes back there again. Sometimes, by mistake, it goes elsewhere. Occasionally it goes to Folkestone, and tries to throw itself into the sea...The SER is profoundly philosophical. Its timetable is the only instance of the human mind fully defining eternity...The SER is going in a tunnel to France, and the government is going to spend twenty millions on fortifications to prevent it ever coming back.'[49] On the other side of the balance, even Hamilton Ellis could say that accidents on the South Eastern were rare compared with other companies, and it was a pioneer in the provision of communication between passengers and staff on trains.[50] Punctuality on the SER, in fact, was better than on the LC&DR, 67% of trains being on time, as compared with 50%.

Intra-company trouble still erupted from time to time, even as late as 1888. In January, a shareholder, William Abbott, FRGS, published a pamphlet entitled *The South Eastern Railway: A Few Facts on its Management under Sir Edward Watkin, Bart., During the Years from 1866 to 1888...A System of 'Supreme Authority.*[51] In his introduction, Abbott made sarcastic reference to Watkin's account of his experiences in his book *Canada and the States, 1851–1886*, and declared his intention of 'supplying what Watkin had omitted from his personal narrative'. This consisted of a list of the usual and wearily inaccurate accusations about the Grand Trunk Railway and Hudson's Bay Company of Canada, the Humber Ironworks Company, the East London Railway, and other 'matters of concern for Stockholders and Investors in the South Eastern Railway'.[52] Abbott referred to an attitude of 'hostility and aggression', and 'meddling and muddling' in the company's relationships with neighbouring companies, and went into long detail on relative financial policies.[53] In his summary he

---

[48]*Ibid*, pp. 47 and 48.
[49]15 March 1884.
[50]C. Hamilton Ellis, Vol. 1, p.307.
[51]London: Bates, Hendy and Company, Walbrook, EC; document in the Archives of the Institution of Civil Engineers, London SW.
[52]*Ibid*, p.3.
[53]*Ibid*, p.11.

argued that 'surely the time has arrived when this policy of restless combativeness and aggression was brought to a close, and that a more healthy system in accordance with commercial principles, the intelligence of the proprietors and...sound common sense...should now be inaugurated...'[54]

At the shareholders' meeting of 26 January 1888, Abbott[55] moved the resolution 'that the Directors are respectfully requested to consider what steps they propose to take to give effect to the wishes of those shareholders who desire, through the instrumentality of a new Chairman, to inaugurate and carry out a policy of peace and harmonious working with our two neighbouring companies'.[56] The seconder, Mr Henderson, remembered the events of 1879, when there was a smouldering fire going on within the directorate for eighteen months or two years, the shareholders knowing nothing about it until it broke into open war. 'Sir Edward got his vote of confidence on that occasion (Cheers)...but he was promising at that time great extensions of traffic with [five other companies]. In his speech today he has almost repeated the words he used on that occasion. He has exercised autocratic control', he concluded, to much interruption. Lord Brabourne, the Deputy Chairman, who had taken the chair, dismissed the charge that he and the other gentlemen of the Board were 'creatures of Sir Edward Watkin (Laughter and cheers). Mr Henderson said that he had condemned Sir Edward nine years ago because we had a disunited Board, and he condemns him today because we have a unanimous Board in his favour (Laughter and cheers)'. A vote of confidence was passed with only one hand raised against it.

In February 1893, yet another Bill for the amalgamation of the South Eastern and the 'Chatham' was withdrawn, the 'temper' of Parliament being Watkin's reason for not pursuing it.[57] In fact, the

---

[54]*Ibid*, p.19.

[55]Who was a shareholder of both the SER and the LCDR, and who clearly preferred Forbes's brand of autocracy and aggression to Watkin's, and to favour or oppose amalgamation of the two companies, depending on which shareholders' meeting he was attending. Abbott was a constant thorn in Watkin's flesh at shareholders' meetings, but when he died and left his widow unprovided for, Watkin headed the list of subscribers to her welfare (*Vanity Fair*, 18 April 1901).

[56]PRO RAIL 1110 426, pp.1421ff.

[57]On 11 May 1885, Watkin had written to Lord Salisbury to ask him to intervene 'to cut the knot, or bundle of knots to expedite matters between the SER and the LCDR, at present in deadlock' and promising 'years of litigation and misery' (*Papers of the Third Marquess of Salisbury*, Watkin Letters, f.134). Salisbury wrote on the letter 'Will look into matter and do what I can'.

two companies were working together fairly well by that time, due, according to the *Railway Times,* to the fact that their respective affairs were increasingly under the control of their managers, rather than their chairmen.[58] From 1 August 1899 they were worked as a unified system, the South Eastern and Chatham Railway, but retained their separate identities, Boards of Directors and shareholders, the net receipts being split 59% to the South Eastern, and 41% to the LCDR[59].

It would seem, from an impartial study of the record, that Watkin's achievement on the SER was good. Despite some provocative and rash enterprises of opposition to its rivals, the company was a greater financial success than the LCDR. Watkin was frequently prepared to discuss joining with the Chatham Company or the LBSCR, and it was not usually he who thwarted the outcome; under his leadership the SER maintained a constructive relationship with the 'Brighton'. The company had an excellent operating ratio of expenditure to revenue and paid better dividends than most others. It is true that the accusations of being autocratic and high-handed had some foundation, as had the criticism of his multiple chairmanships, directorships and consultancies over so wide an area. The list presents an almost unbelievable burden of responsibilities and activity. Such multiple appointments, however, were common with men of exceptional ability and dynamism.[60]

As for being dictatorial, many of the greatest railway administrators were in that particular mould. James Staats Forbes combined the positions of Chairman and Managing Director (which Watkin never did on any of his companies) of the 'Chatham' from 1873; James Allport of the Midland was called 'The Bismarck of railway politics'; Crewe was very much the creation of the LNWR, and as the company's representative in the affairs of the town, Francis Webb, Chief Locomotive Superintendent and mastermind of the works there, was convinced that the citizens ought to do as he said.[61] Anecdotes about the autocratic Chairman of the LNWR, Richard Moon, are numerous. One of

---

[58]Gray, p.50.

[59]George Dow, *Railway Heraldry* (David and Charles, 1973), p.134.

[60]They are features of our own time, too: The *Independent* of 27 May 1997, in an obituary, cited the subject's portfolio of directorships and chairmanships of 'Most of the major companies of Ulster', and named eight of them.

[61]Adrian Vaughan, *Railwaymen, Politics, and Money* (John Murray, 1997), p.347.

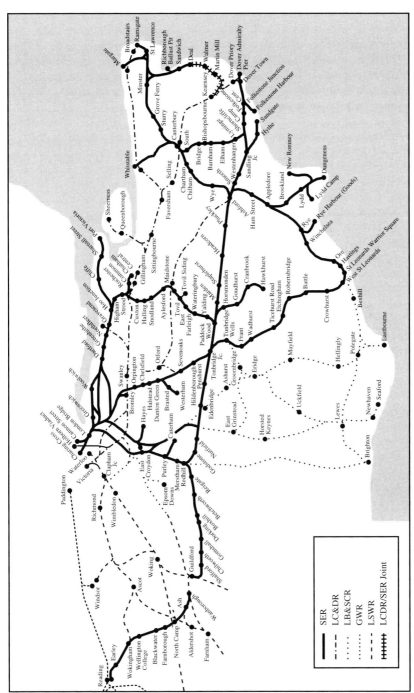

The South Eastern Railway and main connections in the 1890s

SER
LC&DR
LB&SCR
GWR
LSWR
LCDR/SER Joint

123

the directors at a Board meeting kept his newspaper on the table after a meeting had begun. 'It is not the custom at Euston to read newspapers at the Board meetings,' said Moon. Turning to a servant, he said, 'John, take away Mr .....'s newspaper.'[62] In comparison with such gentlemen, Watkin was, as our contemporary saying has it, a teddybear.

T.R. Gourvish has made a study of railway management performance in the four decades following 1860, with special reference to the companies managed by Watkin and Forbes. He chose those two because 'they figure in a great many accounts which stress managerial weakness, being criticised for an empire-building mentality, lack of interest in operation and bitter personal rivalry, [forcing] their companies into unprofitable investment, low levels of service and low profits. In the debate it has been largely assumed that management's goal was, or should have been, a profit-maximising one'.[63] In fact, the decision-making and executive procedures within the company structure were more complex. Managements were concerned also with broader strategies of what Gourvish calls 'utility-maximising' and 'satisficing': concepts which take account of a constellation of economic, psychological and sociological factors which in varying degrees influenced those in authority to make strategic decisions about the company's development.[64] Gourvish concluded that even on the conventional basis of profitability and efficiency, as in return on capital and operating ratio (the percentage of expenditure to income), both companies compared well with others. The outcome of his research was that 'the Watkin/Forbes companies did not perform any less adequately ...than the overall standard for the industry'. In fact, in taking over companies in a poor state, and despite their unprofitable adventures, 'they kept their companies close to a UK standard of efficiency'.[65]

---

[62]John Pendleton, *Our Railways* (Casssell and Co. Ltd., 1896), Vol.1, p.136.

[63]T.R. Gourvish, 'The Performance of British Railways Management after 1860: The Railways of Watkin and Forbes', *Business History,* Vol.20 (1978), p.189.

[64]Definition of the terms in Geoffrey Channon, 'A Nineteenth-Century Investment Decision: The Midland Railway's London Extension', *Economic Historical Review,* 2nd Series, XXV (1972), p.448.

[65]Gourvish, p.198.

9

The Metropolitan Railway

Watkin became Chairman of London's Metropolitan Railway in 1872. He was invited by the Board of Directors to their meeting held on 31 July as a 'large shareholder', to discuss the future of the company, after the disclosure of mismanagement and fraud by some of its officials.[1] At the following meeting his letter of acceptance, 'on certain terms', of an offer of a seat on the Board was read, and a ballot was held to determine which of the directors should resign to make way for him. After his election, it was then resolved that he should become the Chairman.[2]

He was 'of impressive appearance and ability, 52 years old, with an established capacity for hard work, and experience both as a railway manager, and Chairman of two large companies'.[3] He was also 'a walking encyclopaedia of railway knowledge and experience'.[4] Watkin took with him, to be the new secretary of the company, John Bell, from the Manchester, Sheffield and Lincolnshire Railway, ousting the unfortunately-named John Henchman, who was too closely associated with the discredited previous regime.

Watkin had been introduced to the Board in July 1872 by Henry Davis Pochin, a member newly adopted by the shareholders in February 1872. Pochin was representative of the substantial Manchester interest, and had been Mayor of Salford and Member of Parliament for Stafford. Like Watkin, he was a Liberal, being in favour of education reform and disestablishment of the Irish

---

[1] Alan Jackson, *London's Metropolitan Railway* (David and Charles, 1986), p.62.
[2] London Metropolitan Archives, Acc. 1297 Met.1/4; 7 August 1872, Minutes 275, 276 and 277.
[3] Jackson, p.62.
[4] Dennis Edwards and Ron Pigram, *The Romance of Metroland* (Bloomsbury Books, 1986), p.16.

Church, and opposed to all forms of Protectionism.[5] 'Watkin was used to getting his own way and running his own show', and was 'combative, secretive, and empirical in his approach'. Within a very short time he had established himself in his new position, 'and from that time for more than two decades all major initiatives would originate from him'.[6]

If part of what constitutes greatness, or at least great distinction above one's contemporaries, is possession of an overall vision, a 'grand design', which informs all one's actions and decisions, and towards which everything is energetically directed, then Edward Watkin could be so described. It is fairly clear that Watkin came to see his control over the fortunes of the Metropolitan as a link between Manchester, London and the South Coast. As for the greater and even more ambitious goal of linking the North and London to India by means of a tunnel under the Channel, Jackson claims that this is a 'popular legend', and one of which there is 'no hint...in the very large quantity of Metropolitan Railway papers which have been preserved'. 'It seems unlikely', he says, 'to have crystallised in his mind until the MS&LR was at last on its way to London in the early 1890s, by which time his energies were spent.'[7] But, if we are to accept Jackson's description of Watkin as a man who was 'secretive' and 'empirical', then the absence of such an openly declared ambition is not surprising. In those days of ruthless cut and thrust, when the rules of ethical management were still in the making, to have revealed such long-term aims was to have invited much avoidable opposition. In such far-sighted schemes the consolidation of each separate component part needs to be achieved before being slotted into its appropriate position, and thwarting any one of them could have meant frustrating the whole. Jackson does concede that Watkin's long-term intention, in 1872 – the year he joined the Metropolitan – was to connect the 'Sheffield' with the South Eastern Railway, Manchester with the South Coast. He had approached the Great Northern Railway in that year, suggesting that his company and the GN should take over the Metropolitan as a joint concern; and he wrote, as

---

[5]Pochin was the author of *A Plan for Parliamentary Reform,* which advocated the enfranchisement of the working classes - altogether a man with whom Watkin could be at ease.
[6]Jackson, pp.61 and 63.
[7]Jackson, p.76.

Chairman of the MS&L, on 11 November to the Chairman of the Midland Railway to that effect. His interest in the French plans for a Channel tunnel dates from 1856, and he followed closely the development of the international co-operation in the 1870s, before throwing his weight behind it.

The Metropolitan was a distinctly curious railway.. It had been conceived in the 1830s as an underground system to relieve the heavily congested streets of London: 'trains as underground omnibuses', as Watkin later described them.[8] Its prime mover was a lawyer, Charles Pearson (1793–1862, MP for Lambeth 1847–50), solicitor to the City Commissioner of Sewers. He saw, as an additional function for such an underground transport system between parts of the capital, the means by which the urban poor of the mean and disease-infested streets could live in more healthy conditions on the edge of the conurbation – in places like Hampstead Village – and travel cheaply to work by train. Building such railways would also provide improvements to the city in replacing old buildings with new, and with modernised sewage and drainage. These considerations remained with the Metropolitan throughout its development, and these 'social implications' would be part of Watkin's thinking. The company bought up suburban land for housing, far in advance, in some cases, of any perceived need, and developed what became known, from 1915 onwards, as 'Metroland'. The original intention was to connect with the LNWR and Midland at West Hampstead, and go no further. Watkin, however, had more ambitious ideas: it grew northwards, and the whole character of the railway was changed. It thus became a main line railway with an underground system as a southern appendage. 'The Metropolitan is really a trunk line in miniature,' said the Chairman, Lord Aberconway, to the company's annual meeting on 20 February 1930.[9] Eventually, it extended from Verney Junction in Buckinghamshire, southwards through Aylesbury, Amersham, Northwood and Pinner, and into London at Baker Street, with underground lines connecting South Kensington, Paddington, Euston Square, King's Cross and Liverpool Street, making a further junction with the East London

---

[8] *Ibid*, p.15. It became the world's first passenger-carrying underground railway from 10 January 1863.
[9] *Ibid*, p.75.

Railway from Shoreditch, and thus serving as a connection with the SER at New Cross.[10]

Watkin had taken over a very carelessly managed business, with records incompletely or incorrectly kept, dividends paid at highly inflated rates, working expenditure and dividends paid charged to capital, Board activities scrappily recorded, a discrepancy of almost £202,000 in the capital expenditure account, and a near-revolt by shareholders.[11] During his first months in office, Watkin introduced radical changes. At an extraordinary meeting of the proprietors on 15 October, a resolution was adopted that the directors retire, and a new Board be elected, to the reduced total of seven, and Watkin introduced a system which ensured a regular rotation of members.[12] He also engaged one of the most reputable auditors of the time, Edwin Waterhouse, to conduct a thorough investigation into the company's finances, and whetted his appetite for forthright speaking on those – lawyers and contractors – who had been, without much accountability, fleecing the shareholders. On 23 October, he wrote to John Fowler, the company's engineer:

If I am to commit my reputation to this doubtful and anxious work I must have my own way where a principle is involved: and if you and I are to co-operate in the completion of the [Inner] Circle [Line] you must deal with the Company in a far more considerate spirit than that which the papers before me testify to. Even at the risk of giving unpardonable offence to a most influential and able man I intend to say what I have in my mind *now* – before it is too late and in all frankness, while at the same time desiring earnestly not to give just cause of quarrel.[13]

There are important clues here to Watkin's character: first, his seeing the challenges which were set him on the Metropolitan as

---

[10]A connecting line between the Metropolitan at Baker Street and the SER at Charing Cross had been considered briefly in 1891, in connection with the MS&LR entry into London, but no action was taken (Adrian Gray, *The South Eastern Railway*, p.123).

[11]Jackson, pp.60–4.

[12]London Metropolitan Archives ACC 1297 Met. 1/4, Minute 347. The next Minute recorded the award to the Chairman of £2,000 per annum, and that £1,600 per annum 'be distributed, as they determine', between the other directors.

[13]LMA ACC 1297 Met. 1/4, Minute 415.

committing his reputation to either success or failure, and secondly his commitment to frankness and openness, even at the risk, unintentionally, of giving offence. He went on to point out that the sums Fowler had received or claimed to date from the company and the Metropolitan District Railway 'total up to some £330,000...no engineer in the world was so highly paid. You have set an example of charge which seems to me to have largely aided in the demoralisation of the Professional men of all sorts who have laid upon the suffering shareholders for the past ten years...the whole thing with any notion of what is fair *pains* my mind'.[14]

Even allowing for the exuberance of a 'new broom', this seems to be a very rough way of treating one of the nineteenth century's great engineers. John Fowler (1817–98) was born at Wadsley Hall, in the heart of MS&LR territory. He was the engineer of the 'Sheffield' Company from 1844 to 1853, his departure coinciding with Watkin's arrival, continuing, however, as Consultant Engineer. He was knighted in 1885 for his services in the Sudan and Egypt, and made a baronet in 1890 for his work in co-designing and building the Forth Bridge. George Dow said of him that he was a great asset to the MS&L because of his powers of organisation, and his great moral and professional courage.[15] Watkin's letter to Fowler concluded, 'I apologise in advance if I have given any offence (God knows I have not intended to do so) but face to face with a great responsibility I could not, honestly, write in a less open spirit or at less length.' In reply, Fowler pointed out that all the costs were embraced in two agreements, in 1860 and 1864, and it would be 'a grave responsibility to attempt to condemn the conduct of the then Directors of the Metropolitan Railway at the time, who were as prudent, honourable and pains-taking as you or I or indeed any person can claim to be'. This was a grave responsibility which, of course, Watkin had assumed.

The new Chairman also wrote to the company's coal supplier, Alexander Brogden. After a forthright presentation of his view that the company was being overcharged, he concluded that he felt sure 'that if any irregularity had existed you would thank me for

---

[14]LMA, ACC 1297, Met.1/4, Minute 415.
[15]Dow, *Great Central*, Vol.1, p.154.

enabling you to correct it'. A very strongly worded reply included the observation 'I do not understand what is your special qualification for your self-imposed office of "Censor Morum".'[16] The dispute generated by Watkin's letter was taken to law, and dragged on for nearly two years, the Metropolitan finally being awarded damages and costs of £10,000.

These were all signs that a new, honest, open and vigorous regime had begun. Watkin brought to the Metropolitan his great talent and energy for efficient management and organisation, and for expansionist schemes, projecting building well beyond the thinking of the previous regime. His wide experience of contractors and the construction of railways had not, however, included the special problems of building underground in a highly built-up area. One of the problems was that of smoke from steam locomotives in long tunnels, and he had consulted his friend John Ramsbottom, of Mottram in Cheshire. Ramsbottom wrote to the directors on 17 September 1872, saying that he would be happy to look into the problem.[17] He reported on 26 September; ventilation was not needed, but if it were in the future then the successful scheme he had implemented in Liverpool could be adopted.[18]

Another problem centred on the high rates of compensation to be paid to property-owners, whether for shoring up foundations satisfactorily, or purchasing the properties outright and demolishing them. The primitive methods of tunnelling then in use did not make for a swift advance of the works. All of these considerations had deterred the great Robert Stephenson, George's son, from the project in the 1830s. The newness of Watkin to these special difficulties led him to become very impatient with the progress being made with new lines. Thus he told Lucas, of Kelk Brothers and Lucas, the contractor on the Bishopsgate works: '...the work seems only to dawdle on, and in looking at the preparation and the appliances I see nothing that looks like push...'[19] He addressed Edward Wilson, the company's engineer, in the same vein: 'We want energy and work not reports and talk. Are you to blame or the contractors?'

---

[16]LMA ACC 1297, Board meeting of 13 November 1872, Minute 460.
[17]LMA ACC 1297, Met.1/4, Board meeting of 18 September 1872, Minute 326.
[18]*Ibid*, Minute 341.
[19]3 March 1874.

In his reply, Lucas argued that they were having great difficulty with the foundations of a Roman Catholic chapel on the east side of Finsbury Circus. The Board decided, after considering the alternatives, not to buy the school and presbytery of St Mary's but to shore up the foundations of the whole complex. The problem of St Mary's, Moorfields, was to appear regularly in the minutes almost until the line was finished. A temporary iron chapel was provided by the company during the engineering works.[20] St Mary's was a distinguished building, built in 1820 in the Italian style with huge interior columns, on the foundations of the first Roman Catholic place of worship to be built in England after the Reformation. It served as the pro-cathedral for the Vicariate of the London District of the new Archdiocese of Westminster from 1843 to 1869. Watkin could say to the shareholders, when the underpinning had been completed, that he hoped the good people who worshipped there could be persuaded to pray for them, considering the expenditure on their buildings.[21] It is to be hoped, after all the trouble he had gone through, that he did not see the news report in 1899 that St Mary's had been demolished, and replaced, as being too big for the then needs of the parish.

Watkin wrote again to Lucas about the works on the Bishopsgate/Eastern Extension/Liverpool Street line (the terminology varied from time to time), berating him for all the delays. Comparing the works with the same contractors' operation on the 'Hammersmith Aggression' (sc. by the Metropolitan District Company), which was 'swarming with men...the Liverpool Street extension is a Sleepy Hollow...the contrast is painful'. Lucas, replying, hoped that on reflection Sir Edward would realise that he 'is neither just nor generous towards us', pointing out that he must know the difference between forming a railway in the open country and in the heart of the City of London. 'Pray give us credit for acting in good faith'.[22]

Watkin did not get his own way in everything. In 1876, he suggested that the company's administrative staff, spread over several sites, ought to be housed in a new headquarters, on land

---

[20]LMA ACC 1297 Met.1/5, Board meeting of 10 June 1874, Minute 1207.
[21]Alexander Rottman, *London's Catholic Churches: A Historical and Artistic Record* (London: Sands and Company, 1926), p.160.
[22]LMA ACC Met 1/5, Board meeting 25 June 1874, Minute 1236.

24 Aldgate Station, Metropolitan Railway, 1876

owned by the Metropolitan at Liverpool Street Station, on the principle of 'One roof, the master's eye, the concentration of business, economy of staff'. But not all the directors could go along with such a radical reform, which on the face of it was straight economic sense. He also proposed a 'Metropolitan Grand Hotel' at Moorgate Street Station, but lack of financial investment killed it off.[23]

A rival to the Metropolitan, geographically but not in efficiency or financial stability, was the Metropolitan District Railway, which eventually formed the southern part of the Circle Line, from South Kensington to Aldgate. This company was chaired from 1872 by James Staats Forbes (1823–1904), the Chairman, from 1871 to 1898, of the London, Chatham and Dover Railway, the competitor of the South Eastern Railway. This placed him in double opposition to Watkin, and their abrasive relationship, in both roles, proved detrimental to the working of both the railways, preventing their amalgamation – which, by any objective assessment, became increasingly desirable with the passage of time. Forbes was described as possessing a 'suave and charming surface manner, and was able to exercise astonishing powers of persuasion. This exterior concealed an iron will and determination'. *The Railway*

[23]Jackson, p.70.

Magazine's obituary of Forbes said: 'He was a past master in the art of *bunkum* and...by its use...was...able to persuade share-holders...to do as he desired. In private life [Forbes] was an art connoisseur and collector, in contrast to Watkin, who was something of a philistine.'[24] In this judgement, Jackson seems to be following the opinion of Cuthbert Hamilton Ellis, who wrote that:

> Watkin and Forbes were alike in the way they worked, and fought their railways against each other...Both were crafty and unscrupulous. Forbes is supposed to have stimulated War Office hostility to Watkin's Channel Tunnel. As men they were quite different. Watkin was a type of Northern philistine; in the courtly and charming Forbes was the finesse of the Celt. In the old Watkin home at Rose Hill was all that the Exhibitions of 1851 and 1862 could inspire, and money could buy, but Forbes was an aesthete and connoisseur of some renown. Watkin's roots were commercial, Forbes' were professional. Watkin was the only one of his family to achieve eminence in the railway world...James Staats Forbes was brother to William Forbes, General Manager of the Midland Great Western Railway (Ireland), who begat William Forbes the Younger, sometime General Manager of the LB&SCR, and Stanhope Forbes, RA.[25]

Apart from the sulphurous whiff of snobbery here, Ellis is not quite right in saying that Watkin was alone in his family in achieving 'eminence' in the railway world: the son of his brother John, also called Edward, became General Manager and a director of the Hull and Barnsley Railway. More importantly, Watkin was by no means a philistine. There were his activities in the Manche-ster Athenaeum, and the richness of the library he inherited, and valued dearly, from his father. He collected paintings of merit in his travels; when his son Alfred sold Rose Hill in 1901,[26] with its contents, he parted with a large painting called *Icebergs*, the most famous work by the American landscape painter Frederick Edwin

---

[24]*Ibid*, p.332.
[25]C. Hamilton Ellis, *British Railway History* Vol. 1, p.309.
[26]W.H. Shercliff, (ed.), *Wythenshawe* (Manchester: J.Morten, 1974), Vol. 1, p.192.

25 Rose Hill in later days. The glacial boulder mounted on a tree stump was brought by Watkin from Woodhouse Lane Farm about 1892. Inset is the Frederick Church painting *Icebergs*. Its frame was engraved 'To the people of Northenden in perpetuity', a fact which was excited some litigation when it was sold in 1979.

Church (1826–1900). Church was the most prominent member of the 'Hudson River School'; he specialised in painting natural marvels such as waterfalls, mountains, volcanoes, tropical forests, and icebergs. He was noted for his great skill in the management of light and colour, and his plausible and effective renderings of

134

rainbow, mist and sunset, and evoked the 'wildest admiration', and from the beginning sold for extravagant sums.[27] The painting toured the United States, attracting vast crowds, and was auctioned by Sotheby's in 1979, being bought by the Dallas Museum of Fine Arts for £2,000,000.[28]

Watkin also had dealings with Sir John Gilbert (1817–97), President of the Royal Society of Painters in Watercolours, and the Society's Secretary, Alfred Downing Fripp (1822–95), to whom he paid £100 for an example of his art in 1893.[29] A visitor to Rose Hill in 1881 noted a copy of a painting by J.L.E. Meissonier, painted with his left hand by 'Hammer' Nasmyth, and also mentioned that in the main bedroom there was a 'venerable four-poster in which Charles the Second slept after the Battle of Worcester'. In the prime guest room there was a complete set of furniture of Canadian walnut, 'cheval-glass and all'.[30] Of his furniture, Watkin presented to Manchester Corporation in 1892 the chair occupied by George Wilson [31] when he was Chairman of the Anti-Corn Law League, 1841–46. In 1892 he was described as 'recreating himself with fine canvasses, having spent a considerable portion of his wealth in the purchase of rare paintings'[32] As for other family achievements, it depends on one's criteria of value. His cousin Walter Thompson Watkin was a distinguished archaeologist; it was said of his book *Roman Cheshire* of 1886 on its republication in 1974: 'Since its publication...[it] has been essential reading for any serious student of the subject. It stands alone in attempting to survey at length all the evidence relating to the Roman occupation of the County'.[33] His brother John was a priest of the Established Church, with a doctorate from Oxford

[27]*Encyclopaedia Britannica*, 1955 Edition, Vol.5, p.669. The money was used by Manchester Corporation to build a gymnasium at Rose Hill, but it was demolished about 1985 as the house began to be run down to closure.
[28]Derick Deacon (ed.), *Wythenshawe: The Story of a Garden City* (Chichester; Philimore and Co.,1989), p.146.
[29]British Library Add.Mss. 46445, ff 72 and 73.
[30]*Hythe and Sandgate Echo,* 22 October. The reporter added that, above all these things, 'the great charm of the place' was 'the wonderful life and spirit of the host'.
[31]1808–70. Wilson had been a founder-member of the Anti-Corn Law Association. He was President of the National Reform Union in 1864, and Chairman of the Lancashire and Yorkshire Railway from 1867 (*The Concise DNB* (OUP, 1969 Edition), Part 1, p.1419).
[32] *Hythe and Sandgate Echo,* 9 April.
[33]Introduction, by D.F. Petch, Curator of the Grosvenor Museum, Chester.

26 John Woodlands Watkin, Edward's
brother

27 Alfred Watkin, Edward's younger
brother

28 Alfred Mellor Watkin, Edward's son,
in his thirties

29 Catherine Elizabeth Payne Smith,
Edward's daughter-in-law

University;[34] his younger brother Alfred was Mayor of Manchester and founder of a dynasty which included his son Edgar: 'A fine artist, and accomplished pianist, and a good actor'.[35] Edgar's son was the polymath scholar Edward Ingram Watkin (1888–1981), author and translator of books on history and theology, whose own son, Christopher, became Headmaster of Downside School, Abbott of Downside and a writer of books on theology.[36]

An insight into Watkin's methods of working is afforded by an incident which took place in 1874. In that year, a shareholder called Albert George Kitching formed a committee, which at the half-yearly meeting on 31 July pressed, as an amendment to the Board's half-yearly report, for an amalgamation with the Metropolitan District Company. He had previously had a discussion of the idea with Watkin, and referred to the latter's 'courteous manner in which you received me'.[37] The Chairman was of the opinion that such a merger would benefit only the 'District', and secured the defeat of the motion by a large majority.[38] Another shareholder, John Fildes, then demanded a poll, and the following results were announced: those against Kitching's amendment – 58 present and 284 by proxy vote – owned £925,415 of stock in 4,027 shares: 96,524 votes; those voting for the amendment, 10 in number, held £17,090 of stock in 120 shares: 1,829 votes. Of these 10, 5 were also 'District' shareholders. [39]

Though he had crushed the opposition so conclusively, Watkin nevertheless wrote to Forbes with Kitching's proposal, and added his own view: 'At present the position of antagonism of the two companies can only lead to the depletion of each...A union would lead to a single policy, protective of the entire interest, and to some economy, in which all the shareholders would participate.' He told Forbes that he had not joined the Metropolitan out of self-interest,

---

[34]He had graduated BCL in 1856, and was awarded a Doctorate of Civil Law by dissertation on the subject of 'The Civil Law in England' on 21 March 1860 (Oxford University Archives, SP/72a).

[35]Magdalene Goffin, in a private letter.

[36]Obituaries of Dom Christopher appeared in *The Times, Daily Telegraph* and *Independent* in May 1997.

[37]LMA ACC 1297 Met.1/5, Board meeting of 9 July, Minute 1271.

[38]'The District, like the Chatham...never paid a dividend on its ordinary stock'. Edward Cleveland-Stevens, *English Railways: Their Development and Their Relation to the State* (London: George Routledge and Sons Ltd, 1915), pp.304 and 305.

[39]LMA ACC 1297 Met.1/5, 31 July 1874, Minute 1313.

but in the hope of retrieving its fortunes, 'so far as past mistakes rendered it possible', and that the two companies, unified, could complete the Circle Line together. He admitted that he had so far failed to achieve either of these aims, and added that he was willing to retire from his company if an amalgamated board were to vote for Forbes as its Chairman. Forbes's reply to all this was reported by Watkin to be 'unhelpful'. Forbes's explanation to his half-yearly meeting in the same month was: 'We are all agreed about amalgamation, but we cannot agree about the price'; and at a later meeting he said he had rejected Watkin's offer of arbitration on the subject because Watkin was a 'very clever man' and capable of influencing any arbitrator in his favour. Jackson comments that it was surprising that such specious reasoning went unquestioned.

In 1876, Watkin replied to a question about the possibility of a merger that he had exhausted all proposals which seemed reasonable, and they had all been refused. Unless a practicable proposal came from the other side he had nothing further to say. By 1878 matters had changed a little, and Watkin proposed that the 'Met' and the 'District' should jointly support a link between the two and the East London Railway, and thus complete the Inner Circle. This consisted of a jointly owned line from Aldgate to Mansion House via Tower Hill; Parliament, in sanctioning the Bill with an Act of 11 August 1879, insisted that each company allow the other's trains on its own metals, and thus secure the continuous operation of services round the Circle. A rival scheme, proposed by a City lawyer, George S. Newman and threatening to confound Watkin's aims for a connection with the East London, had achieved parliamentary sanction in August 1874. Newman had written to Watkin in the January that he had found 'the unfortunate jealousy existing between the two [Metropolitan] companies . . .an impediment to the completion of the Circle'.[40] Forbes had at first supported Newman's scheme, which was later described by Watkin as 'a miserable confederation. . .to damage the Metropolitan, in the fancied, though not real, interests of Mr. Forbes'. After Watkin's persistent efforts to thwart it, negotiating at length with the Lord Mayor, Forbes had come round to co-operating with the Metropolitan.

As late as 1887, Watkin was still writing aggressive letters to

---

[40]Jackson, pp.72, 73, 106, 107 and 105.

those who were perceived as compromising his interests. In March he chastised J. Grierson, General Manager of the Great Western Railway, for his rumoured support of a projected Regents Canal City and Docks Railway. This would have given the GWR a more direct access to the East End and the Victoria Docks – an obvious threat to the East London Railway and Watkin's carefully constructed web of connections in the area. Persistence in such 'aggression', he wrote, would negate any gains because of the ensuing 'retaliation'.[41] In the following July he wrote to the Chairman of the Great Northern, recalling, equally pugnaciously, the agreements between the two companies. Lord Colville replied with 'a short and simple answer', dismissing any suggestion of a GNR contribution to the Regents Canal scheme, and affirming his company's loyalty to its agreements with the Metropolitan Company.[42] Perhaps the fact that James Staats Forbes was behind the Regents Canal project (which was eventually withdrawn) excited Watkin's old fighting instincts.

All Watkin's years as Chairman of the Metropolitan were marked by his energy in promoting plans to expand to the North – lines to Willesden, Harrow and Aylesbury being successful – and with a keen eye to other lines in promotion which might serve or threaten those aims. He became for a time the Chairman of the Aylesbury and Buckingham Railway (1875) to make sure it followed his plans and not anyone else's.[43] Throughout the 1880s he appears to have been looking in all directions for northern connections with the Metropolitan. His Worcester and Broom Railway (Extension to Aylesbury) Bill of November 1888, to which the Metropolitan had subscribed £100,000, was presented to Parliament at the same time as four other Bills bearing directly on the Metropolitan.[44] Had it been successful (it gained a Second Reading, but a parliamentary committee rejected it in July 1889),[45] he would have taken the Metropolitan to within sixty miles of Ellesmere, the connection with the MS&LR via Wrexham. This astonishing thought was considered to be feasible by the railway press:

---

[41]LMA ACC 1297 Met. 1/15; Board meeting of 20 April 1887, Minute Book p.282.
[42]*Ibid*, Board meeting of 24 August 1887, Minute Book pp.397 and 398.
[43]Jackson, pp. 76 and 78.
[44]*Railway Times*, 5 January 1889, p.12.
[45]LMA 1297 Met.1/16, Minutes 322, 402, 414, 435, 534 and 561.

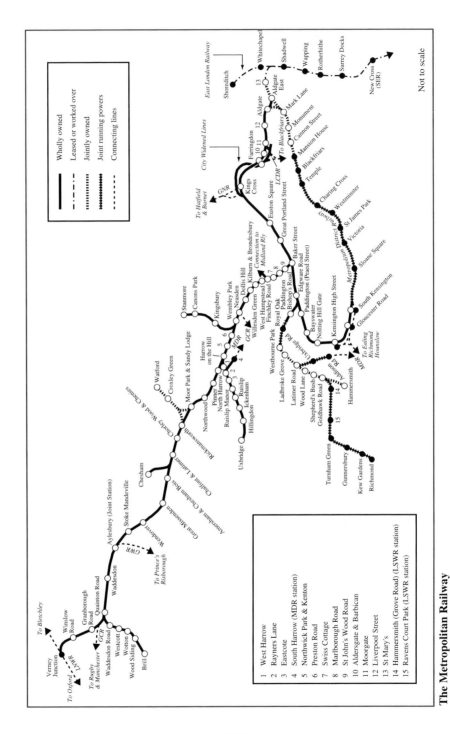

The Metropolitan Railway

Truly it is a grandiose scheme, but whether the 'Railway King' will be allowed to carry war to his neighbours' camp in such magnificent but inartistic fashion remains for the wisdom of Parliament to decide...The entire prospect is, however, quite too vast for the limited vision of ordinary commentators.[46] Should the gap between Worcester and Ellesmere not be filled up, he will have [among the ten Bills in the coming Session of Parliament] another elaborate scheme to fall back on – the Kidderminster, Birmingham and Stoke Railway.[47]

A fuller story of the final connection between the MS&L and the Metropolitan at Quainton Road north of Aylesbury finds its place in the section on his chairmanship of the 'Sheffield' company, but there were other aspects of Watkin's work with the Metropolitan to consider. The company had become, more than any other in Britain, a large-scale landowner. The Chairman in 1902 was Charles B.B. McLaren (1850–1934).[48] He said in a report in that year: 'The Company had a very considerable estate, and large and almost unlimited powers of dealing with it'.[49] This state of affairs had arisen during the expansion north-westwards, when landowners, refusing to sell small strips of land for railway building, insisted on the company's buying large areas of adjoining property. This had happened elsewhere, notably with the Metropolitan District Railway. Watkin's company, however, had retained it when the railway had been built, contrary to the express will of Parliament in an Act of 1845, which required railway companies to sell off all land not needed for their 'special acts', within a maximum of ten years. The Met. manoeuvred special provisions into each of its new Acts as they came along, which passed unnoticed by successive parliamentary committees. At Watkin's personal initiative, the company, in an Act of 21 July 1873, had secured for itself a blanket provision allowing it to retain all surplus lands, 'whenever required, including those acquired in the future'. This was repeated in several later Acts, and such alteration

---

[46]*Railway Times,* 12 January 1889, p.49.
[47]*Ibid,* 4 January 1890, p.15; 11 January 1890, pp.37 and 38.
[48]Made Baronet 1902, Lord Aberconway of Bodnant, Denbighshire, in 1911. He was Vice-President of the National Housing and Town Planning Council in 1911, MP for Stafford in 1880 and 1885, and one of the founders of the National Liberal Club.
[49]Jackson, p.134.

of the parliamentary intentions of the pioneer years of railway development 'presented no problems of conscience in the expansionist atmosphere of 1870 and onwards'.[50]

For a long time the revenues from these extensive tracts of land, progressively developed for housing as the Metropolitan proved its worth as a commuter link, were not distinguished in the company's books from the income derived from fares and charges. This meant that dividends were considerably inflated over and above what a shareholder would have expected from a straightforward railway operation. Watkin saw this unclarity as unhealthy, and set out to streamline the property department and to separate the two sides of the business. As he said to his fellow directors in March 1886: 'It is an anomaly...that a small railway company should have more than one third of its railway dividend on Ordinary Stock made up out of the proceeds of property not needed for the railway', and warned that such a state of affairs gave a false impression of railway profits. From July 1887, the ordinary stock of the railway was split into two portions.[51]

In 1890, the Surplus Lands Committee of the company bought Wembley Park Estate, between Neasden and Harrow. Without Watkin's 'special powers' this would probably not have been possible, but the purpose of the move, though not completely accomplished, was to have historic consequences. A feature of the Paris Exhibition of 1889 had been the Eiffel Tower, at 984 feet the highest building in the world, and it had been retained after the exhibition as a permanent attraction. It had repaid its construction cost of £780,000 within seven months of opening.[52] It rapidly became established as a universal symbol of the city and by 1959 it had welcomed 35 million visitors. The tower made a deep impression on Watkin, and after taking advice from W.E. Gladstone, he decided to provide London with a similar feature. Eschewing more economically viable sites nearer to the centre of London, he chose Wembley as being close to his northward extension line to Harrow, for which land had been bought in the late 1870s from the owner of the estate, the Revd John Gray. Negotiations in the

---

[50]*Ibid*, p.137.
[51]*Ibid*, pp.138 and 139.
[52]Dennis Edwards and Ron Pigram, *The Final Link* (Midas Books, 1982, 2nd Edition, 1983), p.200.

1880s resulted in the purchasing of the whole 280-acre estate in 1890 for the sum of £32,929 18s 7d, including farm implements and two horses.[53] Watkin's scheme was to use some of the land for London's finest sports, leisure and an exhibition centre, and the rest of the area to be developed with commuter housing.[54] The tower, taking up 121 of the acres,[55] was to be the central feature, advertising it for miles around. A 'Metropolitan Tower Company', formed on 14 August 1889, had £300,000 of capital from the Metropolitan Railway.

Watkin first approached Eiffel himself to design the tower, but he declined, in case his fellow-countrymen might think him 'not so good a Frenchman as I hope I am'.[56] Sir Benjamin Baker, FRS (1840–1907), who had worked on the Metropolitan, and was involved with the London tube railways, then took on the job of supervising the work. It was his wrought-iron cylinder which carried Cleopatra's Needle from Alexandria to Westminster, and he was co-engineer with John Fowler on the Forth Bridge (1882–90). The design for the tower was put out to competition in November 1889, offering prizes of 500 guineas and 250 guineas. Drawings were submitted from Germany, France, Italy, Austria, Turkey and Sweden, as well as Britain, and some came from Australia and the USA.[57] Many of the sixty-eight received were totally impractical, and some verged on the fantastic and were in utter disregard of cost. One plan enclosed courts of administration, county council offices, scientific institutions and a library, all surrounded by lodgings, offices and public houses. Another incorporated a locomotive and train which would ascend a spiral railway up to 1,000 feet of a 2,000-foot tower shaped like a multi-layered wedding cake.[58] Eventually the design that was chosen closely resembled Eiffel's graceful construction. It had four stages, however, instead of three, was built of steel, not iron, and had an overall height of 1,150 feet – 165 feet higher than Eiffel's. The legs

---

[53]A.S. Travis, *The Metropolitan Railway in Wembley, 1880-1910* (Typed Manuscript, undated, in Glasgow Public Library), p.5.
[54]Jackson, p.100.
[55]*Railway Magazine*, March/April 1944, p.114.
[56]Felix Barker and Ralph Hyde, *London as it Might Have Been* (John Murray, 1996), p.158.
[57]*Ibid.*
[58]Travis, p.6.

30 The prize winning design for Watkin's Wembley Tower.
The six legs were amended to four in the building

were to rise to 300 feet, and the superstructure for the rest.[59] Even
this included 'restaurants, theatre, shops, Turkish baths, prome-
nades, and winter gardens'. There was to be an observatory at the
summit, a meteorological station, and an 'informal sanatorium'.[60]

Work began on the project, and temporary rail track was laid
from the Metropolitan to the site of the tower foundations to
carry the steel girders, which came from Newton Heath Ironworks
in Manchester. The park, with its boating lake, waterfall, a variety
hall and cycling and sports grounds, was completed within a year,
and became a favourite spot for outings. The tower, however, did
not progress well, and Watkin had to fend off anxious questions at
shareholders' meetings with assurances that there was ample

[59] *Railway Magazine, ibid.*
[60] Barker and Hyde, p.160.

144

31 Watkin's Tower did not progress beyond its first stage

capital, the tower would be completed in, well, eighteen months, and a new station – Wembley Park – was to be opened to cater for the influx of visitors. As with the Eiffel Tower, a quick return on capital was confidently expected. At the mid-1894 half-yearly meeting of the shareholders of the Wembley Tower Company, Francis Pavy, presiding in the absence of Sir Edward, reported that during the last quarter over one hundred thousand people had visited Wembley Park, and expressed great hopes for the completion of the first stage of the tower within three months.[61]

The park was opened in May 1894, with the tower, already suffering from subsidence, still at only its first stage. It was tilting ominously within two years.[62] The possible investors and the visiting public were to show a disappointing lack of enthusiasm for that part of the venture, only £27,000 being raised towards the estimated cost of £220,000. Watkin is said to have invested £100,000 of his own money in it.[63] Despite a further £60,000 from the Metropolitan and its Surplus Lands Committee,[64] the tower

[61]*Herepath's Journal*, 14 September 1894, p.904.
[62]Jeff Hill and Francesco Varrari, *Creating Wembley: The Construction of a National Monument* (British Library Website, 2000).
[63]A.W. Currie, 'Sir Edward Watkin: A Canadian View', p.38.
[64]Jackson, p.100.

did not get beyond its first stage, at a height of 155 feet. Lifts were installed in May 1896 to that level, but of the 100,000 visitors to the park during the first six months, only 18,500 paid for entry.[65] Watkin was the largest individual shareholder in the Tower Company and the construction subsidiary, and had declared that his mottoes were 'Never be beaten', and 'Never admit the word "impossible"'.[66] Nevertheless, the tower was already being called 'The Shareholders' Dismay', and it was soon to become known as 'Watkin's Folly'. It had been hoped at first that the tower would have been named after Queen Victoria, but that high hope, too, was doomed to failure. At the end of 1894 all work on it was stopped, though it remained open to the public, as it was, until 1902.[67] The derelict and rusting hulk remained a blot on the landscape until 1906. In that year the Tower Construction Company, renamed (again) The Wembley Park Estate Company, initiated a programme of housebuilding which eventually overlaid part of the original scheme, and took the decision to demolish 'the spectre at the feast'.[68] It was assailed by about forty men with sledgehammers, knocking out bolts and rivets and sending the girders crashing to the ground. In July 1907, explosives placed under the four legs completed the demolition. The Manchester firm of Heenan and Froude, who had been the builders, administered the *coup de grâce*, and the noise was heard for miles around.[69] The 2,700 tons of scrap metal were exported to Italy.

Donald Hunt, Public Relations Consultant to the Channel Study Group, 1958 to 1989, in his comprehensive history of that venture, says that after what proved to be the final rejection by Parliament of Sir Edward's attempts to achieve authorisation of the tunnel, 'Watkin became more and more eccentric', and cites the Wembley Tower project as evidence.[70] This assessment must take its place among the many summary dismissals of Watkin's aims and activities. The Wembley project, as such, was a failure. But although the tower, as the centrepiece of the grand concept of a huge park

[65]Barker and Hyde, p.161.
[66]*Railway Magazine,* March/April 1944, p.114.
[67]A.S. Travis, p.13.
[68]Barker and Hyde, p.162.
[69]A.S.Travis, p.13.
[70]Donald Hunt, *The Tunnel: The Story of the Channel Tunnel, 1802–1994* (Malvern; Images Publishing Ltd., 1994), pp.64 and 65.

for the recreation of London's masses, was not completed, the sports and leisure facilities were popular, and the area became a venue for large-scale gatherings in the twentieth century. That Watkin's plan was not at all eccentric, can be seen in Blackpool's imitation of the Eiffel Tower, built 1891–94, (though at 520 feet it was not much over half the height), which has been hugely successful ever since.[71] The same architects of the Blackpool Tower, Maxwell and Tuke, also built a higher (621 feet) but similarly-designed version at New Brighton in 1897.[72] The football ground at Wembley was first used for a match on 14 October 1893, which provided the first traffic at Watkin's new station, 'Wembley Park'.[73] The conference centre, arena and assembly hall formed the venue for the highly successful British Empire Exhibition, held in 1924, when the FA Cup Final was first played at the new Wembley Stadium. The Olympic Games were staged there in 1948, and in 1998 it was named the 'English National Stadium'. It became an 'icon of Englishness'.[74] The tower had occupied the land right in the middle of the pitch.

By the end of Watkin's chairmanship, the Metropolitan had evolved almost into two separate railways. There were the original underground lines, referred to by directors and officers as 'The Main Line', and a 50½-mile 'Extension', or 'The Branch', penetrating north-westwards into rural Buckinghamshire: the extension which awaited connection with the southward-questing Manchester, Sheffield and Lincolnshire Railway. These two 'Metropolitan Railways' were linked solely by a single track at Baker Street, which carried no revenue-earning services.[75] It was very different from Watkin's undertaking over twenty years before.

Summing up Watkin's reign on the Metropolitan, Alan Jackson, under the sub-heading 'A Friend to Shareholders', says:

From the time of Watkin's arrival, despite continuing heavy investment in construction in central London, and his bold

---

[71]The builders were the same Heenan and Froude of Manchester (A.S. Travis, p.11).
[72]Roger Dixon and Stephen Muthesius, *Victorian Architecture* (Thames and Hudson, 1978), p.90. This, however, lasted only twenty-three years, being demolished in 1919–21 (*The Wallasey News*, 5 December 1976, p.6).
[73]Jackson, p.337, note 21.
[74]Jeff Hill, Nottingham University, *Creating Wembley;* from the Internet, 19 August 2000.
[75]Jackson p.103.

expansionist policy, which pushed the line into areas yielding only the thinnest [traffic] for many years, his tight financial control on contracts and major purchases, combined with competent management, assured an unbroken sequence of modest but by no means trivial dividends on the Ordinary shares'.[76]

In July 1872, just before he took over the chairmanship, the company had declared a dividend of 1%. From 1877 to the second half of 1884, it was 5%. From then until the first half of 1887, it was 4%, and thereafter it rose again to 5%.[77] After twenty-two years in the chair, he left a well-organised and streamlined company in 1894.[78] In 1883, 'influential shareholders' suggested that he should receive the full £2,500 a year from the date of his appointment in 1872, 'in consideration of the very valuable services he has rendered to the Company'. This was approved by a majority of 92% of the shareholders at the half-yearly meeting of that year.[79] The company's credit was such that it had no difficulty in raising all the money it required from time to time, even the enormous funds needed for the electrification from 1905 onwards.[80]

T.R. Gourvish, quoting George Steiner,[81] described the 'Ideal Chief Executive' as 'a charismatic leader of men...a business statesman in dealing with government and community leaders; a thoughtful person who can look ahead and know how to get there; a man of action who can make decisions for prompt compliance; an innovator; and a vigilant seeker of opportunities who is willing to come to grips with and solve problems.' The requisites for successful management were 'a first-class planning system, charisma, and a sense of competitive urgency'.[82]

Allowing for his failings, it is hard to deny Watkin's qualifying for the title.

Watkin's other commitments were to involve him in responsibilities both close by, and far distant.

---

[76]*Ibid*, pp. 326ff.
[77]*Ibid*, pp.65 and 114.
[78]*Ibid*, p.327.
[79]*Ibid*, p.116.
[80]This had been mooted in the 1880s and 1890s, but was not then considered to be technically feasible.
[81]In *Top Management Planning*, 1969, p.89.
[82]T.R. Gourvish, *Mark Huish*, p.261 and Title page.

148

10

The Great Eastern Railway, And Other Directorships

The story of Watkin's association, as a director, with the Great Eastern Railway has a unique political flavour. The Great Eastern, which was an amalgamation of several smaller companies in 1862, and whose traffic was predominantly agricultural, had overstretched itself in attempting to expand its range of operation to the northern coalfields, and in costly extensions in the London area. Its financial needs were estimated as £1.5 million in 1866, when Parliament, in the midst of monetary crisis, refused permission for them to raise the money. In July 1867, two Great Eastern directors and the Chief Officer travelled to Pitlochry, where Watkin was on holiday, and offered him the chairmanship of the company in order to steer it out of its troubles. The offer was not accepted, but he promised that if the Board was reconstituted so as to command the confidence of the shareholders, he 'would endeavour to obtain for them a Chairman far superior in all respects to anyone then occupying a leading position on railways'.[1]

The Great Eastern Board was not of a mind to agree to such a radical proposal, but shareholder pressure was irresistible. Two days after a meeting of the Manchester Shareholders Association on 6 November, an extraordinary general meeting forced the Board to resign. Six new directors were elected on 3 January 1868, two of whom were Watkin and Lord Cranborne.[2] Lord Cranborne, Robert Cecil, later to become the 3rd Marquess of Salisbury, and one of Britain's greatest Prime Ministers, had about

---

[1]T.C. Barker, 'Lord Salisbury, Chairman of the Great Eastern Railway 1868-1872', in Sheila Marriner (ed.), *Business and Businessmen: Studies in Business, Economics and Accounting History* (Liverpool University Press,1978), pp. 85–8.
[2]*Ibid*, p.187.

149

this time suffered a number of financial losses, the chief of them being due to the collapse of the bankers Overend and Gurney in May 1866. He had asked his father for £1,500, but when he lost his annual ministerial salary of £5,000 on resigning on 9 February 1867 from the post of Secretary of State for India – over the Second Reform Bill – and another of his major investments, the Imperial Mercantile Credit Company, also went into liquidation, he had to go back to his father for a further £1,250.[3] In these circumstances he was open to Watkin's suggestion to become the Chairman of the GER. Watkin, as a Member of Parliament, had early noted Cecil's qualities.

> In 1857, and again in 1864 and 1865...I had formed the notion that honour and truth, the highest capacity, and at the same time class prejudice, were mixed up in him; and I had often said to myself, as I sat listening to him, 'That man wants only the contact and experience of external life only, to make him a great statesman'. I knew something, from a friend of his, of his then private position.[4]

Cranborne replied to Watkin in guarded terms: 'I have thought a good deal over the proposal you kindly made to me...I am not indisposed to accede to your suggestion if I can do so without exciting angry feelings or thrusting aside anyone with a better claim than myself...'[5] He expressed reservations about the GER official's attitude to accounts, and proposed the appointment of two independent auditors 'to protect [his] own honour', given that Watkin might not always be present to advise him. 'If anything happens to make any other arrangement more convenient, I hope you will deal with the matter as if you had never spoken to me on it. I shall retain an equally grateful recollection of your courtesy

---

[3] Andrew Roberts, *Salisbury: Victorian Titan* (Weidenfeld and Nicolson, 1999), pp.101 and 102.

[4] T.C. Barker, *ibid*, p.87. Barker comments: 'This indicates...the rather superior view that Watkin took of his own position'. For the son of a Manchester merchant to assess the qualities and potential of a scion of one of England's noble and ancient houses may seem hubristic. But developments were to vindicate the lad from Salford. Presumably Barker could pray Charles Dickens's 'prayer' (published in *The Chimes*, '2nd Quarter'): 'O let us love our occupations,/ Bless the squire and his relations,/ Live upon our daily rations,/ And always know our proper stations.'

[5] 2 December 1867.

and good opinion', he concluded[6]. He also declined Watkin's offer of a salary of £1,400, despite his difficulties, accepting only £700 on the grounds that a 'highly-paid Chairman is a luxury which should be reserved for the return of a good shareholders' dividend'.[7]

The Board made an effort in January 1868 to persuade Watkin to become Chairman for the two or three months before Lord Cranborne took over, while the most pressing financial and administrative problems were resolved, but they did not succeed.[8] Cranborne became Chairman at the meeting of 16 January 1868, at the age of thirty six. Watkin's prediction that he would 'perform a great public service by taking the chair', and would need only a 'very few months' of experience 'to grasp the policy and details of railway management better practically, and from a higher point of view, than those who call themselves "practical men"',[9] proved amply correct. Cranborne maintained the right to appoint his own accountants, and put in two Board of Trade auditors (Watkin's views on their provenance is not recorded), and 'quickly mastered the complexities' of running a railway, 'with its arbitrations, interlocking compromises, gargantuan ambitions and regular bankruptcies'. 'The Great Eastern', Cranborne said to Gladstone in February 1868, 'is forbidden by Act of Parliament to distribute any dividend till the line [to Bishop's Stortford] is opened. The contractor refuses to open it until his bill is paid, and the Great Eastern is forbidden by Act to pay his bill.'[10]

He made redundancies, abandoned plans for potentially unprofitable extensions, persuaded the support of bankers and Parliament, dismissed the Managing Director, and arranged details of exchanges of traffic with other companies. Only a week after his appointment, he initiated an arrangement whereby individual directors took responsibility for the various departments – Traffic, Ways and Works, Stores, Motive Power, Finance and Steamboats, and he took the chair himself at all meetings of these committees.

---

[6]Papers of the Third Marquess of Salisbury, Hatfield House, *Watkin Letters,* f.2.
[7]T.C. Barker, *ibid.,* pp.88 and 89.
[8]Though he did agree to take a seat on the Board. 'Personally I have no desire for more work,' he wrote to Cranborne on the 5th, 'but I see clearly a public duty before me' (Salisbury Papers, *Watkin Letters,* f.4.)
[9] *Ibid,* f.5.
[10]Andrew Roberts, *ibid,* p.102.

In July 1868 the Official Receiver was discharged, and the next year the Great Eastern paid a dividend again; the cash necessary for re-expansion had been advanced following a conference between Watkin, Rothschild, two other bankers and Salisbury.[11] In Watkinian mode he regularly warned shareholders not to be seduced by engineers or solicitors, 'or persons whose minds are strung to a sanguine degree'. 'Cranborne's accession as the 3rd Marquess of Salisbury in April 1868 did not diminish his commitment to the railway. Indeed, he became more and more immersed in detail as time went by.'[12]

The two men met and corresponded frequently during this period, Watkin continued to advise him in terms of railway politics, as when the brusque manner of the LNWR Chairman, Sir Richard Moon, gave Cranborne to think that he had offended him in some way. Watkin re-assured him: 'I do not think Moon is at all offended. It is his way. He thinks the Chairman of The London and North Western is quite as great a personage as Lord Cranborne who will be Prime Minister in two years, or it will be his own fault, and a hundred times as great a man as Edward Watkin who...he says, taught him his business.'[13] Watkin also gave considerable financial assistance to the Great Eastern in helping to get it out of Chancery, he raised £50,000 to pay off a particularly pressing debt, and switched to the company, at some financial loss, capital belonging to a trust in his wife's name.[14] In 1869 the Great Eastern had been pulled round to be strong enough to think again about its gaining a connection with the Yorkshire coalfield. Salisbury expressed his wish to retire, advocating Watkin as his successor as Chairman. 'All the evidence suggests that Salisbury was a warm supporter of Watkin and all his works.'[15] By 1872, the company was on a sound financial footing, and though its dividend did not attain 2% until 1882, by 1901 it was 6%.[16] It went on to become the operator, from

---

[11]J.F.A. Mason, in *Salisbury: The Man and his Politics* (Eds) Lord Blake and Hugh Cecil (London: Macmillan, 1987), p.19.
[12]T.C. Barker, p.90.
[13]Salisbury Papers, *Watkin Letters*, f.15, 22 February 1868.
[14]T.C. Barker, p.93.
[15]*Ibid*, p.95.
[16]Jack Simmons and Gordon Biddle, *The Oxford Companion to British Railway History* (Oxford University Press, 1997), p.191.

London's Liverpool Street Station, of one of the world's most intensive and efficient commuter train services.

In recommending Watkin as his successor, however, Salisbury misjudged the hostility of the Board, who did not favour Watkin. This may seem harsh, after what he had accomplished, but the new anti-Watkin party in the directorship felt that 'the Chairman of the Great Eastern should not be also the Chairman of two other companies whose interests seem frequently to clash with ours'.[17] This referred to Watkin's policy of saying sweet things on behalf of the MS&LR to companies whose interests were inimical. Such a policy does not necessarily imply duplicity. One man's perfidy can be another man's opportunism within a comprehensive consistency. With an eye to future development, John Fildes, a member of the Manchester Stock Exchange, writing from Mansfield Chambers in Half Moon Street in that city, wrote to Salisbury,[18] commending Watkin's value to the GER as a possible chairman. 'Sir Edward', he said, 'has the interests of both companies [i.e. the MS&LR and the GER] before him...I hope that we, the Great Eastern Board, shall not alienate him, his great services to the Great Eastern Company, and his frank conduct to your Lordship is a sufficient guarantee that Great Eastern interests will be duly protected.'[19] On 20 February 1872 Salisbury resigned, still expressing his faith in Watkin as successor.

Watkin did not succeed him, but he did continue as a director until his own resignation on 15 August. In July 1871 Salisbury had given instructions that £2,000 should be paid to Watkin for the loss he had sustained in 1868 to his wife's trust money, to be paid not out of company funds, but from those set aside for the Chairman. Watkin waived his own fees, of about £100 per year, as a Great Eastern director, either by returning them or giving them away to charity.[20]

Salisbury's chairmanship was 'an event unique in British Railway History...and he left the GER in a very different position from that in which he had found the Company', said the historian

---

[17]T.C. Barker, *ibid*, pp.96 and 99.
[18]6 July 1871.
[19]Salisbury Papers , *Watkin Letters,* f. 57.
[20]T.C. Barker, *ibid.*, pp.98 and 99.

of the GER, without once mentioning Watkin's part in it.[21] The Great Eastern Board had a change of heart four years later, for in early 1876 Watkin received an invitation from them to become their Chairman. He consulted two close friends, who advised him against it, on the grounds that public feeling would not agree to his taking a fourth chairmanship, the others being the Manchester, Sheffield and Lincolnshire, the South Eastern, and the Metropolitan. Watkin replied to the Board that 'if the possibility were offered by general desire, coupled with the condition that I should be consulted in reference to the new list of Directors to be submitted to the shareholders, I should be prepared in such event to request my colleagues on the Board of one of the companies I represent to release me...'[22] He rejoined the Board of the Great Eastern on 5 August, but resigned on 12 November 1877. The Great Eastern was not really in his scheme of things; it might have represented a possibility of a route to London for the MS&L, but on 6 August 1878 he accepted the chair of the East London Railway, having been asked to be the Receiver of that company, which was an important link between between his South Eastern and Metropolitan railways. The counsel of his friends against a fourth chairmanship had clearly been outweighed by superior strategic considerations.

The suspicion of the Great Eastern Board about Watkin's divided loyalties had been fuelled largely by his struggles to achieve a new 'coal railway' between South Yorkshire and the Metropolitan. His efforts arose from disputes between the Great Northern and the Midland over such traffic, with the 'Sheffield' a seriously interested party. This, as we have seen, was a concern also of the Great Eastern, who thus regarded Watkin's association with the GNR with anxiety. The South Yorkshire coal owners had complained in 1870 about the GN and the Midland joining together to give preference to coal from the North-East and Derbyshire, which had the effect of making South Yorkshire coal more expensive. Watkin proposed to a Board meeting of the MSL on 7 October 1870 a new coal railway which would be promoted by the South Yorkshire coal owners, but supported by the

[21]Cecil J.Allen, *The Great Eastern Railway* (London; Ian Allan, 1967), pp.55 and 56.
[22]G. Dow, *ibid*, Vol. 2, p.108.

MS&LR and (Watkin hoped) by the Great Eastern.[23] It was reported to the meeting of 22 April 1871 that the GER liked the idea but preferred a line ending at March rather than Huntingdon.[24] It was prepared, however, to back the Bill in principle, and the MS&L agreed to support it.[25] However, 'after a contest lasting no more than a month...this was rejected by a Committee of the House of Commons'.[26]

Also in 1871, Watkin, in discussing the problem of the South Yorkshire mine owners, and probing the possibility of arrangements with the GNR, succeeded in offending the Great Northern hierarchy. The discussion was confused by counter-proposals from the Midland, and the Great Northern's offer to help the 'Sheffield' and the Great Eastern to carry coals from Yorkshire over existing lines to Shoreditch. Watkin clouded the issue further with an impulsive statement, in May 1871, to the effect that the GN could not be trusted to safeguard South Yorkshire interests. This provoked a justifiably acid response from E.B. Denison, and in the following year there was a renewed attempt by the Great Northern and the Midland to absorb the MSL.[27]

Other amalgamations were then in the air: the Midland and the Glasgow and South Western; the North Eastern and the Great Northern; the Great Western and the London and South Western, among others, but the one which caused the greatest governmental misgivings was the LNWR's Bill to unite its system with that of the Lancashire and Yorkshire Railway. These two companies together would have controlled over one-fifth of all receipts on UK railways, and one-seventh of their total capital. Parliament, alarmed by the monopoly implications, and the petitions against it from Chambers of Commerce in South Lancashire, rejected the scheme, and did so again on its re-presentation in 1873.[28] And so the several schemes, including the 'absorption' of the MS&LR, came to nothing.

---

[23]PRO RAIL 463/11, Minute No. 1369.
[24]*Ibid*, Minute 1717.
[25]Minute 1718.
[26]Cecil J. Allen, p. 49.
[27]G. Dow, Vol. 2, pp.61 and 63.
[28]Edward Cleveland-Stevens, *English Railways: Their Development and their Relation to the State* (London; George Routledge and Son Ltd., 1915), pp.241–5.

The East London Railway was built in 1865 to connect all railways entering London north and south of the Thames. This was clearly an important function in Watkin's mind, and he occupied the chair from 6 August 1878 to his retirement in 1893. It was well-linked at its southern end, near New Cross (it was vested in the Southern Railway in the grouping of 1923), but it never had an adequate connection with the northern lines entering London.

In security of that consideration, Watkin was Chairman of the North London Railway, from the 1870s to 1893. This enterprise was efficiently worked, and declared a dividend of 7.5% in the years 1880 to 1899, except for two years at 6.75%. 'It was the most efficient of all the smaller British railways.'[29] On the East London, one of Watkin's opponents, Albert Grant, circulated a printed pamphlet, dated 5 July 1878, to warn the shareholders of 'the character of the man who seeks to become Chairman of your Company'.[30] His accusations consisted of the usual criticisms regarding the Erie Company, The Grand Trunk Railway and the Hudson's Bay Company in North America, and the Humber Ironworks, all of which, on dispassionate enquiry, are perfectly explicable and defensible by the highest standards of judgement. The shareholders were to express their considered opinion when they accepted his chairmanship a month later.

The Great Western Railway, of which Watkin was a director from 1863 to 1867, was certainly not one of Watkin's 'rescue' appointments. He went onto the Board when the West Midland Railway, of which he was a director, was taken over by the Great Western in 1863.[31] His seat on the Board of the Boston, Sleaford, and Midland Counties Railway dated from about its completion in April 1859.[32] He was in support of his friend Herbert Ingram, MP for Boston and founder of the *Illustrated London News,* who had helped to finance the company. The line was worked by the Great Northern Railway from the outset, and it lost its independent Board of Directors when it was totally absorbed by that company in 1864.

---

[29]Simmons and Biddle, pp.352–353.
[30]The Archives of the Institution of Civil Engineers, 25 Great George Street, London, SW.
[31]Dow, Vol. 1, p.266, and Volume 2, p.17.
[32]Isabel Bailey, *Edward Ingram Esq, MP* (Boston: Richard Kay, 1996), p.57.

He was also a director of three foreign companies. The Danube and Black Sea Railway of 1860 was projected to overcome the fact that although the River Danube was navigable over much of its huge length, where it approaches the Black Sea and access to the world's oceans, it forms a delta of swamps and marshes which posed problems for barge traffic. The shareholders included a large contingent of Manchester investors who asked Watkin to oversee its financial security during the 1860s.

The Belgian Congo Railways had their origin in the great personal interest taken by King Leopold II of the Belgians in the development of the Congo. Unfortunately, his 'civilising mission,' with its core economic impetus, employed forced labour on a large scale, and 'it has gone down in history as a very bad example of colonial administration'.[33] Henry Morton Stanley, the British explorer and journalist, and adviser to Leopold, said 'Without the railroad, the Congo is not worth a penny', and the King asked Edward Watkin to go out to advise on the building of the railway system. The success of his work was indicated in 1885 by Leopold's making him a Knight Commander of The Order of Leopold of Belgium. One wonders how Watkin coped with the labour relations he encountered.

The Athens–Piraeus Railway was $5\frac{3}{8}$ miles long, and ran from Thesion, on the outskirts of the Greek capital, to the Piraeus, with one intermediate station. It was opened in 1869, but was bankrupt by 1874. In 1877 Watkin was called in, and he re-organised the line. It 1880 it was extended to the centre of Athens (Omonia Square), with another intermediate station. This brought its length to $6\frac{1}{2}$ miles, and took the line into solvency. For this success Watkin was awarded the Knights' Cross of the Greek Order of the Redeemer. The line was electrified in 1904 and further extended later. It is now 'Line 1' of the Athens Metro, carrying 90 million passengers a year.[34]

Further directorships held by Watkin were the Blackpool Railway Company, the Wigan Junction Railway and the chairmanship of the Trustees of the New York, Lake Erie and Western

---

[33]*Encyclopaedia Britannica*, 1995 Edition, Vol. 15, p.649.
[34]*The Railway Magazine* Editorial Consultant, John Slater, in a private letter to the author, 18 May 1998.

Railway; he was also and on the board of several non-railway businesses such as the Brazilian Electric Telegraph Company and the Manchester Fire Assurance Company.[35] Many of these were *ex officio*, or held only as long as he was able to continue with them.

Some of them, of course, were in the category of securing his influence on possible developments towards the grand strategy of linking South Lancashire with France and beyond. One possibility was raised in 1875. He had heard that the LNWR and the Midland were planning to absorb the North Staffordshire Railway, and he proposed to the Great Northern that they should forestall them. This would have given a route from Manchester, via Stockport and Macclesfield, to Stoke on Trent, and thence to London, but the talks lapsed in the absence of mutually agreed terms. A sequel was a scheme for the fusion of the MS&L and the NSR, but that fell through in May 1876 after a failure of agreement on an effective date.[36] In August 1878 Watkin was invited to become the Chairman of the North Staffordshire Railway, which was in an insecure financial position, but he declined. Clearly the NSR Board had no hard feelings against him for the failure of the amalgamation talks, nor, equally clearly, did they entertain any doubts about Watkin's financial abilities after twenty-five years on the MS&LR.

Watkin's restless manoeuvring on behalf of the 'Sheffield' was noted by the shareholders, and they passed unanimously at the first half-yearly meeting of 1872 a resolution which was considered by the Board on 23 February. Readers of the standard histories of the period, which describe Watkin variously as 'scheming', 'devious', 'tricky'[37] and a 'great manipulator' [38] and so on, might at this point expect a huge corporate rebuke to the man. But on the contrary the resolution read 'That the best thanks of the meeting be given to Sir Edward Watkin and the Board of Directors for their attention to the interests of the Company, and that the Board of Directors be requested to recognise in some substan-

[35]*The Directory of Directors,* 1892 Edition, Quoted, *The Yorkshire Post,* obituary, 1901.
[36]Dow, Vol. 2, pp.106–8.
[37]T.C. Barker, pp.83, 84 and 93,
[38]F.M.L.Thompson, in *Salisbury: The Man and his Policies,* Edited, Lord Blake and Hugh Cecil (Macmillan,1987), p.258.

tial way the devoted services of Sir Edward Watkin as Chairman of the Company.' The Board resolved that 'the sum of two thousand pounds (£2,000) be voted to the Chairman as a recognition of the eminent services he has for years past rendered to the Manchester, Sheffield, and Lincolnshire Company'.[39]

---

[39]PRO RAIL 463/12, Minute 2309.

11

Grimsby

Watkin's administration on the 'Sheffield' was to transform a small fishing town on the Lincolnshire coast into one of the greatest ports in the country. The Sheffield, Ashton-under-Lyne and Manchester Railway came, by amalgamation of three companies, to incorporate 'Lincolnshire' into its title.[1] The access to Grimsby was to have important effects. The company, under Watkin, threw itself into developing the port with great energy and enterprise. In 1855 the tonnage of fish landed there was 188; in 1861 it was 5,300, and in 1891, 64,000 tons.[2]

Fishing had been the main commercial activity of Grimsby for many years before the nineteenth century: in the tenth or eleventh century, Grim sailed from Denmark and landed in the Humber Estuary, and established himself there as a fisherman. He was very successful, and sold his fish as far away as Lincoln.[3] His loyalty to local chiefs and to the king is supposed to account for the special trading privileges enjoyed by the town named after him.[4]

During the 1830s, the population of Grimsby had actually declined, and though attempts were made to establish industries other than fishing, they failed, and by 1841 one house in every eight was uninhabited. One reason the function of the docks could not be extended was the lack of inland communications, and so the landowners and the dock company urged the corporation to establish a rail connection with the town. In 1844 a group was formed under the inspiration of Lord Yarborough, the Squire of

---

[1]See Chapter 5, p. 50.
[2]Edward Gillett, *A History of Grimsby* (Oxford University Press, 1970), p.301. By 1911, the figure was 190,000 tons. The peak, in 1951, was 198,000 tons.
[3]Maude I. Ebbutt, *British Myths and Legends* (Senate Press, 1996), p.81.
[4]*Ibid*, p.74.

Grimsby, which resulted in the formation of the Great Grimsby and Sheffield Junction Railway Company.[5] In 1845 a new Docks Company took over the Haven Company: five of its directors were also on the Board of the Railway Company. These two concerns were absorbed, as noted earlier, by the MS&LR in 1846. A new dock was opened, on reclaimed land, in March 1852 (on a royal visit in 1854 it was named the Royal Dock), with further rail connections established, and a new era of enterprise had begun to transform the town. New dock and rail installations brought a weekly passenger service to Hamburg and Rotterdam, and later to Königsberg and other ports, as well as cargoes of coal, cotton, salt, iron, and machinery.[6] 'At almost every point, the [town] council was aware of the dependence of the town on the MS&LR.'[7] Politically, it became a 'sort of pocket borough'.[8]

Further dock and rail developments reflected growth in trade, and stimulated further activity. In 1856 £1 million worth of goods were exported; by 1875 this had increased to £10 million, and the tonnage of shipping using the port had increased six-fold in twenty years.[9] The *Grimsby News,* summarising Watkin's influence on the town's fortunes, said that when he joined the MS&L in 1854, he found very fine dock installations but practically no trade. The efforts of Lord Yarborough and his colleagues, and their considerable financial outlay, had borne little fruit and were in danger of coming to nothing. Watkin had set about the job, devoting 'his vast experience and unwearied energies to the immense task of creating a trade in the port'. Characteristically, rather than create enemies and needless competition, he began by encouraging the fishermen of Kingston-upon-Hull to share the splendid facilities, both natural and man-made, of a prosperous Grimsby. He invited them to a 'sumptuous banquet' and conference,[10] but his eloquent persuasiveness was not, on this occasion, the match of his large-scale organising ability: the men of Hull were not to be enticed

---

[5]Gillett, p.213.

[6]*Ibid,* p.222.

[7]*Ibid,* p.224.

[8]P.W. Kingsford, *Victorian Railwaymen: The Emergence and Growth of Railway Labour, 1830-1870* (London: 1970) Quoted in *Railways and the Victorian Imagination,* Michael Freeman (New Haven and London: Yale University Press, 1999), p. 162. A pocket borough is one where representation was controlled by a single person, family, or group interest.

[9]Gillett, p.224.

[10]*Grimsby News,* 25 July 1879.

away, preferring, as a disappointed Watkin put it, 'their wretched huts on the bank of the river twenty miles away'.[11]

Another of his ideas – far more enduringly successful – was to persuade the Midland Railway and the Great Northern to join with the 'Sheffield' and the South Yorkshire Railway to form a joint stock company, known as the Grimsby Deep Sea Fishing Company. This proved to be the first of many such ventures, and, as soon as it was well-established, the railway companies sold it to local merchants as the basis for Grimsby's future prosperity.[12] He also promoted passenger steamships from Grimsby to Hamburg, Rotterdam, Antwerp, and as far afield as St Petersburg, first by persuading certain shipowners, then directly by the MS&L, for which parliamentary powers were obtained on 29 July 1864.

The pace of growth of trade and facilities meant the frequent acquisition of new land by the MS&L, which began to test the town's capacity to expand. The company started to explore the possibility of building docks elsewhere, and the consulting engineer, in a report dated 17 April 1874, suggested Killingholme, to the west of Grimsby. Land was cheaper there, and it had the advantage that the tide differential was easier for the docking of ships. The scheme was not pursued, due, according to one historian, to Watkin's lack of attention to the details of what he already controlled because of his appetite for fresh conquests.[13] This seems a little self-contradictory. The plan for a new dock took another thirty years to reach ground level, when the company, as the Great Central Railway, placed a Bill before Parliament for a deep-water dock at Immingham – about six or so miles further up the Humber Estuary from Grimsby (NGR 198162), which was opened by King George V and Queen Mary on 22 July 1912.[14]

Meanwhile, Grimsby continued to grow, and in 1875 a new customs house, an extension to the Fish Dock, and further rail connections were put in hand. As well as prospects for exporting coal, Watkin, from experiences in North America, had begun to see Grimsby as an important grain port. A warehouse was built,

---

[11]*Ibid.*
[12]*Grimsby News,* 16 April 1901.
[13]G. Dow, Vol. 2, p.164.
[14]Dow, Vol. 3, p.242.

32 Old Grimsby in the 1870s

and an extension eastwards of the rail line from the Old Dock to the main line near Great Coates. Watkin wanted a grain elevator, but that was considered too radical at the time: a visit by the company's secretary and its chief accountant to look at such installations in the USA resulted in their reporting negatively. 'The prejudices of the Old Country, and jealousies of trade interests' were the reasons given.[15] Feelings on the matter had changed by 1912. A grain elevator was included in the facilities at Immingham.[16]

A further royal visit took place on 22 July 1879, when the Prince and Princess of Wales opened a canal link between the Old Dock and the Royal Dock.[17] To mark this occasion, Watkin proposed that a statue of the Prince Consort be erected in front of the Royal Hotel, near the docks. The MS&L Board gave its blessing at the meeting of 23 May, and added its desire that 'in the event of the land being required for railway or dock purposes...another site would be found for the statue'.[18] These were prophetic words.

---

[15]Dow, Vol. 2, p.164.
[16]Illustration, *A Bird's Eye View of Immingham Dock*, by Fortunio Matania, painted for the Great Central Railway promotional book, *Per Rail*, of 1913.
[17]Gillett, p.224.
[18]Dow, Vol. 2, p.167.

33 The Royal Hotel, Grimsby in the 1890s. On the left is Watkin's statue of the Prince Consort of 1879

Eighty-six years later, the Royal Hotel, which had been taken over by the MS&L in 1890, and sold off again in 1946, was demolished to make way for new roadworks.[19]

The Great Central had offered in 1914 to move the statue elsewhere if the local council could find a place for it. They finally decided on a position outside Grimsby General Hospital, but nothing was done about it.[20] It was maintained very carefully by the GCR and the London and North Eastern Railway until 1939, when care for its appearance and that of the Albert Gardens in which it stood lapsed. The statue had been the target of anti-German sentiments in the First World War, and of depredations by pigeons and starlings during and after the Second.[21] Royal permission was granted to move the statue the short distance to the forecourt of the Royal Dock offices; it stood in the way of a new container terminal.[22] In 1983 the 30-feet-high, 20-ton statue

[19]*Lincolnshire Life*, August 1967.
[20]*Grimsby News*, May 1914; *Grimsby Evening Telegraph*, 1 November 1966.
[21]*Grimsby Evening Telegraph*, 10 May 1966.
[22]*Ibid*, 22 December 1966.

was moved again, though only 15 feet, to make way for road improvements.[23]

The *Grimsby Evening Telegraph* of 10 May 1966, hoping that the statue would be saved, stated that Sir Edward Watkin 'got much *kudos* in the town at the time by insisting on paying for the statue, instead of raising a public subscription'. Displaying the fashionable cynicism towards Watkin, the writer went on, 'whether this was entirely disinterested, who can say?' But he nevertheless continued, 'All snide remarks aside, it was an enlightened thing for a railway, of all bodies, to do in those days of devil-take-the-hindmost, to lay out a garden for public enjoyment, and let us give them the credit for it.' He clearly had no knowledge of Watkin's thirty-five-year-old interest in the provision of public amenities.[24]

According to the *Grimsby* News,[25] 'The Railway Company have favoured Grimsby by giving it precedence over other ports...The rapid development of the trade and commerce of Grimsby have frequently induced a train of thought of interesting speculations as to what might have been the position of the port had it not been for the enterprising genius of Sir Edward Watkin. The commercial history of our country is fruitful of striking instances where the progress of towns and districts owes its chief impulse to the vigour, determination, and prescience of individuals. But it may be doubted', went on the writer in laudatory mood, 'whether any one man has conferred greater or more signal benefits on a town than the Chairman of the Manchester, Sheffield and Lincolnshire Railway Company. The inhabitants of Grimsby', he concluded, 'know this, and appreciate the fact to the fullest extent. Sir

---

[23]*Ibid*, 14 August 1983.

[24]The statue of Prince Albert, by William Theed, was cast in Nuremberg and it was a replica of one by the same sculptor, executed for Queen Victoria, which stood in Coburg, Bavaria. The plinth has inscriptions on all four sides. That on the front records: 'Albert Prince Consort, born 26 August 1819, died 14 December 1861, laid the foundation stone of the Royal Dock, Great Grimsby, on 18 April 1849, and the Dock was opened on 27 May 1852'. William Theed (1804–1891) was born at Trentham, near Stoke-on-Trent, the son of the sculptor William Theed (1764–1817), who revived ancient Classical sculpture and was responsible for the Cambridge statue of Byron. Theed the younger executed the Africa group on the Albert Memorial, Kensington Gardens, London (1863-72), which was designed by Sir George Gilbert Scott, (*Chambers Biographical Dictionary*, ed. Magnus Magnusson (Chambers, 1995), pp.1446 and 1447: Roger Dixon and Stefan Muthesius, *Victorian Architecture* (Thames and Hudson, 1978), p.164). The previous royal connection would perhaps account for Watkin's choice of sculptor for his own royal statue.

[25]25 July 1879.

165

Edward Watkin years ago saw the immense advantage of developing this branch of industry.' One hundred years later, the *Grimsby Evening Telegraph* carried a similar panegyric, concluding that the Manchester, Sheffield and Lincolnshire Railway 'had in fact virtually invented modern Grimsby. Before the MS&L, a village. After the MS&L, a Victorian boom town'.[26]

One of Watkin's projects for increasing the prosperity of Humberside did not materialise. In 1882 he supported the idea of a railway tunnel under the river, and he approached the North Eastern Railway, with whom the MS&L had been on good terms for many years, so that the two companies could co-operate. In September of that year the 'Sheffield' company started experimental borings, under the guidance of Professor Boyd Dawkins, who was Watkin's consultant for the Channel Tunnel.[27] By 1885, however, the North Eastern Board had begun to lose interest, and the proceedings lapsed. Watkin attempted to revive the idea in 1885 and again in 1891, but received a firm negative from the NER Chairman.[28] Humberside suffered from continued 'inadequate communication between north and south' for a further ninety years, until the opening of the Humber suspension road bridge in July 1981.[29]

To the credit of Watkin must go the success story of Cleethorpes as a seaside holiday resort. The MS&L had reached there in 1863, and despite the construction of pier by the Cleethorpes Pier Company in 1872, the village, with its ancient windmill and cottages and shops, had not developed greatly. In the winter, raging North Sea storms would bring down parts of the cliff, and so in August 1880 the Urban Sanitary Authority asked the MS&L to preserve the cliff, and the company responded by applying for parliamentary powers to do so, and to develop the foreshore as a place of recreation. The needful powers were granted on 18 July 1881 by the MS&LR (New Works) Act of that date. Seventeen acres of land were bought at a cost of £1,670, and in 1883 a beginning was made on sea defence measures running to over £33,000. Watkin tackled the enterprise 'with gusto',[30] He took over the pier

---

[26]20 July 1979.
[27]Board Minute 8761 of 5 October. PRO RAIL 463/19.
[28]Dow, Vol. 2, pp.185 and 186.
[29]*Encyclopaedia Britannica,* 1995 Edition, Vol. VI, p.878.
[30]Dow, Vol. 2, p.172.

company, under the MS&LR (Additional Powers) Act of 14 July 1884, and spent some £10,000 on swimming baths, refreshment rooms, stalls, a colonnade, a restaurant and a photographic studio.[31] The promenade was lit up by electricity and the gardens completed: he had the public opening performed by Prince Albert Victor on 2 July 1885. In the late 1890s, a pavilion on the pierhead, more stalls, a grotto in the cliff gardens, timber groynes and an extension of the sea walls (completed in 1892) were added. In May 1892 the remaining stretch of foreshore between Cleethorpes and Grimsby not already owned by the company – totalling 33 acres – was bought by the MSLR for £4,500. Dow records that by the end of the century more than £100,000 had been spent on the resort, 'which attracted as many as 30,000 people in a single day'. Truly, as he said, Cleethorpes was one of the MS&L's best investments.[32]

Grimsby, 'The monument of Sir Edward's enterprise and foresight',[33] admitted Watkin as a Freeman of the Borough in 1891. The scroll is dated, under seal, 27 February.[34] A street near the docks was named 'Watkin Street'.[35]

Watkin's enterprise and foresight were being exercised at the same time some 110 miles to the west, in Cheshire.

---

[31] *Ibid.*
[32] *Ibid.*
[33] *Grimsby Observer*, 23 October 1889.
[34] Scroll in possession of Watkin's great-granddaughter, Dorothea Worsley-Taylor.
[35] County Borough Official Guide (London: Batiste Publications, 1961), map facing p.96.

12

Cheshire Activities, 1870–1881

The Cheshire Lines Committee

There were several joint lines (owned by two or more companies) in which the MS&LR was a partner. By far the most profitable of these proved to be the oldest of them, the Manchester South Junction and Altrincham Railway, owned with the LNWR (from 1844, in their days as the Manchester and Birmingham, and Sheffield, Ashton-under-Lyne and Manchester companies). Between 1850 and 1863 the annual profit on its operations rose from £9,600 to over £34,500; the number of passengers conveyed annually from just under 639,000 to over 1,750,000; its season ticket holders from 172 to 736; and goods traffic from 114,600 tons to 679,000 tons a year.[1] Part of the increased traffic during the 1850s was generated by the Manchester Art Treasure Exhibition of 1857, held in an enormous 'Crystal Palace'-type building built on a site to the west of the line, between Old Trafford Station[2] and the present Lancashire Cricket Ground. Over one million people paid for entrance.[3]

The Oldham, Ashton-under-Lyne and Guide Bridge Junction was also jointly owned with the LNWR, while the Macclesfield, Bollington and Marple was vested, with the North Staffordshire Railway, as the 'Macclesfield Committee'. Of several smaller

---

[1]Dow, Vol. 2, p.115. By 1947 it had contributed, like the Metropolitan Railway, to the suburban growth of housing along its route, and two of its stations – Timperley and Altrincham – ranked second and fourth respectively in the whole country for the number of tickets booked, (from verbal information at the time from J.T. Greaves, Chief Booking Clerk of the MSJ&A).

[2]Renamed Trafford Bar from 1992, (John Senior and Eric Ogden, *Metrolink* (Glossop; Transport Publishing Company,1992), p.96).

[3]F. Dixon, *The Manchester South Junction and Altrincham Railway* (Oakwood Press, 1973), pp.17 and 18.

concerns, some were operated with the Great Northern Railway in South Yorkshire, and others with the Midland, via the Sheffield and Midland Committee, notably the Manchester and Stockport Railway, and the Marple, New Mills and Hayfield Junction (MNM&HJ). Part of the Sheffield and Midland Committee's remit was in Widnes, on lines promoted by local enterprise with support from Watkin.

By far the largest and most widely influential of the joint lines, and 'destined to become the most important jointly owned system in Great Britain',[4] was the Cheshire Lines Committee. As part of the battle for traffic in South Lancashire[5] the MS&LR the GNR and the Midland co-operated in this invasion of traditional LNWR territory. The joint operation of several small local railways was authorised by an Act of Parliament, the Great Northern (Cheshire Lines) Act 13 July 1863. These were the Stockport and Woodley Junction Railway (incorporated on 15 May 1860); the Cheshire Midland Railway (14 June 1860),[6] which ran from Altrincham Junction to Northwich; the West Cheshire Railway (11 July 1861), Northwich to Helsby Junction; and two lines (29 July 1862) from Hartford and Greenbank Junction to Winnington, and Cuddington Junction to Winsford; and, finally, the Stockport, Timperley and Altrincham Junction Railway (22 July 1861). On 5 July 1865, the Cheshire Lines Transfer Act was passed. This made the MS&L and Great Northern Railways joint owners of all the above, plus the Garston and Liverpool Railway (authorised on 17 May 1861) and the Liverpool Central Station Railway (29 July 1864). It also empowered the Midland Railway to become an equal partner, which it did on 18 July 1866, thus forming the Cheshire Lines Committee. Two other lines, making useful connections, were later absorbed: the Godley and Woodley Line (authorised in 1862), and the Chester and West Cheshire Junction Railway (1865). This latter completed, with the MSJ&A, a direct line from Manchester to Chester. In addition, a line which was worked by the CLC but always retained its separate identity, was the Southport and Cheshire Lines Extension Railway, opened

---

[4]Dow, Vol.2, p.129.
[5]Than which 'there is no richer railway field', John Pendleton, *Our Railways,* Vol. 1, p.164, quoting in 1896 a population of 1,511,000.
[6]Promoted by local landowners, with MS&L support.

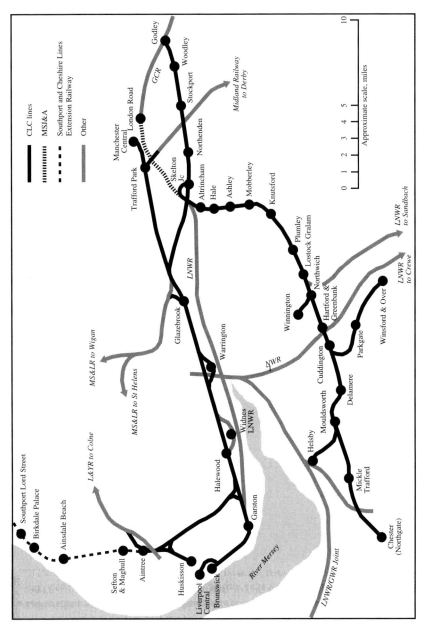

The Cheshire Line Committee

on 1 September 1884, to run from near Aintree Station to Southport Lord Street Station.

The CLC was one of only three joint lines to survive as separate bodies until the nationalisation of the railways in 1948.[7] All these developments are ascribed to 'the forceful leadership of Edward Watkin' by the CLC historian, R. Prys Griffiths.[8] With the triple ownership established, Watkin then proposed a new direct line from Manchester to Garston, connecting with the Garston and Liverpool Railway. This, he argued, was necessary because the 'running powers' route had become untenable. This was the arrangement in which the three companies had to use the LNWR line from Liverpool Lime Street via Garston to Timperley Junction, and from there along the MSJ&A into Manchester London Road – a circuitous route with no fewer than ninety-five level crossings, and the LNWR's attitude to such running powers gradually hardening.[9] The Bill was put before Parliament under the name of the MS&LR only, but Watkin assumed, rightly as it happened, that the other two partners would support it. In view of the stiff competition from the LNWR and the Lancashire and Yorkshire Railway, they had little option but to follow Watkin's initiative. The MS&L Railway (Extension to Liverpool) Act of 1865 authorised a new line from Old Trafford (Cornbrook) on the MSJ&A Railway, to a junction with the Garston and Liverpool (Brunswick) Railway near Cressington.[10] Brunswick was still $1\frac{1}{2}$ miles short of the city centre, and the Act to close the gap, authorised earlier, in July 1864, did not quite complete Watkin's new main line, which had to wait until 6 March 1874 before it was opened to traffic. It ran at first from Manchester London Road until a temporary site was opened at Manchester Central in 1877. It was in competition with two other routes: the LNWR (virtually the same as the 1830 Liverpool and Manchester Railway) from Liverpool Edge Hill to Manchester Exchange; and the Lancashire and Yorkshire Railway line from Liverpool Exchange to Victoria Station in Manchester. With the opening of the permanent Central Station (designed by John Fowler on the same lines as William

---

[7]Paul Bolger, *The Cheshire Lines Committee* (Heyday, 1984), p.6.
[8]In *The Cheshire Lines Railway* (Oakwood Press, 1978) p.1.
[9]*Ibid*, p.6.
[10]R.P. Griffiths, *The Cheshire Lines Railway*, p.5.

34 Watkin's contribution to the Manchester skyline: Central Station, CLC, in the 1890s

Barlow's magnificent St Pancras Station in London), on 1 July 1880, and the building of the Warrington avoiding line in 1883, express trains performed the journey of 34 miles between the two cities in 40 minutes. This was the fastest all-year regular express service in the world at the time.

Watkin's own 'Liverpool and Manchester Railway' must be counted as an unqualified success, though all his obituary notices, apart from one, failed to mention it, or indeed the Cheshire Lines Committee at all.[11] As result of this enterprise, and the introduction of cheap fare facilities, the receipts went up by £10,000 in six weeks. Because of this, Watkin urged his partners, the GNR and the Midland, to agree to increase the inter-city service from hourly-interval to half-hourly. He wrote to Denison and Ellison on 18 June 1877, 'I proposed half-hourly trains because I did not think any less service would bear successful competition. I desired also to abolish timetables: and, further, to deal with the traffic as

---

[11]The exception was *Transport*, 19 April 1901, which said of it that it was 'perhaps the most popular piece of railway improvement with which [his] name is associated'.

35 Cheshire Lines Committee Liverpool to Manchester Express: MS&LR 2-2-2 Locomotive No.502, in the early 1890s with five 12-wheel coaches

if it were a constant and not a fluctuating quality. My train would pendulum between point and point, as the trains of the Metropolitan and Greenwich lines do at present. Thus there would be no attaching and detaching'.[12] The GNR and the Midland were slow to see the value of these revolutionary ideas; Watkin had to be content with an hourly service, and he complained to the MS&L shareholders that he was being impeded by the joint ownership system from going ahead with sufficient 'steam' and 'go'.[13] The reduction in fares, forcing the LNW and L&Y to follow suit, caused the *Manchester Guardian* of 7 July 1877 to praise this initiative of the Cheshire Lines Committee: '... it is to them, and to Sir Edward Watkin in particular, that thanks are due for the substantial advantage which is gained by the travelling public'.[14]

Two short branch lines were built, from Hartford to Winnington, 2½ miles, destined to carry very heavy limestone

[12]Dow, Vol. 2, p. 136.
[13]Griffiths, p.9.
[14]Quoted, Dow, Vol. 2, p.136.

traffic from Tunstead in the Peak District, and the other of 6½ miles from Cuddington to Winsford and its salt deposits, via the village of Whitegate, on 1 June 1870.[15] But Watkin's idea for the extension of the latter from Winsford south-eastwards to Sandbach (about 7 miles) to connect with the North Staffordshire Railway, was not shared by his Great Northern and Midland partners. He went ahead nevertheless, with support from the local communities, and the Sandbach and Winsford Junction Railway was incorporated on 27 June 1872. The MS&L undertook to supply one half of the cost, but Derby and King's Cross were still against the scheme, and within two years the project had lapsed. Dow laments the needless parliamentary expenditure, and Watkin's 'pigheadedness'.[16] But the mid-nineteenth century was littered with such unfulfilled plans, and some eventually successful lines were achieved only by doggedness in the face of difficulties. The Midland's Settle and Carlisle Railway may be cited as an example of the latter. 'Watkin, a clever, energetic, and restless man...for his company,...was always looking ahead, planning the next move, and the one after, before previous schemes had been completed. His adversaries were rarely given time to regain their breath after a previous setback at his hands before he mounted his next assault...even his allies were often taken aback, because each of his schemes was a precursor to the next – and very logical – promotion.'[17]

Another venture of Watkin's, conceived in 1884, was supported by the other two partners of the CLC but came to nothing because he was carried away too quickly with its further development. This was an underground line through Liverpool from the CLC between the stations St Michael's and St James's – connecting with the new Mersey Railway at Liverpool Central Low Level Station. Such a line would have given the Cheshire Lines access to the Wirral, and had a great influence on Watkin's South Lancashire/ North Wales intentions. His suggestion of extending the budget of the scheme from £150,000 to £500,000 quickly caused the Midland and the GN to lose interest, and although Watkin went ahead

---

[15]*Ibid*, p.129.
[16]*Ibid*, p.130.
[17]Peter Hay, article on the Cheshire Lines Committee in *Steam World* Magazine, August 1992, pp. 14–6.

alone, the parliamentary powers he obtained in 1888 lapsed. The Mersey Railway, engineered by Sir John Hawkshaw, one of the engineers involved in the planning of the Channel Tunnel, did, however, connect a Low Level Station at Liverpool Central (opened on 11 January 1892), with the North Wales and Liverpool Line, on which Watkin had been so keen, in 1896.[18]

The Weaver Navigation Trustees.

One of Watkin's many directorships held at this time was as a Trustee of the Weaver Navigation, a water-transport company in central Cheshire. The River Weaver rises in the Peckforton Hills, part of the sandstone ridge in the south of the county, at a point about 2 miles due south of Beeston Castle.[19] It flows southwards for 13 or so miles then winds its way north through Nantwich, Northwich and Frodsham, to join the River Mersey some 55 miles from its source. Because of the almost level terrain, it winds considerably, its depth seldom more than a metre or so, and it was seen in the seventeenth century that a programme of straightening and canalisation, at any rate from Winsford onwards, would make it an effective way of transporting salt from the deposits in Winsford and Northwich, and china clay from Liverpool to the Potteries. The Weaver Navigation was formed in the third period of canal building, 1719–21, after three abortive attempts, the first Weaver Act being passed on 23 March 1721.[20] Most of the straightening and dredging work was completed in 1732.[21]

From 1760 until nationalisation under the Transport Act of 1947, the concern was publicly owned by the Cheshire County Council and run by County Trustees. This arrangement was not unique, but it was 'the main British example of what happened …often on the Continent'.[22] The Act of 1721 appointed a body of

---

[18]The completion of this project marked the first instance of the opening of a major sub-aqueous tunnel. G.W. Parkin, *The Mersey Railway* (Oakwood Press, 1978), p. 11.

[19]OS NGR 535558.

[20]T.S.Willan, *The Navigation of the River Weaver in the 18th Century* (Manchester: The Chetham Society,1951), p.120.

[21]*Hadfields British Canals,* 8th Edition, ed. Joseph Boughey (Stroud: Alan Sutton, 1994), pp. 9 and 65.

[22]*Hadfields, Ibid*, p.161.

Commissioners, eighty-six of the leading gentry of the county, who took little part in the day-to-day running of the canal, leaving that to a team of 'Undertakers'. After complaints about poor management, an Act of 1760 reconstructed the Commissioners as 105 named 'Trustees', with overall responsibility. They consisted of 'six peers, six honourables, thirteen baronets and knights, seventy-two esquires, eight reverends and doctors of divinity'.[23] A further Act of 1894 reduced the total to thirty-eight, only ten of whom were 'traditional Trustees', and 12 County Council representatives, who had to possess the original property qualification: 'A seizin[24] of land or buildings in the County of Chester of the value of at least £100 per annum'.[25] These Trustees stood up against railway opposition in the 1840s 'so formidably that the railway companies treated them with respect'.[26] At a special meeting of the Trustees on 6 January 1862, they voted unanimously to oppose the deposited plans of the West Cheshire Railway, the Birkenhead Docks Railway and the West Cheshire Junction Railway, among others.[27] By 1830 they were making some £30,000 a year from its business, and contributing significant sums to the County Council in relief of rates.[28] From 1820 onwards the new and growing chemical industry in the Northwich area added to the traffic of the company. Alkali and chlorine production is based on salt as a raw material.[29] In 1876 the tonnage of salt shipped down the River Weaver from Winsford and Northwich was 1,015,337 White (i.e. evaporated), and 115,803 Rock.[30]

The list of the Trustees at that time read like a roll-call of the wealthy and influential of Cheshire life, and one historian[31] said that 'it was only natural that the landed gentry were in control of the navigation, not because of the social structure of Cheshire' (though a perceptive observer might be forgiven for assuming that such was the reason), 'but because it was not a private enterprise

---

[23]Willan, p. 73.
[24]Or seisin – a freehold possession.
[25]Albert F. Calvert, *Salt in Cheshire* (E. & F. Spon Ltd., 1915), pp.472 and 473.
[26]*Hadfield's*, p.161.
[27]PRO RAIL 888/110.
[28]*Hadfield's*, pp.66 and 166.
[29]Harry Wardale, 'The Weaver Navigation', in *Transactions of the Lancashire and Cheshire Antiquarian Society*, Vol. XLIX (1910), p.9.
[30]Calvert, p.490.
[31]Willan, pp.136 and 137.

but a public trust of which the profits went to the County. It was', he argued, 'natural and fitting therefore that the men who governed the County also control its Trust.' It is noteworthy that in 1951 in Cheshire, over a hundred years after the first Reform Bill, the landed gentry could still be spoken of as 'governing the County'. He admitted, however, that as society changed in the late eighteenth century 'pressure grew to expand the constituency from which the Trustees were drawn', and the 'self-elected body of landowners, gentry and clergy' began 'to admit representatives of the trading communities'.

Still, three-quarters of the way through the nineteenth century, the Trustees were a solid Tory phalanx to disturb the composure of many a calmer man of Liberal disposition than Sir Edward. He was admitted to their number as one of ten new Trustees at their meeting of 7 July 1870.[32] He fulfilled the qualification of a person of standing and influence in the county as a JP for Chester (as was his fellow-Trustee and director of the MS&LR, John Chapman, who had been Deputy Lieutenant of the County and, in 1855, High Sheriff), he was a knight of the realm, and had only recently (1868) ceased to be an MP for a Cheshire constituency. Further, as Chairman of the MS&LR he had considerable involvement in canals in Cheshire, South Yorkshire and North Derbyshire owned or leased by that company.[33]

Watkin was, in fact, unlike most railway managers, strongly in favour of canals, where, in the interest of free trade and competition, they afforded advantages. When the Manchester Ship Canal was proposed in June 1882, he advised the MS&L Board not to oppose it, out of respect for the wishes of the people of Manchester, and his Cheshire Lines Committee was the first railway to establish a rail connection (at Cornbrook) with the new Manchester docks in 1891.[34] 'The railways' hostility to the scheme never wavered', said one historian.[35] That was true, with the exception of the MS&LR. At the half-yearly shareholders' meeting on 24

---

[32]All quotations and facts are from the Trustees Minute Books, Chester County Archives, except where otherwise acknowledged.

[33]*Hadfield,* pp.188 etc. Dow, Vol. 1, pp.113–16; Vol. 2, pp.219 and 220.

[34]D.A. Farnie, *The Manchester Ship Canal and the Rise of the Port of Manchester* (Manchester University Press, 1980), p.124.

[35]Jack Simmons, *The Railway in Town and Country,1830-1914* (David and Charles, 1986), p.138.

January 1883, Watkin reported 'The Board, acting, I admit, upon my advice, and I take the responsibility of it, did not think it was their duty to oppose the Ship Canal upon its merits. They thought that if the population of Manchester thought it fit to find the capital for a great work of this kind[36]...it did not lie with them to oppose it (Hear, hear).'[37] He said he never had any jealousy on the question of competition between water and rail, there being a trade for each of them. In this neighbourhood, he pointed out, 'there are only two canals [whose] competition is worthy of being estimated at one farthing'. These were the Bridgewater Canal and the River Weaver Navigation. 'The River Weaver Navigation is a powerful element of competition, because by the sagacity of the River Weaver Trustees...they can bring steamers of respectable size almost up to Northwich bridge.'[38]

The Cheshire Lines Committee was also helpful to the project in accepting the necessity for the gradients to enable the railway to cross the new canal at a height of at least 75 feet, where the LNWR and the GWR went to litigation for compensation.[39] Alfred Watkin, the second son of Edward's brother Alfred, was the fifth chairman of the Manchester Ship Canal Company, from 1931 to 1933. Edward's idea, with Cobden, of including the working class in the Liberal Free Trade movement in the 1840s, mapping out the whole city and dividing it into organisational sections, was influential in the 'Popular Capitalism' approach of the Ship Canal planners. It was one of Watkin's employees on the MS&L working on the purchase of the Bridgewater Navigation, Joseph Lawrence, who became manager in 1882 for the Ship Canal Provisional Committee, and he used the same methods.[40]

At the Weaver Trustees meeting following Watkin's admission, the clerk drew their attention to some Notices of Application to Parliament, one of which concerned a proposal for 'making a railway from Sandbach to Winsford and a branch therefrom'. It is not clear how many of the twenty-six Trustees present were aware

---

[36]It was financed by the City Council and large and small people acting together, and not by great capitalists alone, in true Lancashire Co-operative tradition (Ian Harford, *Manchester and its Ship Canal Movement* (Keele, Ryburn Publishing, 1994), p.9).

[37]PRO RAIL 463/77, p.11.

[38]*Ibid*, pp.12 and 13.

[39]David Owen, *The Manchester Ship Canal* (Manchester University Press, 1983), pp.60 and 61.

[40]Ian Harford, p.79.

of the presence in their midst of the originator of that Notice. Watkin was not recorded as saying anything at that meeting, but at the one following on 6 July 1871[41] he proposed an application to Parliament over the Trustees' desire for a boat lift and basin at Anderton, near Northwich, to enable the interchange of traffic between the River Weaver and the North Staffordshire (Trent and Mersey) Canal. Consideration was postponed to a special meeting on 12 October, which 'ordered that the Finance Committee and Works, with such of the Trustees as are members of either House of Parliament, with the addition of Sir Edward Watkin', and three others, 'be a Parliamentary Committee to instruct our Clerk from time to time with respect to the proposed Bill'.

The Committee's Draft Bill was approved on 4 December 1871. A special general meeting was held on 8 January 1872 to discuss a requisition from three of the Trustees – Sir Edward, Thomas Ashton and John Laird.[42] This was 'to reconsider the form of the 8th Clause of a deposited Bill respecting payments to the County ...in order that any alteration to be made in such Clause may be proposed to the Committee in Parliament, to whom the Bill may be referred'. The Minutes record agreement on certain itemised amendments which bear the stamp of Sir Edward's acumen in parliamentary procedures. Another special meeting was called on 18 April 1873, to decide upon 'the steps to be taken with respect to the Bills in Parliament [affecting the Trustees' interests]'. One of these steps was to empower the Trustees' parliamentary committee to confer with the promoters of the Bills in order to achieve mutual agreement, failing which Parliament should be requested to oppose them. At the meeting of 2 June, the Trustees expressed gratification that the Cheshire Lines Committee had withdrawn certain development proposals (unspecified) to which the Trustees had objected. These particular negotiations placed Watkin on both sides of the discussion, and clearly he had been willing to come to conciliatory decisions.

However, signs began to emerge that his natural impatience was beginning to be provoked. He was not present at the meeting of 4 October 1875, at which the clerk 'read a letter from Sir Edward

---

[41]Meetings were held monthly, at Castle Northwich.
[42]Conservative MP for Birkenhead and a prominent shipbuilder there.

Watkin's secretary to Mr E. Leader Williams'. The Trustees responded: 'We direct our Clerk to acknowledge its receipt, and to state that no reflection upon Mr Williams' professional Reputation had been made by the Trustees.' There is no record in the minutes of what Watkin had said, or of what had occasioned his letter, but Edward Leader Williams, jnr, was the Weaver Navigation's consultant engineer for the Anderton Lift Project. From 1856 to 1872, he had been the Weaver Navigation's 'very effective' engineer.[43] 'During his term of office, the "Weaver" rose to new heights of efficiency.'[44] The Anderton Boat Lift, designed by Edward Clarke, was opened in 1875. It 'provided a blueprint for boat lifts all over the world'.[45] It must be assumed that some supposed dilatoriness on Williams' part had aroused Sir Edward's ire. Such an attack on a respected engineer echoes his brusque words of rebuke to John Fowler on the Metropolitan three years before. On the other hand, that all was not well in the Trustees' engineering department emerged fifteen months later, when they met 'to consider the competency of the Company's Engineer', John West Sanderson. He forestalled their judgement by resigning before the meeting. Later, E. Leader Williams carried through the construction of the Manchester Ship Canal, after the completion of which he was knighted.[46] But even on the MSC all was not well. With the work well under way, it emerged that another £1.49 million was needed to complete the canal, and a leading shareholder declared that the problem was due to bad engineering, and proposed that a younger engineer be put in charge.[47]

Watkin was present at the 8 January 1877 meeting, but for the last time. He had attended only 13 of 234 possible occasions – an unusual record for him in any of his responsibilities. John Chapman ceased to be a Trustee in that year, having died on 18 July.[48]

---

[43]Ted Gray, *A Hundred Years of the Manchester Ship Canal Company* (Aurora Publishing Ltd., 1994), p.26.

[44]Edward W Paget-Tomlinson, *Canal and River Navigation* (Wolverhampton, Wayne Research, 1978), p.238.

[45]Restoration Appeal Literature, April 2000.

[46]Harry Wardale, *ibid*, p.8n.

[47]Ian Harford, p.159.

[48]Dow, Vol. 2, p.109.

The Public Benefactor.

From time to time, Watkin was a benefactor in most of the places where he lived, or represented in Parliament. But it was, perhaps, in the village of Northenden, Cheshire, that he played the most significant part. Northenden parish, at the end of the eighteenth century, comprised one village and four hamlets of 187 houses. It was three miles in length and one mile wide. The Diocesan Visitation of 1789 recorded one family 'of note', that of Willam Tatton Egerton, at Wythenshawe Hall, a member of the Egerton of Tatton family who owned most of Wythenshawe as well as Tatton Hall, Knutsford.[49] Absolom had been impressed by Northenden's pleasant rural countryside on his visit to Joseph Johnson, his partner in the reform movement in Manchester, and in 1832 had bought the house called Rose Hill, which Edward inherited in 1861.

Local accounts report that Edward was energetic in support of Northenden Working Men's Club, which opened in 1866 with a programme of speakers, of which he was one. In 1867 it began a series of Saturday evening lectures. The first of these, in February of that year, was by the Rector, on 'Natural History', and at a subsequent meeting 'Edward Watkin MP gave a reading of selections from various authors, including poems by Thomas Hood, and popular ballads in the Lancashire dialect. These afforded much interest and amusement.'[50] In the same year the Free Library moved to the Reading Room of the Working Men's Club. 'Mr.Tatton presented a set of Sir Walter Scott's Novels, and Mr.Watkin gave one hundred volumes of Dickens and other popular writers.'[51]

Five years later the Free Library Movement was inaugurated in nearby Stockport at a public meeting addressed by Watkin, held at the Mechanics' Institute. Watkin offered to present two thousand volumes to start the project. Several years elapsed, due to local administrative difficulties, before the scheme took shape, but

---

[49]Derick Deakin (ed.), *Wythenshawe: The Story of a Garden City* (Chichester, Philimore and Company, 1989), p.16.
[50]W.H. Shercliff (ed.), *Wythenshawe: A History of the Townships of Northenden, Northen Etchells and Baguley* (Manchester, J. Morten, 1974); 2 Vols., Vol. 1, p.268.
[51]*Ibid*, p.269.

clearly, though he had ceased to be Stockport's MP, he was still taking an interest in the town's welfare, and the education of its working men.[52]

From his time in Stockport there has survived a moving testimonial to his work for underprivileged children, a leather-bound gilt-embossed 'presentation' from the Ladies Committee of the Stockport Ragged and Industrial School in 1868, 'to congratulate Sir Edward on his Knighthood'.

> The frequent Annual Excursions, princely in their character and surroundings that Sir Edward W.Watkin has so bounteously provided for the Children and Friends of this institution have produced a remarkably beneficial influence. Sympathy, the universal bond which ought to unite all classes of Society, has been evoked, the germ of many a high resolve has taken root on these Golden Days in the lives of the Juvenile Vagrants, the goodly development of which may be traced in every Annual Report; for of the 352 Children trained in this Institution 150 are known to be doing well.

> The Ladies Committee trust that Sir Edward Watkin may long enjoy the honour conferred upon him, and, as the Knights of old, ever continue to be the chivalrous supporter of the Poor, the Destitute, and the Oppressed.

> 'For his bounty/ there was no winter in't. An Harvest 'twas That grew the more by reaping.'[53] 1 October 1868.[54]

The *Manchester Courier* said of Watkin that he was 'a zealous worker in all causes which tended to the social, moral, and intellectual improvement of the people'.[55]

In Northenden, 'Field Days' – outings for local children, numbering over 200 usually – took place each year to nearby farms, parks and houses, often under Watkin's auspices. In 1872 the outing was more ambitious, when he and his lady invited children and teachers from the three schools – Northenden,

---

[52]*Stockport Advertiser,* 25 September 1925.
[53]Quoted from Shakespeare, *Antony and Cleopatra,* Act 5, scene 2: Cleopatra describing Antony. Shakespeare has 'Autumn' for 'Harvest'.
[54]Book in the possession of Miss Dorothea Worsley-Taylor of Clitheroe.
[55]20 April 1901.

182

Sharston and Shadow Moss – in a special train to Woodhead. 'There, the children enjoyed buns and milk, a ramble on the hills, then tea and cakes before returning to Northenden for seven o'clock. On these occasions, Watkin was a genial host.'[56]

In 1872, the parish church, dedicated to St Wilfrid, built in the sixteenth century on Saxon and Norman foundations, was found to have been weakened by alterations made over the years. The decision was taken in 1873 to rebuild it. The architect was Joseph Stretch Crowther (1832–93), who was well-known for his restoration of Manchester Cathedral. The foundation-stone of the new parish church was laid on 11 April 1874 by T.W. Tatton of Wythenshawe Hall, and 'many influential families attended the ceremony'. A procession was formed at the Rectory, led by fifteen clergy, including the Rector, Edward Ralph Johnson, Archdeacon of Chester, and the Rural Dean, R.H. Brown. They were followed 'by a large company of ladies and gentlemen, including the High Sheriff of the County Sir Edward W. Watkin, and Lady Watkin, Mr Hugh Birley, MP,[57] the Mayor of Manchester (Mr Alderman Watkin), officers and children of the Sunday School, and Mr T.W.Tatton'. The new church was to the old design, and the cost was £13,000. The cost of the rebuilding was raised by appeal, and the largest amounts contributed were recorded as 'Thos W. Tatton, £850; Gibbs, Bailey and Worthington, £850; Sir Edward W.Watkin, £500; Lady Watkin, £350.0s.9d.'; plus two other donations of £500.[58] Mary Watkin's figure is curious. Could it be accounted for by the fact that, with her husband's, it made them, jointly, the largest contributor?

As part of the celebration of the Queen's Golden Jubilee in 1887, Watkin and his wife opened Rose Hill in the September for a party for the children, who had been given a special day off school.[59] They later invited fifty 'old women' of the parish to a dinner; the definition was fifty years of age, but a later extension reduced this to forty-five. Two omnibuses conveyed them from

---

[56]Shercliff, pp.266 and 191.
[57]Hugh Birley was MP for Manchester from 1868 to 1883, a Cotton-Spinner and well-known to the Watkin family. He was a Conservative, but not, it seems, of the type of an older member of the clan, H.H.Birley, who had been the notorious Captain of Yeomanry at Peterloo. [Goffin, p.240].
[58]Northenden Parish Church Records.
[59]Shercliff, p.290.

their several homes to Rose Hill (and back again afterwards), and each guest was individually 'received' by their host and hostess. They all were given a shawl and a new Jubilee half-crown, and those unable to attend had their gifts delivered to them. The menu for the 'sumptuous dinner included geese, beef, mutton, veal... vegetables, plum puddings and tarts, and beverages were served according to the several tastes and wishes of the consumers'. The health of Sir Edward was proposed by the steward, Mr Mullett, who said that during the fourteen years he had been in their service, he had never once had an unkind word, and couldn't say how many he had deserved. 'Always popular in the district, Sir Edward and Lady Watkin, by their generosity, and their recent distribution of cloaks to the girls of the village, have drawn to themselves a respect and esteem it is given to but few to enjoy.'[60]

There are two alabaster memorials in the parish church. One, on the south wall, to Absolom, was erected by Edward and his sister Elizabeth, and is surmounted by a plain Cross. Opposite, on the north wall, is a similar one to Edward, erected by his two children. This is decorated, from time to time, by a photograph of him, and several verses and pictures by the children of the parish school. Most of the stained glass windows were donated, mainly by the Tatton and Egerton families, and the Watkins. The most easterly window in the north aisle was a gift, on the occasion of a birthday anniversary of Edward's wife, and on the wall to the north of the west door is a window in memory of Absolom Watkin and his wife Elizabeth. It has three lights, depicting St Elizabeth, St John the Baptist and St Anne. The other window in the west wall, to the south, was given by Edward 'To the glory of God and in acknowledgement of many mercies', in memory of Mary Watkin, whose likeness appears in the bottom left-hand corner. The three lights depict St Mary Magdalene, The Blessed Virgin Mary and Mary of Bethany. The window to the west of this memorial is to the memory of Absolom's friend, Joseph Johnson (1791–1822), who was imprisoned for his part on the Speaker's platform at Peterloo in 1819, given by his grandchildren.

Not all was sweetness and light, however, in Edward's relationship with the village. The parish records include a correspondence

---

[60]*Folkestone Gazette,* 6 November 1888, quoting the *Stockport Advertiser* at length.

regarding his attempts to secure the right to one of the church pews for his son, Alfred. He wrote a letter on 12 December 1870 to John Leigh, Churchwarden, to ask if he would allow the pew at present occupied by Mr Leigh to be acknowledged as belonging by right to Alfred, who was the present owner of the Hazlehurst Estate in the parish, to which property the pew belonged historically. One of the previous owners of the house had been a Dissenter, and thus had no need to occupy the pew for his thirty years of ownership. His successors, who were churchpeople, found it occupied and sat elsewhere, but Sir Edward wished the legal position to be properly established. His son, he said, had no desire to cause the least trouble or inconvenience, and was quite prepared to sit elsewhere, so long as his right was acknowledged. Unfortunately, his courteous letter included a reference (though entirely polite) to the way a fence at the corner of the drive leading to Rose Hill from Longley Lane had encroached by a yard on to his property, making the turn into the lane more difficult. He offered to pay what it took to restore the fence's original line; but it might have been more sound psychologically to have written separately on that point. Accordingly, Mr Leigh replied on the next day with a bold summary of the occupants of the disputed pew 'for near thirty years', and considered that he had 'a perfect right to it'. Regarding the fence, 'there had been no encroachment', and he was 'not disposed to make any alteration' to his Northenden property.

Sir Edward then wrote to the Senior Churchwarden, with copies of the letters exchanged, asking him 'to investigate the facts', and to re-iterate that if put in possession, his son would gladly allow Mr Leigh to use the pew, but his right to it 'should not be treated with defiance'. This triggered a correspondence which continued until April 1871, in which the churchwardens argued that the right had lapsed, because the Faculty had originally been issued in the name of the owner of the house or estate of Hazlehurst as an individual, and not to the house or estate as such. They had taken counsel, and the fact was that control of the pews was 'entirely vested' in the Churchwardens. This was true, as when legal faculties were granted, they usually applied to named families (normally only for so long as they remained parishioners) or named places of residence, for the benefit of whosoever lived there for the time being, 'though most usually without intention to make it perma-

185

nent'[61] Watkin had also taken counsel at 'the highest authority', who advised that Mr Leigh had 'no rights whatever, and is in illegal possession'. The correspondence ends there, and it seems that Watkin let the matter drop, and Alfred continued to sit elsewhere in the church, and with his father left to negotiate with difficulty the altered turn into his drive. The 'highest authority' quoted by Watkin, presumably Mr Justice Mellor, QC, was clearly no expert on this recondite area of law. The pew difficulty was a clear example of how Watkin could exhibit the greatest stubbornness when he thought he was in the right, as was particularly true in protection of his son's welfare.

Another well-documented correspondence was exchanged by him and the Rector and Churchwardens between early 1869 and the summer of 1879: this time over a need for the enlargement of the churchyard. Thomas Lings, Senior Churchwarden, set out a proposal to take part of one of Watkin's fields for the purpose, in exchange for a plot of similar size. Sir Edward's response to the Rector,[62] from London Bridge Station,[63] raises some points of his view of the matter. He could never consent to the allied proposal to encroach on the Rectory garden and cut down its hedges and trees; he was not happy with the perceived necessity for a *square* churchyard. 'If it were essential to spoil the shape of my field in the way proposed,' he wrote, he 'would endorse it – *pro bono publico* – but it is not. What witchery is there in a square churchyard?' he asked. 'Our ancestors have slept quietly for ages in odd-shaped pieces hitherto.' Another letter of the same day (some evidence of passion here) makes the same points in more detail, and suggests that there were other pieces of land available without taking a 'single nick' of the Rector's garden, and distorting and prejudicing the future of his [Watkin's] own Belcroft property. This bore some old cottages, which he intended to demolish,[64] with a view to building some half a dozen nice 'modern' houses

---

[61]Alfred Heales, *History and Law of Church Seats* (London, Butterworths, 1872), pp.99, 115 and 116.

[62]29 April 1870.

[63]His letters in this series are written variously from six different addresses: 6 Cleveland Row, St James's, SW; 32 Westbourne Terrace, W (Metropolitan Railway HQ); London Bridge Station, SE. (South Eastern Railway HQ); London Road Station, Manchester (MS&LR HQ); 18 Westbourne Terrace, Hyde Park, W; Holly Bank, Sale, Cheshire (his brother Alfred's home – 7 July 1879).

[64]He did so in March 1879, and built two cottages, The Hollies and Church Villa.

there. He was also concerned about the continued existence of a public footpath to the next village, Gatley, involved in the proposals. However, in reply to the Rector,[65] who had clearly raised wider issues, Watkin, after mentioning the compulsory purchase of lands for public purposes, and the anxiety caused locally by developments taking place in the growth of the village to a suburb, and suburb to town, concluded that 'Whatever you decide will have my poor aid and help so far as I am able to render it'.

The discussion had dragged on for ten years, but in the end both parties were satisfied: the church had its churchyard extension, and a handsomely over-the-odds payment for the release of some of its own land, and Watkin could develop his building plot and a second carriageway.

In 1879, he resigned as Trustee of Sharston School, in favour of someone on the spot 'who can find time to attend to the duties, which at present [he was] far too occupied to be able to do'.[66] In the midst of all his high-level business and political activities, it is revealing that he had continued with such lowly responsibilities.

Throughout the years 1870 to 1879 Watkin's letters[67] mention in passing bouts of illness, and, more seriously, Mary Watkin's deteriorating health. He refers on 7 June 1879 to his obtaining 'medical appliances' for her 'severe illness'. As she had another nine years to live (she died on 8 March 1888), her last years must have been very constrained and painful.

Watkin was High Sheriff of Cheshire in the year 1874. The office, as representative of the Crown in Cheshire, is the oldest in the county, having been established before AD 1000. The High Sheriff was originally responsible for everything that happened in the shire: he had full police powers, was in charge of all Crown property, he judged all cases with the Bishop, and also nominated representatives of the shire to Parliament. In more recent years his role has been far less onerous, but he is still appointed by the Monarch. The main responsibility is to attend upon the High Court Judges visiting the county. Upholding law and order remains partly his charge, as is uniting the Sovereign's subjects in loyalty to the Crown.[68] 'Watkin served his year with due magnifi-

[65] 17 July 1879.
[66] Watkin to Deacle, 7 July.
[67] For example, 29 April 1870.
[68] *Cheshire Life*, April 1999, p.163.

cence.'[69] By the end of his life he had become the oldest Justice of the Peace of the Stockport County Petty Sessional Division, having been made a magistrate for Cheshire in 1864.[70]

In 1875, 'Lord Chief Justice Cockburn visited Manchester[71], and was the guest of Sir Edward Watkin, MP, at Northenden.'[72] On the Friday he went to the Town Hall, where he was presented with an address by the Corporation.[73] Subsequently, the Lord Chief Justice, the Marquis and Marchioness of Salisbury, with John Arthur Roebuck, MP,[74] and his daughter, inspected the loan of pictures and other works of art at the Athenaeum, visited the Owens College (which five years later became the University), and the Royal Exchange. The next day, the Marquess of Salisbury received an address from the Chamber of Commerce, and afterwards, in the company of the Lord Chief Justice and others, visited Peel Park, where they lunched with the Mayor of Salford.[75] Judging by the five places visited, Watkin also arranged the whole event, on the basis of 'personal influence and achievement'.

Another Manchester engagement was an invitation to speak at the twenty-fifth anniversary of the founding, on 4 June 1859, of the Manchester and Salford Co-operative Society, in the form of a tea-party on 8 November 1884 at Belle Vue Manchester, attended by 10,000 people. The principal speakers were the Dean of Manchester, John Oakley, recently appointed from the Deanery of Carlisle Cathedral, Sir Edward, and Mr David Adamson.[76] The Co-operative Movement, as a matter of principle, had been very close to Watkin's sympathies, and 'it was left to him to make explicit the ideological function of co-operation'. He looked upon 'Co-operative Societies as the golden

---

[69]*Momus*, 13 November 1879, p.82.

[70]*Stockport Advertiser*, 19 April 1901.He served also as a magistrate for Manchester, Lancashire and Kent.

[71]On Thursday 21 January.

[72]William E.A. Axon, *Annals of Manchester* (Manchester: John Heywood, 1886), p.347.

[73]Sir Alexander James Cockburn (1801–80) was an intimate friend of Disraeli, who described him as 'A man of transcendent abilities...learning, and majesty.' (*DNB*, Vol. 4, pp.633–7).

[74]Roebuck (1801–79) was Member of Parliament for Sheffield from 1849 to 1869, and from February 1874 until his death. He was the author of, *inter alia*, *The Colonies of England*, and was 'Sometime agent in England for the House of Assembly of Lower Canada'. (M. Stenton ed.), *Who's Who of British Members of Parliament* (Harvester Press Ltd., 1976), Volume 1, p.24).

[75]Axon, *ibid*.

[76]*Ibid*, p.408.

bridge which spanned the interests of competition with the interests of co-operation. It was the resource which, where there were conflicts between capital and labour, came in so usefully and so well, to show men that they had mutual interests provided they had mutual trusts.'[77]

Watkin's benefactions extended also to his other spheres of influence, in Manchester and the South East. A special meeting of the shareholders of the Manchester, Sheffield and Lincolnshire Railway was held on 1 April 1887 to discuss the suggestion, by the Prince of Wales, for establishing a national memorial of the Golden Jubilee of Her Majesty's reign, and the possibility of a contribution from the company. In a long address, Watkin regretted some of the opposition to the suggestion nationally, and certain comments in Manchester that his support for it was 'only another attempt of Sir Edward Watkin to get the proprietors to do exactly as he wishes'. He commended himself as an example of one whose advice on giving money was worth following: 'Something I have never told you before,' he said, 'is that during the last eleven years I have given out of my own pocket...£5,000...in connection with the Manchester, Sheffield and Lincolnshire Railway.' He listed compensation to the victims of the dreadful accident of two or three years ago, and the cost of legal proceedings. As the population of Grimsby increased from 7,000 at the beginning of their investment in that place to about the present 40,000 to 50,000, they needed 'schools, chapels, churches, institutions for fishing lads, mechanics institutions, and all the adjuncts that ought to surround and grow up with the advancing prosperity and civilisation of a large town'. He could have mentioned that his wife was a benefactor in her own right: among other things it is recorded that she provided garden seats in Grimsby, near the Alexandra Docks.[78] 'Who was ready for the money for these things?' he continued. 'I was. There is hardly a church or a chapel...that has not my mark upon it, hardly an institution to which I have not contributed. I took what generous men would call a chivalrous, and what ungenerous men would call a Quixotic, course of action (Applause). All this would be taken out of profit and loss if this

---

[77]Ian Harford, *Manchester and its Ship Canal Movement* (Keele, Ryburn Publishing, 1994), p.137.
[78]*Grimsby Observer and Humber News,* Wednesday, 14 July 1880.

were Mr Thomas's Mill, or a joint stock factory, and if anyone thinks all this should have been paid by this co-partnery [sic], [let them] pay it back to me...and I will give the whole to the Imperial Institute.'[79]

Parading one's generosity with the blowing of trumpets on street corners has never been considered a godly virtue. But this was to a gathering of men who had a legitimate interest in financial activities concerning their business, and Watkin was trying to encourage support for a heartfelt project. He appealed, finally, to his view of the British Empire and the benign rule of the Monarch. His resolution was seconded by Sutcliffe-Thomas of Yorkshire, who offered the information that Manchester was the centre of the largest population in the Empire in a given radius, which included both Lancashire and Yorkshire.[80]

In the debate, Vernon K. Armitage objected to 'A considerable amount of what the Americans call "waving the flag". When Sir Edward Watkin confines himself to railway matters we listen to him with great respect. Out of respect for him we let him go further from time to time; we allow him to talk politics to us' (Watkin had begun his address by enlarging on his political position as 'One of the old Radical party, not a Little England Radical, nor a Disunion Radical, but one of the real old sort') 'and we listen to him out of the respect we have for him on other matters; listen to him with...something like a slightly contemptuous amusement, because we do not recognise Sir Edward Watkin's opinion upon political matters as being of the smallest value whatever. On questions of railway matters we listen to [him] with infinite respect, and we draw the line there.'[81] After further debate, the motion was carried with only thirteen votes against.

Watkin arranged, in the name of the South Eastern Railway, to supply food to the city of Paris during Bismarck's siege in the Franco-Prussian War.[82] In recognition of this, a Napoleon III Medallion was presented to him in February 1871.[83]

In 1888 he took it upon himself to restore a decaying monument

---

[79]PRO RAIL, 463/77, pp.7, 8 and 9.
[80]Ibid, p.10–17.
[81]Ibid, pp.11 and 19. Watkin, later in the meeting, dealt with his assailant with some sarcasm.
[82]19 September 1870, for four months.
[83]In the possession of Miss Dorothea Worsley-Taylor.

in the Cheriton Road cemetery at Folkestone, erected by the German Government in memory of officers and men who lost their lives when the battleship *Grosser Kurfürst*[84] was wrecked six miles off the shore with a loss of 284 officers and men. The ship had been in a collision with the German flagship *König Wilhelm* during manoeuvres, while trying to avoid a Norwegian barque.[85] Because it was a national monument, Watkin felt it would be embarrassing to the Germans if it were allowed to fall into ruin, and arranged for its restoration. The Secretary of the South Eastern Railway wrote on 27 April 1888 to the German Embassy, informing the Ambassador of what had been done, and saying that Sir Edward trusted that he was justified in availing himself of the opportunity 'to testify his regard for your countrymen, from whom he and his constituents have experienced unvarying kindness and consideration'. The Ambassador conveyed the sincere thanks of the Imperial Government to Sir Edward, adding that steps had been taken 'to maintain the monument in its present excellent state of preservation to which Sir Edward has so kindly contributed'.[86]

His method of chairing shareholders' meetings was notoriously high-handed, but he was very different when addressing other kinds of gathering, especially when the audience was predominantly of young people. When invited as the main guest at a school prize distribution, he would invariably come well-versed in the details of some recent scientific discovery, and explain it in terms which his audience could understand.[87]

His standing as a local benefactor was particularly high in Hythe and Folkestone, of which constituency he was the parliamentary representative for so long. His eventual retirement from his seat in the Commons, in 1895, was 'to the regret of all. He had not only been the railway king, but the king of Folkestone...From the highest to the smallest social function he was always ready to be in attendance. He exercised a quiet and unostentatious charity, and it

---

[84]'Great Elector' – the title of a Prince of the Holy Roman Empire who had the right to participate in the election of the Emperor.
[85]*Folkestone Gazette*, 3 November 1888; *Folkestone Express*, 18 June 1881; *Folkestone Gazette*, 29 May 1978.
[86]*Folkestone Gazette*, 24 February 1953; *The Herald*, 24 June 1999. The German Government carried out renovations in 1924 and 1953.
[87]*Financial News*, 16 April 1901.

is with gratitude that he will be remembered in Folkestone. He was the grand old man whose pocket was ever open to the needs of his constituents, who combined business with philanthropy, and opulent kindness to a fault.'[88]

[88] *Kent Messenger*, 20 April 1901.

13

Watkin The Politician

'A Parliamentary Political career attracted unprecedented interest among the business community in the period that followed the Second Reform Act. Many who had earlier been content to work through the voluntary associations in pursuit of the social, philanthropic and political aims of their communities, now chose to go directly into parliament themselves, And the result was a fusion of previously somewhat distinct spheres of political and social organisation,' wrote H.L. Malchow.[1] '[Entering Parliament] seemed to them, as it would not have seemed to their fathers and grandfathers, a natural extension of entrepreneurial success.'[2]

As part of a reply to questions after a speech in Hythe Town Hall in 1885, Watkin revealed that he 'began political life as a young fellow of 16 or 17', and at that time he was campaigning against Mr Gladstone, who had gone to Manchester hoping to be elected as 'a High Church Tory candidate. We beat him by two or three to one.' He learnt how to make speeches, he said, with beer barrels, window ledges, and waggons as platforms.[3] In his twenties he was active in the promotion of city parks, the Saturday half-day holiday, and the provision of public baths and wash-houses.[4] He later served as a city councillor for the Exchange Ward of Manchester in the years 1859–62. His most important contribution there was the adoption, at his proposal, of the French system, in street improvements, of buying up vacant land adjoining new buildings. This ensured, when the land was later developed, that

---

[1]H.L. Malchow, *Gentleman Capitalists: The Social and Business World of the Victorian Businessman* (Stanford University Press, California, 1992), p.357.
[2]*Ibid*, p.1.
[3]Sir Edward Watkin, Bart., *Speeches* (London: C.F. Howarth, 1885), pp. 23 and 24.
[4]*Grimsby Observer*, 5 May 1880; Chapter 3, 2nd to 4th pages, above.

36 Manchester Town Hall, 1823–1877

the enhanced value of the street benefited the City Rate Fund, rather than the pockets of speculators. During his time with the Trent Valley Railway, in 1846, he was nominated as an Anti-Corn Law candidate for the forthcoming by-election in Stafford. A Liverpool merchant, Lawrence Heyworth, was asked by the Burgesses to stand as a Liberal and Free Trade candidate, and Protectionism was represented by a Dr Sleigh, of Chiswick, Middlesex. Dr Sleigh had been at a meeting in the Manchester Corn Exchange in 1841, which Watkin chaired, but had left early because of the opposition of the workers there to Protectionism.

At the Stafford meeting for the official adoption of candidates, Watkin was received with enthusiastic cheering. He described himself as 'a humble individual, appearing as a combatant of the scions of aristocratic houses and the nominees and representatives of sacred dukes (laughter), to represent the views of the people at large.' Quoting a *Daily News* report of the complaints from agricultural labourers about Protectionism, he asked the crowd if they were for the labourers or Dr Sleigh. He asked for a show of hands if they were for a total and immediate repeal of the Corn Laws, and a 'forest of hands' was raised. 'All who think that he

194

should go back to [The Duke of] Buckingham, raise your hands (a large show of hands amid laughter and cheering). Protectionism has been tried for hundreds of years, and it has not been to the benefit of the working man...In view of the feelings of this meeting, no defender of the Corn Laws ought to think of representing Stafford (cheers).' However, Watkin continued by stating that there existed on the Statute Book a law, 'made by the Aristocracy (friends of Dr Sleigh)', which says that no man could represent a constituency 'unless he possesses £300 a year, landed property. My property is the labour of my hands,' he went on, 'and the thoughts of my head. On that alone I wish to rely, and not on any broad acres; and on that account they will not allow me to go to the poll. But you have an opportunity of showing to the candidates your opinions; and at the next election you shall have a total repeal candidate, and a man who is in favour of popular principles.' (A voice – 'We'll have you now!') After further pointing out that a vote for Dr Sleigh would support the Duke of Buckingham's opposition to repeal, he concluded, 'There can be no thraldom exercised here by the aristocracy...and to you I appeal to record a vote in favour of the rights and interests of the common people of this country (Loud cheering).'

The Mayor then asked for show of hands for each of the candidates. A decided majority was in favour of Watkin, and the Mayor made his declaration to that effect, but Watkin, thanking him for his impartiality, pointed out that he did not have the necessary qualifications for candidature. If his lack of qualification were eventually upheld, he proposed that those who had voted for him should give their vote to Captain Carnegie, and urged them to do so.[5] Carnegie was adopted by 733 votes to 25.[6]

At the election, David Urquhart, Conservative, Chief of the Clan Urquhart of Cromarty, was elected, receiving 754 votes out of 1,547, Captain Carnegie's total being only 271.[7] Urquhart (1805–77) represented Stafford from that year to his retirement in 1852.[8]

---

[5]The Hon. Swynfen Thomas Carnegie (1813–79), Captain (RN), had been the Member for Stafford from 1841. He was a Conservative, but supported Free Trade, (Michael Stenton (ed.) *Who's Who of British Members of Parliament* (Harvester Press, 1976), 4 Vols. Vol. 1, p.67).

[6]*Staffordshire Advertiser*, 14 May 1846.

[7]*Ibid*, 31 July 1847, p.4.

[8]Stenton, Vol. 1, p.388.

Watkin's appearance at all as a possible candidate is strange, in that he knew all along that he was ineligible. The likelihood is that he wanted to make a point to illustrate the injustice of the statute, and also to try his hand at serious electioneering. Throughout his working life, he preferred to be seen as a politician with railway interests, rather than as a Railway King.[9]

Eight years later, the Home Secretary, Lord Palmerston, invited Watkin to head a Commissariat to investigate into the conditions of the army serving in the Crimean War, conditions which were assuming the status of a national scandal. In April 1855, Lord Ellenborough gave notice that he would move a resolution in the House of Lords censuring the government for their failure to remove incompetent administrators in the Crimea. Palmerston, giving way to public feeling, agreed to act. On 1 May he wrote to Panmure (Fox Maule, 2nd Baron, Secretary for War), telling him to appoint 'Mr Watkins' (sic), the Manager of the Manchester and Sheffield Railway, as head of the Commisariat in the Crimea in the place of William Filder: 'We cannot assign our Troops to the tender mercies of Filder.' He wrote to Panmure again on 8 May, urging him to appoint more efficient men than those at present in positions of authority, or the debate would be damaging to the government and the best interests of the country.[10] Edward declined the offer, on the grounds (revealingly, but reasonably) that without plenipotentiary authority, and that of military rank, the appointment would not carry the weight required for its effectiveness.[11]

It was only two years later that he entered Parliament itself, and, according to the 'Liberals of Exeter', in their panegyric after his work there in the 1873 election, his path to the House of Commons was directed by Richard Cobden. Whatever the impetus, Edward Watkin stood as a Liberal in the election of 1857 for the constituency of the Borough of Great Yarmouth, Norfolk. On 28 March that year he was elected by a majority of 158, William McCullagh being the other Member elected. Unfortunately, a petition was lodged against the result, on the grounds of

[9]*Momus*, 13 November 1879, pp.81–2.
[10]Jasper Ridley, *Lord Palmerston* (London: Constable, 1970), pp.439 and 440.
[11]E.W. Watkin, *Canada and the States: Recollections, 1851 to 1886* (London: Ward, Lock and Co., 1887), p. 8.

Undue Election and Return. A House of Commons Select Committee was set up to investigate, and held sittings between 23 and 29 July 1857. The committee heard evidence that bribery had influenced the election campaign of the two men elected. Several witnesses were called and cross-examined, and it was established that six people had been bribed before the voting, by four men acting as agents of the two candidates; that the two candidates were guilty, by their agents, of bribery; that the two were not therefore duly elected Burgesses to serve in Parliament for the Borough of Great Yarmouth; and, finally, that 'it was not proved to the Committee that the aforesaid acts of bribery were committed with the knowledge and consent of the said William Torrens McCullagh and Edward William Watkin.'[12]

This result was published, and caused 'great excitement' in the borough. '[Mr Watkin] was met at the railway station by several thousands of people, who gave him a most enthusiastic welcome; and, on his entering a carriage to proceed to the hotel, the horses were taken out, and the vehicle was drawn in procession round the town, by ropes, to the Star Hotel. Mr Watkin addressed an immense assemblage, of between ten and twenty thousand people, where he spoke for an hour and a half.'[13] A resolution was unanimously passed to the effect that the meeting deeply regretted the decision of the Election Committee by which the borough had been 'most unfairly and unjustly' deprived of the services of two esteemed and valued representatives. 'There is a great feeling of exasperation' at the committee, 'well known to have been a packed one, with a strong Tory bias'.[14] Whatever his agents had done overzealously in his cause, Watkin was clearly still held in good faith by the people he had hoped to represent, but his efforts to be nominated for the seat in the election of 1859 were unsuccessful. Despite his having been exonerated from the charge of corruption, that was the end of his political aspirations for the time being (though he declined an invitation to stand for Salford in 1859), and the affair was to reverberate during his next campaign. The matter needs to be put in context: 'In the nineteenth century if you

[12]House of Lords Record Office, London: *Minutes and Evidence of the Proceedings of the Select Committee on the Great Yarmouth Borough Election Petition*, 3 August 1857.
[13]W. Finch-Crisp, *History of Yarmouth, from AD 46 to 1877*. From the Internet.
[14]Folkestone Library Archives, newspaper cutting of 8 August 1857.

lost an election, you automatically petitioned for malpractice.'[15] Gladstone's brother Tom once lost an election but retrieved it on petition (1830), and once won an election and lost it on petition (1842).[16]

The Yarmouth affair was not laid completely to rest. *The Pall Mall Gazette* of 18 September 1866 reported that a Great Yarmouth Election Commission, which had completed its sitting of twenty-three days, would not be closing it business entirely, 'as there is some idea of investigating more fully the circumstances of the elections of 1859 and 1857'. This would involve summoning as witnesses six MPs, including Watkin, and 'Mr Justice Mellor', Watkin's cousin-in-law, who was MP for Great Yarmouth from July 1857 (thus having replaced Watkin) to March 1859. John Fildes, the Manchester stockbroker, and John Wintringham, a Grimsby solicitor, bear witness to a great deal of discomfort in Watkin at the prospect of further such high-profile investigations and their possible effect on his future reputation.[17]

The results of the 1866 enquiry by the Yarmouth Election Commission did not incriminate Watkin at all, as it happened. Such positive and repeated evidence of innocence counted for little, however, to those with a different axe to grind. In a House of Commons debate on Corrupt Practices at Elections on 19 March 1867, William Bagge, Member for West Norfolk,[18] rose to ask if certain Members of the House and Justices of the Peace, giving their names, had been found guilty of bribery in the recent past, and if so, 'to remove them from the several Commissions to which they belong'. One of the men so named, Philip Vanderbyl (1827-92), Member for Bridgwater, objected to the inclusion of his name, adding that he thought it was 'pretty well known that there must have been some peculiar motive' behind the hon. Gentleman's question. Watkin, also one of those named, replied to the question, relying 'on the good feeling of the House and its love of

---

[15]Charles Clifton Brown, MP, Channel 3 TV, 1.50 p.m., 23 August 1998, *Political Dynasties, No. 10.*

[16]Roy Jenkins, *Gladstone* (London: Macmillan, 1995), p.37.

[17]Fildes to Wintringham, September 1866. Wintringham Papers, North East Lincolnshire Archives. 223/5/4.

[18]A Conservative, strongly against Free Trade, he was a magistrate and Deputy-Lieutenant for Norfolk. He was MP for West Norfolk from 1837–57, and 1865–80 (Michael Stenton, *ibid*, pp 15 and 16).

fair play on both sides, to allow me to read a letter I addressed to the Lord Chancellor this morning.' He perfectly agreed with the hon. Member for West Norfolk 'that a man who would either give a bribe himself or wilfully and knowingly suffer a bribe to be given on his behalf, was not worthy to hold Her Majesty's Commission'. On seeing the Notice, he decided that the most honourable and manly course for him to pursue – 'and allow me to say that in following an honourable and manly course it is not necessary for me to take lessons in propriety from [the] hon. Gentleman opposite' – was to address the Lord Chancellor immediately. He then read his letter:

> My Lord, I respectfully apply to your Lordship to order a full inquiry into my personal conduct as impugned in the Report of the Great Yarmouth Commission [of 1866]. I entertain the opinion that any man who would himself give a bribe, and knowingly or wilfully would enable, or would knowingly countenance bribery and corruption, commits a serious offence...When the Commissioners first assembled...I volunteered to give evidence, but I regret to say that I was not called till October. I was my own voluntary accuser of an imprudence and indiscretion which I would rather exaggerate than excuse, and the blame of which I will not seek to lay at the door of those who might have protected me. In volunteering evidence, I felt it my duty in the public interest to assist the labours of the Commissioners, however far the truth might condemn me to inculpate myself, and I shall never regret the step I took, although it has enabled a more unjust and ungenerous report, which I challenge as contrary and in excess of the evidence as regards myself...I shall refrain from acting as a magistrate until I learn your Lordship's decision.[19]

This incident had a very happy consequence. On the following day Gladstone wrote to Watkin:

> You will have read the proceedings of the latter part of last evening. I cannot but congratulate you on the speech...by

---

[19] *Hansard*, CLXXXVI, 19 March 1867, c 127, 128.

which you had virtually placed yourself beyond their reach. I did indeed, while you were speaking, endeavour to signify my opinion, and I also had an opportunity subsequently of adverting in debate to the subject...I hope I do not take an unwarrantable liberty in this direct and personal communication. Which I hope, however, you will not trouble to acknowledge.[20]

Watkin's reply of the same date thanked him for his 'most generous aid last night', and for his 'true, genuine kindness'. Referring to his own view of the conflict between 'the manufacturing, managerial and working section of the population, and the leisurely, amateur, and garrulous ruling sector', he revealed: 'Having been brought in the school of *real* people, I have sometimes thought that these party politics dehumanise many. But your kindness shows that there are noble natures in which the heart can never be reduced to a calculating machine – even by politics.' He concluded by declaring 'solemnly that I never gave or authorised a bribe – as the future will show'.[21] Thus began a warm friendship between the two men which lasted for over thirty years.

Eleven years after being unseated at Great Yarmouth, Watkin stood for the constituency of Stockport. There is plenty of evidence that his preparation for this election was a hectic progress. The Earl of Yarborough, of Brocklesby Hall, near Grimsby, a director of the Manchester, Sheffield and Lincolnshire Railway, wrote to Edward[22] to assure him of his support in the candidature, through the agent of his estate, Stephen Gibbons.[23] To John Wintringham,[24] Gibbons said that a letter from his Lordship to Watkin asking questions about Grimsby and the Humber shipbuilding concern in which Watkin had a directorial hand, had received a reply which did not answer the points raised, but promised to see his Lordship personally after the Stockport election.[25] Watkin's reply, from the Queen's Hotel, Manchester,[26]

[20]Gladstone/Watkin Correspondence, BL Add. Mss. 44337, Folio 1.
[21]*Ibid*, ff 2, 3 and 4.
[22]1 March 1864.
[23]Wintringham Papers, 223/3/43.
[24]8 May.
[25]*Ibid*, 223/3/48.
[26]5 May.

is difficult to read, from the obvious haste of its execution. He promises 'to set matters right as soon as I can get rid of the hurry of the moment'.[27] Gibbons had written to Wintringham on 3 May that 'I can't understand Mr.W. I find he is a puzzle to other people as well.'[28]

Watkin's attention to clarifying his actions and intentions as he went along was less than total, due to his multiple commitments. This was in the period when he was criss-crossing the Atlantic in dealing with affairs in Canada. To Wintringham, who was also a local councillor in Grimsby,[29] John Fildes (who became Wintringham's father-in-law in 1864, and Liberal MP for Grimsby from 1865 to 1868), said: 'As I had only two minutes with Mr Watkin all I could ask him to do was to read your letter and reply to it. He has promised to do so but his engagements this week are such that it is doubtful if he will be able to fulfil his promise.'[30] However, when Watkin *could* be pinned down, he was attentive to what was being said. Fildes' letter to Wintringham of 5 January 1864 refers to some sensitive matter not specified: 'I felt a delicacy in mentioning it to Watkin. [But] he was most kind in the matter.'[31]

At a mass election meeting gathered before the public market house in Stockport on Friday, 6 May 1864, Watkin was commended as a candidate by Alderman McClure. He said Mr Watkin had done much for the borough during the last eleven years, and assured the crowd that the paucity of railway provision in the town would soon be improved. The proposed candidate had been well chosen from several worthy gentlemen, all of whom were fit and proper for the nomination. Alderman Wilkinson reported that not only was the Liberal Party united in their sponsorship of Mr Watkin, but so also were the Conservative Party. Watkin's less than complete commitment to party adherence was a feature of his whole political career. His becoming a Unionist in the Home Rule debate, in defiance of his personal friendship with Gladstone, and his standing as an Independent or as a joint candidate in his Hythe days were examples.

---

[27] *Ibid*, 223/3/75.
[28] *Ibid*, 223/3/47.
[29] 19 May 1863.
[30] *Ibid*, 223/2/14.
[31] *Ibid*, 223/3/1.

Unanimously accepted on a show of hands, Edward, in his acceptance speech, paid tribute to the MP for the previous sixteen years, Mr Kershaw, who had been 'a good merchant, a good employer, a faithful citizen, and a good subject'. He also praised him for remaining plain 'Mr Kershaw', 'without seeking to attach to his name some of those meretricious titles which political subserviency could always obtain. Peace to his memory.'[32] Watkin's speech also referred to foreign affairs, the high current rate of taxation, and the iniquities of a franchise which made 300 votes on the estate of a Southern landowner equal to the thousands who voted in Stockport. He stressed, with his customary array of carefully-researched figures, the benefits of Free Trade – to much applause – and ended with an encomium of public opinion, of which, he claimed, this country had more reason to be proud than any other: 'that glorious, healthy, manly, public opinion which...was founded upon the honesty, the truthfulness and love of fair play of the people at large'. This public opinion, he believed, 'could carry everything before it...It was improved, strengthened and purified by those teachings from the thousands of free pulpits which distinguished and illustrated the religious freedom of this land; it was informed and instructed by a free press...This public opinion,' he continued, 'forced Catholic Emancipation from the government of the Duke of Wellington; it extorted free trade from the protectionist government of Sir Robert Peel...' and 'there was no difficulty which it could not disentangle, no wrong which it could not redress (Applause).' He saw England as having a duty, as a great nation, to be just, to set an example of freedom and enlightenment, and 'to succeed in obtaining liberty for enslaved and enthralled people, and hastening that glorious time when "they shall beat their swords into plough-shares, and their spears into pruning-hooks; nation shall not lift up sword against nation, neither shall they learn war any more, but they shall sit every man under his vine and under his fig tree, and none shall make them afraid." '[33]

Stirring nineteenth-century rhetoric? No doubt. But there is also little doubt that he could stand behind his words. He was elected,

---

[32] *Stockport Advertiser*, Friday, 13 May 1864.
[33] *Ibid.*

202

unopposed, on 9 May 1864, and took his seat in Parliament. After his election, Watkin received a letter of congratulation from Montreal which would have gladdened him particularly. J. Curtis Cook, Secretary of the Mechanical Department of the Grand Trunk Railway of Canada wrote to say: '[His election would give] further occasion for the exercise of the Administrative ability and energy for which you are so eminently distinguished.'[34]

There was another contest for the seat as early as 11 July 1865, when a General Election was held. This Watkin won, with 733 votes, his fellow-Liberal John Benjamin Smith polling 658 (the first two candidates being returned), and the Conservative, William Tipping, 595. Because of an Act of extension of the suffrage, another General Election was held on 16 November 1868.[35] In his campaign, Watkin, at a public meeting to propose the candidates, declared that if, during this contest, 'I have uttered one word that has wounded the feelings of any of my opponents, or anyone connected with the Conservative Party, I regret it. I withdraw it, and apologise for it.' About the many things that had been said about him 'of a character that was certainly not kind,' he told them, 'I most freely forgive all those who have uttered anything that has given me pain,' and he expressed the hope that by tomorrow at four o'clock (that is, after the declaration of the result), 'not a single acrimonious feeling will remain in the minds of anyone.' He picked up the singing, by some of the crowd, of *Rule, Britannia*, commenting that at the last election, Britannia had not ruled. 'Who is Britannia?' he asked, and answered himself, 'Why, the British people – the subjects of the Queen in England, Scotland, Wales and Ireland, who, having obtained household suffrage, govern these realms.' Developing this theme, he declared: 'Household Suffrage will only be good and useful as you may use it', and set out three great things for which it ought to be used: 'Universal Education; the reduction of our heavy taxation; and Justice to Ireland (Cheers).' Some had been kind enough to call him an Anglo-Hibernian, he said, but: 'He is no true Englishman who is not an Anglo-Hibernian. Unless you do justice to every part of the Queen's dominions, you cannot have peace and

---

[34] 28 May 1864. Letters of Sir Edward Watkin, Canada Archives, Ottawa, A519.
[35] *Grimsby Observer and Humber News*, 5 May 1880.

progress within her borders; and so long as you have peace you have no barrier to free trade.' He challenged his opponents to state what proposals they had for the problems of Ireland, foremost among which were religious equality and the question of land.[36]

The electorate had been increased almost fourfold by the new Act, and, in what must have been a surprising result, a Conservative candidate was elected, breaking the Liberal tradition which had held in Stockport for several years. William Tipping, the son of a Liverpool corn merchant, 'the type of good old English gentleman' and resident at Brasted Park, Kent,[37] topped the poll, with 2,714 votes. John Smith (Liberal) was second with 2,658, and Watkin narrowly missed election with 2,598. A touch of irony lay in the fact that William Tipping was a director of the LNWR, the company that held sway over Stockport's 'paucity of railway provision' until Watkin built his line through Tiviot Dale in December 1865.

The constituency underwent a change of boundary and name in 1869, becoming the Parliamentary Division of East Cheshire. Watkin was again defeated, this time by Sir William Cunliffe Brooks. Brooks was born in the same year as Watkin, and like him was a magistrate for the City of Manchester and the County of Chester, but there the similarity ended, and their political views were very different. Brooks 'came from an ancient and respectable Lancashire family, was educated at Rugby and St John's College, Cambridge, and was a Barrister in the Northern Circuit'.[38] *The City Jackdaw* of Manchester called Watkin's campaign 'a gallant fight', and reported that 'in the course of an incessant canvass, in which he spoke every night, he...made the newspaper reader familiar with the names of teeming villages of which the majority had never heard before.'[39] A petition was filed shortly afterwards for the voiding of the result on the grounds of corrupt practices. 'The buying and selling of votes had been commonly practised ...and it became notorious under the system of open voting with the increased electorates.' After 'considerable trouble and expense' the petition was later withdrawn.[40] George Cartier, joint Prime

[36]*Stockport Advertiser*, 20 November 1868.
[37]*Stockport Express*, 3 June 1926.
[38]*Stockport Ancient and Modern*, p.364
[39]22 September 1876.
[40]*Stockport Advertiser*, 3 June 1926.

Minister of Canada with Sir John MacDonald, Watkin's friend and fellow enthusiast for the transcontinental railway, a devout Roman Catholic, commiserated with him over this defeat. He offered, as something which had militated against him, the fact that Watkin had attended the laying of the cornerstone of a Roman Catholic school in Stockport, and had drunk the health of the Pope at the lunch which followed.[41] A more likely cause for his defeat was that the boundary changes had included in the new constituency the 'innermost fastnesses of country Toryism'.[42]

The year 1868 saw an important change in the political map of the country. In a speech to a Lancashire audience holding up Manchester Liberalism to the admiration of the country, Grant Duff said 'What Lancashire thinks today, England thinks tomorrow.'[43] 'Such a speech could not have been made after 1868, for in that year and 1874 Manchester deserted its traditional Liberalism and the leadership of the Liberal Party passed to Birmingham.'[44]

Watkin had affected the commercial legislation of the country in a speech on 5 March 1867. Speaking at considerable length (four and a half pages of *Hansard*), he called for a Select Committee on the Acts relating to Limited Liability Companies. He asserted that the Act of 1862 had failed in the anticipations vested in it, and had given rise to a degree of speculation in the stock markets 'unrivalled since the time of the South Sea Bubble in 1720'. Thus 'there were at present 2,200 joint stock companies of all kinds in existence, having a nominal capital of perhaps £1,000,000,000, probably 750,000 shareholders, and 12,000 persons of another class which had grown up, and who were interested in them as trustees and directors.' The whole speech was full of facts and figures, and illustrated the need, as he saw it, for better legislation. The motion was agreed to, and a Select Committee of eight people was nominated on Friday, 8 March. At its first meeting, on Tuesday, 12 March, 'Mr Watkin was called to the Chair', and he presided over all eleven of its meetings. The committee's Report

[41] E.W. Watkin, *Canada*, p.474.
[42] *The City Jackdaw*, 22 September 1876, p.383.
[43] *Manchester Guardian*, 10 August 1868, quoted in H.J. Hanham, *Elections and Party Management: Politics in the Time of Disraeli and Gladstone* (Longmans, 1959), p.286.
[44] Hanham, p.286.

was presented to the House on 28 May 1867. It drew up ten resolutions, regarding the governing of the buying and selling of shares, the conduct of shareholders' meetings, and the formation and winding-up of limited liability companies, under the guidance of Board of Trade regulations, and in conjunction with the Registrar of Joint Stock Companies.[45]

Also in 1867, he raised another matter regarding the efficient operation of the country's trade, when he addressed the need for co-ordination of information in the cotton trade. In a series of letters between November 1867 and April 1868 to the Duke of Richmond, President of the Board of Trade (1867–69), Watkin argued: 'Prices were fluctuating, and the whole trade is anxious for reliable facts.'[46] He recommended a system of returns to be compiled for the benefit of those involved in the cotton trade, so that they would have some comprehension of the national position regarding stocks held, and incomings and outgoings. 'Damage has been done and is occasioned', he wrote, to the persons engaged in the Manufacture of Cotton, and to the public by the want of reliable statistics for the Imports, Exports and Stocks of raw cotton, to, from, and at the various ports of the United Kingdom...It would promote the public advantage', he argued, 'if such...were regularly collected and published under the control of the Board of Trade.'[47]

Watkin apparently organised a gathering of the cotton spinners for Thursday, 26 March 1868 to meet the Duke, for he wrote to the assistant, Captain Peel, to let them have a large room in which to assemble, expecting 'a very large muster'.[48] As usual, he wanted action to be taken immediately, for he asked within a few days, 'Can you tell me what the Duke has decided re Cotton. Our people are most anxious, and the Session wears away.'[49] In the final letter of the collection, marked 'Private', and dated simply 'Wednesday', Watkin ends with the words 'It is a pity the Duke

---

[45]From the full Report of the Select Committee on the Acts relating to limited liability companies, in the Manchester City Library Archives. This legislation 'effected the saving of hundreds of thousands of pounds to investors' (*Birmingham Mail*, 16 April 1901). and 'released £16,000,000 which had been lying dead in securities that were practically useless' (*Stockport Advertiser*, 19 April 1901).

[46]West Sussex Record Office, Chichester, Goodwood Papers, 832/176. 28 November 1867.

[47]*Ibid*, 829/506 (no date).

[48]*Ibid*, 832/289.20 March 1868.

[49]*Ibid*, 832/332.31 March 1868.

does not see his way to appeal to the Cabinet...Many thanks for the trouble you have taken.'[50] It would appear from this that his efforts were finally in vain.

However, a few weeks later, a 'Cotton Statistics Bill' was ordered to be brought in by Thomas Bazley (1797–1885), Member for Manchester, under his and Watkin's name, and those of the Members for Liverpool, Salford and Ashton-under-Lyne. This was presented and read on 27 April 1868. It would seem that Bazley had been appointed by the four to be spokesman for the measure, but Watkin had acted as secretary and mastermind of the negotiations: among the correspondence from him to the Duke of Richmond were the drafts of four forms for the registration of 'Cotton' information, and the draft wording of the Bill itself.[51] After several Readings and Committee Reports, the Royal Assent was given on 25 June 1868 (31 and 32 Vict. c.33), and Watkin had again had a hand in regulating the laissez-faire system.

In June 1868, in one of his last speeches as Member for Stockport, Watkin urged changes to the provisions proposed by the Boundaries Commission as they affected Stockport. He preferred the name 'East Cheshire' to the proposed 'North Cheshire', and this was accepted. His proposal of Stockport, instead of Macclesfield, as the place of nomination for East Cheshire, was, however, turned down.

After his two defeats in Cheshire in 1868 and 1869, Watkin stood down from political activity until 1871. In that year 'he was in communication with the Liberal Party in Plymouth, with a view to taking Sir Robert Collier's seat'.[52] Nothing came of this, but in 1873 he was invited by the Liberals in Exeter to stand in the election of December that year.

In the 1870s the main concern of the Liberal Party, as a coalition of many sectional and interest groups, was to unite the efforts of the party behind a single issue. The Anti-Corn Law and the Reform organisations had represented such a system in the early days, but nothing had taken their place to unify party policy.[53] Gladstone's snap dissolution of Parliament on 24 January 1874,

---

[50]*Ibid,* 833/335 (no date).
[51]Goodwood Papers, 892/308.
[52]*Exeter Flying Post,* 12 November 1873.
[53]D.A. Hamer, *Liberal Politics in the Age of Gladstone and Rosebery* (OUP, 1972), pp.1ff.

after six months' searching for a means to restore the vitality of the party, caused nationwide dismay. The *Durham County Advertiser* spoke strongly for many when it expressed the hope that the English people had not forgotten their love of fair play, which denounced 'striking a man unprepared in the back'.[54] After the election defeat of 1874, Lord Hartington was to speak of three components in the Party – Whig, Radical and Irish – and went so far as to advocate three leaders 'if one was not capable of unifying the Liberals as an effective party of political power'.[55] Chamberlain suggested that one of the 'Nonconformist' concerns, such as national education or disestablishment, could provide a rallying point, and that of these disestablishment should be the first article of the new Liberal programme. He had shown, to his own satisfaction at any rate as Mayor of Birmingham, the value of 'single issue' programme politics.[56] The 'Newcastle Programme' of October 1891 was a late panic reaction to the fissiparous state of the Party.[57] None of these issues seems to have emerged in the Exeter by-election, though Watkin was to deal with them in his Hythe campaign in 1874. Chamberlain's Nonconformist attitude to disestablishment formed another sharp distinction between the two men, a distinction which was to emerge as open hostility in the Channel Tunnel debates of the 1880s.

The by-election campaign of 1873 was a hard-fought one, with both Conservative and Liberal Parties laying claim to be the natural expression of the city's character. The Tory newspaper, *Trewman's Exeter Flying Post*, missed no chances of discrediting the Liberal candidate. Reference was made to his multiple railway chairmanships, asking how he was going to 'do his duty to his three railway companies when he adds to those Parliamentary duties?' No opportunity was overlooked to make slighting references to the finances of those three railways (the MS&L, the Metropolitan and the SER), which 'had to eke out rather scanty dividends by a rather low rate of wages', said Arthur Mills, the Tory candidate. He went on to assert, 'that his electioneering project in the extreme South West interfered with his railway

---

[54]William Henry Maehl, 'Gladstone, the Liberals, and the Election of 1874', *Bulletin of the Institute of Historical Research,* Vol. 36 (London: 1963), pp.60 and 53.
[55]Hamer, p.39.
[56]*Ibid*, pp. 44 and 45.
[57]*Ibid*, p. 173.

duties in the North was evident'. References to Great Yarmouth were plentiful: 'The stranger comes with soiled hands from the disenfranchised borough of Norfolk.'[58]

Such charges were usually defended by Watkin in *his* hustings with facts and figures, to try to defend his character against such accusations as 'The great I AM, full of vainglory, bombast, egotism...purse-proud vulgarity...and pusillanimous...ungentlemanly attacks on his opponent.' Sir Stafford Northcote described him at this time as 'something of a snob'.[59] As if this catalogue of contumely were not enough, fears were insinuated about his alleged 'ambiguous' attitude to English Church Disestablishment: 'The great Church and State struggle will come if only the Liberals of Sir Edward Watkin's stamp are returned to Parliament: this would endanger the sacredness of the Sunday. Sending such a man to the Houses of Parliament would swell the ranks of the enemies of the Church of England.'[60] The term 'Radical' was often used, with deliberate suggestions of Republicanism. Exeter was the first city to congratulate Her Majesty the Queen on the approaching marriage of the Duke of Edinburgh to the Grand Duchess Marie of Russia, and thus dispel, 'despite the presence of Sir Edward Watkin in the city', any thoughts of its 'leaning away from Royalty'. The Tory newspaper spoke proudly of the large numbers of Conservative working men in the constituency, and claimed that 'the intelligence of the Exeter working man was outside Watkin's previous experience, and too much for him'. Scorn was poured on Watkin's background: 'Exeter was not only a Conservative City, but a place of some culture', and 'it would be a disgrace to return a hard-grained, coarse-minded man like Sir Edward Watkin to represent it in Parliament...He knows nothing of the Education Act and its working – we fear very little of education in any sense.'[61]

The Liberals' campaign committee did not exactly serve him

---

[58] *Exeter Flying Post*, 19 November 1873.

[59] Robert Newton, *Victorian Exeter* (Leicester University Press, 1968), p.194. If the word was used in the usual sense of 'a vulgar and ostentatious person who strives to flatter, imitate, or associate with people of perceived higher status or prestige, and despises supposed inferiors', then this was an inaccurate and unfair description, which itself could have been snobbish.

[60] *Exeter Flying Post*, 19 and 26 November 1873.

[61] *Ibid.*

particularly well. A poster addressed 'To the Electors of Exeter' read, acrostically:

Silver, copper, brass in plenty / In my pockets mix with gold,
Railway shares enough for twenty / Endless wealth and power untold,
Dividends at all the quarters / Wondering clerks my agents pay;
Artisans and Guards and Porters / Railways three my words obey.
Doubt not I can help you greatly, / Work for thousands I can bring,
And with parks and mansions stately, / Try to prove a 'Railway King.'
Know that I am now Director / In the Chair of Railways three,
Never was so great Protector, / King or Kaiser, Pope, as me.
Now's your chance, my wise Elector, / Take me for your new M.P.

Sir Edward W.Watkin, Knt.,SER., MS&LR, and MR. Exeter, 3 December 1873.[62]

Watkin's opponents, in ripe sardonic mood, could hardly have bettered this effort. It is doubtful that Watkin saw it all before it was pasted to the billboards. Apart from the obvious bombast, he would never have sanctioned the attribution to him of chairmanship of the Midland Railway: the abbreviation for the Metropolitan was usually 'Met.Rly.'

Watkin has been characterised as a 'new type of candidate for Exeter, one who was a creator of a modern world in which the city had little share.'[63] Not until 'the end of the 60s did the tides that had been sweeping through the main channels of national life and had raised the country as a whole to the peak of its economic power, reach the remoter creeks and inlets.' The Conservatives, who had been uncharacteristically out of power in Exeter since 1868, welcomed 1873 as a trial of strength, and a large proportion

---

[62]Exeter Public Library Archives
[63]Newton, pp.194 and 173.

210

of their planning for it had been directed at winning the vote of the working man. Much was made of Gladstone's Licensing Act of 1872, as all the brewers and wine-merchants were Conservatives.[64] His Education Act had stirred up considerable opposition. 'The 1870s were not an edifying time in the city's history.'[65]

From the reports of his speeches, which may have been highly selective, of course, Watkin does not seem to have been at his best in this campaign. There is too much special pleading, and rather more of politicians' rodomontade than usual, searching for the subject which brings most applause, and fewer of his customary declarations of principle and solid statements of intent. Nevertheless, Arthur Mills, a director of the North Staffordshire Railway,[66] won the contest with a majority of only 321 (2,346 to 2,025, with eleven spoiled papers).

Notwithstanding the fact that he had not been successful, Watkin was presented by the Liberals of Exeter, at a great public demonstration on 7 December 1874, with a substantial leather-bound volume, in illuminated Gothic script, bearing upon its forty-three pages the names of about 1,200 of them. Presented along with a 'handsome service of plate,'[67] to 'Sir Edward William Watkin, Kt., Bt., Sheriff of Cheshire', page two of the book states that it was given 'as a token of our respect for your public and personal character, and our admiration of the talent, the energy, and the unflinching courage, you displayed in the arduous contest of December last.' Page three continues, 'We know by the published record of your life that you have been, from your youth up, devoted to the great principles which direct the progress of humanity...We are grateful to you for your manly efforts...We tender you this token of our regard because we desire that your family should see that the great sacrifices which you make of personal comfort and pecuniary means in serving the public, bring you the love and confidence of the people.'[68] It concludes by wishing him and his 'excellent lady' many years to enjoy the respect of the public, and the hope that others will follow his

---

[64]*Ibid*, pp.109, 110 and 194.
[65]*Ibid*, pp.191 and 193.
[66]Geoffrey Alderman, *The Railway Interest* (Leicester University Press, 1973), p.62.
[67]*City Jackdaw*, Manchester, 22 September 1876, p.383.
[68]pp.4 and 5.

bright example. 'Tory Exeter slandered your good name beyond the ordinary bounds of electioneering license [sic]...Liberal Exeter tenders this token of respect as an abiding answer to the slanderers.' The methods adopted to discredit Watkin apparently crossed the line of permissible practice: the presentation volume records: 'The Dissolution of Parliament prevented any exposure by Judicial Enquiry of the foul means' by which Watkin's efforts had 'been frustrated'.[69] The perennial subject of electioneering corruption was not effectively dealt with until the Corrupt Practices Act of 1883. Even then, this was seen as 'an unambiguous interference with what many still regarded as virtually a "free trade" in votes.' [70]

A fascinating incident arose from Watkin's Exeter campaign. Frederick W. Evans, a clerk employed by the Great Western Railway at Bristol, helped to raise support for Watkin among railwaymen in Exeter. Evans was a pioneer member of the Associated Society of Railway Servants, one of the early trade unions, and Watkin agreed that if he were elected he would give his backing in Parliament to a 'Workman's Compensation Act'. Sir Edward was not elected, but when in January 1874 the GWR gave Evans a month's notice because of his union activities, Watkin immediately offered him employment on one of the three railway companies of which he was chairman. However, he made the proviso that Evans discontinue his work for the ASRS. Evans would not accept this condition, and turned down the offer, whereupon Watkin headed a subscription list, started on Evans' behalf, with a gift of £50.[71] On 25 May 1875, having been elected a few months earlier as Member for Hythe and Folkestone, Watkin honoured the spirit of his promise to Evans, and moved for leave to bring in a Bill 'to provide for Compensation to Workpeople engaged in common employment in cases of injury by accidents when Employed.' The motion was agreed to. However, Evans and the Parliamentary Committee of the TUC were unhappy with the Bill when it was formulated, mainly because it limited the compen-

---

[69]p.4.
[70]K. Theodore Hoppen, *The Mid-Victorian Generation, 1846-1886* (Oxford: Clarendon Press, 1998), p.647.
[71]Philip S. Bagwell, *The Railwaymen: A History of the NUR* (George Allen and Unwin Ltd., 1963), pp. 72 and 73.

sation to a sum equal to one year's wages.[72] In summer 1875, Watkin proposed the raising of the figure to £300, but in spite of Evans's support the TUC opposed this suggestion, and it was dropped. The matter was then taken up by Alexander McDonald, the member for Stafford, who brought in a more radical Bill on 9 February 1876. After a Select Committee of Inquiry, and much counter-proposing and petitioning, an Act was finally passed into law in 1880.[73]

Given Watkin's abiding sympathy for 'the ordinary working man', and his regular speaking up on his behalf in the House, it seems strange that he did not support the nascent trade union movement. The explanation is probably twofold. First there was his fundamental belief in the oneness of mankind: that in a comprehensive framework of the wholeness of human activity, in mutual trust and interdependence, undertaken without adopting adversarial positions, lay the key to harmony and progress. Secondly, as a theological presupposition, he held the Victorian notion of the goodness (perhaps, indeed, the holiness) of England as the most advanced expression of Christian civilisation and development, with the concomitant responsibility to spread this abroad in the Empire and beyond.[74] Social responsibility, in this view, was of the essence, and best expressed in benevolent paternalism. Thus, the ultimate best interests of the working man lay in a unified and co-operative system, based on Christian honesty and trust and love on both sides, rather than in the opposition of self-interested groups battling out issues to the ultimate happiness of neither capital nor labour. Watkin's position was uncomfortably close to being aphorised by Karl Marx when he said that Christian social principles 'preach the necessity of a ruling and an oppressed class, and all they have for the latter is the pious wish that the former will be charitable.'[75] In the late nineteenth century this

---

[72]And also because Evans mistrusted Watkin's motives in introducing the Bill, (Alderman, p.62).

[73]Bagwell, pp.117–19.

[74]Watkin seems to have held (perhaps unconsciously) to Hegel's 'synthetic' view of reality, in the ascendancy at the time, of perceiving all elements as holding together in a synthesis, based on the emergence of England as the embodiment of the Classical and Christian virtues; as distinct from an 'analytical' view, which considered all elements in isolation and then sought to relate them.

[75]Quoted, Jonathan Luxmoore and Jolanta Babiuch, *The Vatican and the Red Flag* (Geoffrey Chapman, 1999), p.6.

measurement of human social principle was fading. Watkin's Victorian high optimism was in decline until its final expiry only thirteen years after the Queen's death and his own.

Undismayed by his defeated exertions in Exeter, Watkin stood for representation of the Borough of Hythe in the General Election of 1874. His agent in this election, as in Exeter and the subsequent campaign in Hythe in 1880, was 'the eminent solicitor' Richard Hart, who had been Disraeli's agent in the contest for Maidstone in 1837. According to Watkin, 'Mr Hart had many interesting reminiscences of Mr Disraeli to recount which he hoped to relate on another occasion, but probably never had opportunity.'[76] He was elected unopposed in 1874, to represent the united boroughs of Hythe and Folkestone. A local newspaper reported, on his acceptance by both Conservatives and Liberals, that there was in Sir Edward 'a thin veil between the two parties.' He was returned unopposed again in 1880.

In preparation for the election of 1885, Watkin addressed two large meetings of his constituents on Friday, 23 October 1885: one in the morning at Folkestone Town Hall, and one in the afternoon at the Town Hall in Hythe. In his morning speech, which was by no means the same as the later one, he raised several key questions, and declared his position on each one of them. The first was electoral reform. He was of the opinion that the Reform Act needed reforming, so that suffrage was made so complete – with no 'class or sort of persons being excluded from the franchise', including women, spinsters and widows – that 'further extension. . .would be entirely needless'.[77] He objected to the property qualification, which excluded 'several hundred men, worthy, respectable, intelligent, honest men'. He quoted the story of an American voter in the State of New York, which in the old days had a property qualification: a man had to be in possession of twenty dollars. 'One of the claimants, in computing his qualification, had to bring in the value of his donkey and the cart. . .One day the donkey died, and the vote was objected to and the man was disenfranchised. He said he had made a discovery of a thing that had never struck him before: that the vote did not rest in himself, but in the donkey.'

---

[76]E.W. Watkin, *Canada and the States: Recollections, 1851-1886* (Ward Lock, 1887), p.495.
[77]*Speeches of Sir Edward Watkin, Bt., MP, at the Folkestone and Hythe Town Halls, Friday 23 October 1885* (London: C.F. Rowarth, 1885), p.7.

Watkin spoke of the need for a cheaper and simpler system of land transfer from one owner to another, mentioning his own experiences in Greece. He mentioned the problem of Ireland, which 'may perplex and puzzle the most astute statesman', and the need for a thorough modernisation of the Channel harbours, citing the example of the ones on the French side. A question from the floor regarding the disestablishment of the Church of England he answered by quoting Gladstone's address at Midlothian: that it was a matter for the consent of the nation.[78]

In the afternoon his main point was universal franchise, which he developed in a different way, emphasising the need for the availability of education. His convictions in this area are well attested in many of his words and actions, but he went further here and stated his belief, quoting his kind and dear friend, the Bishop of Manchester, only yesterday suddenly deceased,[79] that unless education was accompanied and associated with religious instruction, it was worth very little. 'You may teach a man', he went on, 'the culture of this world, but there is another world, and if the country had simply a secular education...that education would be a curse among us instead of a blessing.' In a revealing statement he declared that he was 'speaking old-fashioned language very likely, because the fashion of the day is to believe nothing'. By 1885 the Christian Church and Faith were no longer the constant constituents of social and political endeavour that they had been. Science and scholarship seemed to have undermined them, and 'with Bishops and University professors going over to the camp of those who were regarded as the enemies of the faith', many people were losing what Christian confidence they had.[80] Nevertheless, Watkin believed that social questions (still referring particularly to education, free and compulsory, paid for or voluntary, but speaking from a general principle), required us to bring Christian charitableness to bear, asking of each issue: 'What is just and honest and Christian?'[81] Clearly he was convinced, like Wilberforce, Shaftesbury and Gladstone, that Christian theology

---

[78]*Ibid*, pp.8, 11, 5, 13 and 22.
[79]This was Edward Fraser, the second Bishop of Manchester, from 1870 to 1885.
[80]J.R.H. Moorman, *A History of the Church in England* (Adam and Charles Black, 1953), p.380.
[81]E.W. Watkin, *Speeches*, p.36.

had a bearing on political ideology and action. However, 'The 1890s showed that Gladstone's moral politics stood little chance against [the appeal] to the economic self-interest of a disparate popular electorate.'[82] Lord Salisbury, though also a committed Christian, was of a more pragmatic mould: 'No one dreams of conducting national affairs with the principles which are prescribed for individuals...and the common sense of Christendom has always prescribed for national policy principles diametrically opposed to those which are laid down in the Sermon on the Mount.'[83]

He also spoke on the reform of the House of Lords. He deplored the suggestion that the bishops should be 'kicked out' of the Upper House. He knew of no 'nobler man' anywhere than the late Bishop of Manchester, and the present Archbishop of Canterbury (Benson) and his predecessor (Tait). If he could do what he pleased, he would – far from removing the bishops – include also 'the President of the Wesley Conference, The President of the Congregational Union, and the President of the Baptist Union.'[84] The fact that he did not mention the Archbishop of Westminster cannot be construed as obdurate bias: his sympathy for Catholic Emancipation, and for the Catholic people of Ireland and Canada, gives the lie to that. The Roman Catholic bishops at that time gave no indication that they would be interested in upholding the Establishment in such a way. In his reference to Ireland, he said it seemed to him 'it would be very much better if Ireland were handed over to the United States as a State of America, rather than continue the horrible condition of things which exist at this moment.'[85]

Watkin declared himself as an Independent in his Liberal views, owing his loyalty to his constituents and to his own principles rather than to the exigencies of the Party Whips. There were times when he felt like crossing the floor of the House, during his tussles with Joseph Chamberlain over the Channel Tunnel,[86] and other

---

[82]Richard Jay, *Joseph Chamberlain: A Political Study* (Oxford: Clarendon Press, 1981), p.146.

[83]David Goodall, Review in the *Tablet*, 20 November 1999, of Andrew Roberts, *Salisbury: Victorian Titan* (London: Weidenfeld and Nicholson, 1999).

[84]Watkin, *Speeches*, p.37.

[85]A BBC Radio programme on the Americanisation of Eire in the late 1990s was entitled *The 51st State* (reported in the *Tablet*, 4 September 1999, p.1202).

[86]In the early 1880s he did submit himself at times to the Conservative Whip, though this may have been during a phase of gratitude for his baronetcy from Disraeli.

times when he could be very radical. In the latter category must come his support for an Amendment proposed by John Stuart Mill (Member for Westminster, 1865–67) in the Debate on the Representation of the People Bill, on 20 May 1867. Mill's amendment[87] was to leave out the word 'man' in order to insert the word 'person' instead. The Reform Bill of 1832 had for the first time excluded women, by the use of 'male persons'. The 1867 Bill used the word 'man', which was generally interpreted as 'mankind', and taken to include women. Mill wanted to remove all ambiguity, and enfranchise women.[88]

In the vote on the Amendment, Watkin was one of those supporting Mill's proposed alteration, as part of what Mill called an 'unexpectedly large minority of 73', out of a total vote of 269.[89] 'Men think me a Radical', Watkin declared. 'I am a Radical: but I am a Conservative Radical: I want to see everything reformed that ought to be reformed in order to preserve the fabric of the State. I am strongly for reform. I am totally opposed to revolution.'[90] Joseph Hoare (1814–86), speaking in favour of the Conservative Party candidate at a Lancashire election campaign in 1868, said 'The difference between the Conservative and the Liberal creed was as great as that of light and dark...Liberals boasted that it was better to destroy everything than let anything alone; the Conservative creed [was] to preserve, and, if possible, increase the usefulness of what was good, and to sweep away all that was bad.'[91] Small wonder that the Conservatives in Hythe and Folkestone should be content with being represented by Sir Edward.

The Blackburn Telegraph said of him that '[Despite being] a Cobdenite, he was not a robust Liberal. There was more of the old Whig than of the new Radical in his political leanings.'[92] The only sign of dissatisfaction with Sir Edward's performance emerged late in his incumbency at Hythe and Folkestone. Some Liberals in Folkestone held a meeting and called upon him to render an

---

[87]Page 2, line 16.
[88]Roger Fulford, *Votes for Women* (London: Faber and Faber, 1957), pp.68 and 69.
[89]Hansard, CLXXXVII, cols. 817–29, and 842–3.
[90]Watkin, *Speeches,* p.37.
[91]H.J. Hanham, *Elections and Party Management: Politics in the Time of Disraeli and Gladstone* (Longmans, 1959), p.317. Hoare contested Manchester himself, unsuccessfully, in the same year.
[92]15 April 1901.

217

account of his stewardship. They received a kind and courteous reply, but the resolution was widely publicised, and Watkin was uneasy about it. Enquiry revealed that the meeting was held in a coffee shop, and only fifteen persons were present, only eight of whom were voters.[93]

In the elections for the Hythe Division of Kent in 1885, and again in 1886, Watkin was re-elected, and on 12 May 1886, he was given the Freedom of Hythe.[94] A special album was presented to him by 400 Burgesses of the Municipal Borough of Hythe, in recognition of his services to the electorate.[95] He was returned again in the elections of 1892 and 1895, when he resigned through ill-health. He thus completed an unbroken service there of twenty-one years.[96]

The subjects on which Sir Edward made speeches during his parliamentary career fall roughly into seven categories (excluding the Channel Tunnel): overseas concerns, Ireland, railway matters, the army, individual justice, merchant shipping, and 'government' – the latter comprising home affairs and Standing Orders and Motions of Procedure. Under the 'Overseas' heading, there were sixteen speeches all told, mainly on relations between Canada and the USA; eight on Ceylon, primarily concerned with government policy and its effect on native labourers, and probably on information from his old friend and cousin-in-law, George Wall, who held a government appointment in the administration there. Surprisingly, he participated only seldom in the discussion of Bills affecting home railways, even in support of the MS&LR's London Extension, and only once on one of his favourite bugbears – the duty charged on income from passenger fares.[97] This tax on travel, one of several sore points of government interference in railway operation and accounting, was originally imposed in 1832 and not removed until 1929.[98] Watkin also spoke to the Manchester Central Line Bill in 1866. The army seems to have engaged his

---

[93] *Kent Messenger,* 20 April 1901.
[94] A letter dated 14 June 1999 from Kent County Archives.
[95] Listed in E.W. Watkin, *Catalogue of Rose Hill Library* (Manchester: Henry Blacklock, 1891), p.3.
[96] *Grimsby Observer,* 18 April 1901.
[97] On 7 March 1876, *Hansard* CCXXVII, col. 1593. 'A tax on locomotion', he claimed, 'was, next to one on food, almost the worst that could be imposed'.
[98] Simmons and Biddle, *Oxford Companion to British Railway History,* (OUP, 1997), pp.501 and 502.

interest and attention to a surprising degree, considering the lack of tradition and connection in the family.[99] He spoke ten or eleven times on army matters, his very first speech in the House[100] calling attention to new inventions in the field of firearms and military machinery and urging an imitation of the 'worthy system' in the United States, 'which ensured that the army was brought up to date every five years'. He also advocated in the same speech a coastal telegraph system for the effective deployment of the army in the case of an invasion of England.

The subject of merchant shipping is not surprising, as an MP for Great Yarmouth, and for Hythe and Folkestone, and considering his continuing interest in the port of Grimsby. In April 1878 he raised a Question in the House concerning the arming of the merchant marine against privateers and pirates in time of war.[101] The favourable reception of his suggestion encouraged him, when in 1885 war with Russia seemed inevitable, to buy six 9-pounder guns from Sir Joseph Whitworth and Company Ltd to equip some of his MS&L ships in Grimsby.[102]

He made no fewer than ten contributions to debates on electoral practices – a subject painfully close to his experience. After his defeat in 1873, he twice spoke up on matters concerning Exeter: one on the Endowed Schools Commission there in 1875, and the other on the subject of borough magistrates, in 1878. Very early in his membership of the House, he saw himself as a spokesman for the working man. In his first words after being returned in the election for Stockport, he spoke in the long debate on 11 March 1864 on the Second Reading of the Borough Franchise Bill, which proposed the extension of the franchise beyond the aristocracy and the middle classes. The vote, however, went against the Bill by a majority of 56. By 17 May 1867, this discussion, on an amended Bill, had been resumed, and had touched on a consideration of what constituted a dwelling house for the purpose of determining the eligibility of a vote for a working man. Watkin proposed an amendment which required a 'dwelling house' to be of at least two rooms. 'No civilised being', he argued, 'should live in less than two

---

[99]Though his paternal grandfather had served in the Brigade of Guards (A.E. Watkin, p.8).
[100]*Hansard,* Vol. CXLV, 25 May 1857, Cols. 867–9.
[101]*Hansard,* Vol. CCXXXIV, 8 April 1878. Col.854.
[102]Dow, Vol. 2, p.154.

rooms.' He did not want 'Household Suffrage' to be degraded to 'Hovel Suffrage', because that would encourage the building of large numbers of tenements not fit for human habitation, in order to increase the number of votes available.

His sympathy for the working man did not attune him to the rise of organised labour.[103] The emergent trade union movement was forged largely in the heat of many injustices and cases of exploitation, which Watkin must have known, but would regard simply as bad managerial practice. The formation of confrontational bodies to correct malpractice was not a good foundation for goodwill and a creative relationship between capitalist and worker. This would explain his objection to 'Strikes and Lockouts' in a debate on 10 August 1887. He drew attention to a circular issued by the Amalgamated Society of Railway Servants 'Threatening strike breakers ("blacklegs")'. Watkin urged protection of workmen who wished 'to dispose of their labour in their own way'. An apparently harsh question on 10 May 1875, was whether a threat by the National Federation of Coal Miners to withdraw their labour, in a dispute over wages, constituted 'an illegal combination, thus rendering its promoters liable to penal consequences?' The reply he received was that as the proposal in question was not adopted by the Federation, 'the question of penal consequences did not arise'.

On 9 March 1880, the House debated the Railway Servants (Compensation for Injury) Bill, mentioned above. He objected strongly to what he saw as an 'Election ploy' – singling out the railways among all other industries in the country. He compared the number of deaths and injuries on railways (642 killed, 2,163 injured – the previous speaker's figures) with the national overall figure of 100,000 killed and injured. He moved an Amendment requiring a national system of adequate insurance, to which 'both the capitalist and the workman should contribute in just proportion'. This proposition was not voted upon; there were only forty members present. Later in that year, on 4 August, in the discussion of the Employer's Liability Bill, Watkin expressed his fear of multiple cases of legislation if the Bill were to be passed. 'The bulk of the sensible working classes', he said, 'were already connected

---

[103]See also p.213 supra and p.235 infra.

with insurance funds, and they did not wish to substitute a harassing system of litigation for the quiet, regular, and fair compensation between master and man which at present had done so much for them.' He may have been describing the men in his own immediate employment, but how far what he said was true of the relationship between capital and labour generally was debatable: he was speaking more of his own ideals and practices than of the overall picture. He was a firm believer, not only in universal education, but in each worker insuring himself and his family, and he promoted self-improvement classes on his railways, and in the principle of company savings banks for employees, who might set aside some proportion of their pay each week as they went along. This principle endured on the Great Central and LNER companies, and after nationalisation in 1948.

The Second Reading of the Friendly Societies Bill on 22 June 1875 gave rise to a dispute over how much should be paid on the death of a child (this had been £3 originally, then raised to £6), and what the minimum age for a child should be for insurance purposes. William Thomas Charley (1833–1904), MP for Salford, argued that as the Bill stood, the life of a baby of one day could be insured for £6, and he thought that it was undesirable to continue such a temptation for the very poor: he proposed a minimum age of six months. Sir Edward said the concessions (£6 compensation, no minimum age) had been wisely made by the Chancellor of the Exchequer, 'and they had been most gratefully received by the working classes'. He 'regretted that the poor people of this country had been so grievously libelled. What right had anyone', he asked, 'to suppose that they would be tempted to murder their children for the sake of obtaining £6?' He trusted 'that the Chancellor of the Exchequer would remain firm on that point, and not accept the amendment'. At the end of the debate, Watkin moved the inclusion of the clause 'that the sum charged by the Registrar of Deaths for...a certificate shall not exceed one shilling'. This was accepted, and the Bill itself, in a form agreeable to Sir Edward, was passed on 24 June.

In what was only his third speech after entering the House, on 14 July 1857, Watkin supported a motion proposed by the member for Newport, IOW, that Her Majesty would 'employ all the means in her power to put down the African Slave Trade.' Watkin observed that 'the people of this country were...responsible more than any other in the world for the slave trade: at present four millions of our population were employed, or at least fed, by the cotton manufacturers.' But he warned that though 'violent means of oppression might go a long way to put down the slave trade...still the chief source of the trade would remain' (i.e., its profitableness). But 'if England were to divert her attention more to the means of substituting free-labour cotton for slave-labour cotton, she would be doing greater things for the suppression of the slave trade than by addressing remonstrances, however just, to the Emperor of the French, or by increasing her squadron on the coast of Africa.'

Under the heading of 'Personal Injustice', he took up cudgels on three occasions on behalf of men he perceived as not having been fairly treated. On 21 November 1867 he raised the case of Thomas Maguire, Marine, who had been tried for murder in Manchester, and since received an unconditional pardon.[104] 'Was the Home Secretary', asked Watkin, 'prepared to recommend that he be restored to the service?' The Home Secretary assured him that the man had been so restored.

In June 1875, Watkin first raised questions from the floor about the case of Gunner Henry George Charlton, a soldier of thirteen years' service who, 'for some slight error of discipline', was committed for 112 days to Milbank Prison. Through being kept in a dark cell below the high water of the river, with a perpetual cold draught (Watkin had visited the cell for himself), he had fallen ill, been set to hard labour, and then to solitary confinement for 48 hours, on bread and water. He was discharged on 1 March 1875 on a bitter winter's day, suffering from frostbite, without an outer garment, or any food or drink. He arrived in Exeter almost totally disabled, having lost most of one foot and the toes of the other. Speaking in the House again on 5 March 1877 Watkin claimed that this was cruelty, and called upon the Secretary of State for War to explain. *He* had ascertained from a doctor he had sent, and the man's chaplain, that the authorities were quite wrong in

---

[104]Maguire had been one of 26 men charged with attacking a police van carrying two prisoners, with intent to release them, on 18 September 1867. Police Sergeant Brett had been shot dead in the attack (*The Manchester Guardian*, 29 October 1867; *The Times*, 12 November, 14 November 1867). Maguire was acquitted of any offence, and wrote to *The Manchester Guardian*, thanking all who had raised a petition for him, and hoping for restoration to the Royal Marines (*The Times*, 15 November 1867).

claiming that Charton was responsible for his own condition. After unsuccessfully appealing for official financial assistance for the man, Watkin sent him some money to keep him out of the workhouse, and when Charlton died not long afterwards paid for him to have a Christian burial. He was sure the Strangers in the Gallery would tell the story to the public, so that it was impossible to starve a man to death again in a military prison. In 1876 he outlined a proposed minimum diet, and this was adopted by a special committee for all prisoners.

The third case came in a debate on 16 May 1890, on the proposed award of £300 per year to the widow and children of Sir William Palliser, the late Member for Taunton, who by his inventions had saved the country £5 million.[105] Watkin said that he could not but 'protest against the mean and shabby character of the speeches with which the First Lord and the right hon. Member for Derby[106] [had] opposed this matter. I am quite sure', he said, 'the First Lord would never apply such principles to his transactions in the Strand...I will be no party to such a settlement', and went on to offer £300 of his own money if the First Lord of the Treasury and the Member for Derby went with him to make a personal offer to increase the award. The next speaker proposed an additional allowance of £150 per year, and this was carried by 105 votes to 85. This event prompted *Vanity Fair* to comment that Sir Edward's charity was 'sometimes unostentatious, sometimes not'.[107]

In one of his more provocative moods, but still reflecting the radical side of his political nature, Watkin enquired in the House of the Attorney-General on 25 March 1884 if he would 'lay upon the table, and cause to be circulated, Copy of the Bill now pending in the Parliament of the Dominion of Canada, which provides for the political enfranchisement of women possessing the qualifications fixed for men; and also Copy of the Ordinance passed by the "House of Keys" of the Isle of Man, which provides for the political enfranchisement of women.' After much stalling, the Attorney-General (Sir Henry James) replied that he saw no means

---

[105]His main inventions had been in rifled ordnance and projectiles, which were ignored by the War Office for years until adopted in 1890 (DNB, Vol. xliii, p.119).

[106]Sir William Harcourt.

[107]18 April 1901.

why the printing of these documents should be gone into, as any private person could have access to them. Watkin's opinion of the reply is not recorded.

Sir Edward made no fewer than thirteen interventions in debates concerning Ireland. He spoke in January 1881 on a Bill concerning the protection of persons and property; on peace preservation in the country (July 1875 and January 1881), applauding Parnellian statesmanship, but condemning Fenian threats and violence; on recompense for mistaken arrest (1884); and on local government in Ireland (1888). He was persistent in urging proper lighthouse and telegraph provisions on Ireland's coasts. On 2 August 1866, he spoke in the debate on the Habeas Corpus Suspension (Ireland) Act Continuance Bill (Second Reading). The Attorney-General for Ireland (Walsh) stated, in favour of the Bill, that the great mass of Fenians were adventurers and strangers who had come from America, having learned habits in the Civil War there that rendered life and property insecure. Watkin said that he had determined to vote against the Bill, because it represented the holding in suspension of the rights of 6 million Irishmen for the sake of 300 Fenian prisoners. He agreed with the Attorney-General that the source of the evil lay in America, and he thought the solution was by representation to the government of that country.

Perhaps his most substantial contribution to the debates on Ireland concerned the proposed disestablishment of the Irish Church. On 27 April 1868 he argued for the substitution of the voluntary system for the Establishment in Ireland. He quoted Dr Arnold of Rugby, on: 'Whether Ireland remain in its present barbarianism, or grow in wealth and civilisation, in either case the downfall of the present Establishment is certain: a savage people will not endure the insult of a hostile religion; a civilised one will reasonably insist on having their own.' Watkin claimed that '[the Irish people] see a church richly supported by the spoils of their own Church Establishment, in whose tenets not one tenth of the people believe. Is it possible to believe this can endure?' He admitted, however, that the problem was deeper than that of the mere confiscation of the Church of Ireland's property. That would not reduce difficulty, seeing that Protestants, as individuals, owned more land and were of a higher social standing than the Catholics.

The most pressing Irish problem in the latter part of the nineteenth century was, of course, that of Home Rule. Watkin, with his politically 'holistic' views, was against Home Rule, and in 1886 aligned himself with the Liberal Unionist position. (There were, in fact, several positions within Liberal Unionism, the principal ones being Whig Unionism and Radical Unionism.)[108] In a speech on 26 March 1886, Watkin expressed agreement with those members of the Liberal Party

> who would offer a most determined opposition to the estab-lishment of a separate Irish Parliament, as it would be certain to produce a disastrous collision between sections of the people holding conflicting views on social, economic, and reli-gious subjects, and would produce a feeling of insecurity which would jeopardise all industrial and commercial pursuits, and that the maintenance of the Union between Great Britain and Ireland was the best safeguard of the peace, prosperity and liberty of all classes in Ireland.

In his view, the interests of Irish prosperity were best secured by British investment in projects which would benefit Ireland econom-ically, and not by casting them off in their present poverty. For all Stafford Northcote's jibe of 'snobbery', he was not afraid to be outspoken against Gladstone on Home Rule. He wrote on 28 April 1888, 'Alas, Mr Gladstone – no one of you great men will make any concessions...If only you would, capital would flow to Ireland, and confidence would bring every blessing! I venture to think that if you and Mr Parnell would go for a Royal Commis-sion – sit in the Recess and report next year – the door of unity might be opened!'[109]

He cited the idea of a tunnel between northern Ireland and southern Scotland, which would connect the island by rail with Britain (and the Continent, through a Channel Tunnel). 'An Irish Channel Tunnel', commented the *Dundee Courier,* 'would have been an enormous boon and would have gone far to settle the Home Rule problem...we might...have had a United Kingdom by

---

[108]Michael Hurst, *Joseph Chamberlain and Liberal Re-Union* (Routledge and Kegan Paul, 1967), p.33. The sadness of 20th century Ireland may be attributed to the Ulster Unionism of 1922, rather than the work of these 19th century Liberals. The term itself within Irish politics, both Protestant and Catholic, was of a 'transfiguring vagueness', allowing the support of all shades of opinion (S.J. Connelly, (ed.), *The Oxford Companion to Irish History* (OUP, 1998), p.245).
[109]BL Add. Mss 44337, f 32.

this time.'[110] He also proposed a canal from Dublin to Galway, through which transatlantic liners would travel, on a shortened journey between Liverpool and New York, creating employment and new businesses along its route, and draining the central bogs.

For these schemes he received the customary odium from twentieth-century railway historians, but it is possible to argue that if his vision of building up an economically sound Ireland, and repairing the errors of the past, had been shared by a sufficient number of politicians, the history of the two islands might have been far more peaceful and meritorious. Such public works would mean prosperity and progress for Ireland, and, he said, would be 'worth more than a dozen Home rule Bills'.

The canal plan was explored in some detail, and was designed and costed by T.A. Walker, who constructed the Severn Tunnel and most of the Manchester Ship Canal. The interest costs on the outlay on both projects, argued Sir Edward, would not exceed £600,000 per year over a 99-year lease, 'about a fifth of the cost of keeping a hostile force in Ireland'. [111]

In the meantime, from 1869 onwards, he was investing in Irish railways and cross-Channel traffic, notably with the Newry and Greenore Railway (which eventually came under the control of the LNWR), and, in conjunction with the Cambrian Railway, links with the Great Southern and Western Railway. He supported the proposal to build the Dublin Trunk Connecting Railway, but it was violently rejected by both Houses.[112]

He retained to the last a paternalistic concern for Grimsby. His son Alfred was MP there for three years,[113] and was himself involved, controversially, in an election there in 1892. The two main candidates were the Liberal Unionist Edward Heneage (1840–1922), who had been the MP for Lincoln between 1865 and 1868, was unsuccessful in Grimsby in 1874, but served there

---

[110]16 April 1901.

[111]E.W. Watkin, letter to *The Times*, 18 July 1892, following a Paper on the feasibility of the project given by Sir Roper Lethbridge, KCIE, MP, to the Society of Arts on 11 February 1891 (Journal of the Society, 13 February 1891, pp.235–43). Watkin also supported the idea of a canal across the Wirral from Hilbre to Leasowe to avoid the approach problems of liners into Liverpool. This was first proposed in 1824, and explored in 1827 by Thomas Telford and Robert Stephenson (Transactions of the Historical Society of Lancashire and Cheshire, Vol. 124 (1973), article by W.R.I. McIntyre, pp 108–27).

[112]Dow, Vol. 2, p.160.

[113]The *Daily Chronicle*, 15 April 1901.

between 1890 and 1892; and Henri Josse (c1828–93), who described himself as a National Liberal. Josse was born in France, but was expelled from that country for his part in the disturbances of 1848. He was naturalised as a British subject, and settled in Grimsby. Watkin had been expected by his fellow-Liberal Unionists to commend Heneage's candidature, but he threw in his weight on the side of Josse, a follower of Gladstone, on the grounds that Josse had played an important part in the development of the town and the foreign trade of Grimsby. He was a JP, and President of the Grimsby Liberal Association from its foundation. Josse was elected in July 1892, but resigned just before his death in February 1893. Heneage contested the ensuing election, at which Watkin's choice was Henry Broadhurst (1840–1911), but this time Heneage won.[114]

Watkin's contributions to parliamentary procedures thinned out after 1891. In fact, only three more occasions appear in *Hansard*. The first of these, on 31 March 1892, was about who was to bear the cost of a proposed water and drainage tunnel through the Rock of Gibraltar; and the other two, on 7 and 15 November 1893, concerned the sanitary state of the principal hotel (The Palace) in Birkdale, near Southport. Thus, his first political activity was, domestically, in Manchester, and his last official speech, after circling the globe and influencing the formation of the British Empire, was concerned with a domestic issue in Lancashire, at the northern end of his Cheshire Lines Committee railway.

The Earl of Radnor[115] said of Watkin, during the 1895 election campaign for Hythe, and Watkin's standing for both the Conservatives and Liberals for the previous twenty-one years: 'No one (not even himself) knew what his politics were, excepting that he would vote for anyone or anything to get support for his Channel Tunnel.'[116] Conceding Sir Edward's all-embracing enthusiasm for the Channel Tunnel in all its commercial and philosophical impor-

---

[114]Broadhurst was described as 'an advanced Liberal', and was in favour of Home Rule; but he was prominent in work concerned with the juvenile reformatories, working class housing, and old age pension provision.

[115]In a letter to Aretas Akers-Douglas, First Commissioner of Works in Salisbury's 3rd Cabinet, 4 April 1895 (Kent Studies Centre, Maidstone, U564 C440/4).

[116]In the same letter he remarked that Watkin had taken 'his name off the British Unionist Association', but 'his reasons for doing so have not come down to us'.

tance, the facts would still seem to require a judgement both more objective and more charitable.

Certain principles and standpoints remain constant throughout all Watkin's political utterances. In his Stockport election campaign of 1864, he was described in the local newspaper as 'an independent Liberal and Unionist', even at that stage, and he said himself that he voted 'for what he saw as right, without caution for the official party line.' This was why he could be accepted at times by the Conservatives as a candidate they did not need to oppose. To the constituents in Hythe in 1885 he could express admiration for Gladstone, in his 'moral courage to change his opinions'.[117] Watkin's attendance record in the House of Commons, his contribution to its debates, and his influence upon legislation, reflect very creditably upon him. Apart from the 'career' politicians, his performance shows up well in comparison with other 'businessman' Members, and especially against those who hardly ever rose to speak, even in their constituents' interests. On the other hand, in all fairness to such Members, the 'widespread view that Parliament in the mid-nineteenth century was an undemanding occupation for gentlemen of leisure' is a distorted view. Even those who perceived the sum of their duties as simply listening to the debates, and voting accordingly, served by 'their assiduity in providing an attentive audience'.[118]

[117]E.W. Watkin, *Speeches*, p.35.
[118]Jenkins, *Gladstone*, p.255.

14

Watkin and Labour

The accident at Hexthorpe in 1887 had an interesting sequel. The crash occurred on 16 September, when a Liverpool to Hull MS&LR train collided with a Midland Railway excursion to the Doncaster Races. The directors discussed the circumstances at their meeting of 30 September.[1] It had caused the 'death of twenty-four persons and injuries to 200 others, 40 seriously'.[2] At the coroner's inquest, Sir Edward expressed the great sorrow and grief of the directors, and 'thought it right to state that in order to save trouble and reassure the minds of many poor people...it was not the intention of himself and his colleagues to dispute the legal liability for the consequences of the accident, and all those who would meet the question in a fair and just spirit would be dealt with quickly and generously'. In fact, two inquests were held, and in both, the juries had returned a verdict of manslaughter against the driver and fireman of the Liverpool train for their culpable negligence in disregarding the danger signals exhibited to them, which was the cause of the accident. The Chairman reported that large meetings of the company's employees, had been held at Mexborough, Sheffield and elsewhere, at which resolutions had been unanimously passed, offering to contribute a week's wages per man 'towards the cost which may be incurred by the Company' in consequence of the accident. This was 'an expression of their sympathy with the Directors in the sad calamity'. The Board was unanimous that the offer could not be accepted, but expressed their gratification at finding such proof of the good feelings of the staff, inviting a deputation from their body to meet

---

[1]PRO RAIL, 463/21 Minute 10984.
[2]These figures were consolidated later to 25 killed and 94 injured (Dow, Vol. 2, p.202). Pendleton, Vol. 2, p.450, gives 60 injured.

the Board, so that adequate expression might be given of their appreciation of the course taken by the men.[3] The meeting took place on Tuesday, 4 October 1887 in the boardroom at Manchester London Road Station. A report of the meeting was printed, to twenty-one pages, and was interleaved in the minute book. There were ten directors, four senior officers and fifty men present. Before the men spoke (having been assured by the Chairman that they would be invited to do so after he had said a few words), several of the directors expressed their sorrow at what had happened, and their gratitude for the actions of the men, but Watkin was at his best in his introduction to the meeting.

He said he had read with great emotion some of the expressions that had been used at the various meetings held by the men, and observed, to cheers, that the meetings were merely the beginnings of what he called a 'great movement'. 'I need not tell you', he said, 'because many of you know perfectly well from long experience in the service of your employers, that the desire of the Board has always been to treat the undertaking as a great partnership between the silent partners who have supplied the capital out of their individual savings, on the one side, and the more active partners who do the hard and the mental labour in connection with the undertaking on the other'. In sentences that would invite the wrath of a mid-twentieth-century trade union official, he said: 'We have always desired that it should be a partnership on just and equal terms, and that we should, whatever we do, avoid those complications which every now and then have marked as well as disfigured the great history of labour'. The shareholders on the one side, and those who work for pay are very much an equality, he suggested. 'Taking the last year as a test, I find that the total net profit earned was £770,056. On the other side we paid in regular wages and salaries...£685,609. There are 11,396 shareholders', he told them, and their share of net profit on the year was £67 11s 0d a head. The company employed 9,935 persons, and their share came to £69 0s 2d per head. Therefore', he concluded, to several ('Hear, hear') affirmations, 'there is not so much of a difference...between the man who finds the capital and the man who works.'[4]

---

[3]Minute 10985.
[4]Printed supplement to the minutes, p.4.

This is an interesting comparison (except, presumably, from the point of view of the Marxist doctrine of Surplus Value), and one which puts a different perspective on the slender dividends most of the MS&LR investors received. And also on the comment, intended as a rebuke, of Mr Fielden, a shareholder of the South Eastern Railway, at a shareholders' meeting of that company, that 'Sir Edward had raised the salary of every railway worker in England'.[5] It is difficult to avoid the speculation of what result the same method of comparison would have produced on the LNWR and the Great Western.

While being 'immensely debted' to them for what they had suggested, 'and I cannot find words to say how much we thank you,' he told them, 'the Directors have come to the conclusion that it would not be consistent...with their duty to tax those who labour in the sweat of their brow to the extent that you have proposed...And so', he concluded, '[you] must allow us to respect-fully decline'.

It says a great deal for the *esprit* of Watkin's main railway company that such an upswelling of corporate sentiment and co-responsibility should have taken place at all. The Marx/Engels doctrine of the inevitable enmity and total conflict of interest between Capital and Labour was already permeating industrial relations by 1887, and the attitude of some railway chairmen and directors gave some warrant for that argument. Watkin's patern-alism, as well as his conservative religious beliefs, might have been in the process of being rendered obsolete by the current of events in theology and political and scientific philosophy, but that it was not mere idealism was illustrated by the actions of those locomen, inspectors, guards, signalmen and warehouse operators of South Yorkshire and Lancashire.

Watkin then gave some details of the costs and liabilities in the matter in hand, and went on to encourage the men to continue to invest their savings in the various funds and schemes – Mutual Provident, Reserve, Accident, Staff Savings Bank – which the company had set up for the purpose of their security. He mentioned that the directors had tried to establish a superannua-tion scheme for those who work for daily wages, on the lines of

---

[5] *The City Jackdaw*, Manchester, 22 September 1876, p.383.

the existing arrangements for salaried staff, which would be funded partly by contributions from shareholders and directors and partly by contributions from the men. Their efforts had not, so far, overcome the very great difficulties they had encountered, but the hope was still alive.[6] There followed a short discourse on those who regarded capitalists as 'bloated plutocrats', for whom they worked for hours before they were able to secure anything for themselves ('But if a hard-saving man had not provided the capital ...there would be no employment for the workman'), and those, 'rare among shareholders', who say that 'the duty of a Joint Stock Company is to get the work done as cheaply as it can, and to get as much work for a sovereign as it possibly can, and to leave the workmen all the chances and accidents of life'. He pointed out that though there might be these wild elements on either side, 'this is not the language by which you have been met by this Board of Directors when any proposition has been made to them' [Cheers]. 'They have felt that we are all partners in a great undertaking, and that we have a mutual interest in it'. Watkin's view that 'workers' and 'capitalists' were in partnership for the success of their common enterprise cannot be attributed solely to 'paternalism', whether the word be used pejoratively or not. In fact, it was:

> One of the most deep-rooted concepts that Liberals had of their role in politics. The philosophy, the idealism even...was that between working men and employers there was fundamental identity of interest, that prosperity or lack of prosperity in industry affected all alike, that working men benefited if capitalists prospered. All belonged to 'the industrious class'. In so far as there was class division in human society it was between working men and their employers, on the one hand, and the parasites, the non-industrious, landowning class, on the other.[7]

A further look at how Watkin viewed the function and welfare of employees in his various companies may help to give some insight

---

[6]This distinction between salaried and waged employees had not been overcome by the time of nationalisation in 1948.

[7]D.A. Hamer, *Liberal Politics in the Age of Gladstone and Rosebery* (OUP, 1972), p.14.

into his practice of business management. Not long after he had taken over as General Manager of the MS&L Railway, he initiated projects for Staff Benevolent Funds and Savings Banks, in June 1854. He presented as a Christmas present to every station clerk (station master) on the line a turkey, goose or leg of mutton. In 1855, company schools for the children of employees were established. He was a strong supporter of Staff Improvement Classes and Mechanics' Institutes. In the day when various methods of shorthand writing, including Isaac Pitman's, were considered merely a harmless eccentricity, Watkin had his office staff taught the Pitman method, and this fact was known by the Pitman family. On 30 August 1887, they held a public meeting in Manchester, and Watkin was invited to preside.

He gave a practical account of his pioneer work in utilising the art for the dictation of correspondence in the offices of the railways with which he had been associated. It was their custom...when they engaged a young man as a clerk, to compel him to learn shorthand, and Mr Henry Pitman[8] had been their first teacher. I am bound to say, said Sir Edward, that the Pitman system had been an unmixed blessing to all those connected with railway work to whom phonographic ability had been of the utmost service.[9]

Pitman's is still the predominant system in use today.[10] The MS&LR was 'a training college for the railway service'[11], and this characteristic remained throughout its existence as the Great Central Railway, and into the LNER period. It was a company characterised by 'contented workmen'.[12]

Following a request from some of the company's clerks whose salaries were £100 per year that these be reduced to £99 10s 0d, in order to avoid income tax, the company declined, but eighteen months later, in 1855, the Board ruled that the company would pay the income tax on all staff salaries of between £100 and £120

---

[8]The younger brother of Sir Isaac, who had settled in Manchester.
[9]Alfred Baker, *The Life of Sir Isaac Pitman* (London: Sir Isaac Pitman and Sons Ltd, 1913), pp.15, 118 and 266.
[10]*Encyclopaedia Britannica*, 1995 Edition, Vol. 10, p.762.
[11]*The City Jackdaw*, Manchester, 22 September 1876, p.382.
[12]*Ibid.*

per annum.[13] Always keen on encouragement, Watkin launched a plan which gave enginemen monthly monetary incentives to work more than the prescribed daily mileages, and to effect savings in locomotive working. Unpunctual running, however, on more than one train per week, incurred a fine of one shilling in normal circumstances within the enginemen's control, or half a crown if due to shortage of steam through bad firing.[14] In 1874, he built forty-nine cottages at isolated places on the line for employees who were having difficulty finding homes; these were built, for instance, at Torside, Crowden, Woodhead, Woodhouse, Barnsley Junction and Dodworth. This scheme was extended during the following year, and hundreds of staff houses were erected by the company up to the end of the century.[15] Most railway companies built some houses for their workers, but Watkin stands out in this respect.[16] His programme of building houses in Grimsby from 1860 was intended primarily to attract fishermen to the town, but the provision of 'healthy workingmen's dwellings with proper sanitation and municipal improvements' was quickly appreciated.[17] He once remarked: 'If I were to walk through a workhouse and see any employee of the MS&LR dying there, I should not consider we had done our duty as Christian men and employers'.

From the start he initiated a progressive and enlightened policy with the business community; traders were offered six-monthly and yearly tickets for those whose business with the company amounted to not less than £250 per annum. A scheme to encourage residential traffic took the form of the issue of free tickets, valid for ten years, from Sheffield to any station as far as Retford, to anyone who built a house of an annual rental value of £35 or more, within two miles of any station on the line.[18]

Watkin was in the forefront of widespread co-operation between railway managers, becoming the first president of the Railway Club, inaugurated at the Clarence Hotel, Manchester on 2 November 1855, to facilitate mutual help and exchange of infor-

---

[13]Dow, Vol. 1, p.160.
[14]*Ibid.*
[15]Dow, Vol. 2, p.73.
[16]Jack Simmons, *The Victorian Railway* (Thames and Hudson, 1991) pp.67 and 381, n.186.
[17]William Ashworth, *The Genesis of Modern British Town Planning* (Routledge and Kegan Paul, 1954, repr.1972), pp.129-30.
[18]Dow, Vol. 1, p.160.

mation between railway officers.[19] He was a member of the Railway Companies' Association, which first met on 4 November 1858. This sprang from a conference of delegates of various railway companies, who had met to resolve difficulties of conflicting interests, especially those arising from the bitter warfare with the LNWR, who wanted a more permanent organisation. Its object was 'Railway Improvement by all and for all'. This body existed, in visible continuity, to the nationalisation of the British railway system in 1948.[20] This organisation was distinct from the Railway Companies' Association which held its first meeting on 29 July 1858, which was formed to promote parliamentary Bills, and was dedicated to increasing profits and cutting down wasteful competition. Little attempt was made to involve railway MPs, and the association was dissolved, after divisions and falling attendances, on 12 September 1861.[21] These organisations emerged at the same time as the need had been felt for a 'railway clearing house', to facilitate the correct allocation of receipts and costs, and general co-operation between the companies.

Watkin's just and compassionate treatment of his workforce (with possible exceptions where he was defending his son's welfare) might seem to be at odds, as we have noticed, with his hostile attitude to moves towards organised labour and the emergent trade unionism. The key to this apparent inconsistency is in his view of the unity of interest of capitalist and worker. Some of the newly rich merchant classes adopted the worst characteristics of the aristocracy they were beginning to replace: an attitude of power over their workers, and ambitions in the area of ostentatious riches, private landowning, and large, castle-like houses.

An example of this was Joseph Priestley Edwards (1816–68), son of a Halifax manufacturer, who bought an estate at Fixby Park, near Huddersfield, and the valleys and moors at Saltenstall, above Luddenden in Yorkshire. The moors had been used from time immemorial for rights of turbary[22] and grazing; they were criss-crossed by paths and packhorse ways, but appropriated and closed to the public by Edwards. In 1859 he began the construction of a

---

[19]*Ibid.*.
[20]*Ibid*, p.190.
[21]Geoffrey Alderman, *The Railway Interest* (Leicester University Press, 1973), p.19.
[22]The common right to dig peat or turf.

mock-baronial pile called Castle Carr, with appropriated landscaped gardens and follies – lording it over the land and common folk around it in aristocratic style.[23] This attitude to the workers (in Marx's definition, those who had to sell their labour to live) was indeed the extraction of as much work from them as possible, for the payment of as little money as possible.

Watkin, however, did not forget his origins, and respected his employees. He adopted from the best of the previous generation of land-owning gentry the view that power and influence carried with them great and binding responsibilities. Those called to management had a duty to compassion and humanity as well as to efficiency and leadership.

The concept of 'organised labour' set the two halves of a business against each other. The formation of trades unions had been attempted 'after the repeal of the ineffective Combination Acts of 1824, and the...Reform Act of 1832, which, while welcomed by the middle classes, was a profound disappointment to radicals and the militant working class'. Early efforts were dissipated by internal disagreements, and in 1834 matters came to a head when six trade unionists in the Dorset village of Tolpuddle administered oaths to fellow workers, were charged under the Mutiny Act of 1749, and sentenced to seven years' transportation.[24] The influence of 'Socialism' emerging from the eighteenth century 'Enlightenment' gained strength during the nineteenth century. Robert Owen (1771–1858) was a strong influence on the formation of 'Collectives' among the working class, but his own methods were actually an enlightened paternalism. [25]

It has been remarked that the railwayman was an ideal employee for the disciplined work of the system, coming, as most of them did for the first half of the era of railway building, from a rigidly authoritarian life in the countryside.[26] It took nearly a generation for the less scrupulous railway managements to force the necessity for some sort of labour solidarity in organisation. Examples abound. 'The Great Northern would suspend for the most trivial

---

[23]Michael Harding, *Walking the Peak and Pennines* (London: Michael Joseph, 1992), pp.204-5.
[24]Christopher Hibbert, *The English: A Social History, 1066–1945* (London: Guild Publishing, 1987), p. 492.
[25]Trevor May, *An Economic and Social History of Britain, 1760-1970* (Longmans, 1987), pp.229-30.
[26]Frank McKenna, *The Railway Workers, 1840-1970* (Faber and Faber, 1980), p.27.

offence; the North Western discharged a ganger for leaving his post to obtain a cup of tea'. 'In 1848, the Great Western dismissed a clerk for betting on a horse race...It was this bullying and arbitrary treatment management were anxious to preserve'.[27] In the 1890s, 'Mr.Forbes, Chairman of the London, Chatham and Dover Railway wrote that railwaymen were not overworked and were well paid..."I sometimes work myself seventeen hours a day". Asked if his work compared with that of his workforce, whose seventeen hours a day were arduous, uncomfortable, and dangerous, he declined to reply'.[28] Such attitudes were never part of Watkin's style, and as late as 1891 this was borne out by the staff themselves. It was recorded in the minutes of an MSL Board meeting held on 5 June of that year that William Pollitt (the General Manager) had received a letter from the drivers at Mexborough. This was written to Thomas Parker (the Locomotive, Carriage and Wagon Superintendent), regarding the hours of duty question, a subject 'about which Evidence had been given before the Labour Commission which the Directors consider Satisfactory as showing the good feeling Existing between the men and their Employers'. The letter is printed in full in the minutes:

Mr Parker [Locomotive, Carriage and Wagon Superintendent]

Mexboro'

10 May 1891

Dear Sir,
Having seen the Evidence given before the Parliamentary Committee re the hours worked by Railway Servants, at the instigation of Mr Harford, Gen. Sect'y, Amalgamated Society of Railway Servants, We, the Engine Drivers and Firemen employed by the M.S.& L. Rly Co'y at Mexboro' consider it our duty as Loyal Servants to enter a protest against the unfair manner in which undue weight is brought to bear upon our Company by the fact, that the Evidence adduced is by discharged servants, and therefore is not in accordance with the much improved system of operation at the present time,

---

[27]*Ibid*, p.35.
[28]*Ibid*, p.71.

and we consider it our pleasure to offer our services, should you feel disposed to require them, to give evidence in the Company's behalf before the above-mentioned Committee. We consider, 'taking the past for our guide', anything conducive to our welfare and that of the General Public by the shortening of hours worked, can and will be dealt with as far as possible by yourself, in conjunction other officials of the Company, without the interference of Legislature.

We are also desirous to state that Mr Harford's action is directly contrary to the wishes of the Engine Drivers and Firemen of the M.S.& L. Co., neither has he any authority to represent us. On behalf of the Enginemen at Mexboro' – Committee's signatures over – [29] I remain your Obedient Servant,

[Signed] A. Fox Engineman' [30]

It is clear that Watkin had successfully communicated his ideals of mutual respect, trust, and co-operation.

Brakes and other Technical Matters

After the accidents at Bullhouse in 1884, in 1887 at Hexthorpe, and in other parts of Britain, the question of brakes for trains, and which was the most effective of the several methods which developed, was raised with greater urgency. Watkin has received more than his share of unfair criticism from railway historians for the widespread conservatism which characterised nearly all companies towards the acceptance of new developments. The early trains had brakes on the locomotive tenders only, the engine itself reducing speed by being put into reverse gear. In the 1850s a brake compartment or van was specified, in which the guard had a screw brake, acting on the wheels of his vehicle, to assist the stopping of trains. Later, engines were fitted with steam brakes, as more

---

[29]The signatures of the other ten members of the representative committee at Mexborough are appended to the letter.
[30]PRO RAIL 463/24, Minute 13,954.

reliable construction materials were evolved, but the increase in train weights and speeds made a brake which acted on all the wheels of each passenger vehicle very desirable.

From experiments in the 1840s and onwards, various methods were tried and the issue came down eventually to a choice between 'simple' brakes, which could be applied by the enginemen throughout the train, and 'automatic' brakes, which applied if the engine, or part of the train, were to become detached. The Board of Trade wanted a universal application of the automatic system, but the railway companies, always averse to being told what to do in their engineering and commercial activities by the government, procrastinated, mainly on grounds of needless expense in the circumstances of continuous development and new refinement. Three systems of continuous brake emerged as the main contenders: the 'simple' vacuum, designed by James Young Smith, in which a pipe running the length of the train through cylinders on each carriage had its air extracted by a pump on the locomotive. When steam was introduced to the pipe, the vacuum was broken, and the brakes were applied. If the train pipe was severed for any reason, however, the brake became useless. The 'automatic' vacuum system, perfected by James Gresham, had the advantage that if the brake pipe was broken, the brakes were applied on all vehicles automatically. The third was the compressed air brake, designed by George Westinghouse and Steel-McInnes, which worked, basically, in the same way but used compressed air instead of a vacuum as the brake power.

There was a long-running debate in Parliament. Queen Victoria wrote to Gladstone on 30 October 1873, expressing concern over the number of train accidents. A Royal Commission on Railway Accidents proposed full brake trials, and these were duly held at Newark, near Nottingham, in June 1875. Of the seven types tested, including the 'cheap and dreadful'[31] chain brake of the LNWR, the trials found in favour of the continuous compressed air brake, but companies remained reluctant to adopt it.[32] James Staats Forbes told the shareholders of the LCDR in February 1876 that

---

[31]Adrian Vaughan, *Railwaymen, Politics, and Money* (John Murray, 1997), p.210. As late as 1883, the LNWR Chairman, Richard Moon, could declare. 'It was the best brake in the world' (Jeffrey Wells, *Backtrack Magazine*, March 1999, p.156).

[32]Simmons and Biddle, *The Oxford Companion to British Railway History* (OUP, 1997), p.42.

he had been urged for some tome to adopt continuous brakes, block telegraph, and signal/point lever interlocking, but he 'had been reluctant to involve the shareholders in a single shilling of outlay which could be avoided'.[33]

In answer to one of the questions raised from time to time in Parliament about the protection of the travelling public, the President of the Board of Trade (Viscount Sandon) replied in 1880 that he 'could hardly say that the steps taken by the Railway Companies as to continuous brakes have been as energetic and satisfactory as I could wish'. But after giving some figures in illustration, he went on to say:

> It is fair, however, to observe that the continuous improvements that are being made in continuous brakes explain to a certain degree the hesitation of the Companies in coming to a decision on this matter, and they certainly show how inexpedient it would be that Parliament, unless absolutely compelled by the want of action on the part of the Companies, should lay down the rule as to the adoption of some particular form of brake.[34]

Watkin's inveterate hostility to the Board of Trade must have melted considerably at such a perceptive and balanced reply.

During his time in North America in the 1860s, he had met James Young Smith, who was Superintendent of Machinery to the US Military Railroads. After the Civil War, Smith did not achieve much success in marketing his simple continuous vacuum brake, and he came to Europe. He persuaded Watkin and the MS&L Chief Engineer, Charles Reboul Sacré, to adopt his brake. After several serious accidents – notably on the London and South Western Railway on 3 June 1884, and on the MS&LR at Bullhouse, near Penistone, on 16 June 1884, and Hexthorpe, near Doncaster, on 16 September 1887 – the limitations of the Smith brake were exposed, though in none of these cases was it the cause.

The historian Cuthbert Hamilton Ellis seemed to blame Watkin for everything that could be attributed subsequently to the Smith

---

[33]Adrian Vaughan, p.210.
[34]*Hansard*, 9 March 1880.

vacuum brake: he claims that his decision for its adoption was 'destined to be more disastrous than any other error of mechanical judgement perpetrated on a British railway.'[35] This statement seems even more comprehensively unjust than most of the unexamined blackenings of Watkin's character. A Bill introduced in Parliament in 1873 to enforce the installation of continuous brakes was defeated by the influence of no fewer than 124 railway director MPs, and a fair sprinkling of railway directors in the House of Lords.[36]

The MS&L Board, discussing on 5 September 1884 the Company Secretary's reply to the Board of Trade's recommendations after the Bullhouse accident, recorded: 'Blame is cast upon the Company for the non-adoption of a particular form of Automatic Break [sic], presumably the Westinghouse Break, which appears to be considered as the "Board of Trade Break", a late inspecting officer of the Board being the Chairman of the Westinghouse Company.' The Secretary, Edward Ross, quoted the Boards of Trade's Inspecting Officer, Colonel Yolland, as saying in his report on the accident that the Westinghouse Automatic Air Brake was 'a very clever and ingenious piece of mechanism of a very great number of separate parts...but, as is well-known, the greater number of parts in any piece of mechanism, the greater is the liability of failure.'[37]

Some months earlier, addressing a Metropolitan Railway meeting, Watkin had exuded a premature self-satisfaction with the Smith brake, on the grounds of simplicity and cheapness, and with characteristically colourful phrase had criticised the air brake and the Board of Trade. This earned him an adverse report in the railway press, and demonstrated, again, that sometimes he was not his own best advocate.[38]

The relative virtues of the continuous vacuum brake and the compressed air system were still being debated well into the twentieth century. At the 'Grouping' of the main line companies in 1923, all four companies standardised on the vacuum brake for all

---

[35]C. Hamilton Ellis, *British Railway History* (George Allen and Unwin, 1953), Vol. 2, p.42.
[36]Adrian Vaughan, p.207.
[37]Board Minute 9305.
[38]As a matter of record, not a single passenger was killed on the Metropolitan or the SER while Watkin was Chairman.

locomotive-hauled trains. Electric units all had the compressed air system. The latter became universal, though vacuum-fitted goods trains were still running on the main line as late as 1997.[39]

The question of the adoption of one particular form of technology while other systems are still being developed has remained as a problem to railway operators into the present century. The commitment of vast sums of money to any one of the several designs of train safety equipment is a serious business while technology is still advancing and the method adopted could soon be outmoded. Watkin, in addressing the MS&LR half-yearly shareholders' meeting of 21 January 1885, had said, in a debate on the safety at speed of coal wagons, 'If it is necessary to secure public safety in the smallest degree, a money sacrifice is nothing in comparison to the protection of life and person from injury.'[40] But this must be must be taken in the context of securing the design of rolling stock to as high a standard as possible, rather than lavish spending on elaborate operating devices. Only a year before he had characterised safety systems as 'over-machining', which had 'the tendency to make men more and more like automatons and less personally responsible'.[41]

He has been quoted by the railway historian O.S. Nock as saying at a Board meeting after the Bullhouse accident that he preferred 'an occasional Penistone' to fitting something he did not want.[42] This, commented Nock, 'might have rendered Watkin liable to a charge of corporate manslaughter by twentieth century standards'. But Watkin was putting into blunt Mancunian phraseology what the management of all transport operations – shipping, airlines, and railways – have always considered prudent, but have expressed in more circumlocutory ways or left unrevealed. In the same issue of the *Railway Magazine* just quoted appear these words, regarding the enquiry into the accident at Clapham Junction in 1998: 'When the expenditure needed to install ATP [Automatic Train Protection] had been fully assessed, it became apparent that the cost per likely life saved was extremely

---

[39] The bogie hopper wagons built from 1935 for the conveying of limestone from Peak Forest (Tunstead) quarries to the Northwich (Winnington and Lostock Gralam) plants of the ICI Company.

[40] PRO RAIL 463/77, p.24.

[41] 23 January 1884. PRO RAIL 463/77, p.10.

[42] Quoted, *Railway Magazine*, May 2000, p.19.

high, and successive governments have jibbed at providing the money for its widespread installation.'[43] A television programme broadcast on BBC2 on the subject of railway safety[44] stated that cost-effectiveness was always taken into account, and quoted the figure of £3 million per life as a calculation when deciding upon an expensive safety system.[45] This was precisely Watkin's point.

Throughout his career, he was always willing to examine new technology. At first he was not impressed by the 'Block' system of train safety, in which trains were kept clearly apart from each other by regulating the space between them, arguing that it removed responsibility from the engine driver, and advocating closer adherence to existing rules on safety.[46] But by the development of the Block system by Edwin Clark, which was introduced in 1854, Watkin had changed his mind sufficiently to have it installed on the whole of the MS&L main line from Guide Bridge to New Holland by the end of 1857.[47]

He was in favour of catch points[48] in the face of his consulting engineer, in the 1860s. A good example of their desirability was seen on 23 June 1864, when thirty-three wagons broke away from a train at Dunford Bridge on the gradient up to the eastern end of the Woodhead tunnel. The wagons ran for no less than twenty-two miles, through Sheffield Victoria Station and as far as Darnall, before they stopped, fortunately without meeting another train.[49] Watkin was also successful, in 1884, after trying for many years, in introducing an electrical system of communication between passenger and guard, to supplement the existing mechanical provision. He was to go on record as saying: 'A man was safer in an express train than anywhere else in the world'.[50] He was also

---

[43]*Ibid,* p.28.

[44]18 September 2000.

[45]The cost, in millions of pounds, of the various systems at the time was: ATP, 1,000; Train Protection and Warning System, 485; TPWS +, 555; European Train Control System, 3,000 (*Railway Magazine,* May 2000) pp.10 and 11.

[46]Jack Simmons, *The Railways of Britain* (London: Sheldrake Press, 1986), p.195.

[47]Dow, Vol. 1, p.257.

[48]These are turnouts which are trailing to the direction of travel, permanently set against the traffic flow, but sprung so as to be forced in passage, to act as a trap for wagons breaking away from a train which may otherwise collide with a train following.

[49]Dow, Vol. 2, p.25.

[50]*King* magazine, 20 April 1901. The statistics still bear him out. European Commissioner figures for the year 2001 show the following risk of fatality for each mode of transport: Per 100 million passenger kilometres, Road – 1.10; Ferry – 0.33; Air – 0.08; Rail – 0.04. Per 100 million person/hours, Road – 33; Ferry – 10.5; Air – 36.5; Rail – 2.

energetic in pursuit of electric lighting systems. Manchester London Road Station was one of the first places in the city to use it in place of oil-lighting, and his chalet at Beddgelert was lit by electricity generated on the premises by water-power from the building's own reservoir. In 1887 he installed an electric hoist at Rose Hill, to enable Lady Watkin to be moved from her room about the house and grounds in her wheelchair. It was his idea to introduce, in 1889, electric bell signalling in the notoriously smoke-filled Woodhead tunnel,[51] and at his suggestion, carriage warming apparatus was installed on the Manchester to New Holland expresses in 1854.[52]

His restless ingenuity could at times verge on the risible. At the Board meeting of 31 May 1861 he 'called the attention of the Directors to the Contract with the Electric Telegraph Company which would expire in about 11 years from the present time', with a view to seeking their approval for taking steps 'anticipatory of such Contract [renewal]'. He suggested, 'Trees of a proper kind might be planted at the required distances along the line which might be done at a small expense, and they would grow to the required height by the time the Contract was terminated.' He submitted the following estimate, which had been supplied by G.T. Smith, the company's rating agent, of the cost:

25 trees to the mile, to be planted 5 feet high in growth at 5d each:	1s 5d
Labor [sic] in planting, say 2 men, would be only one mile per day:	6s 0d
Stakes, say, 1 score per mile:	1s 0d
[Total]	8s 5d

Far from raising a smile, and a motion for Next Business, this proposal was adopted.[53]

Watkin, however, in common with the chairmen of most companies at the time, including the LNWR, took very unkindly to a revolutionary proposal of Allport, of the Midland, to take effect

[51]Dow, Vol. 2, p.206.
[52]Dow, Vol. 1, p.218.
[53]Minute 10.

from 1 April 1872. This was to carry third-class passengers on all trains, instead of only on certain services, which was the custom. Allport followed that by proposing to reduce all first-class fares to 1s 5d per mile and abolish second class altogether. This, with effect from 1 January 1875, gave third-class passengers cushioned seats, and the hard wooden-seated third class coaches were scrapped. The MS&L Board saw this as an 'unfriendly act, calculated to do damage to railway property'. The directors decided to support the other companies in their opposition, 'in whatever course they may deem expedient for mutual protection'.[54] A spirited debate took place, including a leading article in *The Times* of 12 October 1874, which argued that as there were three classes in society, the railways should go on respecting them. Such protective conservatism, and questionable sociology, were doomed to fail in the open market, and all companies had to follow suit eventually, the MS&L and the Cheshire Lines doing so in 1891–2.[55]

---

[54]Dow, Vol. 2, p.58.
[55]Simmons and Biddle, p.85.

15

The Channel Tunnel

Watkin's part in the promotion of a land link between England and France occupied much of his energies between the 1870s and the 1890s. From the beginning, the Channel Tunnel forms a fascinating study of how the Victorian characteristics of vision, passionate commitment and unquenchable energy and enterprise, clashed in their commercial and economic boundlessness with the imperial manifestation of these qualities in the military and political fields. It is not altogether clear how Sir Edward – 'One of the most formidable men who ever ran a railway from a financier's desk'[1] – first became interested in the idea of a Channel tunnel. Absolom had recorded in his journal[2] that during a visit to London he and Edward had been to the Panorama of the overland route to India, '[With] which we were much pleased.'[3] The idea of a continuous rail connection from his father's Manchester cotton trade to its biggest customer could have been sown in conversation at that time. One of his arguments for the tunnel forty years later was that it would 'connect England with her great dependency of India',[4] and he never lost his interest in that country. In 1857, in one of his earliest speeches in Parliament, he argued at length for more energy in pursuit of an arterial railway system there, which would ensure greater efficiency in the administration of the country. Merely a practical question, he would be told. 'But these practical questions were at the foundation of all political success', which was attained by 'labour and forethought'.[5] He had discussed

---

[1]Humphrey Slater and Correlli Barnett, *The Channel Tunnel* (London: Allan Wingate, 1958), p.53.
[2]13 June 1850.
[3]A.E. Watkin, p.262.
[4]*Hansard*, 5 June 1890, col. 27.
[5]*Hansard*, CXLVI, cols. 1713–30, 17 July 1857.

with Richard Cobden, with whom he visited Paris during the Anglo-French Commercial Treaty in 1860, the idea of saving time and avoiding the distress of the sea crossing. The *Illustrated London News* had given good coverage to the Frenchman Thomé de Gamond's detailed French plan of 1857, and Watkin was a close friend of the founder and editor of the *ILN*, Herbert Ingram, dining with him in London in that year.[6] What is certain, however, is that without his vision, energy and ability, the whole project would have foundered in the 1870s for lack of leadership on this side of the Channel.

The idea of a submarine tunnel connecting France with England dates back to 1802 when, after the Treaty of Amiens had brought the French wars to a temporary conclusion, Albert Mathieu, a mining engineer from Northern France, submitted to Napoleon Bonaparte his plans for a road tunnel for stage coaches. In 1833 Mathieu's plan was taken up, as a railway tunnel, by Joseph Aimé Thomé (later de Gamond), whose name was to dominate discussions of the Channel tunnel thereafter. He was confident of support from the English side, having received encouragement in 1827 from Isambard Kingdom Brunel and Joseph Locke, and the Prince Consort spoke very warmly of the project. In 1856, de Gamond submitted to Napoleon III his latest research and proposals: Watkin claimed later that it had been his suggestion to de Gamond that he spoke to the Emperor about his plans. The Emperor set up a commission, which reported favourably, but insisted that before a comprehensive technical survey could be made, there must be full co-operation between the British and French governments.[7]

By April 1866 the *Moniteur Universel* could carry an item reporting that 'a campaign had begun on the Straits of Dover for the last verification of a project for a submarine tunnel', the plans of which would be on view in Paris at the Universal Exhibition of the following year. It was probably at this time that de Gamond met William Low, one of several engineers on the English side who had been assiduously preparing schemes for a tunnel. The co-operation between de Gamond and Low rapidly became a full-

[6]Isabel Bailey, *Herbert Ingram Esq., MP* (Boston, Lincolnshire: Richard Kay, 1996), p.55.
[7]Slater and Barnett, p. 16.

37 Aimé Thomé de Gamond, leading French proponent
of the Channel Tunnel (1807–1875)

scale Anglo-French venture. Low involved two other British engineers who were interested, James Brunlees, and John Hawkshaw, who constructed the Lancashire and Yorkshire Railway.

In the summer of 1868, the Emperor received a delegation of some twenty people to look at the latest development of Low's original plan. This group represented the newly formed 'Anglo-French Channel Tunnel Committee'.[8] The Emperor responded by forming an official commission to investigate the new plans. 'The presentation of the Low–de Gamond scheme to Napoleon III was a turning-point in the history of the Tunnel',[9] and 1868 was a turning point also in other areas. France's Napoleonic prestige and influence was fading, and Bismarck and von Moltke were plotting its final demise. In July 1870, the action was joined, and interest in the Channel tunnel was overwhelmed. But not for very long. Public opinion in England, which had combined a sullen fear and dislike of France with a fellow-feeling for the Germans, swung in

[8]Donald Hunt, *The Story of the Channel Tunnel* (Malvern, Images Publishing Ltd.,1994), p.31.
[9]Slater and Barnett, p.23.

248

favour of the post-Napoleonic France, and a recognition that an ally was now needed on the Continent as a counter-balance to the new united Germany. In July 1871, Lord Granville wrote to Viscount Enfield that he had been informed by the French that the time had come to resume negotiations.[10]

On 15 January 1872, the Channel Tunnel Company Ltd was incorporated and registered in London by the Anglo-French Tunnelling Committee.[11] It projected a tunnel from Dover to Sangatte, connecting the LCDR and the South-Eastern on the British side, and the Chemin de Fer du Nord on the French. The estimated cost was £10m.[12] In 1873, a disagreement between Hawkshaw, with his plan for a double-tracked single tunnel, and Low, who favoured self-ventilated twin tunnels, came to a head, and Low formed his own 'Anglo-French Submarine Railway Company' in opposition.[13] In 1874, the Foreign Secretary, Lord Derby, sought the view of the Board of Trade on the project, which replied that it had 'no doubt of the utility of the work, and that it ought not to be opposed'. The military implications of the project they referred to the War Office, who replied that 'there were no objections to the undertaking on military grounds'.[14]

The promoters thus had the blessing of both countries. The French Chamber passed a Bill which ratified a convention between Michel Chevalier, of the French Channel Tunnel Company, and the Minister of Public Works, giving permission to drive a tunnel from the French side to meet its English counterpart, and to conclude an agreement with the British for co-ordination of the work[15] The speed of the French Government's response, and the detail it had entered into, had the effect of unsettling the calm and unhurried attitude hitherto thought appropriate by the British. There was at the Foreign Office and the Treasury a sudden emergence of problems requiring solutions, including limits of jurisdiction between the two countries and the railway companies involved.[16]

---

[10]Keith Wilson, *Channel Tunnel Visions, 1850*-1945 (Hambledon Press, 1994), p.10.
[11]Wilson, p.11.
[12]Thomas Whiteside, *The Tunnel Under the Channel* (London: Rupert Hart-Davies, 1962), pp.28–9.
[13]Hunt, p.35.
[14]*Ibid*, pp. 35–6.
[15]Slater and Barnett, p.34.
[16]*Ibid*, p. 41.

In 1874, Watkin, who had been judging the best time to enter the field, put forward his own scheme, under the auspices of the South Eastern Railway, and Parliament empowered him, and the rival LCDR, to spend £20,000 each on tunnel research. The SER had taken the place of Low's by then defunct Anglo-French Submarine Railway Company, and adopted his twin-tunnel plan. But as early as 1875 the Board of Trade said that defence considerations must be safeguarded, despite the War Office's *Nihil Obstat* of 1874. At the time, Britain was at peace with the world, and confident in her ability to cope with any military emergency. But the threat of invasion by Napoleon Bonaparte was still a living memory. As Gladstone put it in 1870, 'Happy England! Happy ...that the wise dispensation of Providence has cut her off, by that streak of silver sea, which passengers so often and so justly execrate...Maritime supremacy has become the proud – perhaps indefectible – inheritance of England.'[17] These sentiments, with their Shakespearean echoes, made a deep impression, and for many years his imagery was part of the vocabulary of those who opposed a Channel tunnel.

Yet in August 1875 the Channel Tunnel Company received the Royal Assent to its Bill and a concession of ninety-nine years was granted, enabling the company to proceed with the purchase of the necessary land. Preliminary work began at St Margaret's Bay, Dover, but the site was later abandoned because of the constant ingress of water. In 1876, when his zeal and undimmed visionary fervour seemed about to be realised, Thomé de Gamond died. Watkin was later to pay him tribute as the pioneer of the project.[18]

Watkin had already come to an understanding with some of the French promoters, who must have been pleased to find a purposeful collaborator on the British side. In 1880 he put forward another scheme, and was now really to apply himself to the project. He set about acquiring lands near Dover to start his own exploratory work, as the site in St Margaret's Bay was still in the hands of the Channel Tunnel Company. He went to the west of Dover, to Abbot's Cliff and Shakespeare Cliff – roughly halfway between Dover and Folkestone – where the first shaft was sunk.

---

[17]Quoted, Whiteside, p. 45.

[18]de Gamond's biography is overdue for writing. At least as late as mid-1998 there had not been one (Bibliothèque nationale de France, Paris. Private Letter).

Watkin made sure that all the details of the scheme were brought regularly to the attention of the shareholders of the SER, the press and the general public. He was a firm believer in large-scale junketings, and had long experience in organising them, and in securing plenty of space in newspapers. He was energetic in promoting all sorts of causes in Parliament, as well as his own projects, and was well known for his practice of conferring friendly gestures on influential people. Week after week, as the boring of his tunnel progressed in the pilot gallery at Shakespeare Cliff, Sir Edward exploited his gift for public relations, inviting large groups of important people, as many as eighty at a time: politicians, statesmen, editors, reporters, artists, members of great families, financiers and businessmen, members of the Church and military establishments. These included General Sir Garnet Wolseley, already firmly against the whole idea, and to become crucially influential in its fate.[19] A sketch in the *Illustrated London News* records a champagne party held in the tunnel, a little distance from the boring machine, but clearly 'in a solidly-timbered cave-like area', the party having arrived there by the narrow-gauge train which ran in the tunnel.[20]

At one of the lunches, held in the Lord Warden Hotel in Dover in February 1882, the General Manager of the SER read a telegram from Watkin, who was unable to be present, expressing the hope that by Easter Week a locomotive compressed-air engine would be running in the tunnel, of which it was expected that the first mile 'would by that time have been made'.[21] Advantage was taken on such occasions to excoriate the rival tunnel scheme of Lord Richard Grosvenor's Channel Tunnel Company – still on paper and in the process of preparation. In the opening battle between the two schemes, Watkin acquired a private letter from Grosvenor to James Staats Forbes, in 1881, which amounted to a plea for concerted action against the South Eastern Railway, and which Watkin exploited with more zeal than tender scruple. In the ensuing correspondence he poured scorn on the lack of coherence in the Chatham company's plans and financial arrangements.

Going down from London to be part of Sir Edward's tunnel

[19]Whiteside, pp.38–9.
[20]*Ibid*, p.40.
[21]*Ibid*, p.41.

parties appears to have become one of the fashionable things to do in English society in the early part of 1881. Visitors to the tunnel workings included, by the spring of that year, the Lord Mayor of London, the Archbishop of Canterbury and the Prince of Wales.[22] An eyewitness, writing some years later, described Watkin's 'spirit' for the project: 'He went down the shaft in a bucket, rode to the end of his mile and a quarter drift, and turned on the boring machinery, making no secret of his belief that the hole could be continued to the coast of France without a hitch.'[23] In all these preparations, Watkin showed himself to be fully abreast of the latest technology.[24]

Twice during 1881, Watkin wrote to Joseph Chamberlain, President of the Board of Trade, suggesting that a work of such magnitude and importance should not be left to private monopoly, but be funded by the government. The reply was an emphatic negative, though Watkin was assured there would be no private monopoly of the tunnel.[25] In September 1881, Watkin, having obtained his new Act, empowering him to go ahead with his tunnelling operations – subject to certain restrictions – applied to Joseph Chamberlain for public funds to enable his SER company to bore the eleven-mile stretch to meet with the French operation in mid-Channel. Chamberlain refused the application, whereupon Watkin decided to float a new company. The Submarine Continental Railway Company, with a capital of £250,000, was formed in December 1881, and by an agreement of January 1882 this Company took over the SER's existing shafts and headings.[26]

However, developing alongside all this commercial and technical activity, the peace of mind of the Board of Trade, troubled since 1875, had been quietly eroding away. The pace of Watkin's progress was gradually building up serious alarm at the military implications of what was taking place. The misgivings had been brought to the public notice in an editorial in *The Times* in June 1881: '...as a relief to the tender stomachs of passengers who dread sea-sickness, the design is excellent,' but '...it must not the

---

[22]*Ibid*, p.42.
[23]*Newcastle Chronicle,* 16 April 1901.
[24]Slater and Barnett, p.56.
[25]P.A. Keen, 'The Channel Tunnel Project', *Journal of Transport History,*Vol. 3 (1985), pp.138–9.
[26]Hunt, p.44.

less be received with caution. Shall we,' said the writer, 'be as well off and as safe with it as we are without it? Will it be possible for us to guard the English end of the passage that it can never fall into any hands other than our own? A force of some thousands of men might be able by surprise to seize the English end of the tunnel and use it for a bridgehead for the general invasion of England.' Becoming more specific in its fears, the article concluded that 'a design for the invasion of England and a general plan of the campaign will be subjects on which every cadet in a German military school will be invited to display his powers...Nature is on our side at present...the silver streak is our safety.'[27]

About this time, Sir Edward told an extraordinary meeting of the Submarine Continental Railway Company an anecdote he was to use in his speech supporting the First and Second Readings of the 1888 Channel Tunnel Bill, that '...the great strategist, Count von Moltke, and other German officers had distinctly declared that the idea of invading England through the tunnel was perfectly absurd. Count von Moltke said they might just as well try to invade England through his library door.' Watkin dismissed the threat to national security as founded on 'hobgoblin arguments' by 'men who would prefer to see England remain an island for ever, forgetting that steam had abolished islands, just as telegraphy had abolished isolated thought.' He maintained his view that the tunnel was at once idealistic and practical, and said that the company's motto was the same as that of the SER – 'Onward'.[28] He believed firmly 'that the tendency of nations was, and ought to be, towards union and not backwards, towards isolation...England is outgrowing the "streak," as it outgrew canals and roads.'[29]

In mid-January 1882, the Board of Trade wrote to Watkin, drawing his attention to Section 77 of the South Eastern Railway Act of 1881. This forbade any tunnelling beyond high-water mark without further permission, in consideration of foreshore rights. Early in March, Watkin received another letter from them, reminding him that if he were to continue digging beyond the high-water mark, he would be in violation of the foreshore rights of the Crown. Watkin replied that as the land from which he was

---

[27]Whiteside, pp.46 and 47.
[28]Whiteside, p.53. Hansard, 27 June 1888.
[29]Address to the Society of Arts, 19 April 1882. In the journal of the Society, 21 April 1882.

working had been bought from the Church of England, it was therefore, according to traditional ancient rights, no longer Crown property. This could be called casuistry in the service of procrastination: a characteristic of Sir Edward which could be turned by his enemies into charges of 'slipperiness' and 'dishonesty'. The Board of Trade replied, predictably enough, that the Crown had overall rights over the coast from high tide to the three-mile limit. A parliamentary diarist noted under the date 28 June 1882 the following:

It has been decided to stop the Channel Tunnel works pending the report of the Departmental Committee; and Mr Chamberlain, as President of the Board of Trade, is charged with seeing that behest carried out. In this undertaking he has secured for himself the implacable and undying animosity of Sir Edward Watkin. If the irate baronet follows up his present intention, his little quarrel with the President of the Board of Trade will be perpetuated in an original form. Sir Edward declares that in the event of the Channel Tunnel works being permanently stopped, he will erect on the site a stone pillar high enough to be seen by all vessels passing up and down the Channel, and on a clear day visible even from the coast of France. On this he will have engraved an inscription setting forth how the tunnel was visited by the Prince of Wales and other royal personages, by Mr Gladstone, the Speaker of the House of Commons, and by a large contingent of peers and commoners; and how, when all seemed prosperous and all the world applauded, the works were peremptorily 'stopped by Joseph Chamberlain, of Birmingham.' 'Joseph Chamberlain' and 'Birmingham' are each to have a line of bad pre-eminence to themselves, for Sir Edward Watkin does not know which is the more hateful to the ears of good men and honest politicians.[30]

The 'lines of bad pre-eminence' need further explanation. Joseph Chamberlain was in several ways like Watkin. Both came from mercantile backgrounds, and both were men of restless energy and

---

[30]Henry W. Lucy, *A Diary of Two Parliaments* (London: Cassell and Company, 1886), Vol. 2, pp.265–6.

organising genius.[31] Both their fathers were born in London, though Chamberlain's was from a long succession rather than fortuitous, as was Absolom Watkin's being born a Cockney. Chamberlain's father was a shoe manufacturer, and withdrew his son from school at the age of sixteen to work with him. From the age of eighteen, young Joseph went to work in his cousin's screw-manufacturing business in Birmingham, from which he retired at thirty-eight with a substantial fortune, to devote himself to politics. He was Mayor of Birmingham in 1873, and entered Parliament in 1876. Like Watkin, he had a strong religious upbringing, though in his case as a Dissenter: his political opponents despised him as a 'Dissenting upstart'. In fact, Unitarians were, strictly speaking, like Deists, on the very fringes of Christian belief. Chamberlain had no firm conviction of an after-life, and no sense of the Divine. He once said that Christ was not the only teacher, and of other Unitarians, 'If they believe in only one God, they pay twenty shillings in the pound.'[32] His ruling conviction was that doing as much good for mankind as one could in this life was the only way. But clearly his self-discipline and his idealism were founded on a firm Protestant work-ethic.[33]

The parallels with Watkin in their respective spheres, however, and any suggestion of personal animosity, are not the full reason for the latter's antipathy. The Birmingham Liberal Association had been founded in 1865, and three years later it was remodelled and became the platform for a new kind of Liberalism. By the autumn of 1865, due to Chamberlain's energy and initiative, a programme of Radicalism, entitled the 'Unauthorised Programme', was proposed. The seven principal propositions of this programme bore a strong resemblance to those of the Radicals and Chartists against whom Absolom Watkin and Richard Cobden had argued thirty years earlier. This time the message was irresistible and it was a turning-point for the party. 'The epoch of middle-class Liberalism had passed; the signposts pointed to democracy.'[34] The editorial preface to the 'Programme' said clearly that its proposals sounded 'the intervention of the State on behalf of the weak

[31]J.L. Garvin, *The Life of Joseph Chamberlain* (Macmillan, 1932) (2 Vols.), Vol. 1, pp.34–9.
[32]*Ibid.*
[33]*Encyclopaedia Britannica,* 1987 Edition, Vol. 3, pp.64–5.
[34]Garvin, Vol. 2, p.55.

against the strong, the interests of labour against capital, of want and suffering against luxury and ease.'[35] The era of a comprehensive, Christian-based paternalism was fading, to be replaced by differently motivated groups and factions engaged in a struggle for power and influence.

Thus Birmingham became the centre of Liberal political development, replacing Manchester's hegemony of half a century, and generating the long-standing argument as to which was the 'Second City' of the realm.[36] The 'Unauthorised Programme' was claimed to be the death-knell of 'the fatal *laissez-faire*...the hoary shibboleth of the Manchester School'.[37] Watkin and, in this sense, Gladstone were gradually falling behind the times politically, and Watkin could be excused for wanting to enshrine prominently his double aversion. Chamberlain, whether aware of Sir Edward's monumentary intentions or not, argued that the tunnel heading must have reached the limit authorised by the 1881 Act, and demanded that he cease operations.[38]

The Secretary of the Submarine Continental Railway Company agreed to the demands to stop the work, but Watkin, in a telegram to Chamberlain, said that the boring machine had been stopped, but the ventilating air in the shaft, transmitted by the machine, was giving cause for alarm for the safety of the workmen. Chamberlain, in reply, conceded that if lives were in danger the machine should continue to work, and that an investigation would be ordered to see if any workmen would need to remain in the heading. Colonel Yolland, RE, Chief Inspector of Railways to the Board of Trade, was appointed to lead the investigation, but Watkin argued that no visits could take place for another week because the Duke of Edinburgh was expected to visit the works on 18 April. Chamberlain was angered by this, and asked what Colonel Yolland's visit had to do with that of the Duke, to which Watkin replied that he would be happy to welcome Chamberlain personally. Chamberlain did not take up his offer, but Watkin, with the support of his fellow directors,

---

[35]*Ibid*, p.57
[36]The Lord Mayor of Manchester in 1973–4, when asked by the author for his view on this question, replied that the subject of which was the second city of the realm was a dispute between Birmingham and London.
[37]Garvin, Vol. 2, p.105.
[38]Hunt, p.54.

continued to thwart the Board of Trade's attempts to put a stop to their endeavours. They persisted, during the following three months, in putting forward reasons why Colonel Yolland could not make his inspection. In the meantime, the boring machine continued to cut through the chalk, watched by a variety of visitors, one of whom was the President of the Board of Trade himself, though he remained unmoved by Watkin's hospitality and enthusiasm.[39]

In the early summer of 1881, the Board suggested to the War Office that a departmental committee should be appointed, with representatives from the War Department, the Admiralty and the Board of Trade.[40] These were Colonel J.H. Smith, RE, Vice-Admiral Phillimore and Mr Farrer, Chairman, and the Farrer Committee was appointed on 22 August. Evidence was heard from Watkin on 13 December, Sir John Hawkshaw on 16 December – these two giving evidence on the 'rival schemes' – from Sir Garnet Wolseley on 25 January 1882, and from Sir John Adye on 26 January. Wolseley and Adye were two serving army officers selected to present memoranda by the Secretary of State for War.

Watkin, in his evidence, assured the committee that, in an emergency, the tunnel could be destroyed 'in half a dozen different ways' by touching 'a button at the Horse Guards'.[41] Asked about how long it would take to go through the tunnel, Watkin replied, 'I am sanguine enough to believe that we shall work through the tunnel in less than half an hour', compared with the boat passage of an hour and a half, or exceptionally an hour and twenty minutes. He continued, 'That a man gets into his carriage at Aberdeen, or Liverpool, or London, or anywhere, and he goes through, without change, to Marseilles, or anywhere he pleases...It is an untold advantage as a matter of health, and a great economy of time; in fact it is an immense economy of health and life to have it so agreeably and quickly done.'[42]

In reply to a question of how many rails he was proposing to lay in the tunnel, Sir Edward informed the committee that 'I

[39]Garvin, Vol. 1, p.432.
[40]Lord Forbes, *Shall we have a Channel Tunnel?* (Aberdeen: A. Brown and Company, 1883), p.17.
[41]*Ibid*, p.25.
[42]*Ibid*, p.26.

38 Sir Edward repulses the French invaders in the Channel Tunnel (contemporary newspaper cartoon)

should make two separate Tunnels side by side, with one line of rails in each, and for this reason, that we expect the two tunnels will ventilate each other. In addition to that, in case of an accident, of course we are not likely to have an accident in both tunnels at once.'[43] Sir Edward's plan for twin cross-ventilating tunnels, following William Low's studies, was substantially the one which was subsequently built, and his estimated journey time through the tunnel compares well with the present Eurostar time of thirty-five minutes, terminal to terminal, which is slightly further than his scheme.[44]

On 1 February 1882, the Chairman of the Farrer Committee wrote to Chamberlain that the national security question had assumed great importance during the enquiry, and requested further military and naval evidence. Chamberlain's reply, of the following day, was to the effect that the final decision on a question of such

---

[43] *Ibid.*
[44] Thomas Abbott (ed.), *Jane's World Railways* (Thomson, 37th Edition, 1995–6), p.17.

magnitude could not be taken by a departmental committee, but by the government as a whole, and therefore need not prolong any further the proceedings of the committee. The Farrer Committee having been thus wound up, the Secretary of State for War, on being told of the circumstances, decided that before the Channel Tunnel scheme was brought to the government, a scientific committee should be assembled, comprising both military and civilian experts, to ascertain the practicability of effectively closing such a tunnel, if it were built.[45] On 23 February such a committee was formed, under the presidency of Major-General Sir Archibald Alison, Bt, KCB. The committee met four days later, and on 28 February its composition was announced to the House of Commons by the Secretary of State for War, who made it clear that they had not been charged with considering the Channel Tunnel scheme generally, but simply from the point of view of national security.

Sir Edward gave his evidence to the Alison Committee on 28 March 1882. Amongst other things, he assured the members that if the tunnel were filled with water as a security measure, it would be very unlikely that the enemy could pump it out, because the sea water would run in as they did; and, with reference to the use of explosives, he knew from experience how easy it was to 'bring down half a mountain almost in a second or two'.[46] The evidence of Lord Richard Grosvenor, MP, Chairman of the Channel Tunnel Company, also spoke of the ease of defending the tunnel entrance by artillery and troops.

The Alison Committee completed its report on 12 May. Its main features included recommendations that the end of the tunnel should not emerge within range of effective fire from the sea; it should be capable of being sealed off by a portcullis; by temporary demolition of the land portion; and by flooding, temporarily by sluices, and permanently by allowing access of the sea into the tunnel. Any mechanical arrangements for activating such obstructions ought to be within fortresses, and also from one or more distant places; it would be presumptuous to place absolute reliance upon even the most comprehensive arrangements for making the tunnel useless for an enemy. The report considered both the

---

[45]Forbes, p.19.
[46]Ibid., p.26.

schemes for which a Bill was before Parliament, and decided that neither tunnel could be recommended because they both failed the above safety requirements.[47]

Possibly the evidence and testimony which carried greatest weight was that of Sir Garnet Joseph Wolseley. Born in Dublin in 1833, he was from 1882 the Adjutant-General of the British Army. A veteran of the Crimean War and the Indian Mutiny, among several other campaigns, he was regarded as an expert in the art of surprise attack. He had a reputation for efficiency in the field of army supplies, and the phrase 'all Sir Garnet' was used in the army as meaning 'all correct'. There is a tradition that he was the model for W.S. Gilbert's 'Modern Major-General' in *The Pirates of Penzance*. He later (1885) became a Viscount, and in 1895 Commander in Chief of the British Army. His memorandum to the Alison Committee began forcibly:

> The proposal to make a Tunnel under the Channel may, I think, be fairly described as a measure to annihilate all the advantages we have hitherto enjoyed from the existence of the 'silver streak', for to join England to the Continent by a permanent highway will be to place her under the unfortunate condition of having neighbours possessing great standing armies, a state of things which prevents any of the Continental nations from disarming, as long as any one of them refuses to follow suit. The construction of the Tunnel would place us under those same conditions that have forced the powers of Europe to submit to universal service. It is to be hoped, therefore, that these measures may not be treated simply as 'private bills' but that the question may be dealt with as one of great national importance.[48]

Britain had never had to maintain a standing army strong enough to repel, at short notice, a powerful and resolute invader, having had for centuries control of the seas.[49] Wolseley warned against such a radical change in national thinking, and the threat of

---

[47] *Ibid*, p.21.
[48] *Ibid*, p.32.
[49] Fukuzawa Yukuchi (1835–1901), a Japanese visitor to Britain, and an influential observer and writer in Japan on Victorian England, commented that measured as a proportion of the general population, Britain had the fewest regular soldiers of any country in Europe (Andrew Cobbins, *The Japanese Discovery of Victorian Britain* (Japan Library, 1998), pp.185–6).

hugely increased taxes for spending on the army. In his Memorandum to the Farrer Committee, he added, 'Why should a new
danger be added to those that already existed? The Tunnel would
directly tempt invasion...the successful invasion of England, with
the Tunnel in enemy hands, would be the permanent ruin of the
country.'

The report submitted to the committee by Lieutenant-General
Sir John Adye, the Surveyor General of the Ordnance, did not
support these fears. 'A French strategist', he argued, 'who wanted
to invade England would never regard the tunnel as the answer to
his problems...even if invading units started moving through the
tunnel, a small force of artillery could destroy them with ease as
they emerged at Dover.'[50] However, his measured arguments
carried less weight eventually than the melodramatic case of Sir
Garnet Wolseley.

Within four years, the Channel Tunnel Company and
Hawkshaw's single tunnel plan had become virtually moribund.
Watkin offered them a chance to collaborate with him, but his
offer was refused. In April 1882 he invited members of the Société
Chemin de Fer Sous-Marin for a private visit to the works at
Abbot's Cliff and Shakespeare Cliff, at which they had expressed
great satisfaction – no doubt to Watkin's own. About this time, a
party of Watkin's guests included Ferdinand de Lesseps, the
builder of the Suez Canal. He, in his toast to the Queen, declared
that the completion of the work was required in the interest of
mankind.[51]

On the evening of Wednesday, 19 April 1882, Watkin addressed
a meeting of the Society of Arts on the subject of the Channel
Tunnel. In anticipation of over-attendance, special tickets were
issued, and the discussion ensuing from Watkin's paper had to be
continued at a further meeting, on Monday 24 April. Both gatherings were chaired by Lord Alfred Churchill. Watkin, before going
on to a technical description of the engineering involved, and the
objections to such a project, introduced his address by expressing,
first, his confidence, in that hall, of an impartial consideration of
the subject; and secondly, took it for granted that his hearers

---

[50]Hunt, pp.45–6.
[51]Whiteside, p.84.

would agree that 'increase of the intercourse...between nations means...the augmentation of wealth...the expansion of civilisation...a great breaking down of barriers, a great letting in of light, the softening of national prejudices, and an extension of career for the workmen especially, but for all men of work, alike – all tending to peace and goodwill amongst men. Bishop Hall', he continued, 'records that Bacon said truly there are three things which make a nation great and prosperous – a fertile soil, busy workshops, and easy conveyance for men and commodities from one place to another. To which', Watkin said, 'let me add knowledge and freedom.' After a digression, dealing with the opposition which had arisen to the enterprise – 'The black darkness of prejudice – vulgar, selfish, ignorant...often spiced with envy, hatred, and all uncharitableness' — he concluded with a tribute to 'the father' of the enterprise, the man to whom the great credit ought to be given, 'M. de Gamond...that enterprising and far-sighted Frenchman. He is dead. But...dead or alive, you and I would not rob him of one atom of his fame' for his convictions. 'He worked, *mente, corde, manu.*'[52]

All the papers relating to the project since 1870 were published as a Parliamentary Blue Book It was formally presented to Parliament on 15 August 1882, and on 26 February the following year, the Foreign Secretary, Lord Granville, announced the formation of a Joint Select Committee of Parliament as the next step to decide the matter.[53] It was justified by Chamberlain in the House of Commons on 3 April, by the argument that 'there had been no attempt to exhaust...the effect of the Tunnel on Commerce', and that 'the general military question had not been fully discussed ...[and] it was desirable that further evidence should be taken on the subject...before [the House and the Government]...were asked to come to any conclusion in the matter.'[54] The remit of the Joint Select Committee, under the chairmanship of Lord Lansdowne, was 'To enquire whether it is expedient that Parliament sanction a Submarine Communication between England and France.' The underlying question, as before, was 'would the economic and social advantages of such a tunnel be greater than its military

[52]*Journal of the Royal Society of Arts,* 21 April 1882, p. 566.
[53]*Hansard,* CCLXXVI, cols. 813 and 814.
[54]*Hansard,* CCLXXVII, cols. 1363–8.

disadvantages?'[55] The committee held fourteen meetings, beginning on 20 April and finishing on 21 June 1883. In the course of these meetings they interviewed forty people, asking 5,396 questions.

The contributions of Watkin and the other common members were similar to those in the previous committee of enquiry, except that Lord Wolseley's was more elaborate and better calculated to raise the passion of patriotic xenophobia in the public at large. His arguments, which overshadowed the committee's consideration of the economic and commercial advantages of a submarine tunnel, were those of a highly experienced soldier wedded to the rhetoric of preacher: 'Since the day when David secured an entrance by surprise or treachery into Jerusalem through a tunnel under its walls, how often have places similarly fallen? And...will again similarly fall?'[56] Admiral Selwyn, in the Society of Arts debate on the subject of the tunnel,[57] argued, on the contrary, that given the threat of invasion, it was better for England to know exactly where it was to take place, because the secret of success in such an attack was the surprise of where the landing was to be.[58]

However, his argument did not reflect the gathering mood of the nation.[59] The spectacle of a horde of armed Frenchmen speeding through the Tunnel and decanting itself onto English soil did not appeal to the British public. Sir Edward came under waspish attack in *The Sunday Times*[60] for his advocacy of such an unpatriotic enterprise. His perseverance was likened to 'the persistent gnawing of a mouse behind the wainscot'. 'The grinding of Sir E.Watkin's rock-boring machines...working night and day to put an end to that insular position which has in past times more than once proved our sheet anchor of safety, had precisely the same disquieting effect upon us as the operations of the mouse.' The writer did, however, concede to him 'the leonine energy, strength, and courage of which the British race furnish so many admirable examples'. He concluded 'We sincerely hope that Sir E.Watkin's project will shortly receive its final "coup de grace",' but allowed

---

[55]Hunt, p.60.
[56]Whiteside, p.50.
[57]24 April 1882.
[58]*Journal of the Society of Arts*, 28 April 1882, p.600.
[59]The scheme could 'claim more letters to the *Times* than the proverbial sea-serpent' (*Black and White*, 20 April 1901).
[60]16 April 1882.

'No doubt he will not yield without a resolute struggle.' The article reported that Watkin had recommended the Channel tunnel on wider grounds than the commercial, social, or even political. He argued it would 'promote a religious rapprochement' between English and Continental peoples. He quoted Thomé de Gamond as saying that 'a manifest sign of the religious spirit of the times is the general propensity of nations to throw down the national or artificial ramparts behind which they have so long entrenched their antagonisms.'

Parallel to these debates on overall policy, the correspondence between Watkin and the Board of Trade had gradually become more and more acrimonious, and eventually communication ceased from both sides. On 5 July 1882, Chamberlain took Watkin to the High Court, and obtained a ruling which reinforced his 'explicit directives' of 28 April. The SER Board protested again, through its solicitors, that it had no desire to persist in invoking previous correspondence, 'but when the Government has been asked in vain, and over and over again, to declare its policy on the main question – tunnel or no tunnel – surely my clients might fairly claim to more considerate treatment.'[61] The Submarine Continental Railway Company wrote to Gladstone at the same time, requesting his intervention as the head of the government 'to protect us from a course which we believe to be entirely unprece-dented in the industrial history of the country.' Clearly Watkin's position was that here was a completely straightforward piece of industrial and commercial enterprise, perfectly in keeping with all the other achievements of Victorian engineering, ingenuity and financial boldness. If there were strategic reasons why this parti-cular one was undesirable, then the government ought to say so unequivocally.

Gladstone replied on 31 July that he did not want to interfere with the Board of Trade, but agreed with the company that their whole correspondence on the matter should be laid before Parlia-ment, and within a fortnight. In July 1882, the Board of Trade applied for an order from the High Court of Justice which gave legal access to the No.2 (Shakespeare Cliff) Heading. Gentlemanly persuasion having failed, the law was invoked to get the work

---

[61]Wilson, p.41.

stopped. Colonel Yolland went to the Shakespeare Cliff operation on 15 July, having visited on the eighth, and discovered that over 1,800 feet of pilot tunnel had been bored beyond the limit of Crown property, that the heading could have been ventilated without the use of the boring machine, and that provision for channelling off ground water was inadequate. His perceptions of the safety of the operation were not improved by the fact that during the investigation he slipped and struck his head against a truck rail. In his report to the Board of Trade he recommended that the company should be forced to cease its work at once. On 15 August the SER and the Submarine Continental Railway Company were accused of a breach of the injunction of 5 July, and thus of contempt of court.[62]

By the end of summer 1882, the Submarine Continental Railway Company had tunnelled 897 yards from Abbot's Cliff, and the No.2 pilot tunnel at Shakespeare Cliff was 2,040 feet long. At this point the company had expended about £100,000. The French were puzzled about the Board of Trade's intervention. The British could not be serious about the security problem?[63]

On 6 April 1883, Lord Forbes delivered a lecture in Aberdeen on the subject 'Shall we Have a Channel Tunnel?' He quoted Lord Wolseley's warnings about the military dangers which this 'mercantile activity' and 'hunt after riches' would set in train, and he ended by asking 'a favour of the promoters and doers of the work, if the Tunnel should be made: that they will agree to have inscribed in large and conspicuous letters on our end of it, these words, SIC TRANSIT GLORIA BRITANNIAE.'[64]

The Lansdowne Committee's draft report went through several stages, none of which met with the approval of a majority. Lord Lansdowne's personal report ended with the words, 'We have no course open to us except to recommend that this enterprise should not be prohibited on merely political grounds, and that it should be allowed to proceed.' However, his was a minority view. Only three members of the committee were prepared to support him; the other six were firm in their belief, expressed in the final report, that it was 'not expedient that Parliamentary sanction should be given

---

[62]Hunt, p.57.
[63]*Ibid.*
[64]Forbes, pp.38–9.

to a Submarine Communication between Britain and France'. The report was adopted on 10 July 1883.

On 24 July, Chamberlain informed the House of Commons that the government had accepted the six to four verdict of the committee, and the following day he wrote to Gladstone, 'I do not think that any encouragement should be given to Sir E.Watkin.'[65] A result of this negativity was that on 18 March 1883 the French company, the Société Concessionaire du Tunnel Sous la Manche stopped work, having reached a limit of 1,840 metres – approximately the same as the English heading. The French shaft then closed, but Watkin insisted on keeping the English workings open, and continued with maintenance work. Colonel Yolland visited the workings again in August 1883, and reported to the Board of Trade that a further 70 yards had been dug since his previous visit, in gross violation of the injunction; but the Chief Engineer, Francis Brady, replying to the consequent Board of Trade court action, replied that only ventilation had been carried out, so that Colonel Yolland did not suffocate during his inspection.

After another visit, Yolland conceded that he had miscalculated. By that time, public feeling was running high, and angry citizens smashed the windows of the Westminster offices of the Channel Tunnel Company.[66] Confirmation of Watkin's takeover of the rival company came at an extraordinary general meeting held on 24 February 1887, when a resolution was passed 'That the name of the Submarine Continental Railway Company Limited be in future "The Channel Tunnel Company Limited".' This was confirmed at a further meeting on 11 March. And so, after all the skirmishing and to-ing and fro-ing, Watkin was left in sole charge of the field, albeit an unproductive one for him, and his company (renamed 'Channel Tunnel Investments' on 15 June 1971) existed, still quoted on the Stock Exchange, until the harvest finally came in 1994.

Meanwhile, however, he was not giving up. The mouse was even yet gnawing at the wainscot.[67] In August 1887, the company introduced a new Bill into Parliament, aimed at permitting it to resume its experimental borings. At the same time, in true Watkin fashion,

---

[65] Wilson, p.47.
[66] Whiteside, p.89.
[67] *Vanity Fair* described him later as 'the bore of the Channel Tunnel' (18 April 1901).

it launched a public petition, pointing out that it was a 'commercial enterprise of vast mercantile value, and an international work which cannot fail to promote peace.' This last claim was a bold attack on the military diehards, turning their arguments on their heads. The petition was signed by nearly fifty prominent men in commerce and politics. In his speech on 3 August, Watkin said

> *The Times* of today accuses those promoting the Bill of having selfish interests...On the contrary, those who have been engaged in promoting the tunnel have done so patriotically in a national, and not a money-making, spirit. The board of directors is an honorary board, the secretary is an honorary secretary, the engineers are honorary engineers, and, strange to say, the solicitors are honorary solicitors also. A high road under the sea to connect the Continent of Europe with England ought to be an international work, and ought not to be trusted to private enterprise.

Expressing again his broader view of the whole project, he continued:

> While Europe is becoming more and more one country only by the piercing of mountains, the bridging over of rivers, and the breaking-down of old-fashioned ideas of exclusion...we, in England, on the other hand, are becoming more and more isolated.

Assuring the House of the geological soundness of the Channel bed, Watkin said it was of old grey chalk, consisting of one third clay and two thirds chalk, in an unporous seam 300 feet thick. He continued:

> I do not wish to say anything that the most captious might construe into irreverence, but I may say that the late Archbishop of Canterbury [Tait], after I had explained the geological facts to him, said he believed that Providence had placed that wonderful material between the coasts of England and France with a view to ultimate intercommunication.[68]

His geological and theological enthusiasm almost carried the day:

---

[68] *Hansard,* CCCXVIII, cols. 1037–55.

267

at the Division only 46 votes separated the Ayes (107) from the Noes (153). Moving the Second Reading on 27 June 1888,[69] Sir Edward said 'The Bill was promoted by 600 or 700 gentlemen and a few ladies, among whom were the Members of this House, and Members of the other House of Parliament, together with representatives of the great staple industries and commerce of the country.' He referred to a considerable amount of misconception and misrepresentation in regard to the proposals, citing an article in *The Times* of that morning, which stated: 'The Continental railway gauge is different from ours.' Sir Edward pointed out that the Prince of Wales's carriage, built in England on the English gauge, had travelled almost over all of Europe without break of gauge. Replying to another objection, Sir Edward told the House that on the lighting of the tunnel he had taken the advice of Sir William Siemens, 'undoubtedly a very high authority...and the Tunnel could be made as light as day'. In a sharp reference, he went on to comment that 'Simple-minded people had an idea that the Board of Trade was intended to protect enterprise and not to obstruct it. France was our best foreign customer save one', and the trade between the two countries 'amounted to £51,000,000 sterling per annum. People talked of France as if we had no interest in it at all. But', he continued, 'our colonies were almost to a man in favour of [the tunnel]. Everybody in the United States laughs at our fears, and they know very well that if England belonged to the United States, which, perhaps, might be the case some day...did they think that twenty-four hours would elapse before they began to connect themselves with France?'[70] The vote on this occasion was 165 for, and 307 against. Lord Randolph Churchill poured ridicule on Watkin's suggestions for securing the tunnel in case of national emergency, and remarked 'The hon. Baronet seems to exercise that extraordinary power of absorption and devouring every rival scheme which he has so often shown in connection with other projects.'[71] Watkin's supporters would perhaps have seen that as a tribute, rather than a derisive criticism.

---

[69] *Hansard*, CCCXXVII, cols. 1427–42.

[70] 'Watkin tried to persuade the European and American powers with a view to the complete neutralisation of the work,' (*Stockport Advertiser*, 19 April 1901). Needless to say, this early attempt to establish a North Atlantic Treaty Organisation was not successful.

[71] *Hansard*, CCCXXVII, cols. 1495 and 1496.

In June 1890, Gladstone, whose attitude towards the tunnel had initially been hostile – with his 'silver streak' reference – was eventually won over to the idea by Sir Edward himself. He reflected, in a speech supporting Sir Edward's Motion for the Second Reading of the Channel Tunnel (Experimental Works) Bill, that 'there are states of feeling which thrive on what they feed on; and that what is true of the love of money is also true of the love of panic.' He concluded, 'I believe this to be a considerable measure and a useful measure, and that the arguments opposed to it deserve neither acceptance nor respect.' The danger of a Channel tunnel was not to be judged by the military professionals, he said.

During this debate, Watkin put forward a new argument for his project: 'It would extend the British Empire some eleven or twelve miles in the direction of France.'[72] This was hardly more felicitous than his excursion into creation theology in a previous debate, when, pointing out that the British Isles had once been joined physically to France, he claimed that those who opposed the present plans for restoring the connection were casting doubt on the wisdom of Providence.[73] On this occasion the motion was lost by 153 votes to 234.[74] The *Railway Times* blamed this defeat on Joseph Chamberlain and his jingoistic sentiments.[75] Francophobic feelings, however, have deep roots in the English consciousness. Siegfried Sassoon, even after the 1914–18 War, could write, 'Please, no more war...except against the French!'[76]

Watkin continued to introduce parliamentary Bills and Motions, but all were defeated or withdrawn. One of them, The Channel Tunnel (Experimental Works) Bill of 1894, was sent on to the War Office by the Treasury. The Permanent Under Secretary wrote that he was 'strongly opposed to this Tunnel, and I believe its construction would be a national misfortune.' The War Office returned the Bill to the Treasury on 19 February, saying that 'on each occasion of a Bill being brought forward for the construction of a tunnel between this country and France [previous Secretaries of State for war] have, on military grounds, expressed themselves as opposed

---

[72]*Hansard,* 5 June 1890, col. 26.
[73]Whiteside, p.92.
[74]Wilson, p.47.
[75]Gray, p.281.
[76]Quoted, Jacques Darras, *Beyond the Tunnel of History* (Macmillan, 1990), p.58.

to the measure and [the present Secretary] sees no reason for adopting a different course as regards the present Bill.'[77] Up to the year 1895, the Channel Tunnel scheme had been brought forward to Parliament no fewer than eleven times.[78]

After frequent attempts during the twentieth century, the British and French Governments finally agreed, on 20 July 1986, to the construction of a rail-only tunnel, and the work was completed in December 1993, when the contractors handed over the tunnel to the operators.[79]

Let the last word be with a Frenchman, as was the first. The BBC Reith Lectures for 1989 – the centenary year of the birth of Lord Reith, and the bi-centenary of the French Revolution – were for the first time delivered by a foreigner. Jacques Darras, Dean and Professor of English and American Literature at the University of Picardy, Amiens, called his series 'Beyond the Tunnel of History'. His words would have been seen by Watkin as a total endorsement of all that he had held dear throughout the vicissitudes outlined in this chapter. 'What is being eroded by the Tunnel', he said, 'is nothing else than the imposition of an Eighteenth-Century Enlightenment rationality upon the spaces we inhabit.' His wider vision was a revival of the pre-Enlightenment, pre-Renaissance medieval notion of a city, or cluster of communities, linked with a wider cultural hinterland that stretched far beyond what we now think of as the nation-state. 'Six hundred years ago, in the High Middle Ages, students would pass in a regular flow from the Sorbonne to Florence, to Montpelier, to Oxford, then down to Padua and back...travelling our way from both sides of the Channel will help achieve a mutual transfusion of history...Nationalism itself will be a thing of the past.'[80] Expressing wider and deeper issues, glimpsed only fleetingly by de Gamond and Sir Edward, Darras expressed

---

[77]Wilson, p.49.

[78]Keen, p.141.

[79]It was formally opened by Her Majesty Queen Elizabeth the Second and President François Mitterand on 6 May 1994. The oldest living direct descendant of Sir Edward, his great-granddaughter Dorothea Worsley-Taylor, of Clitheroe, Lancashire, was invited to the ceremony, and was presented with a bronze medal in commemoration of the occasion. The first trains ran on 19 May 1994.

[80]Darras, p.45.

270

the opinion that 'the gradual, inexorable process of European unification presents us with a unique opportunity to remould our values, to create an almost Hegelian synthesis of the values of Novelty and Continuity, of the interests of the individual and those of the wider society. The cultures of Europe', he suggested, 'are in many ways converging.[81] Perhaps we will learn that Nationalism was a recent invention...and the most valuable legacies of the past have been bequeathed by those cultures most open to enrichment from external influences.'[82]

Postscript: The Kent Coalfield

Watkin may have been thwarted in his attempt to build a Channel tunnel, but his burrowing activities produced an important side-effect. Professor Boyd-Dawkins FRS,[83] scientific adviser to the Channel Tunnel undertaking, contributed an article to the *Contemporary Review* of 1890 entitled 'The Discovery of Coal near Dover'.[84]

> The discovery of coal near Dover is one of those events which mark a new era in our industrial development...it forms a striking example of the relation of faith to works in the scientific world. The faith has been proved by experiment to be true, and the works necessary for the proof would not have been carried out without the faith,

he wrote. The idea of buried coalfields in the area was advanced by Robert Alfred Cloyne Godwin-Austen (1808–84), the English geologist, who in 1855 brought before the Geological Society of London a paper 'On the Possible Extension of the Coal-Measures Beneath the South-East Part of England'. Acting upon this theory, Boyd-Dawkins, in 1886:

---

[81] *Ibid*, p 89.
[82] *Ibid*, p.106.
[83] (Sir) William Boyd-Dawkins, born Welshpool, 1838; died Bowdon, Cheshire, 1929 (Manchester Central Library, 910.6, M1). Sociologist and anthropologist, he was Professor of Geology for 35 years, and a Member of the Senate, at Manchester University (H.B. Charlton, *The Making of a University* (Manchester University Press, 1951), p.178).
[84] pp.470–9.

271

presented a report to Sir Edward Watkin, Chairman of the South Eastern Railway and the Channel Tunnel Company…and recommended on both scientific and commercial grounds that a boring should be made in South-East Kent, in the neighbourhood of Dover, and that the Channel Tunnel works, now so unfortunately suspended, offered the best site for the trial…Sir Edward acted with his usual energy on my report, and the work was begun in 1886, and has been carried on down to the present time, under my advice, and at the expense of the Channel Tunnel Company. There can be no doubt as to the value of these coalfields…it is obvious that a large addition to the supply of coal may reasonably be expected from Southern England, though it cannot reasonably be expected that many such enterprises as this, which has been so energetically pursued by Sir Edward Watkin, will be carried on under the present conditions of the law as to minerals.[85]

All the advantages go to the landowners, and all the risks to the adventurous. This contrasted this with the state of affairs in France, where all mineral deposits belong to the state, and every encouragement is given to private enterprise. Across the Channel, the mines had been, by a system of concessions, developed continuously over the last hundred years 'to within thirty miles of Calais. We may ask why, until this boring by Sir Edward Watkin, enterprise should have stopped short on the Calais shore?' Boyd-Dawkins asserted that the answer was clear: 'We are at least a century behind our neighbours in this work…and our system has prevented the 'Garden of England' from being studded with busy centres of industry in places where a few farmers and farm labourers gain a precarious livelihood.' [86]

He was later beset by a problem of attribution for the opening-up of the Kent coalfield. In an article entitled 'On the History of the Discovery of the South-Eastern Coalfield', he found himself having to contradict a claim for the sole credit by the SER Chief Engineer, E. Brady.[87] Boyd-Dawkins set out to the Manchester Geological Society the true course of events as he saw it,

---

[85]*Ibid*, p.477.
[86]*Ibid*, p.479.
[87]E. Brady, Paper to The Federated Institution of Mining Engineers, 14 July 1896.

concluding 'The responsibility for the conduct of the geological part of the enterprise was mine, the higher responsibility for carrying out the work to a successful result was Sir Edward Watkin's. To Sir Edward Watkin, is due the credit for translating geological theory into ascertained fact.' [88]

The area of the coalfield proved to be about 206 square miles, of which 56 were under the sea, but workable.[89] Fifteen years later, the Kent Coalfield project drew as much from Watkin's detractors as any of his endeavours: 'The enterprise is remarkable for the fact that it has not yet produced a single scuttle full of coal.'[90] 'What have we today to represent the lost capitals of the...several moribund or defunct Kentish "Colliery" companies? A few bore-holes in the chalk and clay.'[91] Difficulties *were* at first encountered in getting the mines started, mainly due to water flooding the workings, and to obstruction by landowners.[92] But a new railway company, the East Kent, was promoted in 1910 and built in 1911–12 to meet the need for rail connections with the collieries which were being sunk, and by 1919, forty Kent coal companies were registered, with a total capital of over £9 million.[93] In 1984, production was over one million tons a year, and new pits were being projected,[94] until the change in government energy policy.

The Channel Tunnel and the Kent Coalfield were both Watkin projects to mature after his death. But in the meantime he had been involved in other explorations.

---

[88]*Ibid*, pp.160 and 159.
[89]*Encyclopaedia Britannica,* 1955 Edition, Vol. 13, p.330.
[90]W.J. Stevens in the *Financial Times* of 15 April 1901.
[91]*Railway Times,* 20 April 1901.
[92]John Hilton, *A History of the Kent Coalfield* (1986), p.179.
[93]A.E. Ritchie, *The Kent Coalfield* (1919), p.302.
[94]Hilton, p.180 (These last three references via Kent County Council Libraries).

16

Expansion into Wales

Part of Watkin's 'Master Plan' was to unite various small railways in South and North Wales – under the noses of the GWR and the LNWR – and feed their traffic Merseywards and via a Mersey tunnel to Liverpool and Manchester, 'A bold enterprise, which would overshadow the largest and most important of our existing systems...an example of [Sir Edward's] fertility of resource and indefatigable perseverance.'[1] Among other traffic considerations, such as the thousands of tons of bricks, tiles and drainage pipes produced annually, and the rich deposits of limestone and lead which could be developed, the Cheshire salt industry produced about a million tons a year of white salt, and 'at least one ton of poor quality coal or slack' (lying about in abundance at the Welsh coalfields) 'was needed to make two or three tons of salt'.[2] Of the fifty-four salt works in mid-Cheshire at the time of the formation of the Salt Union in 1888, all but a handful were owned by the Cheshire Lines Committee.[3]

Accordingly, Watkin proposed in 1866 that the CLC take over the Mid-Wales line, from Tal-y-Llyn Junction, Brecon, to Llanidloes This was a mountainous line, with all the attendant operating and maintenance problems. He was not supported by the GNR or the Midland. A team from the MS&LR which was sent out by Watkin to survey the traffic potential advised him against it, and he abandoned the idea. Some of these smaller Welsh lines were very small. At least one of them, the Swansea Vale and Neath and Brecon Junction Railway Company, 'had

---

[1]*Stockport Advertiser*, 19 April 1901.
[2]Mary Rochester, *Salt in Cheshire* (Cheshire Libraries and Museums, 1985), Part 1, p.13.
[3]*The Salt Union Limited* – official copy of Contracts with Vendors, 1888, pp. i–iv, The Salt Museum, Northwich.

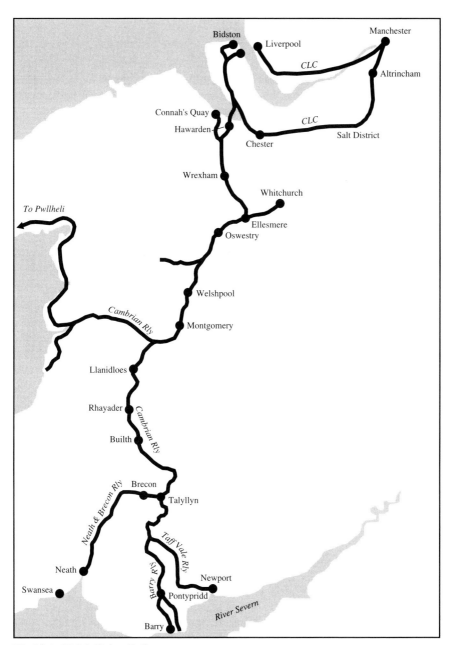

Watkin's Welsh Union Railways

275

more words in its title than miles of track $(7\frac{1}{2})$'.[4] By 1888, further developments had taken place, and in that summer Watkin himself made a tour with fellow-director J.W. Maclure to survey the Welsh railways which, taken together, formed a route from the South to the Dee. These included the Taff Vale, the Neath and Brecon, the Brecon and Merthyr, the Cambrian, and the Wrexham Mold and Connah's Quay Railway. The last of these was already earmarked for takeover,[5] and together with the MS&L it promoted the Welsh Railways Union Bill, which achieved parliamentary sanction in 1889, largely due to support from Gladstone.

Watkin had assumed the chairmanship of the Neath and Brecon on 27 February 1889, as a preliminary move.[6] The Neath and Brecon had been formed on 13 July 1863, when the Dulas Valley Mineral Railway changed its name after only one year of operation to suit an ambition to become a through route between Swansea and the Midlands. It opened throughout on 3 June 1867. It was, in the words of one historian, 'physically arduous, and commercially precarious'.[7] Its most prominent claim to fame was that Craig-y-Nos Station was used by Dame Adelina Patti (1843–1919), the Opera *grande dame*, who had a large house, Craig-y-Nos Castle, nearby.[8] But its importance to Watkin was that it connected Mid-Wales with the coalfields of South Wales. With '20-20 hindsight', as the composer Igor Stravinsky once said, it is possible for us to see how the Neath and Brecon connection was not so much part of a visionary concept as a hopelessly optimistic dream.[9]

Other preliminary moves had taken place in 1884. The River Dee was a barrier to lines coming from Central Wales to West Cheshire, and as early as 1861 there were suggestions for crossing it. In 1866, representatives of the three CLC companies had given evidence to Parliament of a scheme for a tunnel. The financial

---

[4]D.S.M. Barrie, *A Social History of the Railways of Great Britain* (David and Charles, 1980), Vol. 12, p.20.

[5]It was absorbed by the Great Central Railway in 1905.

[6]Dow, Vol. 2, pp.13 and 216.

[7]Barrie, p.205.

[8]Christopher Awdry, *Encyclopaedia of British Railway Companies* (Patrick Stephens, 1990), p.36.

[9]*The Times* commented later that the whole scheme, 'though a large-minded one', was 'almost as hopeless from the outset as the invasion of Russia by Charles XII of Sweden' (15 April 1901, p.6.).

crisis of that year caused it to be abandoned, but in 1873 a high level bridge was mooted. This was well supported locally, and by Parliament, but it was never built. Watkin proposed a 'Chester and Connah's Quay Railway', linking the CLC near Chester to the Wrexham, Mold and Connah's Quay Railway by means of an iron swing bridge. This was passed by both Houses on 28 July 1884. Work on the bridge was soon put in hand, and the lowering of the first cylinder of the bridge supports, near Hawarden, was marked, on 16 August 1887, by a ceremony of which Watkin, as usual, made the most. It attracted a large crowd of local people, as well as the numerous invited guests.

He invited his friend Gladstone to perform the inauguration ceremony – a master stroke, for the great man lived nearby, in Hawarden, and had always shown great interest in the local railway system. After the cylinder had been lowered, Gladstone delivered an appropriate speech, and all the guests then went to lunch in a nearby tent – all 500 of them: civic dignitaries and traders, landowners and railway officers, journalists and contractors. After the loyal toasts, Gladstone proposed success to the

39 Mr Gladstone's train at Hawarden Station, 28 March 1896, for the formal opening of Watkin's new North Wales line. MS&L 2-4-0 Class 1 B locomotive no 89

277

Chester and Connah's Quay Railway, and at great length. He praised the MSLR, and spoke of its chairman as being 'of the utmost experience and renown in the railway world. Sir Edward Watkin', he said, 'is one of those men who is wicked enough to desire that a tunnel should be constructed under the Channel to France; and what is truly painful to me is that I am compelled to confess before you – and I do it publicly – that I am one of those men who are wicked enough rather to agree with him.'[10] Watkin must have grown visibly at these words, for at that time he was short enough of support for his tunnel project. More was to follow: as soon as Gladstone had finished, a local Bard, R.D. Roberts of Rhyl, recited a fourteen-verse ode he had written specially for the occasion. The penultimate verse ran:

40 Watkin, aged about 70

[10]Dow, Vol. 2, p.214.

All hail Edward Watkin/ Pioneer of the world!
Who united great nations/ His banners unfurled.[11]

After such dual eloquence, even Watkin, not especially known for brevity and conciseness on the public occasion,[12] was brief in his response.

Watkin wrote to Gladstone on 2 August 1887, declining an invitation to stay at Hawarden because his wife 'had a fit three months ago, and was for a long time insensible'. She had gradually regained strength, but he felt 'he should not be away from her'. He was sure that Gladstone might 'sympathise with two people who [had] pulled together – often against the system – for 41 years of married life!'[13] On 21 February 1888 he reported that 'Mrs Watkin, I regret to say, makes little, if any, satisfactory progress. She is still confined to her room.'[14] But she 'desires to be remembered to Mrs Gladstone, for whose longer life and health – and also for yours – she offers up humble, but hopeful, Christian's prayers, daily.' On 6 March he had to leave her sickbed for urgent business in London. She improved slightly on the seventh, which encouraged him to stay to complete his work in the capital, but she died later in the day, and he did not arrive until 4 a.m. on the eighth.[15] Her last hours were spent in devotions, with her daughter Harriette and grand-daughter Mary.[16] She was sixty-five years old.

Watkin was devastated by Mary's death. Despite the fact that his manner of life must have entailed many and long absences from home, and tensions when they were together, he had been devoted to her. He was particularly sad that he was not by her side during her last hours, and he expressed his regret in a memoir, dated March 1888, 'In Loving memory of Mary Briggs, Wife of Sir Edward William Watkin, Bart, MP, Rose Hill, North-

---

[11] *Ibid.*

[12] Though he had never achieved the heights of grandiloquence of Mr Gladstone, 'to whom nothing is easier...than to pour out a stream of eulogistic commonplaces', (*The Times,* 22 October 1892), whose speeches had an 'anaesthetising eloquence', and to whom 'obfuscation became an art form', (Roy Jenkins, *Gladstone*, pp.154 and 101), Watkin agreed with the judgement of (Sir) John A. Macdonald, of Canada, who said that Gladstone was 'a great rhetorician, but not an orator', (E.W. Watkin, *Canada and the States,* p.504).

[13] Glynne-Gladstone Mss 1537, Hawarden.

[14] Watkin–Gladstone Correspondence, BL Add Mss 44337, ff 27–8.

[15] *Memoir*, March 1888, p.6.

[16] *Ibid*, pp.14–15.

enden, Cheshire', written in the third person. It was privately printed, 'handsomely...and bound in silver and dark grey cloth',[17] and the title page is headed by the IHS monogram, with the 'I' in the form of a cross, and footed by a logo of the intertwined Greek letters alpha and omega. He described her as: 'Loving and devoted wife, the best friend, and the truest counsellor of her husband' for the forty-three years of their marriage.[18] He credited her with 'entering into and grasping the complicated problems of his daily work', and giving him counsel 'based always on the one cardinal maxim: "Do the thing which is right."' He ascribed to her the credit for the creation of employees' savings banks on his three main railway companies, opening many accounts with her own private money, and through which 'more than one million pounds of the savings of working people had been passed'.[19] He praised warmly her constructive and administrative capacity, citing as an example her extension and remodelling of Rose Hill,[20] and her personal kindliness to all, including her husband's colleagues, who found in her a listening ear and sound advice, always urging them to 'put their consciences into their work'. 'Her charity knew no bounds': a statement borne out by the numerous obituaries.

At a special meeting of the Folkestone School Board on 12 March, she was praised for the great interest she had always shown in education in the town, and for her liberal subscriptions to the various schools.[21] It noted her unostentatious promotion of the welfare of young people and the large sums she had given to the poor of the borough.[22] During the time of the funeral in Northenden all businesses in Folkestone closed, and many houses had their blinds drawn.[23] The funeral took place on 10 March in the parish church, messages of sympathy being received from, among many others of family and railway company connection, the King

---

[17] *Folkestone News,* 17 March 1888.
[18] Memoir, p.6.
[19] *Ibid,* pp.6–7.
[20] Watkin and Mary greatly enlarged the house during their ownership, adding a library and further rooms (including, according to tradition, a chapel). It was sold off, except for a few buildings, by Alfred after Edward's death.
[21] She had opened the Dover Road schools only a year before, at great inconvenience to herself because of her illness.
[22] Similar tributes came from the borough of Hythe.
[23] *Folkestone News,* 17 March 1888.

of the Belgians, the Bishop of Manchester, Gladstone, the mayors of London, Manchester, Folkestone and Hythe, Mr Hickson of Montreal, the Dean of Canterbury, Lady Sophia Cecil, Miss Alderson (sister of Lady Salisbury), Mr Sebag Montefiore, Mons. Felix Matthias (Commander of the Legion of Honour, Paris), The Folkestone Fisherboys Band, and the Folkestone fishermen.

On 3 August 1889, Watkin and Gladstone came together again at Hawarden. This was for the formal opening of the bridge, which was 'a great engineering work, and an important link of communication between Liverpool and North Wales, and which has been constructed by the Manchester, Sheffield and Lincoln-shire Railway Company...opened by Mr and Mrs Gladstone'. He and his wife 'travelled from London with Sir Edward Watkin, MP, and other directors of the company by a special train on the Great Northern Railway, which was joined near Altrincham, on the Cheshire Lines, by carriages from different places on the Manchester, Sheffield and Lincolnshire Railway, and the lines associated with it, including those of the Midland Railway.'[24] The

41 Hawarden Bridge, opened 1899

[24]*Illustrated London News,* 10 August 1889, p.184.

bridge was named 'The Hawarden Bridge', and crossed the River Dee at the head of its estuary, where it is 480 feet wide. The structure consisted of 'two fixed spans, each of 120 feet, and a large opening swing-bridge, weighing 752 tons, 287 feet long', which gave a 'free passage of 140 feet' for shipping. Hydraulic machinery 'opened and closed the bridge in forty seconds'. It gave the Cheshire Lines and the Wirral line from Liverpool 'direct connection with the Welsh system of railways which the Bill now in Parliament proposes to amalgamate for through working to Cardiff and South Wales.'[25] Among those assembled at the bridge were Gladstone and his wife, Herbert Gladstone, MP, Henry Gladstone, Watkin, the Mayor and Mayoress of Chester and of Wrexham, with railway and local business dignitaries. Mrs Gladstone touched an electric bell and the huge structure gradually rotated, taking only forty seconds to complete its 90 degree turn, and swung into position amid great cheering, while a band played *The March of the Men of Harlech.* Gladstone made a speech declaring it a great day for Wales, making its struggling railways part of a great system.

The first traffic from Wales to Merseyside passed over it on 31 March 1890.[26] In anticipation of the new railway, new collieries had been sunk near Hawarden, and in an attempt, before it opened, to syphon off business, the LNWR established a goods office in the centre of Hawarden village, at the Fox Inn.[27] To minister to the 'large numbers of navvies and other workpeople' coming into the area to build the new line, a missionary or evangelist was engaged to minister to their spiritual needs, though because of a long delay in starting the work, he had to be stood off in February 1889.[28]

Watkin's correspondence with Gladstone, from March 1867 to April 1896, was largely on political and party subjects, but they exchanged views also on personal and religious matters. They sent each other books of mutual interest, and in December 1890, Watkin thanked his friend for a copy of his recently-published *The Impregnable Rock of Holy Scripture,* which he was already

---

[25] *Ibid.*
[26] Dow, Vol. 2, p.222.
[27] *Hawarden Parish Magazine,* May 1886 and May 1887.
[28] *Ibid,* April 1888 and February 1889.

re-reading. He had been disturbed, early in his life, by a varied rendering of the Hebrew word *Nakash* by 'Llydr-Adam Clarke, the great commentator of the Wesleyans of the last century'. Adam Clarke (1762–1832) wrote a Commentary on the Old and New Testaments in eight volumes; published in 1826. It remains in print to this day, largely because of its remarkably original interpretations that 'continue to startle'.[29] But Edward had decided that wherever doubts were raised it was 'better to think no more about it'. With three main line railway companies and a parliamentary constituency to run, and one or two large projects in hand at any given time, there could not have been many spare moments for theological speculation. It is not possible, from such glimpses, to draw any conclusions about the depth of his theological understanding, but although, from the evidence there is, it was nowhere near as comprehensive or profound as Gladstone's own, it would be reasonable to deduce that his faith, particularly about the nature of God, and the Gospel and its application to politics and business, was very much in line with Gladstone's. On 12 November 1888, the latter, in connection with his plan to establish at Hawarden 'An Institution for the Pursuit of Divine Knowledge', set out his credo on the relationship of faith to the rest of human life, in these words:

The negative movement of the age aims at establishing a severance between the Christian system and the general thought of the time; its history, philosophy, physical science, poetry and literature at large. But no enlightened Christian will admit that our Christianity was intended to be an isolated thing, standing apart from all other conditions of our life. The comprehensiveness of Creation and of human nature are a perpetual lesson to us, teaching that we should aim at nothing narrower than a Christianity which is to cover the whole ground of our complete existence. This is our Charter: and we cannot consent to its mutilation or contradiction…God is to

---

[29]John H. Hayes, *Dictionary of Biblical Interpretation* (Nashville, Abingdon Press, 1999), (2 Vols.), Vol. 1, p.199. A particular example given by Hayes is that of *nachash* in Genesis Chapter 3, verse 1, where Clarke argues that the word, which is traditionally translated 'serpent' actually meant 'devil', 'ape', 'baboon', or 'orang-utan', drawing on his extensive knowledge of Arabic as well as Hebrew.

be glorified...We should improve and maybe perfect our means of maintaining the harmony between Christian knowledge and all other knowledge.[30]

Far from conforming to merely 'common currency' late-Victorian religion, Gladstone and Watkin attested their positive commitment to a *Weltanschauung* which was decaying in the face of assaults from science and the Enlightenment.

On 8 October 1892, Watkin wrote to Herbert Gladstone from the Royal Pavilion Hotel, Folkestone,[31] to say he was attending a meeting of the Church Congress in the town. The Church Congress was a body which first met in King's Hall, Cambridge, in November 1861, the inspiration of a group of Cambridge men who wanted to bring together clergy and laity to discuss important questions facing the Church. It was held yearly in different parts of England, and its success led to similar meetings in Scotland, Canada, Australia and the USA. Although not part of the statutory or legal structure of the establishment, the Congresses were intended to give expression to the living voice of the Church on current issues, and to ways of sharing new views and methods in the conduct of Church life.

The agenda of the 32nd Meeting,[32] which was presided over by the Archbishop of Canterbury (Benson), and at which Edward was listed as one of the seventy-two Lay Presidents, included sessions on such subjects as 'The Relationship between the Authority of the Bible and the Authority of the Church;' 'The Attitude of the Church Towards Labour Combinations, in Respect of their Aims and Methods;' 'Working Mens' Meeting;' 'Christian Ethics, Individual and Social;' 'Thrift and the Poor Law'; and 'Christian Doctrine and Christian Life.'[33]

It was through his friendship with Gladstone that Edward made the acquaintance of his third son, Henry Neville Gladstone (1832-1935). On 31 July 1889 Watkin invited Henry and his father to

---

[30]Quoted, T.W. Pritchard, *A History of St Deiniol's Library* (Hawarden: Monad Press, 1999), pp.10-11.
[31]British Library Add. Mss. 46054, f.8.
[32]'A major event in the town.' Kent County Council, Folkestone Library Heritage, Private Letter, 30 October 2001.
[33]*Folkestone Chronicle,* Special Congress Issue, 8 October 1892, p.8.

visit the Eiffel Tower,[34] 'just completed by M. Alexandre Gustave Eiffel...[it] was ascended by Gladstone, Henry, Sir Edward' and three others, in the September.[35] He invited Henry to an event in Grimsby in October 1889, an invitation which made 'some slight acknowledgement...for India kindnesses.'[36] Henry had originally been in shipping, but had gone on to the building and managing of railways and jute mills, among other undertakings. He sailed for India on 3 December 1874 to work for the family-related firm of Gillanders, Arbuthnot and Company of Calcutta. He had 'an invincible love of trains, which persisted until he was able to finance and manage railways,'[37] and helped to promote in 1880 the first narrow (metre) gauge railway in India, the Darjeeling Steam Tramway Limited, opened 4 July 1881, which was renamed, on 15 September, The Darjeeling Himalayan Railway Company Ltd.[38] 'Henry was a model employer, idolised by staff, and he made the Company's fortune and his own.'[39]

It was, then, at Henry Gladstone's invitation that Sir Edward went out to India in 1888 as an adviser. As early as 1857, in one of his earliest speeches in Parliament, Watkin had argued for more energy in the establishment of a good railway system in the subcontinent.[40] After his visit in 1888 he wrote a book[41] in which he by no means restricted himself to railway matters. The *Hythe and Sandgate Echo* published an extensive review of it[42] which declared that the book was 'not intended to hit off the public taste or to advertise the author, but is written with a purpose, aimed at influencing the public policy of this nation towards its vast Eastern dependency.' It reads like 'a big speech in Parliament', and contains statistics and extracts 'liberally enough for all the weight of a state paper'. The book was based on 'the knowledge, the

---

[34]Gladstone/Watkin Letters, ff 53-54. A suggestion encouraged by M.Léon Say, the French Ambassador in London, ibid., ff.55-58.
[35]Ivor Thomas, *Gladstone of Hawarden* (London, John Murray, 1936), pp.140-141.
[36]*Grimsby Observer*, 23 October 1889.
[37]Ivor Thomas, p.18.
[38]Tony Martin, *Halfway to Heaven: Darjeeling and its Remarkable Railway* (Chester, Rail Romances, 2000), pp. 29 and 36.
[39]Francis W. Hirst, *Memoir* [Of Lord Gladstone of Hawarden] (OUP, June 1941), pages not numbered.
[40]*Hansard* CXLVI, cols. 1713–30, 17 July 1857, (cf p.246, supra).
[41]*India: A Few Pages About It* (C.F. Rowarth, 1889).
[42]29 June 1889.

experience, and the financial skill acquired by half a century of successful work in the highest ranges of industrial enterprise'. It gave 'the impressions produced upon a vigorous, original, and receptive mind when brought into contact with problems... Probably no man has pledged himself more definitely at home to the principle that the state should never undertake what can be done by private enterprise', but considering the difficulties that faced the development of India, 'he has the courage to throw overboard the doctrines of his school' and 'boldly proclaim' that 'the state should take up the role of the provider of capital'.

On the subject of public involvement in the development of railways, Watkin, in a paper entitled 'Railways and the State', delivered to a meeting of the Manchester Chamber of Commerce in 1872,[43] argued strongly against State control, speaking on Monopoly, Amalgamation and Competition. His main points were that 'State Control' meant control by party politics, creating 'charming nests' for redundant politicians and raising overhead costs. 'The whole theory of political economy as regards production...was based on motive. It assumes that motive is the parent of action. Why is it that State work is seldom, if ever, as successful as individual work? Because motive is in great measure wanting.' Echoing Adam Smith, he asserted that self-interest, gain and profit were essential to success, and produced hard work. State control would 'take the very soul out of industry, removing competition and the motive to excel'.[44] Competition, he believed, 'was in accordance with sound economic maxims'.[45] However, he saw a distinction between State ownership and control, and the application of State capital to get an industry established. He had made this distinction while he was in Canada, and returned to it for the railways of India. 'English doctrinaire fads do not fit Indian necessities', he wrote.[46] The reviewer set out verbatim Watkin's five-point programme, which 'though not...in the language of Socialism...or of Marx or Lassalle, is decidedly Socialistic in its scope and character':

---

[43]13 May; Printed by Cave and Sever, Manchester (London School of Economics Library, HE1 (42) 293).
[44]*Ibid*, pp.9–11.
[45]*Ibid*, p.8
[46]Watkin, *India;* quoted *Hythe and Sandgate Echo,* 29 June 1889.

1. The establishment of a powerful department of the Indian State, consisting of practical men, which, provided with adequate means and with the fullest powers, shall develop thoroughly the undeveloped resources of India, especially its coal and petroleum.

2. The extension of Indian railways and works by the economical credit and efficient organisation of the Indian State.

3. The commercialisation of the Indian railway system, giving Business rather than Military management.[47]

4. A complete change in the storage and warehousing system. The establishment near railways and in all important centres of great produce, stores...Under government control.

5. The laying down of independent submarine cables by the State and the provision of far cheaper means of passing to and fro between the United Kingdom and India.

He was strongly critical of the wide variety of rail gauge in the sub-continent,[48] contrasting that liability with the way the whole of North America had settled uniformly with the 'standard' gauge of 4' 8½". Point number 3 of his programme was one of Watkin's many side-swipes at the military, with its 'red tape', and at the existence of what he called 'old-womanism' – a ruling class ('which cannot dig and to beg is ashamed'), put into positions which they are unfitted to occupy; a 'disease' he described as 'not so bad in India as in Great Britain', but 'bad enough'. The book was dedicated to his 'old friend', Lord Salisbury – 'wisely', said the reviewer, as being one 'more disposed to sympathise with such Napoleonic projects than any living leader of public opinion'.

On Watkin's return from India, the Parliamentary Borough of Hythe and Folkestone gave a banquet in celebration, at the Pavilion Hotel, Folkestone, on 1 February 1889, with the Mayor

---

[47]Watkin sent a copy of his book to Lord Salisbury, and summarised these points rather differently. He added to Point 3 the words 'With a view to making India the thorough competitor of the United States', (Papers of the Third Marquess of Salisbury, Watkin Letters, 9 May 1889, f.155).

[48]The gauges being 1.676 m (5' 6"); 1 metre (3' 3⅓"); 762 mm (2' 6"); and 610 mm (2' 0").

of Folkestone in the chair. The cover of the official programme bore a sketch, by one H. Johnson, depicting a be-turbanned Sir Edward sitting in *howdah* on an elephant. The elephant and the *howdah* carried an 'SER' monogram, and a banner over his head bore the words 'SALVUS AB INDIS'.

Watkin's months in India had been a long diversion from his work in North Wales, and still to be supplied under his Welsh Railways Union was a connection between the Wrexham, Mold and Connah's Quay Railway at Wrexham Central Station and the Cambrian Railway at Ellesmere, some 12¾ miles. In April 1891, he opened negotiations with the Great Western Chairman, F.G. Saunders, with a view to co-operation between them in the area. His proposals[49] proved unacceptable to the GW at a meeting in September, but by that time the MS&L had committed itself, with the Cambrian, to the project.[50]

Work was started with the cutting of the first sod by Mrs G.T. Kenyon, wife of George T. Kenyon, MP for Denbigh, and one of the directors of the new railway, on 11 June 1892.[51] It was not until 2 November 1895 that the line was opened.[52]

Gladstone had consoled Edward when Mary Watkin died, and when Gladstone lost his son William in July 1891, his friend was able to share with him, in return, the 'sure and certain hope'.[53] Gladstone sent him a copy of the 'very admirable sermon of Mr Wickham',[54] which Edward had passed on to his daughter, 'who inherits her late mother's feeling for all the good!'[55] It was about this time that Watkin wrote to Gladstone to encourage him on his becoming Prime Minister again at the age of eighty-three. 'We do not pray', he said, 'that he will, because we *know* that the Almighty will give you strength to complete your great career.' Regarding effectiveness in old age, he reminded his friend that 'the

---

[49]Recorded in the MSLR Board minutes of 8 May 1891.
[50]PRO RAIL 463/24, Minutes 13,934 and 13,956.
[51]Peter E. Baughan, *A Regional History of the Railways of Great Britain* (David St John Thomas, 1991), Vol. 11, p.161.
[52] Baughan, *Ibid.*.
[53]Watkin-Gladstone Correspondence, BL Add. Mss 44337, ff 72–3.
[54]The Revd Edward Charles Wickham, Master of Wellington College 1873–93, and Dean of Lincoln from 1894, was married to Gladstone's daughter Agnes. The 'Absolutely Perfect' sermon had been preached at the funeral of Gladstone's eldest son, William, who died on 4 July 1891, (Gladstone's Diary, 12 July 1891 (ed.) H.C.G. Matthew (Oxford: Clarendon Press,1994), p.395).
[55]Watkin-Gladstone Correspondence, ff 72–3.

Dandolo became Doge of Venice in troublous times when 84 – and did not die until he was 97, and that it was said that "if he had died at 76, he should have left, unperformed, the most useful years of his life." '[56]

Watkin was heavily weighed by loneliness[57] after the death of his wife. In fact, he had been hit by bereavement several times over the previous years. His brother John had died in 1870, at the age of forty-eight, from congestion of the lungs, which suggests heart failure, and his younger brother Alfred had died in 1875, at fifty[58]. Edward remarried four years after Mary's death, to a lady he had described to Gladstone as a 'plain, farmer-like old lady – if a lady can be said to be old at 79!' [59] He had been a close friend of Herbert Ingram, founder of the *Illustrated London News,* until his drowning in 1860. His widow had turned to Watkin for support, and he placed the fortunes of the paper and her whole estate on a firm basis. Nearly thirty years later, when the management faced serious questions, she appealed to him again, and he turned the paper into a family joint-stock company, Ann Ingram owning one quarter of the shares, her two surviving sons (one had drowned with his father) a quarter each, with her five daughters sharing the other quarter. It was at the height of her difficulties that Sir Edward proposed marriage, and they were married at St George's, Hanover Square by the Rector, Dr. David Anderson, assisted by the Revd H. Russell Wakefield, Vicar of Sandgate, on Wednesday, 7 April 1892; 'the service was much curtailed, lasting only about five minutes'.[60]

This development met with much scepticism in the press, founded on the opposition of the lady's two sons (though the five daughters were completely happy for her). The main accusation was that Watkin wished to gain possession of her fortune, but the facts bear out that she gave large sums to each of her seven children, and that Watkin, despite having settled liberally on his two children, was amply provided for. Before the wedding, it was stipulated that the assets of both of them were to be mutually

---

[56]BL Add Mss 44337, ff 83 and 84, 24 July 1892.
[57]*Folkestone Chronicle,* 9 April 1892.
[58]Their sister, Elizabeth, had died at 46, in 1863, only two years after Absolom, and their mother in 1866, leaving Edward as quite the longest-lived of the children.
[59]BL Add Mss 44337, f.70, 21 August 1889.
[60]Isabel Bailey, *Herbert Ingram Esq., MP* (Boston, Richard Kay, 1996), p.197.

42 Ann Ingram-Watkin, Sir Edward's second wife

exclusive, and both were independent of any financial gain from the union.[61] In the interests of fulness, it should be added that Ann Ingram-Watkin left in her will, of 5 June 1895, the Advowson of the Living of Boston, in the Diocese of Lincoln (an honorary post), to Sir Edward; the property in Caernarvon to Alfred Watkin (and on his death to his sister Harriette's son, James Worsley-Taylor); and the rest to her own children.[62] Their happiness was to be brief: Ann Ingram-Watkin had a stroke early in 1896 and died on 26 May, thirty-nine days short of her eighty-fourth birthday.

---

[61] *Folkestone Chronicle*, 9 April 1892.
[62] *Hythe and Sandgate Echo*, 9 February 1897.

The Hawarden to Bidston line, changed in 1894 to the 'Dee and Birkenhead Committee', was started with a sod-cutting ceremony near the new Hawarden bridge on 21 October 1892, when Gladstone, attended by no fewer than twelve of his family, performed the ceremony, and headed the guest-list of 250 people at the following luncheon.[63] Watkin was accompanied by his second wife, and his son Alfred and nephew Edward were there, as was the budding Welsh politician Lloyd George, and Watkin's friend Professor Boyd Dawkins. The group, in a roped-off area, consisted of Sir Edward, Mr and Mrs Gladstone, and Lady Watkin, 'an aged group whose life-work is writ large on the contemporary history of England...[leaving] deep footprints on the sands of time', waxed the writer of the report in *The Manchester Evening Mail* of 15 April 1901. Gladstone, in spite of his customary exercise of tree-felling in Hawarden Park, could not manage to overturn the clod of earth satisfactorily, and so Sir Edward went his assistance.[64] Although winded, Gladstone then proceeded to deliver his speech on 'the glories of railway competition', but reflected that the LNWR should join with the new enterprise and 'take its share of the valuable traffic'. He observed how much was still to be done to bring Lancashire and Wales together: 'It was a consideration not to be lost sight of from either the economical or the social point of view', and remarked on 'the power of Sir Edward Watkin's winning tongue'. He praised, to cheers, 'the manful and energetic spirit of Sir Edward Watkin'; without him such a 'spirit of courage and enterprise would [not] have been infused into those over whom he presides.[65] I said to Sir Edward Watkin "Will you be able to take me through without changing from Hawarden to Folkestone?" and he said "Yes".' *The Times* leader writer that day added that he fancied 'that the form of the question was rather disappointing to the projector of the Channel Tunnel, who might have preferred to be asked to promise to carry "his eminent friend" right through from Hawarden to Paris.' Gladstone's speech, another of his monuments to pleonasm, occupied 400 lines in the newspaper.

Sir Edward, in response, took the opportunity of Gladstone's

---

[63] *The Times*, 22 October 1892, pp.9-10.
[64] *Ibid.*
[65] *Ibid.*

presence to mention a grievance of the 'railway people': the way that biased regulations enabled landowners 'to take advantage of great public works for private gain'. *The Times* listed the guests present, including directors and officials of the MS&L, and the CLC, the WM&C, Cambrian Railways, the Buckley Railway, the Wrexham and Ellesmere Railway, the Mersey Railway, the Wirral Railway, the Mersey Docks Board, and the mayors of Chester, Birkenhead and Wrexham. The total length of the new line was given as 14 miles, and it was described as an important link in the system of railways under the Welsh Railways Through Traffic Act of 1889.

Watkin's railway developments at Hawarden had an influence on Gladstone's noble scheme to build a library to house all his books when his time came, and make them available for the purpose of theological learning. Gladstone conceived the idea while attending the funeral in Oxford of Dr Edward Pusey in September 1882, and discussed it with his son Stephen. Stephen wrote to his brother in August 1886 about it, saying that their father planned to build a library in Hawarden, 'as future railways will make it soon very convenient for Liverpool etc'.[66]

Although the value of the Chester and Connah's Quay Railway was to prove itself over the years, *Herepath's Journal* commented in 1894 on the 'poor state' of the Mid-Wales railways. The editor saw the Neath and Brecon as the weak link in Watkin's plan, as arrears of interest payments had reached the sum of nearly £48,000. The Wrexham, Mold and Connah's Quay lost £5,000 in the December half of 1893, though it met its absolute internal charges. 'The main problem with all these railways is inadequacy of traffic, and sparse populations, nor any important industries.'[67] Such a negative view was not shared by the *Financial News*. In 1901 it stated boldly that 'The Welsh system will eventually be strung together in a unified system.'[68]

Watkin invited many journalists to the opening of the Dee Bridge, but first he conducted them on a tour of the Manchester Ship Canal workings. His curious headgear was guaranteed to fix the occasion in their minds. It was turban-shaped, of a coarse grey

---

[66]T.W. Pritchard, p.9.
[67]September 1894, p.882.
[68]16 April.

wool with the fluffy side outwards, could be moulded into different shapes, and could not be blown off. Asked where he had obtained it, he explained it had been designed for him by an admirer in a Lancashire factory, and was unique. However, three months later, every member of the party received a facsimile, with Sir Edward's best wishes.[69]

A stylised version of the Hawarden Bridge over the Dee is, in the twenty-first century, the logo of the First Great Western Train Operating Company's Borderlands Line, 'Linking Wales and Merseyside'.

Watkin's new railway across the Dee was not his final contribution to the facilities in North Wales. He was to make his mark in an entirely different way – on Snowdon itself.

[69]*Newcastle Chronicle*, 16 April 1901.

17

Snowdon Fastnesses

In 1889 Watkin bought the estate of Hafod-y-Llan at Nant Gwynon near Beddgelert in Snowdonia. Here, not far up the valley called Cwm Llan, he built a chalet, finished on 22 May 1891, as a place for refreshing his energies 'for the busier life in Cheshire and in Kent'.[1] It was made of wood and white-painted corrugated iron, replacing an old stone cottage called Ty'n y Coedcae ('House of the field in the wood'), a circumstance which would fail to obtain planning permission today, and even in 1899 an observer said that 'the appearance of the painted corrugated iron possesses no charm, and...depends entirely upon its situation for its external attractiveness'.[2] A contemporary account described it as of 'only one story high, but...is a happy compromise between commodiousness and cosiness. All the rooms are panelled with light wood, and every room is abundantly served with electric light.' A reservoir constructed at Braich yr Oen supplies 'the motive power, which is concentrated upon a beautiful little engine in a shed just below the chalet'.[3] The design of the chalet was curiously similar to that of the first Gladstone Memorial Library at Hawarden, though not as large. The contract and specification for the library, from J.C. Humphries, Albert Gate Works, Hyde Park, London, dated 5 September 1890, points out that such a building can be sold after a few years for use elsewhere, as indeed it was when the present brick-built library was erected in 1904. (It was used for many years as a chapel in a

---

[1] David E. Jenkins, *Bedd Gelert: Its Facts, Fairies, and Folk-Lore* (Portmadoc: Llewelyn Jenkins, 1899), p.250.
[2] *Ibid,* p.249.
[3] *Pall Mall Budget,* 15 September 1892; quoted, Jenkins, p.250.

43 Watkin's chalet on the slopes of Snowdon, 1892

nearby parish.)[4] Watkin's chalet was burnt down in 1963, though the name 'The Chalet' remained on the gate until about 1996.

In September 1892 Sir Edward invited Gladstone to open the 'Watkin Path' to the top of Snowdon, a path to be 'free for ever for public use'.[5] His provision of access to the mountains of what is now part of the Snowdonia National Park was of a piece with his motives in the establishment of recreational space for the urban classes in his younger years. His views on mountains differed from his father's. Absolom confided to his diary[6]: 'To risk one's life merely to get to the top of a very high mountain…was a very silly affair, and one that, as it imperilled the lives of the guides also, could be justified neither prudently nor morally.'

Thomas E. Ellis, MP, a Welsh-speaking Liberal, who had been recently been appointed as Deputy Whip of the Liberal Party,

---

[4]The Venerable T.W. Pritchard, in personal conversation.
[5]Jenkins, p.250.
[6]9 May 1855 (Goffin, p.359).

295

suggested, via Herbert Gladstone, that the visit ought to be expanded to a consideration of Welsh affairs generally: the Irish Home Rule debate had aroused Welsh aspirations. Gladstone accepted the suggestion eagerly, and conformed to Ellis's arrangements for the trip to include speeches in Caernarvon and Portmadoc. After his speech in Caernarvon on 12 September 1892, he made his way, by the North Wales Narrow Gauge Railway, from Dinas to Rhyd-Ddû, from where Sir Edward's carriage conveyed him in pouring rain to the chalet.

The following day they made their way to Cwm Llan, where between 3 and 4 o'clock Gladstone mounted a platform fixed to the top of a rock by Watkin's workmen. The platform group included Sir Edward, Lady Watkin, Gladstone's daughters Helen and Mary (Mrs Drew), Herbert Gladstone, the local MP Tom Ellis, and Lloyd George. Sir Edward chaired the meeting, and when the hymn-singing had stopped for cheers for the Prime Minister, asked for the speeches of welcome. Two addresses in Welsh were read, and Gladstone stood up to respond, but Sir Edward told him that another hymn was to be sung first; 'the Welsh have their own way of doing these things, you know,' he said.[7] Gladstone then addressed the estimated 2,500 people assembled there on Land Reform in Wales, which was rather a disappointment to the crowd because they had hoped for something positive on the disestablishment of the Welsh Church, if not Welsh Home Rule.[8] The whole meeting, however, was conducted in the highest of spirits, and further hymn-singing, concluding with *Land of My Fathers*. Later, Sir Edward had a large brass plaque mounted on what came to be known as 'Gladstone's Rock', [9] bearing the following message composed by him, first in Welsh (translated by Tom Ellis) and then in English:

September 13th 1892 – upon this rock
The Right Honourable W.E. Gladstone MP
When Prime Minister for the fourth time and 83 years old
Addressed the people of Eryri upon

[7]C.J. Williams, 'Gladstone, Lloyd George and the Gladstone Rock', *Caernarvonshire Historical Transactions,* (1999), p.65.
[8]Bentley Brinkerhoff Gilbert, *David Lloyd George* (London: B.T. Batsford Ltd., 1987), p.105.
[9]National Grid Reference SH 618523

44 Gladstone, addressing the crowds at Cwmllan, Snowdon, 13 September 1892

Justice to Wales
The multitude sang Cymrig hymns
And 'The Land of my Fathers'
Publicly dedicated by Sir Edward Watkin and Lady Watkin
June 1893.

The odd thing is that no mention was made in the speech that day, or even on the plaque, of Watkin's path up the mountain, the original purpose of the whole occasion. The party adjourned to The Chalet for Dinner, where nine people were present, including David Lloyd George. He was much impressed by this encounter with the great man, and described it at length in his *War Memoirs* forty years later. 'Mr Gladstone did practically all the talking at the dinner-table and afterwards, and the rest of us, only too thrilled to meet and hear this great figure from a past world, were naturally content to listen in silence.' The range of topics of his conversation was varied – political matters, social observations, personal travel anecdotes, and 'a dissertation on corrugated iron

The Chalet, looking northeast

roofing and the difficulty of keeping buildings of this kind warm in winter and cool in summer.'[10] A reference to the Channel Tunnel provoked 'a wonderful panegyric on the people of France'.[11] It would seem to have been one of Watkin's felicitous inspirations to bring together 'the pre-eminent statesman of the Victorian era'[12] and 'the most important and influential British political figure of his time, and probably of the 20th Century'.[13] Ensconced in the 'very pleasing domestic interior'[14] of Watkin's chalet, Gladstone contemplated '...his sessional preparations, especially for the Home Rule Bill.'[15] Mrs Gladstone wrote from The Chalet[16] to her 'dear friend':

---

[10]The specification for the library building at Hawarden included felt lining for all 'Roof, Gables and Walls...to keep the building warm in winter and cool in summer'. (Flintshire Record Office, Hawarden).

[11]David Lloyd George, *War Memoirs* (London: Odhams Press Ltd., 1938), Vol. 1, pp.2–3.

[12]Roy Jenkins, *Gladstone* (Macmillan, 1995), p.xv.

[13]Gilbert, p.9

[14]Gladstone's diary for the day.

[15]Richard Shannon, *Gladstone: Heroic Minister* (Allen Lane, 1999), p.527.

[16]13 September 1892.

I have not time to tell you of the strange wildness and beauty of this spot. The 'Chalet' will speak to your imagination. It is on the very Snowdon range, and we have returned from such a drive! – the late rains enhancing the beauty of the waterfalls; the lights peeping beautifully on one side, while mysterious outlines hung on the other; a large lake on one side, with stupendous rocks solemnly towering above, broken by the dancing many-coloured waters below...'[17]

The next day they set out to climb Snowdon by the new path, Gladstone riding a pony as far as Bwlch-y-Saethau, where, because a mist had descended, he was persuaded to go no further.[18] Mary Drew and Emmeline Watkin (the wife of Sir Edward's brother Alfred's son, Edgar, who was forty-one years old at the time) walked on, to the summit.[19]

The Watkin path goes up Cwm Llan (called Cwm Tregalan in its upper reaches[20]), a fine open valley with impressive waterfalls and hillsides, through the remains of old tramways, to the buildings of the South Snowdon Quarry (closed in the 1880s).[21] From there it continues by the path built by Watkin's workmen up to Bwlch-y-Saethau, 'Pass of the Arrows'.[22] Beyond that point the path is unremittingly steep until it joins the Beddgelert path about 200 yards from the summit.[23]

After his purchase of the land for his chalet at Hafod-y-Llan, Watkin bought in 1893 the estate of Ffridd Isaf, at Rhyd Ddû, making him the owner of a large part of Snowdon mountain (2,038 acres, of which Hafod-y-Llan comprised 1,500), from the summit southwards and westwards. His land included the area

[17]F.E. Hamer (ed.), *The Personal Papers of Lord Rendel* (London, Ernest Benn Ltd., 1931), p. 201.

[18]In his diary he recorded that he rode for only two thirds of the way, and had climbed about a thousand feet on foot.

[19]C.J. Williams, 'Gladstone, Lloyd George and the Gladstone Rock', *Caernarvonshire Historical Society Transactions,* 1999, pp.69 and 70.

[20]E.G.Rowland, *The Ascent of Snowdon* (Pentrefelin, Ciccieth: The Cidron Press, c.1964), p.8.

[21]John and Anne Nuttall, *The Mountains of England and Wales* (Milnthorpe: Cicerone Press, 1989), p.56.

[22]So-called because legend has it that King Arthur was killed there by a flight of arrows (Rowland, p.8).

[23]Herbert R.C. Carr and George A. Lister, *The Mountains of Snowdonia* (London: Crosby, Lockwood and Son Ltd., 1948), p.239.

now occupied by the café and railway station,[24] and also the 'Snowdon' station at Rhyd Ddû on the NWNGR (later the Welsh Highland Railway).[25] After Sir Edward's death, the whole estate was put up for sale at an auction to be held on 5 November 1902. The auctioneer described The Chalet as comprising:

> Porch leading into Entrance Hall, on the left of which is the Drawing Room about 20 feet by 18 feet, Dining Room 16 feet 6 inches square, a Corridor runs through the Building from east to west, and out of it open Two Bedrooms, with south aspect. On the north of the corridor are Bath Room and Lavatory with hot and cold water supply and W.C., Four Bedrooms, Kitchen with Capital Range, Scullery with hot and cold water supply, Pantry, Servants' Hall with range, Larder, Passage and Coal Cellar, all lined with pitch pine, Washhouse, and large detached Larder with slate shelves, Two Servants' W.C.s, Wine Cellar, and Four Servants' Bedrooms...

Part way up the drive from the Beddgelert Road, in an enclosed yard, stood a range of outbuildings – two coach houses for carriages and carts, and a coachman's cottage. These were all stone-built, and, suitably converted, are in use in the twenty-first century. At the last minute, Alfred Watkin withdrew the property, so it was not then sold, but was bought in the early 1920s by the sitting tenant farmer, John Griffith Williams, from whose descendants the area was secured by the National Trust in 1998.[26]

Watkin has been credited with, or accused of, the primary inspiration for the Snowdon Mountain Railway, running from Llanberis to the summit. The *Railway News* and the *Graphic* both reported so on 20 April 1901, and even the *Manchester Evening Chronicle* said confidently: 'It was owing to his enterprise that a light railway was made on the mountain.'[27] Another story attributed to him the intention of placing a huge electric light on the summit, with a generating plant sufficient to cast a light over the

---

[24]Vaynol Papers, 6948, in Gwynedd Archives, Caernarvon.

[25]Map produced for the 1902 sale by Edwin Fox and Bousfield, London.

[26]Emyr Williams, in the *Daily Post*, 1 September 1998. Except for the house at Ffridd Isaf. It is now a privately-owned guest house.

[27]15 April 1901.

greater part of the county, but opposition to such 'vandalism' proved too strong. This was in *The Star* of 15 April 1901; the *Financial News* on the same day added that this went no further than rumour. The *Daily Chronicle*, however, went so far as to say firmly: 'It is true that he vulgarised Snowdon by a railway and electric light.'[28] The railway was attributed to him in a Guide Book as late as 1922.[29] Other rumours were to the effect that in 1896 he was projecting a rival railway from Beddgelert to the summit.[30] In the late 1870s a plan had been conceived by two engineers of the Festiniog Railway to run a line along the present route from Llanberis, over the top, and down to Rhyd-Ddû to join the North Wales Narrow Gauge Railway there.[31] Rumour also credited Watkin with such an idea, but there is no hard evidence. Even *The Railway News* declared that 'he built a railway to the cloud-capped summit of Snowdon'.[32] The fact is that, whatever the proliferation of such stories, there is absolutely no trace whatever of Watkin's involvement in the Snowdon Mountain Railway.[33] Watkin was, however, a frequent user of the train. A contemporary writer, describing a journey in 1897, said 'We had a very distinguished fellow-traveller with us – the doyen of Railway Chairmen, who, in spite of his three-score years and ten, would insist on going up to the Summit Inn, where he was carried in a sedan chair by the engine-driver and guard from the railway station [to the top of the mountain]. It is not the first time he has done this.'[34]

While he was formulating his Welsh plans, Watkin received a request from a strange quarter.

---

[28] 15 April 1901.

[29] *The Book of Snowdon*, quoted by Keith Turner, *The Snowdon Mountain Railway* (David and Charles, 1973), p.81.

[30] John Partington, article in the *Railway Magazine* in 1897, quoted, Turner, p.78.

[31] Turner, pp.32–7.

[32] 20 April 1901.

[33] Personal confirmation from the retired Manager of the SMR, Derek Rogerson, 3 March 2001.

[34] John Partington, quoted, Turner, p.78.

18

Brief Lancashire Excursions

While Sir Edward was working to develop Cleethorpes as a holiday resort, he received an invitation from another watering-place, Blackpool. A deputation from the town and the Lytham Improvement Commissioners went to meet the MS&LR Board on 22 October 1880. They were seeking a new railway between Black-pool and Manchester, notwithstanding that there were three stations in Blackpool already.[1] John Pendleton[2] described Black-pool as the 'greatest holiday haunt in the world', with two million visitors a year. But it was not well served by its railway companies. He described a journey from Blackpool to Manchester on the Lancashire and Yorkshire Railway as so slow that 'a Sunday ride from the seaside resort to Manchester still gives one time for reflec-tion. It requires more patience than Jacob possessed when he served twice seven years for Rachel.'[3] It probably was such consid-erations that induced the burghers of Blackpool and district to approach Edward Watkin.

Acceptance of the suggestion hinged largely upon the success of the Wigan Junction Railway, promoted by local enterprise. This was planned to go from Glazebrook, on the Manchester to Liver-pool line of the Cheshire Lines Committee, to Ince, near Wigan, to serve the large coalfields in that area.[4] Watkin saw the WJR as an extension of the CLC, but the Great Northern disagreed, so the Midland and the MS&LR undertook to support it. Eventually the Midland backed out, and the 'Sheffield' promised financial support

---

[1] These were Waterloo Road, Central, and Talbot Road – the last two of which were termini; all were jointly owned by the LNW and the L&Y (Tom Heaviside, *On Lancashire and Yorkshire Lines* (Ian Allen, 1997), p.71).

[2] In *Our Railways* (Cassell, 1896), Vol. 2, p.85.

[3] *Ibid*, Vol. 1, p.163.

[4] Dow, Vol. 2, p.104.

with a net profit agreement.[5] The line was opened for coal and goods traffic in October 1879. In 1881 the MS&L took over the line altogether, but the resulting financial commitment made it hesitant to accept the proposal to extend from Wigan to Blackpool. The projected Blackpool line has been part of the charge of reckless and megalomaniac empire-building levelled against Watkin by railway historians.[6] The facts indicate that the pressure to expand so far north of Manchester came from local community interests; they approached Watkin again on 5 May 1882, and he personally surveyed the prospects for the line in the Wigan, Preston, and Blackpool area, meeting some of the landowners.[7]

The East Lancashire Railway, incorporated in 1871, was building its line from Southport to Preston, and approached Watkin in 1873, proposing that, on completion, it should be leased to the 'Sheffield'. Watkin expressed his willingness, provided the Midland would 'go halves' with him; but this it was not prepared to do. By summer 1882, with the new prospects, the picture had changed: the West Lancashire could be a useful asset in linking Wigan with Southport, Preston, and Blackpool. Accordingly, the Wigan to Longton (Southport) extension was authorised in 1883, and on 21 September a comprehensive deputation of twenty-eight persons, representing the local authority and leisure facility owners of Blackpool, Preston, Lytham, Freckleton and St Anne's, met the MS&L Board. Watkin listened to seven speakers urging the new line, and responded that he could not remember any occasion when local public opinion had been more unanimously expressed. 'We have always been very chary', he said to them, 'of interfering with the rights or property of anyone else. We have made a line to Wigan, and through the northern coalfields, and...through the town of Preston, where we join the great Dock and Railway project of the Corporation...The MS&LR Board have been pushed by the progress of events into the position of today.' He referred to attempts he had made to work with the LYR, but his speech was not one of his best thought-out, perhaps because his heart was not wholly in the scheme, as well as being heavily

---

[5]Dow, Vol. 2, p.105.
[6]For example, Jack Simmons, *The Victorian Railway* (Thames and Hudson, 1991), p.113: 'rapacious and ill-considered ambitions'.
[7]Dow, Vol. 2, p.173.

303

engaged in Channel Tunnel business. However, he did approach the L&Y, and on 19 April 1884 wrote to their Chairman, Pearson.[8]

It is easy to imagine the position of the directors of the L&Y and LNW at this approach from the most energetic of their opponents. To them it cloaked an attack on the very heartland of L&Y prosperity. The MS&LR minutes of 2 May 1884 record: 'The opposition of the Lancashire and Yorkshire and London and North Western Companies was being proceeded with.'[9] Pearson's reply set out, with great courtesy, the previous decision of the company, namely that Blackpool was 'very well accommodated' already, and offered to take any traffic for Blackpool which the MS&L may have. The reply was aimed at pacifying the 'Sheffield', but ignored completely the consortium of local interests.

The Bill for the railway was lodged, after an unsuccessful attempt, in 1884, and the Blackpool Railway was incorporated on 7 August of that year, to build a line between the West Lancashire at Preston to Church Street in Blackpool, via Lytham. However, making the connection between the West Lancashire and the CLC near Southport caused long delays, and the local promoters began to get restive. The estimated cost of building the line had, by 1887, risen to around £400,000, and on 10 June 1889, Watkin made a final attempt to get the LYR involved in the project. He wrote to George Armytage, the then Chairman of the L&Y, tactlessly both pleading for Armytage's co-operation and complaining of his company's past actions. 'I have been anxious - perhaps too anxious - to co-operate with the Lancashire and Yorkshire rather than act separately or in antagonism, and though many friendly overtures of mine have hitherto been met by delay and the *non possumus* because of your partners, I take upon myself, just once more, and finally, to refer to the condition of things...' He dangled the bait of L&Y entry into Wales over MS&L metals, and the contemplated tunnel lines in Liverpool, and reminded Armytage of the facilities at Birkenhead which had been granted to the LYR. He received a courteous but firmly negative reply.[10]

In the following year, yet further deputations arrived from the

---

[8]PRO RAIL 463/19, 27 May 1884, Minute 9123.
[9]PRO RAIL 463/19, Minute 9118.
[10]Dow, Vol. 2, p.180.

elders of Blackpool and Preston, urging action, and reminding Watkin that his company had already sunk £70,000 in the project, for the purchase of the greater part of the land. On 8 July 1892, another extension of powers was obtained, and the Town Clerk of Blackpool was assured that the MS&L intended to see the line completed. Later that year, a prospectus was issued, but it was becoming clear that Watkin's attention was being drawn away from the project to another concern, much dearer to his heart. The same Act of 28 March 1893 which gave the Blackpool line an extension of time authorised also the London Extension of the MS&LR.

The Blackpool Railway, which had an official seal, never actually existed. After a further flicker of life, the project was abandoned in 1896. The land, amounting to the value, by then, of £302,000, was sold off to the LYR and LNW. An attempt by a London contractor to revive it in 1895 had come to nothing, as did a final request to build it by official representatives of Preston and Lytham, in July 1899. The death of the scheme improved relations with the LYR and LNWR immediately, and the Great Central Railway began through trains to Blackpool over the LYR. The West Lancashire Railway was eventually absorbed into the Lancashire and Yorkshire.[11]

---

[11] *Ibid*, pp.179–82.

19

Forward to London

The earliest intimation by Watkin of his intention to extend the MS&LR to London appears in a document he printed to advise John Chapman and his Board in negotiations with the Great Northern in 1860, referring to 'the importance of obtaining for yourselves an independent access to London'.[1] On 11 November 1872, Watkin, with surprising transparency, said to W.P. Price, the Chairman of the Midland (which had opened its own 'London Extension' four years earlier), that his policy would be 'if I live so long, to connect the...Sheffield line with the Metropolitan and extend it to a junction with the South Eastern. I very frankly expressed my views upon this to you.' He tried to negotiate with the Midland for a joint line from north of Doncaster to Rushton, near Kettering, joining the Midland main line there. Watkin haggled over his plan to connect eventually with the Metropolitan, and the Midland over connections with the GNR and LNWR where the new line would cross them. The Bill was mangled in Parliament, and the plan came to nothing.[2]

At the MS&L half-yearly shareholders' meeting on 24 January 1883, Watkin floated a warning. He referred to the working disadvantages of terminal stations and short-length traffic flows which were handed on to other companies, and said that the MS&L and the Lancashire and Yorkshire, 'and no other companies in England collected a vast amount of traffic for which other people get more than their share of the benefit. When I see the great railway companies, the London and North Western, the Great

---

[1]Dow, Vol. 1, p.197.
[2]Dow Vol. 2, pp. 65 and 67.

46 Watkin's MS&LR Saloon, No. 1033, photographed at Gorton works where it was built in 1890

Western, the Midland, the Great Northern – all extending themselves wherever they can...it makes us occasionally anxious with regard to the future. I know it is said "Sufficient unto the day is the evil thereof", but wise men endeavour to look at what is the tendency of things affecting the future.' It seemed to him 'that with railways like the Manchester, Sheffield and Lincolnshire and the Lancashire and Yorkshire the tendency must either be to absorption, amalgamation, or extension [Hear, hear].'[3]

In September 1889, Watkin wrote to Lord Colville of the GNR, arguing for a joint line through Nottingham and Leicester to join the Metropolitan at Aylesbury, 'to piece together your railway system and the Manchester, Sheffield and Lincolnshire system.'[4] He was clearly testing the reaction of the GNR, and hoping to share the expense of his scheme for his new London line. Having learned from experience, no doubt, to temper his impatience, he was in no hurry at this time to apply for parliamentary powers, but he did begin exploring the costs of building a southward connection with the Metropolitan Railway, and drafted an agree-

[3]PRO RAIL 463/77, pp.4-5.
[4]Dow, Vol. 2, p.236.

ment concerning through traffic, rates and fares in which the MS&L, the Metropolitan and the South Eastern Railway would be participants.

The Great Northern, in its response to Watkin's letter, expressed concern for the vision he had unfolded, referring to the integrity of existing traffic agreements dating from 1 October 1860. By the beginning of 1890, its concern had heightened to anxiety. Watkin wrote to Colville on 3 February:

> No one can deny that the trade of the country demands completion of the through route between Annesley and Nottingham. No one can deny that to have a second string to your bow would give greater strength and profit to the Great Northern, and would in all senses be better than wasting your shareholders' capital on the plastering of your old line. The work is inevitable, and it will be done without you if it cannot be done with you.[5]

The times were propitious for further expansions. In the week ended 18 January 1890, receipts on 33 of the principal lines of the UK amounted to £1,294,158 on $17,964\frac{3}{4}$ miles of line. This worked out at £72 per mile, compared with the figure of £68 for the corresponding week of 1889. The increase of revenue on the MS&L was 7.87%. The figures for the LNWR, the GWR and the Midland were 6.98%, 5.6%, and 10.2% respectively.[6]

A comparison with the way the Chairman of the MS&LR thought, and conducted his business with his opposite numbers in other companies, and the steady, cautious, risk-free way in which his contemporaries spoke and acted, highlights the exceptional quality of his character. In a business such as a railway company existing to move people and merchandise and basic necessities from one part of the country to another, the return on high capital investment is important. But it takes a more open, more adventurous, bolder type of mind to see the possibilities of increased traffic, and then go out on a limb for such developments. Of course, such a policy can bring failures and losses as well as gains. But possibly it was Watkin's ability to communicate his enthusiasm to the shareholders which made them so willing to back him every time.

---

[5]*Ibid.*
[6]*Railway Times*, 25 January 1890, p.96.

It must, however, have bewildered the shareholders of the East London Railway, when, at their half-yearly meeting in January 1890, he reported that results were not as satisfactory as they could be, because of the lack of through communication. He was doing what he could through the MS&LR, the Metropolitan and the SER to bridge the distance between the South of the country and the North. The railway systems of the country wanted supplementing. The great companies – the North-Western and the Midland – were not able to deal thoroughly with the traffic which the increased prosperity of the country had brought about. Some of the great companies and their supporters had condemned him because he was trying to strike out a new line; but he, nevertheless, intended to make the 83 miles of new line which would complete the connection of the southern railways with the north. This was a broad canvas to set before such a tiny line with hitherto strictly limited horizons.

The Great Northern's reluctance did not deter him from pursuing his aim, as he had warned Colville, and in July 1890, the General Manager of the MS&L was instructed to deposit a Bill for the Extension for the session of 1891. Contingency plans for dealing with the expected opposition were also drawn up. On 11 July, five of the Board of Directors, chaired by Watkin, formed themselves into a committee, with the intention of raising support from the towns through which the proposed new railway was to pass, and from industrialists and traders with a possible commercial interest in the project. This committee, which demonstrated Watkin's sound grasp of the function of public relations pressure-groups, immediately gained support from influential men like Baron Rothschild at Waddesdon Manor,[7] Colonel Henry Lowndes at Braunston, and other businessmen who saw in the enterprise a larger opportunity for competitive bargaining; and from the corporations of Nottingham, Loughborough, Leicester and Leeds, and numerous public bodies,[8] who saw convenience and prestige for their communities in the scheme. Sheffield saw the possibility of a third route to the capital, and Grimsby a speedier route for its fish.

---

[7]The Rothschilds were customers of Absolom Watkin when they lived in Manchester (*Manchester City News*, 20 April 1901).

[8]Charles G. Harper, 'The Great Central Railway', in *Fortnightly Review*, April 1899, pp.590 ff.

In his attempts to involve others in the provision of a further station in Leicester, Sir Edward received support from the City, but none from other railway companies. The GNR had already showed its disfavour; the LNWR (which, apart from the profitable co-operation on the MSJ&A Railway, maintained a consistently cool attitude towards the MS&L during the whole of Watkin's reign) was happy to share the Midland station; and the Midland itself, not surprisingly, was unenthusiastic about a rival station in Leicester, the Chairman commenting that it was simply a move in Watkin's chess game. Sir Edward, rather artfully, considered this uncalled for, as the suggestion for the station came not from him but from the civic authorities. Leicester had, in fact, declared its dissatisfaction more than once with the Midland.[9]

Similarly, in Nottingham the LNWR expressed no interest in sharing the cost of a central station, though eight years after it had become a reality it was asking for running powers there for its trains.

Even at this date, a wary eye was being kept by the MS&L on the wiles of the LNWR. Its directors were informed at a meeting on 21 January 1891 that the LNW had deposited a Bill for a branch to a new goods station in Sheffield. The Board decided: 'A watching petition should be presented against the Bill in order to obtain proper protection.'[10]

From the outset of the campaign to obtain powers to build the new line into London, there was great opposition from various quarters. The cricketing fraternity at Lord's was inflamed by the proposed route, which threatened the Marylebone Cricket Club's ground. The artistic community of St John's Wood held several meetings and signed petitions against the Bill. There was outrage generally at the prospect of sacrificing thirty acres of land for a goods depot at Marylebone Station, and the traffic through a residential area, on 'a line for the conveyance not only of passengers, but of coal, manure, fish, and other abominations'.[11] The cricketing world proposed dire retaliation against Watkin, as the perceived threat to its sacred turf at Lord's began to take hold.

[9]John Gough, in *The Adaptation of Change* (ed. Daniel Williams), (Leicester Museums Publication No.18, 1980), p.105.
[10]PRO RAIL 463/24, Minute 13754.
[11]John Pendleton, *Our Railways* (Cassell and Company, 1896), Vol. 1, pp.359 and 358.

The thought of steel rails running through this 'chief bulwark of our national pastime', as W.G. Grace put it, 'was repellent'.[12]

Watkin saw quickly that this constituency could muster widespread resistance. About this time, an interviewer asked him if he had any more schemes in view. 'No,' he replied. 'When I settle with Lord's, I am ready for Father Abraham's bosom.'[13] That particular contest proved to be not quite so terminal. 'With the suavity which is one of his most conspicuous characteristics',[14] he managed to placate nearly all the complainants. He should be sorry indeed, he told them, to despoil such a cherished cricket ground. All he was proposing was to take a narrow strip of the practice area, and to compensate by giving the club the freehold of other land nearby, and take the railway through a tunnel beneath the ground, guaranteeing its quality and providing it with an eight-foot boundary wall. Also, most of the site of the Clergy Orphan School (purchased by the railway for £40,000 early in 1892, and re-sited elsewhere at the MS&LR's expense) was to be presented to the club.

A meeting of the MCC Committee on 8 December 1890 received notice of the MS&L's plans, and instructed the Secretary, Mr Perkins, to '...watch the progress of the case with a view to opposing the scheme in every possible way when the time arrives.' By the meeting of 9 February 1891, the Treasurer and acting Chairman, Sir Spencer Ponsonby Fane, reported on behalf of the sub-committee that they had employed a parliamentary agent to oppose the Bill. 'Since then the Rly Coy have submitted a new scheme by tunnel under the eastern boundary of the nursery', which was so-called because the $3\frac{1}{2}$-acre Henderson's Nursery Gardens had been there before the MCC purchased it in 1887.[15] At the next meeting, ten days later, it was reported that the MCC representatives had agreed to terms offered by the company – 'to make over to the Club the whole of the Clergy Orphan estate transfer and fit for cricket...eight lines of rails are to be made by cutting and covering or tunnel...' The parliamentary agent was ordered to carry out these terms.

---

[12] *Ibid*, p.360.
[13] *Westminster Budget*, 19 April 1901
[14] John Pendleton, Vol. 1, p.360.
[15] Stephen Green, *The Cricketer*, April 1990, p.38.

The committee had been swiftly won over; but the general membership was very turbulent. A special meeting of the committee was held on 16 March at the Lord Chamberlain's office, to decide how to respond to the many verbal and written remonstrations against any bargains with Watkin. It was concluded that the company's terms were so reasonable that they could not oppose the Second Reading of the Bill. The club rules required that a special general meeting be summoned, and this took place on 6 April, with Lord Willoughby de Eresby, President, in the chair, and about 180 members present. It was proposed that the report of the committee be adopted. Denzil R. Onslow moved the rejection of the report, arguing that a special general meeting ought to have been held earlier, and adding his opinion that the committee had been 'Watkinised'. His amendment was lost by 150 to 24, and the original motion 'was then put, and carried by an enormous majority'.

Onslow stoutly maintained his opposition at another meeting held on 7 December 1891, and warned of the dangers of the scheme, and the necessity to oppose it 'with vigour at every stage'. This time the vote went against him by 96 to 65, and his case was lost.[16] But he had added a very useful verb to the language of railway history, with which many railway shareholders would sympathise. Once agreement had been reached, the MCC co-operated with the company in every respect.

The St John's Wood artists' colony continued its opposition, as did the Great Northern, which, having not long before fought a bitter battle with the Midland over traffic from South Yorkshire to London, determined 'to pursue no Quaker-like policy in the competition that the fourth trunk line to town' would accentuate.[17] Watkin tried to placate the GN, but here his efforts were of no avail. Throughout the campaign, he had been the perfect diplomat, surprising those who had noted his tendencies to bluntness and irascibility when confronted by delaying tactics. Only once did he show some exasperation, and that was when, at the same session, the Bill for the Lancashire, Derbyshire and East Coast Railway was passed.[18] Though this concern never reached either Lancashire

---

[16]Minutes of the committee of the Marylebone Cricket Club.
[17]Pendleton, Vol. 1, p.319.
[18]Dow, Vol. 2, p.243.

or the East Coast, it was clearly covering much the same ground as the MS&L. 'It was a brave scheme,' for 170 miles of railway from Warrington, via Knutsford, Macclesfield, Buxton and Chesterfield to Sutton-on-Sea, spanning the Peak District on awe-inspiring viaducts, and expecting coal traffic amounting to ten million tons a year.[19] But it was a strange promotion at this late stage of railway development, and it was to be absorbed by the Great Central Railway in 1907. Sir Edward's comment at the time was that it was 'as mad a scheme as was ever presented to Parliament'.

On 16 June 1891 the parliamentary committee found the preamble to the MS&LR London Extension Bill not proved. The Board of Directors, meeting on 19 June, resolved to renew its efforts in the next session, subject to the agreement of the shareholders.[20] The cost of all the preparation work had been very heavy, and some of the shareholders became uneasy. Sir Edward told them at a meeting in July that some of the railway decisions made during the parliamentary session had been curious, referring to the LD&EC Railway, 'but the Directors were a stolid class of men who didn't admit defeat, and in the interest of the 13,000 shareholders they proposed to go forward again'.[21]

Some further objections were made. A meeting of inhabitants of Marylebone in January 1892 resolved to oppose the railway on the grounds that it would disturb the patients in the Samaritan Free Hospital and Queen Charlotte's Hospital, and dislodge 25,000 persons of the humbler classes from the neighbourhood.[22] Watkin, addressing a shareholders' meeting in Manchester in that month, assured them that most of the objectors had been mollified. He regaled them with a history of how the cricket-ground became known as Lord's, and declared that he liked the game very much himself, and had no desire to do anything to damage such a venerable institution.

Indeed, Sir Edward had close family connections with cricket. Joseph Makinson, a cousin on his mother's side, was a Cambridge Blue, and was 'considered the most brilliant all-round cricketer of

---

[19]Dow, Vol. 3, pp.153–4.
[20]Dow, Vol. 2, pp.243–4.
[21]Pendleton, Vol. 1, p.362.
[22]*Ibid,* p.363.

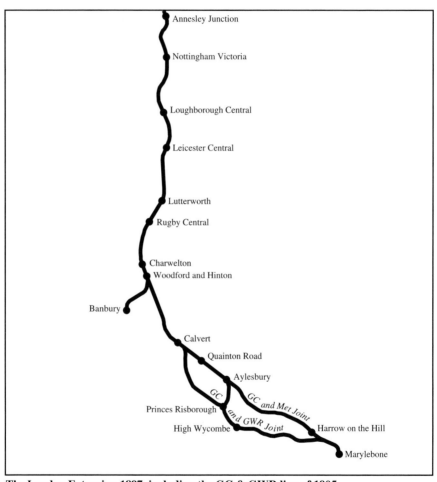

The London Extension 1897, including the GC & GWR line of 1905

his day'.[23] When Edward married for the second time, he acquired a stepson-in-law, Albert Neilson Hornby, the husband of his new wife's daughter, Ada Sarah Ingram. Hornby, the son of William Henry Hornby, a Lancashire cotton magnate and MP for Blackburn, was born on 10 February 1847. He played cricket for Lancashire from 1867, transforming the club from an indifferent side to the County Championship, as Captain, in 1881. He headed the national batting averages that year, being spoken of as W.G. Graces's 'one superior'. He played for them until he was fifty-two years old, the oldest player ever for Lancashire. He captained England against Australia at the Oval in 1882, said by Neville Cardus to be the greatest Test Match ever, the one which England lost by seven runs and which gave birth to 'The Ashes.' He also played for Blackburn Rovers soccer team, was an excellent boxer, and was one of only two men ever to captain his country at both cricket and rugby, playing for England in the latter game between 1877 and 1892. Hornby lived for most of his life in Nantwich, and is buried in the churchyard at the nearby village of Acton, with a marble wicket, bails, bat and ball on his grave. He became a member of the MCC Committee in May 1892, thereby denying by a margin of a few months any contribution he might have made to the club's discussion of his stepfather-in-law's audacity.

There had been 49 petitions against the MS&L's first Bill, but only 31 against the second, and by March 1892 nearly all limited their opposition to the site of the terminus in London and the plans for the station on Marylebone Road with a hotel. The St John's Wood artist's colony, numbering some 200, were still complaining, but their case had descended to arguments like Alma-Tadema's plaint that the vibration from the passage of trains would make it impossible to draw a straight line on the canvas; they were placated by the decision to locate the terminus fronting the Marylebone Road, instead of Boscobel Gardens.[24]

The London County Council saw the project as an opportunity to extract large sums, and tried to make the company pay for street widenings and the building of new ones. Private owners' complaints were satisfied by the company's purchase of their

---

[23]Goffin, p.374.
[24]L.T.C. Rolt, *The Making of a Railway* (London: Hugh Evelyn, 1971), p.15.

315

houses, and of whole squares.[25] The Bill was presented before the Committee of the House on 21 March 1892, and although the opposition was wilting, Watkin and his men prepared by assembling 159 witnesses to plead the case. Mr Bidder, QC, holding a brief for all the Bill's opponents, in a speech redolent of some desperation on the last day of the Committee, declared that the object of the Bill was not to accommodate the needs of the towns and villages which would be served by the new line, but to satisfy the ambitions of the promoters to become a great trunk line to the capital. It was, he went on without restraint, 'to accomplish the long-held ambitious schemes of one man – a man well-known in the railway world – whose hope and dream before he died was to run through carriages from the North to London, and from London to Paris. The Channel Tunnel was integral to Sir Edward Watkin's dream, and now he was leading the shareholders of the MS&L to ruin in the wild belief that this great line would increase their dividends.' Mr Littler, QC, for the MS&LR, replied by assuring the committee that 'there was no better pioneer and guide in railway matters than Sir Edward Watkin', and was as bold as his opponent when he summarised Mr Bidder's utterances as 'rubbish, and highly absurd'.[26]

Unfortunately, as can be seen from Olympian hindsight, there was more than a grain of truth in Mr Bidder's expostulations. The fact that they did not carry executive weight with the parliamentary committee speaks for the respect in which Sir Edward was held at this stage of his life. At the half-yearly meeting of the shareholders in July 1892, Watkin pointed out that they had reached a memorable time in the history of the company, for they were no longer merely the MS&L, but had the powers to build their new line to the capital. Mr Sutcliffe Thomas stood up to point out that Sir Edward had had a notably busy year, and congratulated him on his threefold triumph: he had married a charming lady, he had piloted the Bill through Parliament to give them their new line, and he had again been returned to Parliament.[27]

The way in which Watkin was able to carry the MS&L share-

[25]Dow, Vol. 2, p.244.
[26]Pendleton, Vol. 1, p.365.
[27]*Ibid,* p.366.

holders with him on this huge project is a matter for some surprise. 'One wonders how he did it. He must have had some strange compelling power with business men who would have reckoned themselves hard-headed'.[28] The *Railway Times* commented: 'Experience has taught many a chairman how great is the difficulty of governing timid and recalcitrant shareholders; but Sir Edward Watkin, in the manner in which he succeeds in inducing his constituents to act in accordance with his decisions ...[and] at whose bidding those with whom he has to deal will coincide with any extravagant idea, accept misfortunes with apparent gratitude, or even loosen their purse strings when he blandly says "you must".' After admitting that the MS&L had been doing fairly well, the report commented that Sir Edward intended to cover the 83 miles between the railways of the North and South, but 'we recall that [he] made a similar declaration with regard to the Channel Tunnel, but the tunnel is not made yet'.[29]

Equally surprising is his persuasion of his fellow directors, some of whom were men of considerable stature and pedigree in other walks of national life. The Earl of Wharncliffe (1827–99), a director of the 'Sheffield' from August 1864 to March 1890, vice-chairman from then until May 1894 and Watkin's successor in the chair until his death, was a member of a distinguished family. His father, John Stuart Wortley (1801–55), the second Baron Wharncliffe, graduated from Oxford in 1822 with a first in Mathematics and a second in Classics, and published pamphlets on Commerce and National Finance. His uncle, James Archibald Stuart-Wortley (1805–81), was Solicitor-General from 1865 to 1867, and his cousin Charles Beilby Stuart-Wortley, QC (1851–26),[30] was Under-Secretary of the Home Department, (and later a director of the Great Central Railway).[31] Alexander Henderson (1850–1934), CH, 1st Baron Faringdon (1916), was a prominent financier. He was Unionist MP for Stafford from 1898 to 1906, and for St George Hanover Square from 1913 to 1916. He was Chairman of the Great Central Railway from 1899. Richard Assheton Cross, GCB,

---

[28]Jack Simmons, *The Railway in England and Wales, 1830-1914* (Leicester University Press, 1978), p.93.
[29]25 January 1890, p.97.
[30]Made Baron Stuart of Wortley in 1917.
[31]*Who Was Who* Vol. 1, pp. 754–5; *DNB*, Vol. 19, p.113.

GCSI, PC, DL, LLD, FRS, JP, was Lord Privy Seal from 1895 to 1900, Treasurer of the Inner Temple, 1895, an Ecclesiastical Commissioner for England, Home Secretary twice, and Secretary for India from 1886 to 1892.[32] All of these men might have been thought to be level-headed in socio-political matters, and hard-headed in things financial.

The enormous toll on Watkin's health of these ceaseless labours began to show itself early in 1893. In January he felt ill enough to be unable to attend the shareholders' half-yearly meeting in Manchester, and he wrote to Lord Wharncliffe, his Deputy Chairman, to explain:

> It is forty years since I entered the service of the Shareholders as manager, and thirty years since they elected me a director, and about the same time since I became chairman. In that long period I have never before failed to attend a general meeting of the company. It is a great affliction to me to be incapacitated at a very interesting period of the company's career; but I trust that before long to be able to resume my work in the interest of the shareholders, who have placed me under a debt of gratitude by their confidence and kindness – a debt which I shall endeavour to repay, if that be their wish, by devoting whatever may remain of my life and strength to their services.[33]

Early in the following year, his doctors urged him to take a long rest, and he went to his chalet on the slopes of Snowdon to recuperate. However, the prophetically valedictory nature of his letter to Lord Wharncliffe proved to be justified. In the April he suffered a heart attack, and on 19 May 1894 he wrote to Wharncliffe from The Chalet that he felt he should resign the chairmanship. The Board minutes reproduced his letter in full:

> I write to ask you to tell our Colleagues that I feel the time has come when I must resign the Chairmanship of the Board of Directors at such time as they can conveniently make the necessary arrangements. I need not say that it will be with

[32]*Who Was Who* Vol. 1. p.171.
[33]John Pendleton, Vol. 1, pp.367–9.

great pain that I shall sever myself from the Office which I have held for so long. The hope was held out to me that after a period of rest I might recover my strength, and I am glad to say that I am better. But I fear that I can never be sufficiently strong to allow that constant attention to the affairs of the Company which an adequate performance of the duties of Chairman entails. I therefore think it right – not merely in the interests of my health, of which I hope I have not been unduly careful in time past – but in that of the Company and of my Colleagues that the work should be placed in younger and stronger hands. Will you accept yourself, and kindly convey to our Colleagues, and to the Officers, my sense of the cordial support which you and they have always been ready to give me as Chairman. Also will you say to my successor, whoever he may be (and I think that this is a matter I should prefer to leave entirely with my Colleagues to settle) that if I can be of any assistance to him, especially at the outset, it will give me great pleasure to render it.

On the same day he wrote to his colleagues on the Metropolitan and the South Eastern, also resigning his chairmanship of those two companies.[34] At the Board meeting of 25 May 1894, the directors recorded unanimously their 'appreciation of, and admiration for the great services that he had rendered to the Company', with which he had been so long and intimately connected.[35] They invited him to remain on the Board as a director, and elected Lord Wharncliffe to succeed him as Chairman.

The *Railway Times,* commenting on Watkin's resignation, said, among other caustic comments, that as a consequence the London Extension 'dies a natural death, and it only remains for the board after a seemly and becoming interval to give it decent burial'.[36] The same journal could state confidently, and even more greatly in defiance of fact, seven years later: 'When physical infirmities necessitated his leaving hold the reins, his colleagues lost no time in

---

[34]Dow, Vol. 2, p.250.
[35]PRO RAIL 463/27, Minute 15,453.
[36]2 June 1894, pp. 723-724.

47 The final portrait of Sir Edward, presented to the MS&LR Board on his retirement from the chairmanship in 1894, by William Pollitt, the General Manager

knocking down most of the fabric which they had assisted him in building up.'[37]

At the same meeting of 25 May, the Board had endorsed the negotiations of the General Manager with Alexander Henderson, who had underwritten the raising of capital for the project.[38] A special general meeting of the proprietors of the company was held in Manchester on 22 June, with the object of securing the shareholders' authority for raising the capital. The directors 'hoped Sir Edward Watkin would live to see the pet scheme of his later life carried out'. The meeting 'unanimously agreed to the issue of a prospectus'.[39] At the half-yearly meeting of the shareholders on 25 July, a resolution on Watkin's retirement expressed 'sincere regret', noting that 'the Proprietors have sustained a loss of no ordinary character, they are gratified to learn that he has consented to remain upon the Board and the benefit of his sound advice and exceptional experience will be available to the Company.' It was

---

[37]20 April 1901.
[38]PRO RAIL 463/27, Minute 15,459.
[39]*Railway Times,* 23 June 1894, p.801.

resolved that 'a special fee of £1,000 per annum be paid to him while he retains a seat on the Board'.[40]

Watkin was present on Thursday, 13 November, when the Countess of Wharncliffe cut the first sod for the London Extension on ground adjoining a private house in Alpha Road, St John's Wood.[41] He received the Earl and Countess at the site, and after dedicatory prayers by the Rector of Grendon, Aylesbury, the Revd E.R. Pigott, presented Lady Wharncliffe with a special spade on behalf of the MS&L Board. The Chairman said that although the honour had fallen to him, it was to Sir Edward that the new railway was due. Also present at the ceremony, among the MS&L officers, was Watkin's nephew, Edward, the company's mineral manager. At the banquet which followed, Watkin proposed a toast to the Countess, presenting her with an elaborate silver casket. A further toast to the Chairman marked the end of the scheduled arrangements, but suddenly James Staats Forbes, Chairman of the London, Chatham and Dover Railway and the Metropolitan District Railway, stood up and proposed Sir Edward's health, praising his courage and qualities of character. This unexpected and gracious move was appreciated by all those present.[42] His being invited to the occasion at all was an unspoken tribute to Watkin's magnanimity, which was thus handsomely returned.

The Great Northern, bowing to the inevitable, accepted an invitation to become joint owner of the new station in Nottingham, though not in Leicester. In Nottingham they were also partners in a new hotel, and the MS&L sponsored a similar venture in London. It was the Hotel Grand Central,[43] opposite Marylebone Station, which was leased for operation to private owners.[44] Much thought and discussion was given to choosing a new name for the MS&L, now that it had become a trunk railway. This first appeared in the minutes of the Board on 27 March 1896,

[40]PRO RAIL 463/27. Minute 15,576. Watkin relinquished this award eleven months before he finally resigned. See p.329 *infra*.

[41]Charles G. Harper, 'The Great Central Railway', in *Fortnightly Review*, London, April 1899, p.590.

[42]Dow, Vol. 2, p. 256.

[43]Soon to be changed to 'Great Central', (Dow, Vol.2., p.283).

[44]During the Second World War it was requisitioned by the government, and the LNE Railway bought it afterwards for use as its central offices. The railways were nationalised in 1948, and, as 222 Marylebone Road, it became the headquarters of the new British Railways, (Dow, Vol. 3, p.6). It is now the Landmark Hotel.

48 Local architect George Thomas Hine's magnificent Nottingham Victoria Station. Great Northern Railway Stirling 2-4-0 E2 class locomotive no 78 awaits its next duty

and the names 'Manchester, Sheffield and London' and 'Central Railway' held the field for a while. However, pressure grew for the name 'Great Central', and this was assumed on 1 August 1897. A coat of arms was devised by the new company, and its design, the first authorised by the College of Arms to any railway company,[45] was granted on 25 February 1898.[46] The motto on the device, 'Forward', was probably Watkin's inspiration,[47] as his South Eastern Railway had earlier adopted 'Onward'.[48]

The opening ceremony of the new line was staged at Marylebone Station on Thursday, 9 March 1899. Under the heading 'A Huge Work Completed', the *Daily News* reported the event at length. 'Considerable interest was manifested in the locality...By the free

[45]Dow, Vol. 2, pp.296–8.

[46]A.C. Fox-Davies, *Complete Guide to Heraldry* (London: Orbis Publishing, 1985), p.226.

[47]It was later adopted by the LNER and then by British Rail.

[48]Some irony lay in the fact that the motto of the City of Birmingham was 'Forward', in view of Watkin's attitude to that place and its quondam Lord Mayor, Joseph Chamberlain.

use of walls and roofs some thousands of persons caught a glimpse of the flags which decorated the new station and of the splendid new train ready for dispatch'. It also noted: 'To the delight of his old comrades, the venerable Sir Edward Watkin was, at an early stage of the proceedings, wheeled along the platform in a bath chair, to receive the congratulations of old brother directors, shareholders, and even antagonists in the great fight which he gallantly waged'.[49] To a friend standing by at the time, Watkin said 'Thank heaven I have lived to see this completed.'[50]

Of the 734 guests at the banquet, which took place at the station itself because the hotel banqueting hall could seat only 600, the principal was Sir C.T. Ritchie, representing the Board of Trade.[51] The Chairman welcomed the guests, but had to leave owing to indisposition, and it was his Deputy, Edward Chapman, who proposed the loyal toast. 'What is known as the Extension is a matter of 94 miles,' he pointed out.[52] References by Ritchie, in his speech, 'to the Board of Trade and the railway companies were received with laughter'. He spoke of the preparation and labour which had gone into 'this great enterprise', and of the tribulation through which the company had passed to their crowning triumph. He 'aroused much enthusiasm by his reference to the credit due to Sir Edward Watkin, the promoter of the scheme from its earliest inception, and to the consummate ability of Mr W. Pollitt, the General Manager.'[53]

Ritchie and the guests then made their way to Platform 2, where a special train, headed by 4-4-0 locomotive No. 861, built at the company's Gorton Works in the previous November, surrounded by a special enclosure for directors and heads of departments, was organised to be started by Ritchie with a lever on a dais. The engine and coaches drew slowly out of the platform amidst cheering, echoed from outside the station.[54] 'After a decent interval it returned to the station to become the 4.28 pm special to

---

[49] 10 March 1899, p.7.
[50] *Western Morning News*, Plymouth, 15 April 1901.
[51] Charles Thomson Ritchie (1808–1906), MP for Croydon at the time, and created 1st Baron Ritchie of Dundee in December 1905.
[52] The difference between this figure and the usually quoted one of 83 miles is presumably because of a different calculation of where the new connecting line started in the Sheffield area.
[53] *Daily News*, p.7. Pollitt (1842–1908) was knighted in the 1899 Birthday Honours List, (Dow, Vol. 2, p.345).
[54] *Daily News*, p.7.

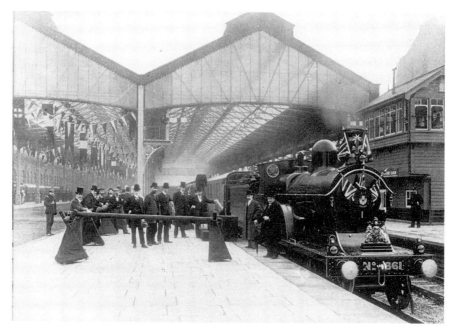

49 The first train from Marylebone, 9 March 1899, about to set off. Locomotive class 11A 4-4-0 No. 861

Rugby and Manchester.'[55] 'The guests before leaving looked over the Hotel Great Central...this is to be one of the huge hotel palaces of the world', said the *Daily News* reporter. Not all opening ceremonies were so well-organised and conducted, or even marked by a grand ceremony at all. Such functions had a history of unruly behaviour, political squabbles, demonstrations, popular takeovers, and even train collisions. 'The opening of the GCR at Marylebone in 1899 was a stately affair, presided over the President of the Board of Trade.'[56]

There was great hope for the future of the new company. The country was prospering, and the Great Central turned the century with a capital of £35,883,489.[57] Even though, financially, the hopes were not to be realised, this section of Watkin's dream had been accomplished, at least in the major part, by the time he left

---

[55]Dow, Vol. 2, p.340.
[56]Jack Simmons and Gordon Biddle, *The Oxford Companion to British Railway History* (Oxford University Press, 1997), pp.357–8.
[57]Dow, Vol. 2, p.347.

50 Marylebone Station at the turn of the century

the scene. He was excoriated, however, for taking yet another main line into London, and this was a feature of railway historical writing for the following eighty or so years. Watkin was 'deluded', and his plan to link Northern England with the Midlands, London and the South Coast was 'quixotic'.[58] He was 'a megalomaniac and a gambler...The "Manchester to Paris" notion was visionary[59] and foolish, a flashy advertising slogan, and no more.'[60] '[The London Extension] was a belated and almost entirely superfluous product of the original era of fighting

---

[58]H.J. Dyos and D.H. Aldcroft, *British Transport: An Economic Survey from the 17th Century to the 20th* (Leicester University Press, 1971), p. 142. A few pages later, they could say: 'The Great Central did much to foster [cross-country services] since it was in the unique position of providing connections with nearly all the major railway systems in England'. (p.150). This echoed the opinion of Sir Edward, when he said, in a parliamentary committee discussion of the Extension Bill, 'It would become a "backbone" to the country's railway system", (*Transport*, 19 April 1901).

[59]Presumably in the sense of 'halucinatory'; but the writer spoke truer than he knew.

[60]Jack Simmons, *The Railway in England and Wales, 1830-1914* (Leicester University Press, 1978), Vol. 1, p.93.

construction.'[61] Watkin was 'ambitious and wrong-headed', and his London Extension was 'a wasteful extravagance, and show[s] Victorian devotion to the competitive principle at its worst'.[62] The railway, as such, was 'a magnificent enterprise. But as an element in the country's system it was a superfluity...it depressed the revenues of the GWR and LNWR as well as the Midland.'[63] 'The Midland's Ordinary shares had been worth 153 in 1893, but had tumbled to 91 at the opening of the GCR's London Extension, and were at 71 four years later.'[64] But that was also true of the effect of the Midland's own London Extension in 1868; it could be said that in 1872 it 'lived to some extent on the traffic of its rivals'.[65]

The Great Central, judged by its financial returns, was not a success. It never paid a dividend on its ordinary stock,[66] despite the excellence of its engineering – laid out for high speed, a ruling gradient of 1 in 176, no curve of less than 1 mile in radius, only one level crossing in its whole length, and all bridges and tunnels built to the Berne Convention loading gauge[67] – and not withstanding its first-class management and technical staff. An 'expert railwayman' said in 1910: 'It is very doubtful whether any capital spent in the last twenty years in competitive schemes has realised an adequate return.'[68] Shortly after the effective date of the 'grouping' of the railways in 1923, Sir Sam Fay, the GCR General Manager, told a large meeting of company staff that 'the London Extension was kept solvent only by the Grimsby fish traffic'.[69] That particular source of revenue was to dwindle steadily, to road haulage, after 1950.

When the Beeching Report was published in 1963, the newest

[61] Sir John Clapham, quoted Rolt, p. 13.

[62] Jack Simmons, *The Railways of Britain* (London, Sheldrake Press, 1986), pp.31–2.

[63] Jack Simmons, *The Railway in England and Wales, 1830-1914,* Vol. 1, p.94.

[64] Adrian Vaughan, *Railwaymen, Politics and Money* (John Murray, 1997), p.265.

[65] Edward Cleveland-Stevens, *English Railways, Their Development and Their Relation to the State* (London: George Routledge and Sons Ltd., 1915), p. 262.

[66] Though it paid out on the others. Its ordinary shares in 1899, rather like those of the MS&LR and SA&MR, represented only 16.22% of the stock, rather than one half, which was the more usual proportion.

[67] Much larger than British clearances, to allow the passage of foreign rolling stock, via a Channel tunnel.

[68] J.H. Clapham, *An Economic History of Modern Britain* (CUP, 1938), Book 4, p.348.

[69] Quoted by a retired 'Top Link' engine driver working on the East Lincolnshire Light Railway, in conversation with the author in 1967.

main line was earmarked for closure, and it ceased to operate as a trunk line on 4 September 1966. However, it had been averred that economic sustainability was not the only consideration in implementing the Beeching Report. A study published in 1994 claimed that the line was deliberately under-utilised and its services run down in the late 1950s and early 1960s in order to present a picture of redundancy. 'Traffic on the [GCR] line was so heavy that it took several years of deliberate neglect and retrenchment before closure could be achieved. It was a unique transport artery ...carrying traffic from the North-East to the South and South-West.'[70] In 1966 the then Prime Minister was finalising negotiations with the French over the Channel Tunnel Project, and at the same time was closing down the only ready-made route between London and Manchester. The French were already planning to build their network of high-speed connecting lines.[71]

Since the opening of the Channel Tunnel, Sir Edward's standing in the minds of railway historians has subtly changed. Writing about the Metropolitan Railway, one writer referred to Watkin's overall dreams as 'megalomaniacal, or more positively, a century ahead of their time'.[72] In 1989, a consortium called Central Railway Group was formed to construct a new, mainly freight, railway from Liverpool to Lille and beyond, via the Channel Tunnel. This would use large tracts of the GCR formation, including the line through the Woodhead Tunnel, between Manchester and Sheffield.[73] A £1.5 billion scheme was promoted in 1996, but it was defeated in the House of Commons.[74] The application, with renewed estimates amounting to £5 billion, was placed in May 2000.[75]

Watkin remained on the MS&LR Board as a director after resigning the chair. Of the thirty-six meetings in the year following, he was present at eighteen, and was appointed in January 1895 to fifteen committees. He may have relinquished the helm, but he clearly had no intention of leaving the ship. His son Alfred was

---

[70]David Henshaw, *The Great Railway Conspiracy* (Leading Edge, 1994), pp.235 and 136.
[71]*Ibid*, p.235.
[72]Nicholas Faith, *Classic Trains* (Boxtree (Macmillan), 1998), p.93.
[73]*The Sheffield Telegraph*, 28 July 2000.
[74]Letter from the Department of Transport, Environment and the Regions, 14 November 1999.
[75]*The Times*, 30 May 2000.

still on the Board, and was elected to the 'Rolling Stock' and 'London Extension' Committees in 1899, at the meeting that his father was elected to the Finance Committee and the New Lines Committee.[76] Sir Edward attended only four Board meetings in 1898 and one in 1899 (Alfred was present at most of them).

Almost to the last, controversy pursued the old warrior. At the Board meeting of 1 April 1898, the General Manager reported a legal action brought by Messrs Whitham and Bernard on behalf of their client Mrs Piercy, against Sir Edward Watkin, Sir John Maclure, and himself. This was to compel them to repay to the GC Company, funds which they, and the other directors of the Company, applied in the purchase of certain shares of the Wrexham, Mold and Connah's Quay Railway Company. The action had been heard on 1 February last. 'Judgement was given on 15 March which dismissed the action, with costs against the Plaintiffs.'[77] Clearly, hatred and malice and all uncharitableness were to follow Watkin for most of his days.

Unfortunately, the co-operation which Watkin had forged between the 'Sheffield' and the Metropolitan began to unravel in July 1898. He had appointed John Bell from the MS&L as Secretary of the Metropolitan on 1 November 1872. Bell went on to be General Manager, then Chairman when Watkin resigned, but rapidly became a thorn in the flesh of the MS&L over the working of the London Extension, because of a long-standing antipathy to the MS&LR Manager, William Pollitt.[78] His obstructiveness to GCR traffic forced the Great Central to look for an alternative, which it found in the Great Western Railway, eager for a quicker route from Paddington to Birmingham. A joint committee planned a line from south of Harrow on the Hill, through Northolt and High Wycombe, and via Princes Risborough to Grendon Underwood, where it joined the GCR main line well clear of Metropolitan metals. This was authorised on 1 August 1899, and opened in 1905.[79]

At the meeting of 17 January 1900, the Secretary (O.S. Holt)

---

[76]Board meeting of 1 February 1899, Minutes 813 and 816, respectively, PRO RAIL 226/2.
[77]PRO RAIL 226/1, Minute 415.
[78]Dennis Edwards and Ron Pigram, *The Final Link* (Midas Books, 1982; second edition, 1983), pp. 20–3.
[79]Rolt, pp.15–17.

read out a letter from Sir Edward, written from 8 The Lees, Folkestone. It read:

Considering the difficulties in which the Great Central Railway Company is at the present moment, difficulties which I hope and believe are only temporary, I desire to forego the special fee of £1,000 a year which was voted to me unanimously by the shareholders on my retiring from the Chairmanship of the Company. Will you kindly inform Mr Henderson and my other Colleagues of my intention.

The Board expressed their appreciation of this gesture.[80] Edward did not manage to attend any of the meetings in 1900, and on 7 December Alfred Watkin laid a letter on the table, submitting his father's resignation as a member of the Board. The Chairman, accepting, expressed the Board's sympathy to him on his retirement, 'after so intimate an association extending for a period of upwards of forty years with the Company.'[81]

---

[80]PRO RAIL 226/2, Minute 1186.
[81]PRO RAIL 226/3, Minute 1592.

20

The Railway Philosopher

the motto of the world's first public railway, the Stockton and Darlington Railway. On the official seal of 1818.

'I have always, as my father did before me, tried to bring my business in aid of better things even than business' Sir Edward Watkin.[1]

There are, broadly speaking, two ways of viewing a railway company as an investment. One is that the maximisation of profit and dividend is the major objective, and all decisions on the company management and development should be governed by this consideration. The other is the wider view that, although a loss-making company is not likely to remain operating in any sense for very long, the objectives of the concern embrace a constellation of economic, social and psychological factors with a wide influence on its operating *esprit* and its cultural environment.

Such an approach by investors and shareholders requires a longer and broader view than its alternative. The point has been made in comparison with education:

> Suppose I was a hard-nosed capitalist [parent] thinking about sending my children for sixteen years' worth of education. This is [poor] investment that no capitalist would ever make...there isn't a way it could pay off. On the other hand, having an educated population does pay off for every society. And the same thing is true for a good [transport] system. If

---

[1]Salisbury Papers, Watkin letters, 9 May 1889; f.154.

you look at it in any moment of time, and judge it [by] very narrow criteria, it probably does not make sense...On the other hand, in the long run, it does. It's the very thing that holds us together, the [transport] system.[2]

One of the main post-mortem criticisms of Watkin has been that of failing to make his railways profitable. This was not true even on its own terms. Because of his part in extricating the Manchester Athenaeum from pecuniary embarrassments which had threatened to overwhelm it, and his signal success when selling the Trent Valley Railway in 1847, he acquired a reputation as a financial expert, becoming known as 'The Railway Abernethy'.[3] 'He possesses the faculty of causing the shares of every railway company with which he connects himself to rise in value. Probably no one has been more successful than Sir Edward in this particular way'.[4]

Nearly all his directorial appointments arose from appeals for help from badly managed and financially threatened companies. He restructured and managed into efficiency and solvency the South Eastern, the Metropolitan, and, by inspired proxy, the Great Eastern, and it is dismissively superficial to say he was responsible for the unprofitability of the Grand Trunk of Canada and the Erie Railroad of the USA.

But Watkin's horizons were far wider than the bottom line of a trading account. He did once say 'My belief is that the whole object in the management of a railway is dividend',[5] but that was part of his argument for basic, and not 'fancy' expenditure, and in the context of a rather turbulent relationship with some of the company's proprietors. The record of his utterances and actions throughout his life shows that such was not his root position.

He told Lord Colville, Chairman of the Great Northern Railway, in reply to the latter's recommending a reduction in the

---

[2]Lester Thurow, Economist at the Massachusetts Institute of Technology, quoted by Nicholas Faith, *Classic Trains* (Boxtree, Channel Four, 1998), p.23.

[3]*The City Jackdaw*, 22 April 1878, p.383. John Abernethy (1764–1831), surgeon at St Bartholomew's Hospital, London, was popularly reputed to have a remedy for all health problems. He had a vigorous and attractive personality, was of blameless life and honourable in all his dealings, despite a bluff and masterly manner which inspired rather than repelled, (*DNB*, Vol. 1, pp.49–52).

[4]*Men and Women of the Day* (London: Richard Bentley and Sons, 1889), (2 Vols.), Vol. 2, p.46.

[5]Chairman's Report to the half-yearly meeting of the shareholders of the South Eastern Railway, 20 July 1882, reported in the *Railway Official Gazette*, August 1882, p.116.

number of trains between Manchester and London: 'I could not be a party to changes which would give to the public less accommodation than they obtain at present. It may be that certain trains do not pay, *per se*, but these trains are run for the advantage of our customers, who in difficult times are running about the country in the strenuous endeavour to obtain business...I think a time of distress is the very worse time therefore to reduce facilities'.[6]

In his book on India, Watkin argued that the net profit revenue did not represent anything like the real gain to the population. He quoted an Indian administrator as saying: 'The existing railways [of India were] worth to the Empire at least £40,000,000 a year, and the increase in land value alone, in wages, and in tax-paying power [had] been marked in all districts through which the iron road passes.' This was a widely held view in India. Railways were socially beneficial in the generation of commerce; in affording an efficient postal system of letters and periodicals, thereby enhancing literacy; and in the rapid relief of famine and natural disaster.[7]

This wider, more profound, perception of the importance of a railway system was of the greatest importance in Canada. Watkin had a great conviction that the British, and the citizens of the Empire, had a divine duty to exploit all the means of modern technology to advance the spread of its culture and civilisation; and the most important of these technologies was the railway. This conviction was 'unwittingly articulated by Watkin's vibrant idealist ideology of technical progress', and it 'shaped his practical business observations'.[8] Professor den Otter offered three examples of railway philosophers in the history of Canada, one of whom was Sir Edward.[9] He took his thesis from an early work, of 1846, by the Canadian engineer Thomas C. Keefer,[10] who called the railway 'The Iron Civiliser', bringing more than economic progress – fostering social integration and stimulating intellectual and moral growth. Keefer argued that Canada would never be great until she

---

[6]MS&LR Board meeting, 116 October 1885, Minute 10,003, PRO RAIL 463/20.
[7]Lawrence James, *RAJ: The Making and Unmaking of British India* (Little, Brown and Co., 1997), pp.176, 184, 304, 306 and 355. It is fair to add the view of Jack Simmons, who described the concept of 'Public Convenience' as a 'great error' which was overtaken by events in the 1920s, (*The Victorian Railway* (Thames and Hudson, 1991), p.314).
[8]A.A. den Otter, *The Philosophy of Railways* (University of Toronto Press, 1997), p.112.
[9]The other two were Francis Hicks (1807–55), and Alexander McKenzie (1822–92).
[10]den Otter, p.34.

built railways.[11] His theory received some support only five years later: 'At the end of 1850 few could express any faith in Canada's future; poverty, lack of communications and transport with cholera rife in places, were pressing heavily on hope. By 1851, they were talking of a "very decided spirit of improvement – a steady progress towards a great and prosperous condition...The change was sudden and complete. It was associated with railways".'[12]

In September 1851, at the opening of the railway between Montreal and Boston, Lord Elgin, Governor General of Canada, declared that he 'appreciated and valued the moral and social, as well as economical effects' of railways. An anonymous speaker at the event allowed himself more imaginative latitude, attributing to God's influence the spread of railways and their universalising effect on society, saying that he used to send 'energy and vitality where before there was silence and barrenness; multiplying cities and villages, studded with churches, dotted with schools and filled with happy homes and budding souls to increase wealth, which shall partially be devoted to his service and kingdom...and make the wilderness blossom as a rose'. Such pious references, notes den Otter, were not glib or insincere, but 'denoted a definitive feature of British North America's philosophy of railways. The overwhelming presence of God in their personal lives and community affairs was a feature of mid-century awareness'.[13]

'It was this paradigm of the age which underwrote Watkin's whole career and which inspired the most utilitarian of businessmen, like Sir Thomas Baring and George Carr Glyn, to take extraordinary financial risks'. It moved even the *Railway Times* to applaud his 'romantic and adventurous call for a transcontinental railway'.[14] He held to his convictions throughout, despite the spirit of retrenchment he found around him, in financial and political circles – a spirit which 'accentuate[d]...regional, partisan and imperial divergencies'.[15]

---

[11]Quoted, Peter Waite, in *The Industrial History of Canada,* (ed.) Craig Brown (Toronto: Lester and Orpen Dennys Ltd.), pp.284–5.

[12]J.J. Talman, *The Impact of the Railway on a Pioneer Community* (Canadian Historical Association. 18pp). From the Internet, 19 May 2001.

[13]den Otter, pp.24–6. A comparative lack of that awareness in the twenty-first century does not diminish the ontological truth.

[14]Quoted, den Otter, p.113.

[15]*Ibid*, p.123.

Watkin refused to be restricted to the dividends, and could open the eyes of others to greater values. 'More than any of his business contemporaries, he understood the political and social implications of rails and steam locomotives'.[16] He believed that to elevate purely economic considerations, in any sphere, above consideration of human development and dignity, was an offence against a far greater reality.

There are other notable examples of such 'railway philosophy'. The Trans-Siberian Railway is even longer than the Canadian transcontinental. Built between 1891 and 1904,[17] it is 5,770 miles (9,288 km) long and connects Moscow with Vladivostok, crossing part of Europe and the whole length of Asia. It connects towns and settlements which have no other means of connection, employs 1.5 million workers, and with the rest of the railway industry of the country is the owner of 64 colleges and universities, 400 hospitals and a vast network of schools – 'a state within a state'. A train driver on the Trans-Siberian commented: 'If the Railway falls apart, the state falls apart.'[18]

Henry Gladstone's Darjeeling Himalayan Railway was, in the year 2000, granted World Heritage status. The line was described in the UNESCO citation as 'An example of an innovative transport system of a multicultural region which was to serve as a model for similar developments in other parts of the world.'[19]

Watkin had reached seventy years of age in the year after his visit to India, and on the ship during his return journey he had fallen, breaking a rib and damaging his hand.[20] He must have fully recovered his health by September 1890, for he could tell Gladstone he had 'had a few days on the mountains, and [felt] more fit for work than I did.'[21] He had always enjoyed robust health, except for the period of stress following the sale of the Trent Valley Railway, but time eventually began to tell. After his

---

[16]*Manchester Faces and Places,* Vol. 2, 10 November 1890, pp.17–20.

[17]From 1916 entirely on Russian soil.

[18]*National Geographical Magazine,* June 1998, pp.17ff. Sir Edward would have been pleased at the 21st century proposal for a tunnel under the Bering Straits to link Siberia and Alaska, (*The Times,* 2 January 2001, p. 12 and third leading article). The possibility of travelling by train from London to New York via Moscow and Canada would represent the ultimate development of his vision.

[19]*Railway Magazine,* March 2000, p.97.

[20]Salisbury Papers, Watkin Letters, 21 January 1889, f.153.

[21]Watkin-Gladstone Correspondence, BL Add. Mss. 44337, f.69; 24 September 1890.

heart attack in 1894 he slowed down considerably, and his last letter to Gladstone was signed in a very large and shaky hand.[22] He mentioned to Salisbury in 1897 that he had been 'laid up for sometime by a serious illness, but I am now about again and equal to general business'; he was hoping to offer himself to his 'old constituents at the next election'. Clearly the relative inactivity in his reduced health did not suit him, and he was entertaining vain hopes.[23]

Though he had moved back from Folkestone to Rose Hill six months before, as if in anticipation, Watkin had shown no warning sign of particular illness or sharp decline when he died peacefully at 3.40 p.m. on Saturday, 13 April 1901. His second grandson, Francis Worsley-Taylor, deputising for his parents, who were ill on holiday in Biarritz, and forbidden to travel by their doctor,[24] and a nephew, were at his side. His son Alfred was in Folkestone and returned to Rose Hill immediately, as did Colonel and Mrs Mellor from Whitefield, Manchester.[25] The death certificate recorded the cause of death as 'Cardiac Failure, Sickness, Exhaustion'. The person reporting the death was 'F.S.Worsley-Taylor, Grandson, Present at the Death, [of] Whalley, Lancashire'. On the day of his death, the flags of the Folkestone Town Hall and over the shipping in the harbour, were flying at half mast.[26]

The funeral, on the following Friday, was a suitably impressive occasion, reported in great detail in the press. The officiating clergyman was the Very Revd the Dean of Manchester, Dr Edward Craig Mclure, brother of the Great Central director, John William. He was assisted by the Ven. Charles Maxwell Woosnam, Archdeacon of Macclesfield, and Vicar of Saint Margaret Dunham Massey; the Revd Granville Bourdas Thurston, Vicar of Lymm, where Alfred and his wife lived; and the Revd Francis Davies Ringrose, Curate of Northenden (there being no rector at the time). A huge and representative congregation included Sir Alfred Watkin, Francis Worsley-Taylor, Alfred Watkin (1858-1947), Colonel J.J. Mellor, the Chairman and Deputy Chairman of the

[22]*Ibid*, ff.85 and 86; 25 April 1896.
[23]Salisbury Papers, Watkin Letters, 14 January 1897, f.164.
[24]Their eldest son, Captain James Worsley-Taylor, was on active service in South Africa.
[25]*The Manchester Evening Mail*, 15 April 1901.
[26]*The Times*, 15 April 1901.

Great Central Railway and a large number of GCR employees in uniform; representatives of the Lancashire and Yorkshire Railway, the South Eastern and Chatham Joint Committee, the CLC, the East London Railway, the Metropolitan Railway, the Midland Railway, the Manchester Ship Canal Company, the Rochdale Canal Company and the Manchester Athenaeum; the Mayor of Folkestone and deputation, F.B. Frith, W.P. Frith and T.E. Tatton, representatives of Northenden Parish Council, and Professor Boyd-Dawkins. There were thirteen carriages of chief mourners and many other private carriages.[27] Numerous floral tributes were also received from the Chairman of the Great Northern Railway, from many individuals including the servants at Rose Hill, and from Lady Hickson of Montreal, Canada.[28] In addition to the many 'official' floral tributes, 'many handsome ones' were sent to Cheshire from private residents.[29]

The long procession, 'gathered from the surrounding country-side', wound its way through the village to the church.[30] The coffin was placed on a catafalque in the chancel, surrounded by flowers.[31] It was an oaken shell enclosed in a lead coffin, with an outer shell of panelled polished oak, which had solid brass mountings, each handle of which bore the letters *IHS*.[32]

The service was fully choral[33] and the first hymn was *Lead Kindly Light*, by John Henry Newman.[34] The psalm was Psalm 90 and for the second hymn, *Now the Labourer's Task is O'er*, John Ellerton's words being excellent for such occasions with the second line particularly suitable on this one: 'Now the battle day is past'. The *Nunc Dimittis* was sung between the church and graveside and *Rock of Ages* on arrival there. The sides of the grave were comple-tely lined with flowers.[35] The tombstone was a massive red granite

---

[27] *The Manchester Dispatch*, 20 April 1901.

[28] *The Manchester Guardian*, 20 April 1901.

[29] *Kent Messenger*, 20 April 1901.

[30] *The Manchester Courier*, 20 April 1901.

[31] *The Manchester Dispatch*, 20 April 1901.

[32] The first three uncial (capital) letters of the name 'Jesus' in Greek, (*Stockport Advertiser*, 26 April 1901).

[33] 'And the ceremony was most impressive', (*The Manchester Dispatch*, 20 April 1901).

[34] The tune was probably *Sandon*, putatively written in the village in the Trent Valley. Unfor-tunately, the strongest tune for this hymn, *Alberta*, was not written until 1924. It came to Sir William Harris when on a train journey across Canada, (*Companion to Hymns Ancient and Modern* (London: William Clowes and Sons Ltd., 1962), p.304).

[35] *The Manchester Guardian*, 20 April 1901.

slab, of sarcophagus shape, with a carved granite recumbent cross on the upper side.[36] It is inscribed with a text from the Book of Proverbs, (Chapter 22, verse 29): 'Seest thou a man diligent in his business? He shall stand before kings.'

One of the most intimate and appropriate of tributes was that from a life-long friend who signed himself simply TRW.[37] He summed up Watkin's life, with an echo of St Benedict, 'Work is Worship'. He concluded that 'the language of the poet is appropriate for putting into fitting language the summary of a life devoted to the uplifting of his fellows by incessant labour':

To dignify the day with deeds of good,
And eve constellate with all holy thoughts
This is to live, and our lives narrate,
In a new version, solemn and sublime,
The grand old legend of humanity.[38]

In 1901 Rose Hill was sold by Alfred to a Mr Parkyn, who sold it on in January 1916 to the Manchester Guardians of the Poor. It was used as an emergency hospital in the Great War, and afterwards as an ophthalmic centre for children from the city, in the fresher air of the Wythenshawe countryside.[39] Later it was an orphanage, and graduated to being a semi-secure house for boys on remand or need of care. Absolom Watkin, as a Lancashire JP, had been a member of the committee for the Manchester Juvenile Refuge; this development would have pleased him.[40]

A visit in 1968 showed it to be a happy, thriving place, with all the original beautiful wood panelling still in well-kept order. By contrast, a return visit four years after it had closed in 1995 because of tighter safety regulations, presented a dilapidated, sad-looking old house hemmed in closely by a seven-foot security fence, and all the grounds built on with some seventy-five modern

---

[36]*The Stockport Advertiser,* 26 April 1901.

[37]Almost certainly T.R. Wilkinson, a friend of Edward's from childhood.

[38]*Manchester City News,* 15 April 1901. The words are by Philip James Bailey (1816-1902), from his poem *Festus* of 1839, an enormous work based on the Faust legend.

[39]Shercliff, p.334. In the March of the previous year he had presented the painting *Icebergs* to the Northenden Church Rooms, but in 1921, the then curate passed it back to Rose Hill as being too big for the functions held there. It was thus placed in the hands of Manchester Corporation for when it was sold in 1979, (see p.140 supra.).

[40]Goffin, p.259.

houses. A builder's notice at the entrance off Longley Lane held out the possibility that the house itself, a listed building, would be converted into luxury flats. Edward's meteorite, or glacial rock, mounted on a tree-stump, was still there before the house, as a feature of the estate. Some of Absolom's 'stones', 4 feet by 3 feet by 2 feet deep, with his texts,[41] survived in the woodland ('Rose Hill Wood', containing many rare trees planted by Absolom) beyond the terrace.

Edward's will, of 8 August 1901, stated effects of £13,636 17s 8d, re-sworn in March 1902 as £17,308 16s 3d. His generosity to his wife and their two children, and elsewhere, accounted for the modesty of this amount. Alfred left £58,407 9s 4d when he died on 30 November 1914, and his wife Catherine Elizabeth £25,141 17s 4d in May 1944.

There was no mention of Sir Edward's death in the minutes of the first Board meeting (10 May 1901) after the event. It was not 'company business', and there had been two valedictory and laudatory mentions already: on his retirement from the Chairmanship, and on his resignation from the Board. Appropriately or not, Minute 1,798 of that meeting recorded that the *SS Northenden* had run aground in the River Elbe on 20 April, in avoiding a collision.[42]

Obituary notices appeared in more than 115 newspapers, from Aberdeen and Glasgow to Plymouth, and from Dublin to Ipswich and Kent. Their assessment of him were extraordinarily varied:

'He could not claim to be a financier or an administrator.'[43] 'As a railway financier, he was unequalled'.[44] 'He was a great railway administrator'.[45] 'He was undoubtedly an able railway manager, but his reputation as…an adviser in cases of financial or administrative disorder stands still higher'.[46] 'A comprehensive failure of his management methods, which produced no financial successes'.[47] 'He has left behind him

---

[41] Mark Chapter 8 verse 36; Psalm 23, etc.
[42] She was refloated on the 22nd, and on arrival in Grimsby was found to be undamaged.
[43] *The Railway Times*, 20 April 1901.
[44] *Finance*, 20 April 1901.
[45] *The Sphere*, 20 April 1901.
[46] *The Manchester Guardian*, 15 April 1901.
[47] *Financial Times*, 15 April 1901.

many a monument to his genius and industry'.[48] 'Of the details of railway management, he had no mastery whatever'.[49] 'A rumour in circulation at one time held him to have been a stationmaster. The story may have arisen from the intimate knowledge he had of the details of railway management'.[50]

Some of the judgements were patently distorted: 'Luckily the Grand Trunk, the Great Western and the Great Eastern failed to appreciate [him] at his own worth, and consequently he left them'.[51] Such judgements helped to establish the pejorative way of writing about Watkin which dominated twentieth-century railway historians, who took up, uncritically and superficially, narrow and negative assessments without enquiry or further evaluation.

Many contrasted his boldness and original ideas with his over-sanguine spirit.[52] But some did not hesitate to use words like 'genius' and 'greatness': 'His talent for reducing chaos to order …was little short of genius'.[53] 'We are dazzled by…this great man's genius',[54] and 'He cannot have lacked some at least, of the qualities of greatness'.[55] He was 'a great and picturesque figure… commanding respect and even admiration'.[56] An especially valuable opinion was expressed by the *Joint Stock Companies Journal*, that he was a pioneer of railway industry and the railway magnate *par excellence* of this country.[57]

The vast majority of notices were good. Some were rather exaggerated, as in the statement '[He was] the greatest railway man England has produced',[58] and, perhaps, 'His great genius… brought the greatest happiness to the greatest number.'[59] But the more analytical Manchester press could assert that he was 'Not a

---

[48] *Finance*, 20 April 1901.
[49] *Engineering*, 19 April 1901.
[50] *Harrogate Advertiser*, 20 April 1901.
[51] *Railway Magazine*, April 1901, p.415.
[52] For example, *Financial Times*, 15 April 1901.
[53] *Commerce*, 17 April 1901.
[54] *Financial Times*, 15 April 1901.
[55] *The Times*, 15 April 1901.
[56] *Financial Times*, 15 April 1901.
[57] 17 April 1901.
[58] *Country Life*, 20 April 1901.
[59] *Manchester Evening Mail Special Edition*, 15 April 1901.

Triton among minnows, but a king above railway kings'.[60] 'His death cannot be seen in any other way than a national loss...[he] played a conspicuous part in the public life of England. In him were blended some of the finest and noblest qualities of which human nature is capable'.[61] Certain of the obituaries, particularly in the Manchester newspapers, expressed regret that he never received from the city or corporation any recognition for his achievements, despite his interest in the place of his birth and youthful activities, which did not diminish throughout his life. 'He was peculiarly "a Manchester Man",[62] and the name he left behind was 'one of which his fellow citizens have every reason to be proud'.[63]

Some commentators attempted to forecast the eventual impact of Watkin's life on the railway culture of the country: 'His name has been so closely associated with the forlorn hopes of our [railway] system, and with many visionary schemes which have not escaped ridicule, for any just estimate to be formed', was one view.[64] Similarly, 'Much of his life's work [is] being undone, being proved useless or becoming obliterated'.[65] On the contrary, 'The Great Central will be [a monument] of his real practical commercial strategy', said another.[66] Yet others attempted prophecy, as on the Channel Tunnel. 'Perhaps towards the end of the present century, when universal peace prevails, Sir Edward Watkin will have been proved only a few generations in advance of his age'.[67] *The Railway Times,* reporting his retirement in 1894, said 'Where so much remains for the future to decide, it would be almost presumptuous to anticipate the verdict of history upon Sir Edward Watkin's life work, and posterity may fairly be left to appraise his handicraft at its true value'.[68]

Perhaps, with the completion of the Channel Tunnel and the growing awareness of railways in the social and economic welfare of the country, these words are only now being fulfilled.

---

[60]*Manchester Evening News,* 15 April 1901.
[61]*Manchester Courier Supplement,* 20 April 1901.
[62]*Manchester Courier,* 15 April 1901.
[63]*The Manchester Guardian,* 16 April 1901.
[64]*The Evening Standard,* 16 April 1901.
[65]*Financial News,* 16 April 1901.
[66]*Investors' Guardian,* 17 April 1901.
[67]*Christian Globe,* 18 April 1901.
[68]2 June 1894, p.12.

51 Great Central Railway 'Director' Class No 438 leaving Marylebone on a Manchester express, 12 years after Watkin's death. The loco is named 'Worsley-Taylor' after his son-in-law.

Appendix 1: The Watkin Family Tree

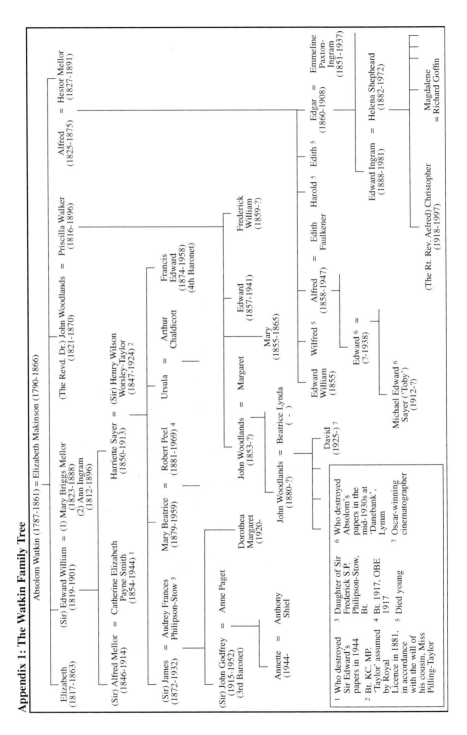

342

APPENDIX 2

WATKIN AS AUTHOR

'You are far too modest in disclaiming literary pretensions. The artistic talent...is in you if it were worth your while to take time to apply it.'

Richard Cobden, in a letter to Watkin, 14 January 1852

A Plea for Public Parks (1845)

The Manchester Examiner, Articles (1845, et seq.)

A Trip to the United States and Canada (London: W.H.Smith, 1 January 1852)

Absolom Watkin. Fragment No.1 (Manchester, 1874)

Absolom Watkin. Fragment No.2 (Manchester, Alexander Ireland, 1878)

Election Speeches, Hythe and Folkestone (London: C.F. Rowarth, 1889)

Canada and the States: Recollections 1851–1886 (Ward, Lock, 1887)

Memoir of Lady Watkin (privately printed)

India: A Few Pages About It (London: C.F. Rowarth, 1889)

Alderman Cobden of Manchester (Ward, Lock, Bowden and Co,1891)

The Library at Rose Hill – The Catalogue (in two parts) (Manchester: Henry Blacklock, 1891)

Addresses to various bodies, published in records of the meetings.

BIBLIOGRAPHY

1. *Manuscript Sources*

Bibliothèque nationale de France
British Library, London.
Canada Archives, Edward Watkin Papers (Ottawa)
Canterbury Cathedral Archives
Chester County Archives, Weaver Trustees' Minute Books
Exeter Public Library Archives
Folkestone Library Heritage, Kent County Council
Glasgow City Library
Glasgow University Archives
Gwynedd Archives, Caernarvon
Hansard
Harrowby Mss Trust, Sandon, Stafford
Hawarden, Flintshire Record Office
Hawarden, St Deniol's Library
House of Lords Record Office
Institution of Civil Engineers, London
Kent County Archives
Kent Studies Centre, Maidstone
London Metropolitan Archives
London School of Economics, Library of Political and Economic
    Science
Manchester Central Library
The Marylebone Cricket Club Archives
North East Lincolnshire Archives
Northenden Parish Church Records
Northwich, The Salt Museum
Privately-owned collections
Public Record Office, Kew
The Reform Club, Pall Mall, SW1
Salisbury Papers, Hatfield House
West Sussex Record Office

2. *Primary Published Sources*

Abbott, William *The South Eastern Railway: A Few Facts on its Management Under Sir Edward Watkin, Bart, During the Years from 1866 to 1888…A System of Supreme Authority* (London: Bates, Hendy and Co, 1888)

Gladstone W.E. *Diaries* (ed.H.C.G, Matthew) (Oxford: Clarendon Press, 1994)

Goffin, Magdalene *The Diaries of Absolom Watkin* (Stroud: Alan Sutton,1993)

Gourvish, T.R. *Mark Huish of the LNWR* (Leicester University, 1972)

Grimsby County Borough: *Official Guide* (Batiste Publications, 1961)

Hamer, F.E. *The Personal Papers of Lord Rendel* (London: Ernest Benn Ltd., 1931)

Hirst, Frances *Memoirs* (OUP, 1941)

Jones, Edgar *The Memoirs of Edwin Waterhouse* (London: B.T. Batsford Ltd., 1988)

Lambton, John George (Earl of Durham)   *A Report on Canada* (London: Methuen Reprint, 1902)

Lucy, Henry W. *A Diary of Two Parliaments* (Cassall and Co., 1886)

Watkin, A.E. *Absolom Watkin* (London: T. Fisher Unwin Ltd., 1920)

Watkin, A.M. *Don't Leap in the Dark* (Manchester: Cave and Sever, 1871)

Watkin, E.W. *Canada and the States: Recollections 1851–1886* (London: Ward, Lock, 1887)

Watkin, E.W. *Catalogue of the Library at Rose Hill* (Manchester: Henry Blacklock, 1891)

Watkin, E.W. *Absolom Watkin: Fragment No.1* (Manchester: Alexander Ireland, 1874)

Watkin, E.W. *Absolom Watkin: Fragment No.2* (Manchester: Alexander Ireland, 1876)

Watkin, E.W. *India: A Few Words About It* (London: C.F. Rowarth, 1889)

Watkin, E.W. *Memoir of Mary Briggs Watkin* (privately printed)

Watkin, E.W. *Railways and the State* (Manchester: Cave and Sever, 1872)

Watkin, E.W. *Speeches* (London: C.F. Rowarth, 1885)
Watkin, E.W. *Alderman Cobden of Manchester* (London: Ward Lock, Bowden & Co.,1891)

3. *Studies*

Chaloner, W.H. *Palatinate Studies: Chapters in the Social and Industrial History Of Lancashire and Cheshire* (Manchester: The Chetham Society, 1992)
Gourvish, T .R. *Mark Huish of the LNWR* (Leicester University, 1972)
Grimsby County Borough: *Official Guide* (Batiste Publications, 1961)
Manchester Corporation Parks and Cemeteries Department: A Short Historical Study (1938)
Manchester Faces and Places, Vol. 2, No.2 (10 November 1890)
Men and Women of the Day (London: Richard Bentley and Sons, 1889)
Parks for the People: Manchester and its Parks, 1846–1926 (Manchester City Art Galleries, 1987)
Trent Valley Railway: Its Origins and Progress of the Undertaking (Manchester: Cave and Sever, 1845)
Watkin, A.E. *Absolom Watkin, Extracts From His Journal* (London: T. Fisher Unwin, Ltd., 1920)
Watkin, W.T. *Roman Cheshire* (1886: Republished, Cheshire County Council 1974)
Wright, N.R. *Lincolnshire Towns and Industry* (History of Lincolnshire, Vol. XI, 1982)

4. *Articles: Technical*

Boyd-Dawkins, William *Transactions of the Manchester Geological Society, 1896–1898,* pp.155ff
Channon, Geoffrey 'A Nineteenth-Century Investment Decision: The Midland Railway's London Extension' *Economic Historical Review;* Second Series, XXV (1972)
Currie, A.W. 'Sir Edward Watkin: A Canadian View', *Journal of Transport History* Vol. 3, Pt 1 (1957)
Gourvish, T.R. 'The Performance of British Railways Management After 1860: The Railways of Watkin and Forbes', *Business History* Vol. 20 (1978), pp.186–99

Keen, P.A. 'The Channel Tunnel Project', *Journal of Transport History,* Vol.III, pp.132–44

Maehl, W.H. 'Gladstone, The Liberals, and The Election of 1874', *Bulletin of the Institute of Historical Research,* Vol. 36 1963)

Mitchell, Elaine Allan 'Edward Watkin and the Buying-Out of the Hudson's Bay Company', *Canadian Historical Review,* Vol. XXXIV, No.3 (1953)

Talman, J.J. 'The Impact of the Railway on a Pioneer Community', *Canadian Historical Association,* (From the Internet: no details given)

Wardale, Harry 'The Weaver Navigation', *Transactions of the Lancashire Antiquarian Society,* Vol. XLIX (1910), p.9

Watkin, E.W. 'The Channel Tunnel', *Journal of the Society of Arts,* Vol. XXX, 21 April 1882, pp.560–6

Williams, C.J. 'Gladstone, Lloyd George, and the Gladstone Rock', *Caernarvonshire Historical Transactions* (1999), pp. 60–70

5. *Journals*

Cheshire Life
City Jackdaw, The (Manchester)
Contemporary Review
Country Life
Cricketer, The
Critic, The (Manchester)
Engineering
Fortnightly Review
Herepath's Railway (and Commercial) Magazine
King Magazine
Lincolnshire Life
Looking-Glass, The (Manchester)
Momus (Manchester)
Railway Magazine, The
Stockport Ancient and Modern
Transport
Vanity Fair

6. *Secondary Sources*

Abbott, Thomas (ed.) *Jane's World Railways* (Thomson, 37th Edition, 1995–1996)

Alderman, Geoffrey *The Railway Interest* (Leicester University Press, 1973)

Allen, Cecil J. *The Great Eastern Railway* (London: Ian Allan, 1967)

Allen, Cecil J. *The London and North Eastern Railway* (London: Ian Allan,1966)

Awdry, Christopher*Encyclopaedia of British Raiway Companies* (Patrick Stephens, 1990)

Axon, William E.A. *The Annals of Manchester* (Manchester: John Heywood,1886)

Bagwell, Philip S. *The Railwaymen: A History of the NUR* (George Allen and Unwin Ltd.,1963)

Bairstow, Martin *The Sheffield, Ashton-under-Lyne and Manchester Railway* (Pub. Author, 1986)

Bailey, Isabel *Edward Ingram, Esq* (Boston: Richard Kay,1996)

Baker, Alfred *The Life of Sir Isaac Pitman* (London: Sir Isaac Pitman and Sons Ltd., 1913)

Barker, Felix, and Hyde, Ralph *London as it Might Have Been* (John Murray, 1996)

Barker, T.C. 'Lord Salisbury, Chairman of the Great Eastern Railway, 1868–1872', in *Business and Businessmen: Studies in Business, Economics and Accounting History*, (ed.) Sheila Marriner (Liverpool University Press, 1978)

Barrie, D.S.M.*A Social History of the Railways of Great Britain,* Vol.12 (Newton Abbott: David and Charles, 1980)

Baughen, Peter *A Social History of the Railways of Great Britain,* Vol.11 (Newton Abbott: David and Charles, 1991)

Bolger, Paul *The Cheshire Lines Committee* (Merseyside: Heyday, 1984)

Borden, Robert *Canada in the Commonwealth* (OUP, 1929)

Boughey, Joseph (ed.) *Hadfields British Canals,* 8th Edition (Stroud: Alan Sutton, 1984)

Boyd, J.I.C. *The Wrexham, Mold, and Connah's Quay Railway* (Oxford: The Oakwood Press, 1991)

Briggs, Asa *Chartist Studies* (London: Macmillan, 1959)

Brown, Craig (ed.) *The Industrial History of Canada* (Toronto: Lester and Orpen Dennis Ltd., 1987)

Burton, Anthony *The Railway Builders* (John Murry, 1992)

Calvert, Albert *Salt in Cheshire* (E. & F. Spon Ltd., 1915)

Carr, Herbert R.C. and Lister, George A. *The Mountains of Snowdonia* (London: Crosby, Lockwood and Son Ltd., 1948)

Chinn, Carl *Poverty Amidst Prosperity: The Urban Poor in England, 1834–1914* (Manchester University Press, 1995)

Christiansen, Rex, and Miller, R.W. *The North Staffordshire Railway* (Newton Abbott: David and Charles, 1971)

Clapham, J.H. *An Economic History of Modern Britain* (Book IV) (CUP, 1938)

Cleveland-Stevens, Edward *English Railways: Their Development and Their Relation to the State* (London: George Routledge and Son Ltd, 1915)

Clifford, Brendan *The Life and Poems of Thomas Moore* (Belfast: Athol Books, 1993)

Cobbins, Andrew *The Japanese Discovery of Victorian Britain* (Japan Library, 1998)

Connelly, S.J. *The Oxford Companion to Irish History* (OUP, 1998)

Creighton, Donald Grant *Dominion of the North: A History of Canada* (London: Robert Hale Ltd., 1947)

Currie, A.W. *The Grand Trunk Railway of Canada* (University of Toronto Press, 1982)

Dale, Peter Alan *In Pursuit of a Scientific Culture* (University of Wisconsin, 1989)

Darras, Jacques *Beyond the Tunnel of History* (Macmillan, 1990)
Deacon, Derick *Wythenshawe: The Story of a Garden City* (Manchester: J. Morten, 1974)

Dendy Marshall, C.F. *A History of the Southern Railway* (Ian Allan, 1963)

den Otter, A.A. *The Philosophy of Railways* (Toronto University Press, 1997)

Dixon, Frank *The Manchester South Junction and Altrincham Railway* (Oakwood Press, 1973)

Dixon, Roger, and Muthesius, Stephen *Victorian Architecture* (Thames and Hudson, 1978)

Dow, George *The First Railway Between Manchester and Sheffield* (LNER, 1945)

Dow, George *Great Central* (3 Vols.) (Ian Allan, 1959–1962)

Dow, George *Railway Heraldry* (Newton Abbott: David and Charles, 1973)

Dyos, H.J. and Aldcroft, D.H. *British Transport: An Economic Survey from the 17th Century to the 20th* (Leicester University Press, 1971)

Ebbutt, Maude I. *British Myths and Legends* (Senate Press, 1996)

Edsall, Nicholas C. *Richard Cobden: Independent Radical* (Harvard University Press, 1986)

Edwards, Dennis and Pigram, Ron *The Final Link* (Midas Books, 1983 ed.)

Edwards, Dennis and Pigram, Ron *The Romance of Metroland* (Bloomsbury Books, 1986)

Euler, Robert D. *The Canada Year Book, 1936* (Ottawa: J.O. Patenaude, 1936)

Faith, Nicholas, *The World the Railways Made* (London: Pimlico, 1994)

Faith, Nicholas, *Classic Trains* (Boxtree (Macmillan), 1998)

Farnie, D.A. *The Manchester Ship Canal and the Rise of the Port of Manchester* (Manchester University Press, 1980)

Finch-Crisp, W. *History of Yarmouth* (from the Internet, 1997)

Forbes, Lord *Shall We Have a Channel Tunnel?* (Aberdeen: A. Brown, Ltd,1883)

Fox-Davies, A.C. *Complete Guide to Heraldry* (London: Orbis Publishing, 1985)

Frangopulo, N.J. *Rich Inheritance: A Guide to the History of Manchester* (Manchester Education Committee, 1962)

Freeman, Michael, *Railways and the Victorian imagination* (Yale University Press, New Haven and London, 1999)

Freeman, M.J. and Aldcroft, D.H. (eds.) *Transport in Victorian Britain* (Manchester University Press, 1988

Fulford, Roger *Votes for Women* (London: Faber and Faber, 1957)

Garvin, J.L. *The Life of Joseph Chamberlain* (Macmillan, 1932)

Gash, Norman *Sir Robert Peel* (Longmans, 1872)

Gilbert, Bentley Brinkerhoff *David Lloyd George* (London: B.T. Batsford Ltd., 1987)

Gillett, Edward *A History of Grimsby* (OUP, 1986)

Gough, John, in Williams Daniel (ed.), *The Adaptation of Change: Essays On the History of 19th Century Leicester and Leicestershire*(Leicester Museums Publication No.18, 1980)

Gourvish, T.R. *Mark Huish and the LNWR: A Study of Management* (Leicester University Press, 1972)

Gray, Adrian *South Eastern Railway* (Middleton Press, 1990)

Gray, John *False Dawn: The Delusions of Global Capital* (London: Granta Books, 1998)

Gray, Ted *A Hundred Years of the Manchester Ship Canal Company* (Aurora Publishing Ltd., 1994)

Griffiths, R.P. *The Cheshire Lines Railway* (Oakwood Press, 1978)

Grinling, C.H. *The History of the Great Northern Railway* (George Allen and Unwin, 3rd Edition, 1966)

Hamer, D.A. *Liberal Politics in the Age of Gladstone and Rosebery* (OUP, 1972)

Hamilton Ellis, Cuthbert *British Railway History* (3 Vols.), (George Allen and Unwin, 1953)

Hanham, A.J. *Elections and Party Management: Politics in the Time of Disraeli and Gladstone* (Longmans, 1959)

Harding, Michael *Walking the Peaks and Pennines* (London: Michael Joseph, 1992)

Harford, Ian, *Manchester and its Ship Canal Movement* (Keele: Ryburn Publishing, 1994)

Hayes, John *Dictionary of Biblical Interpretation* (Nashville: Abingdon Press, 1999)

Heales, Alfred *History and Law of Church Seats* (London: Butterworths, 1872)

Heaviside, Tom *On Lancashire and Yorkshire Lines* (Ian Allan, 1997)

Henshaw, David *The Great Railway Conspiracy* (Leading Edge, 1994)

Hibbert, Christopher *The English: A Social History, 1066–1945* (London: Guild Publishing, 1987)

Hill, Jeff and Verrari, Francesco *Creating Wembley: The Construction of a National Monument* (British Library Website, 2000)

Hobbs, Pam and Algar, Michael *Canada* (M.P.C. Hunter, undated, 1966)

Holt, Geoffrey O. *A Regional History of the Railways of Great Britain* (Vol. 10), (Newton Abbot: David and Charles, 1986)

Hopper, K. Theodore *The Mid-Victorian Generation, 1846–1886* (Oxford, Clarendon Press, 1998)

Hough, R. *Six Great Railwaymen* (Hamish Hamilton, 1955)

Hudson's Bay Company, The *A Brief History* (London: Hudson's Bay House, 1934)

351

Hunt, David *The Tunnel: The Story of the Channel Tunnel, 1802–1994* (Malvern: Images Publishing Ltd, 1994)

Hurst, Michael *Joseph Chamberlain and Liberal Re-Union* (Routledge and Kegan Paul, 1967)

Jackson, Alan *London's Metropolitan Railway* (Newton Abbott: David and Charles, 1986)

Jay, Richard *Joseph Chamberlain* (Oxford: Clarendon Press, 1981)

Jenkins, David E. *Bedd-Gelert: Its Facts, Fairies and Folk-Lore* (Portmadoc: Llewellyn Jenkins, 1899)

Jenkins, Roy *Gladstone* (Macmillan, 1995)

Joy, David, *A Regional History of the Railways of Great Britain* (Vol. 8) (Newton Abbott: David and Charles 1984)

Joyce, Patrick, *Work, Society and Politics: The Cultre of the Factory in Late Victorian England* (California: The Stanford University Press, 1990)

Kidd, A.J. and Roberts, K.W. *City, Class and Culture* (Manchester University Press, 1985)

Lee, Peter *The Trent Valley Railway, Rugby to Stafford, 1847 to 1966* (Trent Valley Publications, 1988)

Lloyd, Roger *Railwaymen's Gallery* (George Allen and Unwin, 1953)

Lloyd George, David *War Memoirs* (London: Odham's Press Ltd., 1938)

Lower, Arthur R.M. *Colony to Nation* (Toronto: Longmans, Green and Co., 1946)

Luxmoore, Jonathan, and Babiuch, Jolante *The Vatican and the Red Flag* (Geoffrey Chapman, 1999)

McDermot, E.T. *The History of the Great Western Railway, 1833–1863* (3 Vols., Vol. I), (London: Ian Allan Ltd Revised 1964)

MacDonagh, Giles *Prussia: The Perversion of an Idea* (Mandarin Press, 1994)

Machiavelli, Niccolò *The Prince* (London: David Campbell Ltd., 1920)

McKay, Douglas *The Honourable Company: A History of the Hudson's Bay Company* (London: Cassell and Co., 1937)

McKenna, Frank *The Railway Workers, 1840–1970* (Faber and Faber, 1980)

McNaught, Kenneth *The Pelican History of Canada* (London: Penguin Books Ltd., 1982)

Malchow, H.L. *Gentlemen Capitalists: The Social and Business*

World of the Victorian Businessman (California: Staffford University Press, 1992)

Martin, Chester *Foundations of Canadian Nationhood* (University of Toronto Press, 1955)

Martin, Tony *Halfway to Heaven: Darjeeling and its Remarkable Railway* (Chester: Rail Romances, 2000)

Mason, J.F.A. in *Salisbury: The Man and his Politics* (eds. Lord Blake and Hugh Cecil), (London: Macmillan, 1987)

Matthias, Peter *The First Industrial Nation: An Economic History of Britain, 1700–1914* (Routledge, 1983)

May, Trevor *An Economic and Social History of Britain, 1760–1970* (Longmans, 1987)

Messenger, Gary S. *Manchester in the Victorian Age* (Manchester University Press, 1985)

Moorman, J.R.H. *A History of the Church in England* (London: Adam and Charles Black, 1953)

Morley, John *The Life of Richard Cobden* (London: T. Fisher Unwin, 1879, 1910 Edition)

Morse, David *High Victorian Culture* (OUP, 1992)

Morton, W.L. *The Union of British North America The Critical Years, 1857–1873* (Toronto: McClelland and Stewart Limited, 1964)

Newsome, David *The Victorian World Picture* (John Murray, 1997)

Newton, Robert *Victorian Exeter* (Leicester University Press, 1968)

Nock, O.S. *North Western* (London: Ian Allan, 1968)

Nuttall, John and Anne *The Mountains of England and Wales* (Milnthorpe, Cicerone Press, 1989)

Novak, Michael *The Catholic Ethic and the Spirit of Capitalism* (New York: The Free Press, 1993)

Owen, David *The Manchester Ship Canal* (Manchester University Press, 1983)

Paget-Tomlinson, Edward W. *Canal and River Navigation* (Wolverhampton: Wayne Research, 1978)

Parkes, G.D. *The Hull and Barnsley Railway* (Oakwood Press, 1948)

Parkin, G.W. *The Mersey Railway* (Oakwood Press, 1978)

Pendleton, John *Our Railways* (2 Vols.) (Cassell and Co. Ltd., 1896)

Pollins, H. *Britain's Railways: An Industrial History* (Newton Abbott: David and Charles, 1971)

353

Pritchard, T.W. *A History of St Deniol's Library* (Hawarden: Monad Press,1999)

Richards, Thomas *The Commodity Culture of Victorian England* (California: The Stanford University Press, 1990)

Ridley, Jasper *Lord Palmerston* (London: Constable, 1970)

Roberts, Andrew *Salisbury* (London: Weidenfeld and Nicolson, 1999)

Robotham, Robert *On Great Central Lines* (London: Ian Allan, 1995)

Rochester, Mary *Salt in Cheshire* (Cheshire Libraries and Museums, 1985)

Rolt, L.T.C. *The Making of a Railway* (London: Hugh Evelyn, 1971)

Rottman, Alexander, *London's Catholic Churches: A Historic and Artistic Record* (London: Sands and Co., 1926)

Rowland, E.G. *The Ascent of Snowdon* (Pentrefelin, Criccieth: The Cidron Press, c. 1964)

Senior, Jack, and Ogden, Eric, *Metrolink* (Glossop: Transport Publishing Co. 1992)

Shannon, Richard, *Gladstone: Heroic Minister* (Allen Lane, 1999)

Shercliff, W.H. (ed.) *Wythenshawe* (Manchester: J. Morten, 1974)

Simmons, Jack, *The Victorian Railway* (London: Thames and Hudson, 1991)

Simmons, Jack, *The Railway in England and Wales, 1830–1914* (Leicester University Press, 1978)

Simmons, Jack, *The Railways of Britain* (London: Sheldrake Press, 1986)

Simmons, Jack, *The Railway in Town and Country, 1830-1914* (Newton Abbott: David and Charles, 1986)

Simmons and Biddle, (eds.) *The Oxford Companion to British Railway History (OUP, 1997)*

Slater, Humphrey, and Barnett, Correlli, *The Channel Tunnel* (London: Allan Wingate, 1958)

Smith, David Newman, *The Railway and its Passengers: A Social History* (Newton Abbott: David and Charles, 1988)

Snelson, Neil J. *Social Change in the Industrial Revolution* (Routledge and Kegan Paul, 1959)

Stevens, G.R. *Canadian National Railways: Sixty Years of Trial and Error, 1836–1896* (Toronto: Clarke, Irwin and Co. Ltd., 1960)

354

Story, Norah, *The Oxford Companion to Canadian History and Literature* (OUP, 1967)

Stretton, C.E. *The Midland Railway* (Bemrose and Son, 1877)

Swindells, T. *Manchester Streets and Manchester Men* (Didsbury: E.J. Morton, 1907)

Thomas, Ivor *Gladstone of Hawarden* (London: John Murray, 1936)

Thompson, F.M.L. in *Salisbury: The Man and his Politics* (eds. Lord Blake and Hugh Cecil), (London: Macmillan, 1987)

Turner, Keith, *The Snowdon Mountain Railway* (Newton Abbott: David and Charles, 1973)

Turner, Michael J. *Reform and Respectability: The Making of a Middle-Class Liberalism in Early Nineteenth-Century Manchester* (Manchester: The Chetham Society, 1995)

Vaughan, Adrian *Railwaymen, Politics and Money* (London: John Murray, 1997)

Vincent, John, *The Formation of the Liberal Party, 1857–1868* (Constable,1966)

Waterman, J.J. *The Aberdeen Railway and The Great North of Scotland Railway in the 1840s* (Aberdeen University, 1873)

Watkin, David, *Morality and Architecture* (OUP, 1977)

Watkin, W.T. *Roman Cheshire* (1886: Republished, Cheshire County Council, 1974)

Webster, Norman, *Britain's First Trunk Line* (Adams and Dent, 1972)

Whiteside, Thomas, *The Tunnel Under the Channel* (London: Rupert Hart-Davies, 1962)

Willan, T.S. *The Navigation of the River Weaver in the 18th Century* (Manchester: The Chetham Society, 1951)

Williams, D. (ed.) *The Adaptation of Change: Essays on the History of the 19th Century Leicester and Leicestershire* (Leicester Museums Publications No 18, 1980)

Williams, Frederick S. *The Midland Railway* (Bemrose and Son, 1877)

Wilson, Keith, *Channel Tunnel Visions, 1850–1945* (Hambledon Press,1994)

Wrottesley, John, *The Great Northern Railway* (Batsford, 1979)

Young, G.M. *Portrait of an Age: Victorian England* (OUP, 1977)

7. *Works of Reference*

Cambridge Biographical Encyclopaedia (CUP, 1994)
Chambers Biographical Dictionary (Chambers, 1995)
Companion to Hymns Ancient and Modern (London: William Clowes and Sons Ltd, 1962)
Dictionary of National Biography
Encyclopaedia Britannica, 1955, 1977, 1987, and 1995 editions
Who's Who of British Members of Parliament (Stenton, Michael) (2 Vols.) (Harvester Press, 1976)
Who Was Who (London: A&C Black)

INDEX

Ellerton, John 336
Ellesmere, Shropshire 141, 288
Ellis, Edward Shipley 172
Ellis, Thomas E. 295f
Employers' Liability Bill, 1880 220
Endowed Schools Commission, Exeter
    219
Enfield, Viscount 249
Engels, Friedrich 19, 20, 231
England 25, 30, 40, 205, 213, 222, 246,
    248, 250, 253, 260–3, 267, 268, 315
England, Church of 10, 215, 254, 284
England, George and Company 94
Enlightenment, The 236, 270, 284
Erie Railroad 115f, 156, 331
European Train Control System 243
Eurostar 258
Eton School 11
Evans, Frederick W. 212f
Ewloe, North Wales 56
Examiner, The Manchester 13, 15, 16–18,
    26
Exchange Division, Manchester City
    Council 70, 193
Exeter 196, 207–12, 214, 219, 222

F.A.Cup Final, 1924 147
Failsworth 29
Fallowfield, The Revd 25
Faringdon, Baron 317
Farrer, Thomas Henry Farrer [(sic)] 257
Farrer Committee 257–9, 261
Faversham 104
Fay, Sir Sam 326
Fenians 10, 224
Fenton, Myles 118
Fenton, William 96
Ferdinand de Lesseps 261
Ffestiniog Railway, Snowdonia 301
Ffridd Isaf, North Wales 299
Fielden, Joshua 113f
Fielden, Samuel 116, 231
Filder , William 196
Fildes, John 92f, 96, 100, 137, 153, 198,
    201
Finsbury Circus 131
Florence 270
Flushing 109
Folkestone 120, 190ff, 212, 214, 217f,
    219, 250, 280, 291, 308, 329, 335
Folkestone Fisherboys Band 282
Folkestone Fishermen 281

Folkestone, Mayor of 281, 284, 287f, 336
Forbes, James Staats 107, 108, 109, 110,
    121n, 122, 124, 132f, 137ff, 237, 239,
    251, 321
Forbes, Lord 265
Forbes, Stanhope, RA 133
Forbes, William 133
Forbes, William Junior 133
Foreign Office 249
Forth Bridge 129
'Forward', Great Central Railway motto
    322
Fowler, (Sir) John 128, 129, 135, 143,
    171, 180
France 39, 64, 143, 158, 222, 227, 246,
    247, 249, 252, 262, 266, 268, 269,
    272, 287, 289, 294, 298
Franco-Prussian War 190
Freckelton 303
Free Library Movement 181
free market capitalism 14, 60
free trade 1, 11, 14, 26, 72, 74, 194, 195n,
    202, 271
Free Trade Hall, Manchester 14, 15, 25,
    27
French Channel Tunnel Company 249
French, Emperor of the 222
French Revolution 270
Friendly Societies Bill (1875) 221
Fripp, Alfred Downing 135
Frith, F.B. 336
Frith, W.P. 336
Frodsham 175

Gainsborough 52
Galway 226
Gamond, Aimé Thomé de 247, 248, 250,
    262, 264, 270
Garston 171
Garston and Liverpool
    (Brunswick)Railway 169, 171
Gatley 16, 187
gauge, railway 43, 65, 74, 268, 285, 287,
    326
Geological Society, London 271
Geological Society, Manchester 272
George V, King, and Queen Mary 162
German Memorial at Folkestone 190f
Germany 143, 248f, 253
Gibbons, Stephen 200f
Gibbs, Bailey and Worthington 183
Gibraltar 227

361

Johnson, The Ven Edward Ralph 183
Johnson, H. 288
Johnson, Joseph 181, 184
Joint Stock (Limited Liability)
    Companies 205, 206
Josse, Henri 226f
Julius Agricola 33

Kay, Alexander 13
Keefer, Thomas C. 332f
Kelk Brothers and Lucas 130f
Kent 218, 272, 294, 338
Kent Coalfield 271ff
Kenyon, G.T. 288
Kersal Moor, Salford 13
Kershaw, James 21, 202
Kidderminster, Birmingham and Stoke
    Railway 141
Killingholme 162
King's Cross, London 55, 127, 174
Kitching, Albert George 137
Knutsford 181, 313
Königsberg 161

Labrador 74
Laing, Samuel 106, 108
Laird, John 179
laissez-faire 207, 256
Lambton, John George, Earl of Durham
    63, 86
Lancashire 51, 91, 108, 155, 173, 186,
    204, 205, 217, 227, 231, 291, 293
Lancashire, Derbyshire and East Coast
    Railway 312, 313
Lancashire and Yorkshire Railway 51,
    55, 96, 107, 155, 171, 173, 248, 302–
    7, 336
Land Reform (Welsh) 296
Lansdowne Committee 262, 265
Lansdowne, Lord Henry (5th Marquess)
    262, 265
Lassalle, Ferdinand 286
Leader Williams, E. 180
Leeds 66, 309
Leicester 42, 51, 57, 307, 309, 310, 321
Leigh, John 185f
Leopold II, King of the Belgians 157,
    280f
Liberal Party, Liberalism 4, 14, 16, 25,
    194, 201, 205, 207–9, 211, 212, 214,
    216, 217, 225–8, 232, 255, 256, 295
library, first free 4

library at Rose Hill 3, 9
Licensing Act (1872) 211
Lichfield 32
Lichfield, The Earl of 31
lighthouse and telegraph provision,
    Ireland 224
Lille 327
Limited Liability Companies Acts 205,
    206
Lincoln 7, 52, 160, 226, 290
Lincoln, Lord (Later, 5th Duke of
    Newcastle) 67
Lings, Thomas 186
Literary and Philosophical Society 4
Literary and Scientific Club ('The Club')
    4, 11
Little, Mr, QC 316
Liverpool 6, 34, 44, 51, 60, 66, 95, 100,
    175, 194, 207, 226, 229, 257, 274,
    281, 282, 292, 302, 304, 327
Liverpool Central Station 169
Liverpool Central Low Level Station
    174, 175
Liverpool Edge Hill Station 171
Liverpool Exchange Station 171
Liverpool Lime Street Station 171
Liverpool and Manchester Railway 7, 31,
    48, 50, 171
Liverpool Road Junction, Manchester
    50
Liverpool St James's Station 174
Liverpool St Michael's Station 174
Liverpool Street Line, London 131
Llanberis 300
Llanidloes 274
Lloyd George, David 291, 296, 297
Locke, Joseph, 247
London 3, 14, 17, 30, 34, 44, 45, 52, 61,
    66, 70, 96, 103, 127, 143, 251, 252,
    257, 279, 281, 310, 312, 315, 332
London and Birmingham Railway 30,
    31, 32, 36
London Bridge Station 186
London, Brighton and South Coast
    Railway 105, 106, 107, 108, 115
London Cannon Street Station 120
London Charing Cross Station 120
London, Chatham and Dover Railway
    104–107, 109–114, 120–2, 132, 239,
    249, 250, 251, 255, 321
London County Council 315
London Euston Station 124

London Extension Bill, MS&LR (1891) 313; (1892) 315
London Extension, MS&LR 218, 319, 325, 326
London Liverpool Street Station 127, 132, 153
London, Mayor of 281
London and North Eastern Railway 164, 221, 233, 321n, 322
London and North Western Railway 32, 34, 36, 37, 39, 40, 41, 43, 45, 46, 51–53, 56–58, 91, 94, 95, 100, 106, 107, 110, 112, 122, 127, 152, 155, 158, 168, 169, 171, 173, 178, 203, 226, 231, 235, 237, 239, 244, 274, 282, 291, 302n, 304–306, 308–310, 326
London Paddington Station 127, 328
London St Pancras Station 172
London and South Western Railway 106, 155, 240
Long Benton, Northumberland 7
Longton, Southport 303
Lord's Cricket Ground 310, 313
Lord's, House of 216
Lord Warden Hotel, Dover 251
Lostock Gralam, Cheshire 242n
Loughborough 57, 309
Lovett, William 14
Low, William 247–250, 258
Lowndes, Colonel Henry 309
Luddenden, Yorkshire 235
Lymm 335
Lytham 16, 302, 303, 304

Macauley, Thomas Babington 27, 28
Macclesfield 207, 313, 335
Macclesfield, Bollington and Marple Railway 168
Macclesfield Committee, The 168
McClure, Alderman 201
McCullough, William 196f
McDonald, Alexander 213
Macdonald, (Sir) John A. 79, 86, 90, 205
Macdonald, Lady 90
McGregor, James 103–105
Machiavelli, Niccoló 43f, 51
McKenzie, Alexander 332n
McKerrow, The Revd Dr William 16
McLaren, Charles B.B. (Lord Aberconway) 127, 141
Maclure, The Very Revd Edward Craig 335

Maclure, John William 276, 328, 335
Madeley, Staffordshire 44, 45
Maidstone 108
Maguire, Thomas 222
Makinson family, the 3, 19, 59
Makinson, Elizabeth (Edward Watkin's mother) 3, 289n
Makinson, Elizabeth's father 3
Makinson, Joseph (Elizabeth's nephew) 313
Mallalieu, Mr 95
Man, Isle of 223
Manchester 1–5, 7, 11, 13, 15, 17, 18, 20, 21, 23, 25–28, 30, 31, 34, 36, 37, 39, 40, 47–51, 53–55, 60, 64, 66, 70, 91–96, 100, 104, 125, 126, 137, 157, 162, 173, 175, 177, 181, 183, 188, 190, 193, 204, 207, 222, 227, 246, 256, 271n, 274, 297, 302, 303, 313, 318, 320, 324, 325, 327, 332, 339, 340
Manchester Art Treasures Exhibition, 1857 168
Manchester and Birmingham Railway 30–32, 36, 50, 168
Manchester and Birmingham Extension Railway 31
Manchester, Bishop of 215, 216 (Fraser); 281 (Moorhouse)
Manchester Cathedral 5, 183
Manchester Central Line 218
Manchester Central Station 100, 171
Manchester Chamber of Commerce 286
Manchester City Council 6, 70, 135, 193
Manchester Corn Exchange 13, 194
Manchester Exchange Station 171
Manchester Fire Assurance Company 158
Manchester Gazette 5
Manchester Grammar School 11
Manchester Guardian 5
Manchester Guardians of the Poor 337
Manchester London Road Station 46, 48–50, 54, 94, 171, 230, 244
Manchester, Mayor of 13, 30, 60, 256n, 281
Manchester and Salford Co-operative Society 188f
'Manchester School' 25, 256
Manchester, Sheffield and Lincolnshire Railway 46, 48–61, 66, 68, 91–102, 112, 113, 115, 116, 119, 125–127, 129, 141, 147, 154, 155, 158–162,

366

Neath and Brecon Railway 276, 292
nepotism 114
Newark 57, 239
New Brighton 147
Newcastle, 5th Duke of (Henry
     P.F.Pelham-Clinton) 64, 67–69, 70,
     76, 77, 86, 87, 89
'Newcastle Programme', The 208
Newcombe, W.L. 56ff
New Cross, London 117, 128, 156
New Holland 243, 244
Newman, George S. 138
Newman, John Henry 336
New Mills 91
Newport, I.O.W. 221
Newry and Greenore Railway 226
Newton Heath Ironworks 144
New York 61, 214, 226, 334n
New York, Lake Erie and Western
     Railway 157
Nietzche, Friedrich 20
Nock, Oliver Stevens 242
'Nonconformist Concerns' 208
North America 61–64, 162, 240, 287
North British Railway Company 51
North Cheshire Parliamentary
     Constituency 207
Northcote, Sir Stafford 209, 225
North Derbyshire Canals 177
North Eastern Railway 96, 106, 110, 155,
     166
Northenden 10, 182ff, 279f, 335, 336
'Northenden, SS' 338
Northen Etchells 181
Northern Star, The 18
Northolt 328
North London Railway 55, 156
North Staffordshire Railway 32, 42, 158,
     168, 174, 211
North Staffordshire (Trent and Mersey)
     Canal 179
North Wales narrow gauge railway 296,
     300, 301
North West Territories 78
Northwich 169, 175, 176, 178, 242n
Northwood 127
Norwich, Bishop of 28
Nottingham 51, 57, 307, 309, 310, 321
Nova Scotia 64
Nuneaton 32, 42
Nuremburg 165n

Oakley, The Very Revd John 188
O'Connell, Daniel 10
O'Connor, Fergus 13, 18
'Old Church', Manchester (Later the
     Cathedral) 5
Oldham 24, 25, 29
Oldham, Ashton-under-Lyne and Guide
     Bridge Junction Railway 54, 105,
     168
Old Trafford (Cornbrook) 171
Old Trafford Station 168
Olympic Games, 1948 147
Onslow, Denzil R. 312
Ontario 64
'Onward', SER Motto 253, 322
Operative Corn Law Association 14, 15,
     16
Oregon 74
Overend and Gurney and Company 105,
     150
Owen, Robert 236
Owens' College, Manchester 13, 188
Owens, John 13, 24
Oxford 7, 10, 26, 135, 270, 292, 317
Oxford, Worcester and Wolverhampton
     Railway 42, 54

Padua 270
Palliser, Sir William 223
Palmerston, Lord Henry John Temple
     55, 68, 196
Panmure, Lord Fox Maule 196
Paris 11, 18, 247, 291, 325
Paris, siege of, 190
Paris Universal Exhibition (1889) 142;
     (1867) 247
Parker, Thomas 237
parks, public 23, 24, 188
Parkyn, Mr 337
Parliamentary Blue Book (Channel
     Tunnel) 262
'Parliamentary' Trains 109
Parnell, Charles Stewart 224
paternalism 232, 236, 256
Patti, Dame Adelina 276
Pavilion Hotel, Folkestone 287
Pavy, Francis 145
Payne Smith, Catherine Elizabeth
     (Watkin's daughter-in-law) 115, 338
Peace Preservation in Ireland Bill 224
Peak District 174, 313
Peak Forest 242n